Interviews with English Filmmakers:
Powell to Pawlikowski

Edited by R. J. Cardullo

INTERVIEWS WITH ENGLISH FILMMAKERS: POWELL TO PAWLIKOWSKI

Interviews with English Filmmakers: Powell to Pawlikowski
Cardullo, R. J., 1948-
Includes bibliographical references and index.
©2018 R. J. Cardullo. All rights reserved.
No part of this book may be reproduced in any form or by any means, electronic, mechanical, digital, photocopying, or recording, except for inclusion of a review, without permission in writing from the publisher or Author.

Published in the USA by:
BearManor Media
P O Box 71426
Albany, Georgia 31708
www.bearmanormedia.com

ISBN: 978-1-62933-253-6
BearManor Media, Albany, Georgia
Printed in the United States of America
Book Text Design: Robbie Adkins, www.adkinsconsult.com

TABLE OF CONTENTS

List of Images v
Acknowledgements vii
Introduction ix

The British Are Coming 1
"'It's Not Too Late to Do It Again': An Interview with
   Michael Powell" 2
"Carol Reed on Directing Orson Welles in *The Third Man*" 19
"'I'm a Picture Chap': David Lean on *A Passage to India*" 27
"Charles Crichton at Ealing Studios: An Interview" 36
"The Filmmaker and the Critic: An Interview with
   Lindsay Anderson" 45
"Novels, Screenplays, and Films: An Interview with Karel Reisz" . . 60
"A Kind of Filming: An Interview with John Schlesinger" 69
"The Movie Lover: An Interview with Ken Russell" 82
"Money Matters/Movie Material: An Interview with
   Tony Richardson" 92
"'Who Would Have Believed It?': An Interview with
   Nicolas Roeg" 101
"'It's Not Just about Me': Ken Loach and the Cinema of Social
   Conscience; An Interview" 115
"The Complexities of Cultural Change: An Interview with
   Stephen Frears" 137

Photo Gallery 160
"Peter Greenaway Holds Court: An Interview at the
   Venice Film Festival" 192
"'Making People Think Is What It's All About': Mike Leigh
   and the Cinema of Subversion; An Interview" 208
"Of Time, Memory, and the Movies: Talking to Terence Davies" . 249
"'Girls Are the New Men': An Interview with
   Pawel Pawlikowski" 266

"Sharing an Enthusiasm for Shakespeare: An Interview with
   Kenneth Branagh" 282

Americans Abroad 303
"Screenwriters, Critics, and Ambiguity: An Interview with
   Joseph Losey" 304
"Only Connect: James Ivory on *Howards End*" 314
"'All Film Is Fantasy': An Interview with Richard Lester" 326

Directors' Feature Filmographies 345
General Bibliography of British Cinema 351
Index 373

List of Images

1. Michael Powell
2. *Peeping Tom*
3. *The Life and Death of Colonel Blimp*
4. Carol Reed
5. *The Third Man*
6. *The Third Man*
7. David Lean
8. *A Passage to India*
9. *A Passage to India*
10. Charles Crichton
11. *The Lavender Hill Mob*
12. *Hue and Cry*
13. Lindsay Anderson
14. *If . . .*
15. *Britannia Hospital*
16. Karel Reisz
17. *The French Lieutenant's Woman*
18. *Saturday Night and Sunday Morning*
19. John Schlesinger
20. *A Kind of Loving*
21. *Far From the Madding Crowd*
22. Ken Russell
23. *Women in Love*
24. *The Music Lovers*
25. Tony Richardson
26. *The Entertainer*
27. *A Taste of Honey*
28. Nicolas Roeg
29. *Performance*
30. *Walkabout*
31. Ken Loach
32. *Kes*
33. *Riff-Raff*
34. Stephen Frears

35. *My Beautiful Laundrette*
36. *Dirty Pretty Things*
37. Peter Greenaway
38. *The Cook, The Thief, His Wife, and Her Lover*
39. *The Tulse Luper Suitcases*
40. Mike Leigh
41. *Secrets and Lies*
42. *Bleak Moments*
43. Terence Davies
44. *Distant Voices, Still Lives*
45. *The Long Day Closes*
46. Pawel Pawlikowski
47. *My Summer of Love*
48. *Last Resort*
49. Kenneth Branagh
50. *Henry V*
51. *Hamlet*
52. Joseph Losey
53. *The Servant*
54. *The Go-Between*
55. James Ivory
56. *Howards End*
57. *Howards End*
58. Richard Lester
59. *A Hard Day's Night*
60. *The Knack*

Acknowledgements

My thanks to the following journals, organizations, individuals, and publishers for granting me the right to reprint material originally contained in their pages or recorded by them: *Films and Filming* (defunct), G. P. Putnam's Sons/Penguin, *Film Comment*, *Film Criticism*, *Literature/Film Quarterly*, Leo Verswijver, *Film Quarterly*, John Stezaker, *The Minnesota Review*, *Cineaste*, *Cinema Journal*, Matt Zoller Seitz, *Sight and Sound*, *The Guardian*, and the British Film Institute.

Introduction

The British cinema had always been a stepchild of the American film industry, and during the 1920s it had almost ceased to exist. But in 1927 Parliament passed the Cinematograph Film Act, setting strict quotas on the number of foreign films that could be shown in the country; this had the effect of stimulating domestic production and investment. The British film industry therefore doubled in size from 1927 to 1928. This expansion continued well into the 1930s, enabling the British to compete with Hollywood not merely nationally, but—for the first time in its history—internationally, on a modest scale. Many of the films produced by the new boom were "quota quickies"—the British equivalent of the low-budget American B-movie—but some were ambitious undertakings by serious producers such as Alexander Korda (1893-1956) and Michael Balcon (1896-1977).

By 1937, the British industry had the second largest output in the world (225 features), and British films were competing strongly with American films on an international scale. Yet British producers were also deeply in debt, and the following year witnessed many bankruptcies and studio closings. In 1938, fewer than 100 features were made and fewer still were released, a reflection of Europe's uncertain political future and the troubled world economy. By the end of the decade most British commercial production was geared toward making second features to accompany American films on double bills.

Before World War II, however, Britain had produced a vastly important contribution to documentary cinema in the government-funded work of John Grierson (1898-1972) and such protégés of his as Alberto Cavalcanti (1897-1982), Basil Wright (1907-87), Harry Watt (1906-87), and Humphrey Jennings (1907-50). During the war, these filmmakers moved toward a blending of narrative and documentary form in such pictures as Watt's *London Can Take It* (1940), Jennings' *Listen to Britain* (1942) and *Fires Were Started* (1943), and Pat Jackson's *Western Approaches* (1944). Meanwhile, the commercial industry produced its own quasi-documentary features praising the armed forces—the navy, in Noël Coward's *In Which We Serve* (1942); the army, in Carol Reed's *The Way Ahead* (1944); the air force, in Anthony Asquith's *The Way to the Stars* (1945); and the home front, in Thorold Dickinson's *Next of Kin* (1942).

Moreover, during and after World War II, a traditional staple of British cinema—literary adaptation—experienced a sharp upswing. The actor-director Laurence Olivier (1907-89) offered distinguished adaptations of three plays by William Shakespeare: *Henry V* (1944), *Hamlet* (1948), and *Richard III* (1955). David Lean (1908-91), after adapting several plays by Noël Coward (*Blithe Spirit* [1945] and *Brief Encounter* [1945] among them), produced two carefully crafted, atmospheric adaptations of Charles Dickens' works: *Great Expectations* (1946) and *Oliver Twist* (1947). Anthony Asquith (1902-68), who adapted Bernard Shaw's *Pygmalion* (1938) before the war, proceeded after it to adapt Terence Rattigan's plays *The Winslow Boy* (1948) and *The Browning Version* (1951), as well as Oscar Wilde's comedy *The Importance of Being Earnest* (1952). And Carol Reed (1906-76) directed *The Fallen Idol* (1948) and *The Third Man* (1949), adapted from stories by Graham Greene, as well as *Outcast of the Islands* (1951), taken from the novel by Joseph Conrad.

Among the most important British films of the postwar period was a series of intelligent and witty comedies made for Michael Balcon's Ealing Studios. These movies were directed by Charles Crichton (1910-99)—*Hue and Cry* (1947), *The Lavender Hill Mob* (1951), and *The Titfield Thunderbolt* (1953); Alexander Mackendrick (1912-93)—*Whisky Galore* (1949), *The Man in the White Suit* (1951), and *The Ladykillers* (1955); Henry Cornelius (1913-58)—*Passport to Pimlico* (1948) and *Genevieve* (1953); and by Robert Hamer (1911-63)—*Kind Hearts and Coronets* (1949) and *Father Brown* (1954). The splendid work of the actor Alec Guinness (1914-2000) in a number of these films made him an international star.

Nonetheless, by the mid-1950s, British cinema had begun to decline into cliché, and Britain was once again in danger of becoming a Hollywood colony. Lindsay Anderson (1923-94) and Karel Reisz (1926-2002) tried to change all that in the mid-1950s by organizing the Free Cinema Movement, which, like Italian neorealism, celebrated, as a manifesto put it, "the importance of the individual and . . . the significance of the everyday." Like the French New Wave, Free Cinema was dedicated to the belief that film should be a medium of personal expression for the filmmaker, who should be socially committed to illuminating the problems of contemporary life. In practice, Free Cinema meant the production of short, low-budget documentaries like Anderson's *O Dreamland* (1954), a satirical assault on the spiritual emptiness of working-class life, set in an amusement park, and Reisz and Tony Richardson's *Momma Don't Allow* (1956), a study of postwar youth in the environment of a London jazz club.

At the time that the Free Cinema movement emerged, a revolution was under way in British theater and literature in which liberal, working-class values emanating from the East End of London and the provinces were overturning the established bourgeois—if not aristocratic—tradition of the preceding decades. John Osborne's diatribe *Look Back in Anger* rocked the world of traditional culture when it was staged at the Royal Court Theatre in May of 1956 by calling into question the whole class structure of British society and assailing the moral bankruptcy of the welfare state. The following years witnessed the appearance of a new group of young, anti-establishment, working-class writers such as David Storey, John Braine, Alan Sillitoe, and Shelagh Delaney, who treated similar themes in a style that can be accurately characterized as "social realism." By 1959—significantly, the year in which the filmmakers of the French New Wave won a number of prizes at the Cannes Festival—the time was ripe for the overthrow of the class-bound British feature cinema in favor of working-class social realism.

In that year, the industry itself produced two films that announced the revolution: the adaptation by Jack Clayton (1921-95) of Braine's novel *Room at the Top*, and the adaptation by Tony Richardson (1928-91) of Osborne's *Look Back in Anger*. Both movies were big-budget commercial productions with well-known stars that nevertheless dealt seriously with the disillusionment and frustration of the British working classes, and both were international hits. Reisz's *Saturday Night and Sunday Morning* (1960), a version of the Sillitoe novel, subsequently became the prototype for what may be fairly labeled British "New Cinema," a social-realist movement whose themes were borrowed from Italian neorealism and whose techniques were modeled upon the Free Cinema documentaries of the mid-1950s and the films of the French New Wave.

The products of New Cinema were generally set in the industrial Midlands and shot on location in black and white against gloomy backgrounds. Their protagonists (usually played by unknown young actors) were typically rebellious working-class youths who used a tough vernacular speech until then unheard in British films, and who were contemptuous of the spiritual torpor that had been induced in their parents and friends by the welfare state as well as by the mass communications industry. Major New Cinema movies include Richardson's *The Entertainer* (1960), *A Taste of Honey* (1961), and *The Loneliness of the Long Distance Runner* (1961); John Schlesinger's *A Kind of Loving* (1962) and *Billy Liar* (1963); Anderson's *This Sporting Life* (1963); Sidney J. Furie's *The Leather Boys* (1963); and Reisz's *Morgan: A Suitable Case for Treatment* (1966).

Like the French New Wave, British New Cinema reached its peak around 1963 and then rapidly declined as a movement while its directors went their separate ways. During the mid-1960s, in fact, a reaction to the bleakness of social realism set in, and the depressing images of the industrial Midlands were replaced by those of "swinging London" in big-budget widescreen color productions like *Alfie* (1966) and *Joanna* (1968). Still, by the late 1960s, with the decline of social realism and the increasing influence of American investment in the now lucrative British cinema (90 percent by 1968), the distinctly national flavor of British films was lost. A number of American directors (such as John Huston and Stanley Kubrick) came to work in British studios during these years, as did such major Continental figures as Roman Polanski (*Repulsion*, 1965), François Truffaut (*Fahrenheit 451*, 1966), and Michelangelo Antonioni (*Blow-Up*, 1966). Meanwhile, British-based directors like Richardson, Schlesinger, and Reisz began to make movies within the American industry or became involved in big-budget international co-productions. (Oddly, the "Britishness" of British cinema was enhanced during the 1960s and 1970s by two American expatriates: Joseph Losey [1909-84], with *The Servant* [1963],

Accident [1967], and *The Go-Between* [1971], and Richard Lester [born 1932], with *A Hard Day's Night* [1964], *The Knack* [1965], *How I Won the War* [1967], and *The Bed Sitting Room* [1969].)

Again like the French New Wave, then, from which it partially sprang, the British social-realist cinema disappeared along with the social context that had motivated it. But its formal and thematic legacy to British national cinema was great. It bequeathed the then-radical stylistic conventions of the New Wave to a cinema stagnant with armchair narrative traditions carried over from the prewar era. And in its concern for the aesthetics of everyday life and outspokenness about the dynamics of sex, class, and power in the post-industrial world, it gave the class-ridden, hidebound British film a vastly wider range of themes than it had ever known before. Social realism also produced a handful of important directors like Lindsay Anderson, John Schlesinger, Tony Richardson, and Karel Reisz, as well as a new pool of international acting talent including young and previously unknown stars such as Albert Finney, Alan Bates, Tom Courtenay, Susannah York, Michael Caine, Julie Christie, Glenda Jackson, James Fox, Michael York, and Vanessa Redgrave.

The fact that British film has rarely been a major force in world cinema is partially explained by America's dominance of the English-language market, and partially by the innate conservatism of British visual and aural culture. Satyajit Ray once said that the British are "temperamentally unsuited" to cinema, and François Truffaut claimed that the terms "cinema" and "British" were incompatible. As if to confirm this, the preponderance of successful British movies in the later twentieth century and early twenty-first century fall into a culturally conservative genre known as "heritage cinema," whose origins can be traced back to the patriotic *Chariots of Fire* in 1981. These are essentially period or costume dramas, which include adaptations from canonical works of national literature—in which the British are exceedingly rich—as well as historical reconstructions based on modern texts. They have conventionally structured narratives and display conservative social attitudes; and, in their heavy reliance on a pictorialist camera style and their fetishization of accurate period detail, heritage films can best be described as having a museum aesthetic.

In the former, canonical category you will find such films as *Sense and Sensibility* (1995), *Emma* (1996), *Mansfield Park* (1999), *Little Dorrit* (1987), *Wuthering Heights* (1992), *Jane Eyre* (1996), *The Portrait of a Lady* (1996), *The Wings of a Dove* (1998), *An Ideal Husband* (1999), *A Handful of Dust* (1988), *Mrs. Dalloway* (1997), *A Passage to India* (1984), *A Room with a View* (1987), *Where Angels Fear to Tread* (1991), *Howards End* (1991), *Much Ado about Nothing* (1993), *Hamlet* (1996), *A Midsummer Night's Dream* (1996, 1999), and *Twelfth Night* (1996), among many others. The category of historical reconstructions would include dramatized portraits of British royalty, such as *The Madness of King George* (1995); adaptations from contemporary literature set in the past, like *Heat and Dust* (1982), *White Mischief* (1987), *The Remains of the Day* (1993), and *Angels and Insects* (1995); political and literary biopics, like *Gandhi* (1982); and, finally, period dramas based on original screenplays—e.g., *Another Country* (1984) and *Shakespeare in Love* (1998).

Despite the conservatism of heritage cinema, the spirit of New Cinema lives on in Great Britain in the work of a handful of directors, some of whom did their apprentice work under its major figures. I am thinking particularly of the social realist Ken Loach (born 1936), with such films as *Kes* (1969), *Family Life* (1972), *Riff Raff* (1990), and *The Navigators* (2001); Mike Leigh (born 1943), who harks back to the "kitchen sink" realism of New Cinema in such films as *High Hopes* (1988), *Naked* (1993), and *Secrets and Lies* (1996); the eclectic Stephen Frears (born 1941), who has directed important films like *My Beautiful Laundrette* (1985), *Prick Up Your Ears* (1987), and *Sammy and Rosie Get Laid* (1988); and Terence Davies (born 1945), noted especially for two quasi-autobiographical films that capture the pathos of working-class life in his native Liverpool, *Distant Voices, Still Lives* (1988) and *The Long Day Closes* (1992). To this list may be added the Irish filmmakers Neil Jordan (born 1950) and Jim Sheridan (born 1949), the Scottish directors Bill Forsyth (born 1946) and Danny Boyle (born 1956), and the Welshmen Chris Monger (born 1950) and Paul Turner (born 1945).

The independent producer Bill Cartlidge once said that the British film industry is "permanently ill, but goes into remission now and then." *Interviews with English Filmmakers: Powell to Pawlikowski* is a collection interviews chiefly on that cinema when it has been in remission—that is, on the British art cinema as it emerged particularly in the post-World War II period and prospered until the turn of the twenty-first century (when Internet piracy began to put more and more pressure on producers and directors to make strictly commercial, international, blockbuster-style films that could turn a huge profit within the first few weeks of their release).

Interviews with English Filmmakers: Powell to Pawlikowski includes interviews with seventeen British filmmakers: Michael Powell, Carol Reed, David Lean, Charles Crichton, Jack Clayton, Lindsay Anderson, Karel Reisz, John Schlesinger, Ken Russell, Tony Richardson, Ken Loach, Stephen Frears, Peter Greenaway, Mike Leigh, Terence Davies, Pawel Pawlikowski, and Kenneth Branagh. Also included are interviews with the following three Anglo-American directors: Joseph Losey, James Ivory, and Richard Lester. Supplementing all of these interviews are a historical introduction to English cinema, a feature filmography for each director interviewed, director-specific bibliographies, a general bibliography on British film, and a comprehensive index.

Interviews with English Filmmakers: Powell to Pawlikowski is hardly designed to be an exhaustive book on the art of British film, but it is intended to be a representative one. This volume is aimed not only, as one might think, at scholars, college students, and teachers of university-level courses in British cinema and the history of film. *Interviews with English Filmmakers* is also aimed at cultivated moviegoers and theater patrons. It is thus not an erudite or pedantic tome targeted only at a limited audience of specialists; instead, this volume is meant to be a highly accessible yet subtly expressive and copiously illustrated collection of interviews, all of which deal with cinematic (as well as dramatic) questions of interest to many educated readers and spectators—not just British ones.

The operative term in *Interviews with English Filmmakers: Powell to Pawlikowski*, it should be clear, is "art." I have nothing against money (who really does?), but I like my film art—British or otherwise—divorced from it, or divorced from dependence on it, as much as possible. I hope the reader will agree and read on—or carry on, as the English say—with pleasure as well as profit.

INTERVIEWS
The British Are Coming

"'It's Not Too Late to Do It Again': An Interview with Michael Powell," by Tony Williams. From *Films and Filming*, no. 326 (Nov. 1981): 10-16.

Michael Powell (1905-90) graduated from "quota quickies" of the thirties to a distinguished career in partnership with Emeric Pressburger, directing such classics as *49th Parallel* (1941), *A Matter of Life and Death* (1946), *Black Narcissus* (1947), *The Red Shoes* (1948), and *The Tales of Hoffman* (1951). The Powell and Pressburger team came to be relied upon for superbly crafted, highly individual, emotionally, imaginatively, and visually intense works that show the British cinema at its most creative and accomplished.

Although he made a string of British cinema classics—including, in addition to the above-named films, *The Life and Death of Colonel Blimp* (1943)—Powell was for many years a somewhat neglected figure, until rediscovery on both sides of the Atlantic brought him back into the limelight at the start of the 1980s. One of the reasons for this neglect was Powell's most controversial work, *Peeping Tom* (1960), made after an amicable split with Pressburger in 1957. This film damaged his career but has experienced a sharp turnaround in critical opinion since Martin Scorsese led its revival in the late 1970s. In 1986, at the age of eighty-one and four years before his death in 1990, Powell issued the first volume of his autobiography, *A Life in Movies*.

In 1981, Tony Williams interviewed Powell at the Zoetrope Studios in Hollywood where he is based, working as a consultant to Francis Ford Coppola.

Tony Williams: What are you currently doing at Zoetrope Studios?
Michael Powell: I came down last year in March to look things over. At that time they were shooting *Hammett* [1982], a film about the early days of Dashiell Hammett in San Francisco. He was writing detective stories for a magazine called *The Black Mask*. This is really a story within a story. You see Hammett creating the charac-

ters with whom he has to deal. They're not just fictional characters but people who walk off the street and start behaving immediately like Dashiell Hammett characters. It's a nice idea.

Frederic Forrest plays Hammett, a nervous, imaginative, almost white-haired, moustached man. He also plays the lead in Coppola's *One from the Heart* [1982], which we're just finishing, as a very sturdy young American who owns half a junkyard at Las Vegas, a man in his thirties, tough, sentimental, brutal, and kind—like most Americans. It's an American comedy, sort of *It Happened One Night in Las Vegas* in 1981. He and Teri Garr are two young Americans, both attractive, always fighting, surrounded by every possible modern gadget that they don't even notice, ordinary supermarket Americans but filled with immortal longings, passions, hatred, and love. I think the film will be a bigger success in Europe than here. It all takes place in Las Vegas on July 4th, so it's got plenty of production.

TW: The usual impression about your role, in England now, is: "How unusual it is for a British director to be working in an American studio!", but throughout your career you've always had a Hollywood connection. I believe you began as an assistant to Rex Ingram in France in 1925?

MP: Yes, that's quite right. I spent the weekend with Walter Strohm, who used to be studio manager at Culver City and MGM. He and I both joined Rex Ingram together in 1925. He was filling me in over what had gone on in those fifty fabulous years in between. We hadn't met since those early days but had hundreds of acquaintances in common. When I went to England first, I was determined to get into British pictures and make big British films, but after I made *The Edge of the World* [1937] I got such a bad reception. Nobody wanted to know about the film. The only people who praised it really (apart from one English critic called George Atkinson—I'll always remember him with gratitude) were the Americans. The American film critics chose it as the best foreign film of the year. So, I thought I'd go to Hollywood. I had a lot of friends there from the old Rex Ingram-*Ben Hur* [1925] days. In fact I had a job waiting for me at MGM. Then my agent, Christopher Mann, asked Alexander Korda to *see The Edge of the World*. Although he didn't have much money at the time he gave me a year's contract without quite knowing what I could do for him, but just to keep me in the country. I'll always remember that.

TW: Didn't you direct *The Thief of Bagdad* [1940] in America?

MP: No. People got that wrong. We all knew the war was coming but not when, of course. Alex had already promised Churchill that as soon as war was declared, all the top technicians he had working on *The Thief of Bagdad* would immediately pitch in under the leadership of Ian Dalrymple, who was a very good editor as well as producer, and make the first propaganda film of the war, which was *The Lion Has Wings* [1939].

When war was declared, I was working on the flying carpet sequences with Sabu. That was on Sunday. On Monday I was already shooting for the Royal Air Force (RAF). We were flying over the balloon barrage and going down to Mildenhall, which was a bomber station, so I was able to get them leaving on the first air raid of the war to Kiel. Others took over various parts of *The Lion Has Wings*, so filming on *The Thief of Bagdad* came to a complete stop. Then Korda tucked the whole thing under his arm, including Conrad Veidt and Sabu, his brothers, the whole production, really all that was left—the big scene in the Temple with the all-seeing Eye and the Spider and the Grand Canyon scenes. That was all filmed here in this studio (i.e., the present site of Zoetrope). The scenes were constructed here and were shot either by Alexander or Zoltan Korda.

TW: What led to your collaboration with Emeric Pressburger and who did what?

MP: Emeric's the writer and I'm the director. We only called ourselves producers to stop others from calling themselves producers. Korda introduced us. Emeric was a contract writer for Korda and I was a contract director. When Korda and Irving Asher, the producer, decided to make *The Spy in Black* [1939] with Conrad Veidt and Valerie Hobson, Emeric was brought in to re-write the script because Veidt's part was not good enough. I was taken over from the contract I had with Korda to direct it and we made a big success of it. It opened during the first week of the war and was a huge success—about a heroic German! By that time I was working on *The Lion Has Wings* and so I said to Emeric, "Sit down, old chap, and write an original—*Contraband* [1940] with Conrad Veidt and Valerie Hobson—because it looks like the film business is folding up, so, before that, let's make another picture." It turned out to be the first of hundreds during the war.

TW: One scene in *Contraband* intrigued me. Toward the end of the film there is a fight in an attic room with all these busts of Chamberlain. When one character knocks another out cold with a bust, he speaks the line, "The old boy still has some fight left in him yet." Wasn't this the period when Chamberlain had left the office of Prime Minister?

MP: No, he was still in office. When France fell, Chamberlain was out and Churchill in. But, at the time, Churchill was Lord of the Admiralty and Chamberlain still Prime Minister. But, of course, he was already the laughing stock of the Nazis and of his own people.

TW: I notice the influence of America even in your British films. In *The Life and Death of Colonel Blimp* [1943] you have the World War I American Negro soldier, there's John Sweet in *A Canterbury Tale* [1944], and, of course, the final romantic alliance between Briton and American in *A Matter of Life and Death* [1946].

MP: We were following a rough propaganda line dictated by the Ministry of Information but, as you rightly say, I've always had this link with Hollywood because there were always people here I'd either met when we were quite young or knew about. We had mutual friends as when William Wyler first came over to England to do one or two propaganda films for the war effort. I've always been a great believer in London and Hollywood being closely in touch. Hollywood very badly needs a flourishing industry with London because of all the actors, writers, and general talent. We need an exchange of talent all the time and it's very bad for the business if everything is concentrated in Hollywood as it is now, with only one or two pictures being made in London. It's out of balance.

TW: So what exactly is your present role as a creative consultant?

MP: I come in on nearly everything. My advice is asked. It doesn't have to be taken. Quite often Francis will ask my opinion about sequences and rushes even when we're shooting. We also discuss other films that are going to be made here. Scripts are written. I read them and give my opinion. There's a good deal to do. I'm pretty busy. I find I'm busier advising than making a film!

TW: Your special project is Ursula Le Guin's *The Earthsea Trilogy* [1975]. What attracted you to this project in particular?

MP: Ten years ago, the first book in this trilogy—*A Wizard of Earthsea*—was published by Puffin in England. It got the most fabulous review in *The Times Literary Supplement*. I liked the sound of it and went right out and bought it. I read it and could not believe that such a distinguished piece of writing was published by Puffin. That's not saying anything about Puffin but Puffin's for kids, and this is by no means only for kiddies. It's for everybody. So I wrote a letter saying, "It's great!" "Who are you?" "Who did the map?" and "Why are you being published by Puffin?" This started a correspondence that went on for the next ten years. She published two more books in the trilogy. Each one was just as good as the other, so gradually when I gave up the idea of doing *The Tempest* in England—because people said, "Oh Christ! Now he wants to do *The Tempest*! It's a good script but you know Micky Powell and you never know where it will end!"—I began to rough out a script of the Ursula Le Guin trilogy. Having done a few sequences, I summoned up courage and sent them to her. She was delighted with them. I said, "In that case, let's do the script together." We have done it so by correspondence. We have met only twice, once in San Francisco and Portland, Oregon, where she lives. It's been a most happy collaboration and it's still going on.

TW: Throughout your career you've had several fruitful collaborations with actors—Conrad Veidt, Anton Walbrook, Pamela Brown, Esmond Knight, and, of course, the best screen performance from Wendy Hiller in *I Know Where I'm Going* [1945].

MP: I love working with good actors. It's really a creative process, what goes on between you, if you trust each other. It's the way that Scorsese is cultivating a wonderful relationship with Robert De Niro. They now understand each other's slightest thoughts. It makes for wonderful support on the screen, not just in life. Esmond Knight was an old friend and I knew what a versatile actor he was. Everyone else just knew him as a handsome leading man.

TW: I find in your English films an interesting critique of British institutions and insularity, particularly in *Colonel Blimp*. What gave you the idea for this film?

MP: It was the previous film—*One of Our Aircraft Is Missing* [1942]. It had Godfrey Tearle playing an old rear-gunner based on the character of Arnold Wilson, who was lost but said, "I'm going to fight this war and not hide behind the bodies of young men!" He had a scene with the pilot (Hugh Burden) in which they talked about the girls (one of whom was Pamela Brown) and he said, "You know, you're very like me when I was young and you'll be just as I am when you're old." The young man said to him, "Do you feel all right, George?" This scene was cut out of the picture. It came at an awkward time and was a bit too long. But Emeric said to me afterwards, "Let's make a film about that idea"—the young man who can't understand what the old man was talking about and the older man who remembers how he was when he was young.

TW: We've now seen the full version In England, particularly the opening confrontation scene (properly restored) between James McKechnie's young officer and Roger Livesey's Blimp.

MP: He says all sorts of insulting things and the old Blimp says, "How on earth can you know what I was like forty years ago?" We then go back and see that he was just as hot-headed, only the War Office cracked down on him or he decided to settle down to being a jolly good soldier.

The full version is an entirely different picture, because it was central really to hear the incomprehension of the young man and then go back to relive the life of the old man. Emeric Pressburger and I owe that to the BBC (British Broadcasting Corporation) and BFI (British Film Institute) because they got together and decided to reconstitute it.

TW: There's a remarkable scene between Blimp and a South African soldier in World War I. The latter believes in torturing information out of captured Germans while Blimp still holds to the anachronistic British sense of fair play.

MP: That was a good sequence later completely cut out. The actor was Reginald Tate, who had played Rochester in the stage version of *Jane Eyre* just before that.

TW: It was quite forward for a movie made at that time to show that Britain has to adopt some unorthodox methods to survive.

MP: Oh, sure. We meant it to be hard-hitting. It wasn't cut at the time, just criticized. The War Office was shocked about it.

TW: Didn't Churchill try to suppress the whole film?

MP: That was because old James Grigg at the War Office was making such a fuss about it. "It's bringing the Army into disgrace!" I don't think that Churchill ever read the script.

TW: Though I haven't seen it for over ten years, *49th Parallel* [1941] seemed to have a certain degree of complexity.

MP: Not really. It's a very simple idea, like the one in Agatha Christie's *Ten Little Indians* [1939].

TW: As a propaganda movie it seems to have a simple idea, but in the film I end up admiring Eric Portman's German officer. He does make it to the U.S.A. but he's brought back to British territory by very unfair means. There are characters supposed, at the time, to represent the best of Allied ideals but I find them very difficult to believe in—Olivier's obnoxious French-Canadian, Walbrook's weak Huttie, and Leslie Howard's silly Englishman. At one point in the film he's criticized by a German character for escaping to Canada to avoid conscription. At no point of the film is this ever refuted.

MP: Well, what about it? People are complex. They're not just black and white.

TW: It seems very remarkable for a film of its time, when Germans were generally painted very black elsewhere.

MP: It's certainly remarkable in that we were both very civilized people. We thought—and still think—that the best propaganda is insidious propaganda. Nobody believes black-and-white propaganda.

TW: I believe you once described *A Canterbury Tale* as a crusade against materialism?

MP: One of the themes of the story was that. Emeric said, "Why don't we make a film about the sort of ideals we are fighting for?" Obviously, one of the most interesting characters in a discussion of that kind is the complete materialist played by Dennis Price.

TW: At the climax he does get to play in Canterbury Cathedral.

MP: Yes, but he's only one of the pilgrims. They all get their desire. The girl finds her young man, whom she thought was dead;

John Sweet learns that his fiancée has gone to Australia with the WACs; and Dennis Price plays the organ before going overseas and probably getting killed. All get their desire except Mr. Culpepper.

TW: I find that the three pilgrims who get their desire are all learning. They have their traditions behind them, like Dennis Price, who wants to play the organ properly. The American is interested in the English heritage. Eric Portman also reveres England but his other side is "The Glue Man," pouring glue on English girls to stop them from fraternizing with GIs.

MP: The trouble with a man like that is that he's a loner. If he had had a wife, she'd have told him not to be so silly and taken his glue away from him. But he's a typical Englishman in that way. I tried to indicate that by the type of things he was interested in. You see in his room mountain climbing and walking scenes—things you do alone. So a chap on his own gets a bit cracked sometimes—monomaniacal.

TW: The opening scenes of a falcon transferred into an aircraft and the falconer into a soldier to abruptly show the passage of time in a second seemed very reminiscent of what happens to the bone in the "Dawn of Man" sequence from Kubrick's *2001* [1968].

MP: Others have pointed that out to me. We always borrow from one another. Martin Scorsese always says he borrowed this or that from *Peeping Tom* [1960] or *The Red Shoes* [1948].

TW: What was your basic intention in making *A Matter of Life and Death*?

MP: We were asked by the Ministry of Information to make a film about Anglo-American relations. They said that, as long as we were losing the war, relationships were very good but, when we started winning together, relationships were deteriorating a bit. People started to criticize each other. You remember some of the things that General Patton said. So they suggested we make something amusing and witty about American relationships with the British. The whole film was based on that. All the different characters are designed towards that end. The man who does not die falls in love with an American girl when he should have reported in Heaven. From then on, it's a fight on Earth and in Heaven for the love and happiness of these two people—quite a simple idea but a *big* idea. I liked it very much. It's my personal favorite of all my films. But I don't think I could have made a fantasy of it. That's why all the miracle stuff came in. I got all that from all the doctors who'd been in the war and had seen so many brain injuries happening around them.

TW: What made you decide to do the Heaven scenes in monochrome and the English scenes in color?

MP: We thought they should be opposed to each other. It seemed pretty obvious. It was Emeric's idea that one should be in monochrome and the other in color. Then it seemed quite natural that the world everybody knew should be in color and the world they didn't in monochrome. As the angels were going to have white wings anyway, it would be all right. It all fitted in.

TW: Was there a critique of British insularity and imperialism along with the sexual repression themes in *Black Narcissus* [1947]?

MP: Not really. There was some of that in the book and we admired the book very much. It was one of the few films we made taken from a book, Rumer Godden's 1939 book. It was very well balanced about the Indians and the British, as in her 1946 novel *The River*, filmed by Renoir in 1951.

TW: Were not the nuns destroyed not only by their personal flaws but also by the nature of the environment?

MP: It was because of the *special* environment. They were obviously successful down in Calcutta where the mother monastery was. But when they were put in this extraordinary, windy palace, it was too much for them—the atmosphere and the loneliness and, as they say, the wind. And, of course, Deborah Kerr in her big scene when she describes to David Farrar and Kathleen Byron how she had a lover in Ireland and he went away. Because she was so ashamed at being deserted, she became a nun.

TW: I notice that, in contrast to Hitchcock, as a director you seem fascinated by red-haired women in your films—Kathleen Byron, Pamela Brown, Maxine Audley, and Moira Shearer, to name a few.

MP: I do like red hair very much. It usually goes with a quick temperament and lovely skin.

TW: *Gone to Earth* [1950] was a co-production with David Selznick?

MP: It was. Funnily enough, I'm gong to have dinner with Jennifer Jones this week.

TW: One reference work mentions narration by Joseph Cotten.

MP: There was some narration in the American version—that is the Selznick version—but not in ours. It was slightly different from Selznick's. He shot some extra scenes and they were directed by Rouben Mamoulian. He told me about them and said they were not very important changes.

TW: Was Jennifer Jones's role similar to her *Duel in the Sun* [1946] image?

MP: No, it was a very much more moving role. She was a very simple childlike sort of girl. Esmond Knight played her father, a coffin-maker. She was a real Shropshire country girl, very simple and attractive. She marries the parson and runs off with the squire.

TW: Was this a project you wanted to do yourself?

MP: No. But many English filmmakers were interested in Mary Webb. At one point they were going to make a film of her novel *Precious Bane* [1924], which was a very big bestseller. Robert Donat was going to star in it but because of the war they did not make it. Korda had bought the rights to the Mary Webb book *Gone to Earth* and so he asked us if we would like to film it. All my family on my mother's side come from Worcestershire and Shropshire (my father's side is from the Welsh Marches), so I was quite keen to do it as I knew the people, the country, the voices. It was a very good story but rather melodramatic. *Gone to Earth* was our most popular film in France up to that time, where it was called *Le Renarde*—*The Vixen*—and still is.

TW: Were you satisfied with the final version?

MP: Yes, I thought it was a beautiful film. If you want to criticize it, it was a little long-winded. It's a simple theme. There wasn't much complication in it except, "Will she run away with the squire?" and "Will she run away from the squire to the parson?" That was about it. So I made a gorgeous picture with marvelous hunting scenes. I re-created the country of my childhood with all the horses, dogs, dog-carts, traps, and the kind of people I knew when I was a child.

TW: I find in British criticism, particularly journalism, a suspicion of the operatic use of cinema. Anything highly visual and colorful that cannot be confined within the canons of good taste, straightforward narrative, and low-key control, is regarded as being in "bad taste." It's a smear that has been used unjustly against your films, particularly *The Red Shoes*, *The Tales of Hoffmann* [1951], and *Oh . . . Rosalinda!!* [1955], which are based on the operatic effect.

MP: Yes, that's right. Of course, they can always criticize my taste. I don't mind that.

TW: *The Red Shoes* was considerably successful at the time?

MP: The film went considerably over budget because we did not realize that when we had a ballet company we also would have to see them quite often in the course of the story, because it's all about a ballet. So we found that we used them about every day for scenes and rehearsals. This took us over our original budget for the dance part of the film, but it was still the most commercially successful film we ever made.

TW: Was *The Tales of Hoffmann* a difficult project to get off the ground?

MP: Not terribly, because we weren't too happy with the films we had made with Korda up to that time. This was the second time we were with him after the war and they hadn't quite come off. We couldn't agree on a subject between us. Thomas Beecham, who enjoyed working with us on *The Red Shoes*, asked us to come and see him and suggested we do an opera—*The Tales of Hoffmann*. We liked the idea and, when we suggested it to Korda, he asked one or two people and they were all enthusiastic. Korda had never seen the opera. So it was quite a happy picture because everybody agreed to do it. We got all the old gang from *The Red Shoes* together again—Helpmann, Massine, and Moira—and got happily to work. It was a very happy picture and got quickly done. We worked for some time with Sir Thomas on the cutting and arranging of the score. It was not new music but the themes had to be developed a little bit differently from the opening—the "Dragonfly" ballet and things like that. When we were quite satisfied with all that on the piano, Sir Thomas did the orchestration and we recorded the picture with selected voices. They were selected to look like the actors, actresses, and dancers who played the parts in the film. Then the whole film was made to playback. It only took about forty-five days and was what I call a "composed film." What had been done before—and I always thought it was a good idea—was a film called *The Robber Symphony* [1936], in which Friedrich Feher wrote the music, recorded it, and then did a film to the music. I said, "This must be the only way to do an opera, so let's record it with singers and mostly record it with dancers, then we'll have a wonderful picture." In effect, that's the way it worked out. We had the first night in America at the Metropolitan Opera.

TW: This is very reminiscent of silent film directors who had an orchestra on set to play to their actors for inspiration.

MP: Yes. I go back a long way. I worked with big directors who had their four-piece orchestra on the set, like Rex Ingram. The first film I worked on—*Mare Nostrum* [1926]—had a theme tune continually being played, "The Serenata to Shelley."

TW: Was your idea with *Oh . . . Rosalinda!!* to make a popular version of an opera with general appeal, using star names of the time?

MP: It was Emeric's idea. The girls were very good. Mel Ferrer was a good comedian. I liked the idea but I think we tried too hard on that. It became a little complicated and wasn't simple enough.

TW: I found problems of synchronization with the music.

MP: Yes. An operetta's a very tricky thing to produce, much more than an opera. It's difficult to make into a film because the plot is stupid, intentionally stupid, and you don't go out of your way to make a stupid plot in a film. Sometimes they arrive on your lap but you shouldn't try to do them. An operetta has to have excuses for misunderstandings like a farce, nice frothy numbers, everybody having a good time. It's not quite on the same level as a fine film.

TW: Obsessiveness and creativity link many of your characters—Anton Walbrook in *The Red Shoes* and *The Tales of Hoffmann* and Mark Lewis of *Peeping Tom*.

MP: All artists are more or less obsessed. They're more interesting when they are—and more obsessive.

TW: What led you to make *Peeping Tom*?

MP: I got in touch with Leo Marks because I'd heard that he'd done a very clever scene involving a cryptogram for *Carve Her Name with Pride* [1958]. It was just after I'd parted from Emeric Pressburger. He first suggested a story of a double agent who betrays both sides, but I said I didn't want to do a spy story. We talked for two or three weeks. Finally, he came to me with this idea, "Would you like to make a film about a young man who murders people with his camera?" I said [*clicking his fingers*], "Yes! You're on! Just tell me the idea." He gave me some ideas and I commissioned him. After that he came round twice a week with more sequences and I would criticize them and he would re-write them. Gradually the script was done that way but he wrote the whole script. It was his idea: Leo Marks.

TW: Was the idea of audience identification with the killer there from the start?

MP: Yes. It's the way you shoot it. You can look on at a thing or you can preach about it or you can absolutely identify yourself with the young cameraman. Since any good director turns himself into a camera—*I Am a Camera* [1955] is the story of every director—I decided to do it that way. I did the horrifying sequence with the young boy with my son Columba, who was about seven at the time, because I knew he wouldn't be frightened if he did it with me. The, as he played my son, I played his father in the film-within-the-film. It gradually grew like that, so the whole thing became a family affair and the family practically turned into a lens.

TW: Did you anticipate the storm that arose when the film was released?

MP: No. I was very surprised because they weren't just bad reviews but vicious attacks. They more or less said that I was morbid and diseased in my mind and was trying to influence other people to be the same. I don't think any director ever had a worse attack. I was completely taken aback, very surprised, and it did me a lot of harm professionally. It meant that any subject I wanted to do that was unusual—and I have a whole shelf of them—I wasn't allowed to. I could not raise the money. What I should have done when I realized this, was that I should have come straight here. They have not got the prejudices here. I knew my films were known there. I didn't know they were so admired, although I've kept friendships here for the forty or fifty years since I started with an American company. But I clung to England because I'm English and naturally wanted to make English films. But I should have seen the writing on the wall and cut and run.

TW: Was *Peeping Tom's* voyeurism influenced by Hitchcock?

MP: No, not at all. In *Psycho* [1960], which I think is his best picture, there's so much humor inside that saves it. I think he got criticized, but they didn't take it as seriously as they took *Peeping Tom*.

TW: Don't you think England has a particularly negative attitude towards creativity, and people doing things in new directions, which is harmful in the end?

MP: I don't know whether it is a general thing. If they do attack an artist, they're worse than anybody because a certain amount of hypocrisy comes into it as well. Look at Francis Bacon. He really got severely mauled. But I don't think the English public and cognoscenti are worse than any others. Perhaps there is a source of hypocrisy that gets added to it. Also, being islanders, they really are insular. They're a bit isolated from Continental thought and I never have been. I've always been very closely identified with everything that's happening there. I know a lot about it, a lot about art, and they may be a little bit jealous of that.

TW: I've read that you originally wanted Pamela Brown to play Anna Massey's mother instead of Maxine Audley.

MP: Yes, because she and Anna Massey could easily be mother and daughter. They look a bit like each other and have almost the same color hair. Pamela's was a deep red. Anna's was more chestnut. They would have made a wonderful mother and daughter.

TW: Mark's stepmother is blonde. So are the prostitutes he kills. Was he taking something against his stepmother out on them?

MP: Well, I didn't go that deeply into it except instinctively.

TW: You've done cameo appearances before in *One of Our Aircraft Is Missing* and in *The Edge of the World*.

MP: In both cases it wasn't just as a show-off, because the kind of actor we'd have had to take to the island of Foula in *The Edge of the World* would have been unbearable, so I played the part and my wife played the girl. Then the part in *One of Our Aircraft Is Missing*—it just happened that the actor didn't arrive at the airfield where we were shooting or else he didn't have his pass. So I just stepped in and did the part for him.

TW: For the BBC-TV showing of *The Edge of the World*, you shot a new prologue and epilogue, returning there forty years later. The North Sea oil was proposed as something that changed the situation of the islanders. I've heard from some people living on the Scottish coast that the oil has not preserved the communities but scattered them even more. Accommodation, particularly in Aberdeen, is now very expensive.

MP: On the mainland, yes. But you'll find that it's had a tremendous effect in Shetland. What it's done for Lerwick is known. They are frightfully good negotiators. The Shetlanders did the deal themselves with the oil companies. They only leased them the port. The big oil port up there is leased only for twenty years. After that, they own it. It's revolutionized the economy of Shetland. They're a very hardheaded and good-humoured people. Very difficult to get round them.

TW: I read somewhere that you have stated your admiration for Walt Disney.

MP: He was one of the great innovators in film. One of the things I disliked was that, when talkies came in, a lot of the timing of silent films went out the window and nobody made those marvelous slapstick comedies anymore, because there were only verbal jokes. But Disney kept on making those wonderful cartoons for at least another ten years, so he kept alive the whole idea of film comedy and narrative-through-image. People don't realize that they owe an enormous lot to him. His films still move. For five years pictures just bogged down in a welter of talk. He was a great inventor and innovator. I was very fond of him; whenever I was in Hollywood after the war, I always spent a day with him.

TW: There are surrealistic and fantasy elements in all of your films, particularly *The Small Back Room* [1949]. Which branch of surrealism interests you?

MP: I don't altogether agree about surrealism because, trained as I have been from the very early days, films are surrealistic. Any film. Because anybody who can start to tell a story in a street or a field just using a camera and an actor—that's pure surrealism. Anything may happen. It's more expressionism that you are referring to. There was a sequence where David Farrar was waiting for the girl to come back to the room. There's a wonderful shot of him underneath, with the bottle falling over on him. We made several bottles of different sizes and shot them from different angles and had great fun doing it. But the critics jumped on me immediately, "Oh, Michael Powell with his German tendencies and German art director must have these German expressionist ideas!"

TW: There are some things that have worked very well, like those giant pencils in Mark's pocket in *Peeping Tom*.

MP: They were about three-and-a-half feet long. That's the only way you could have done that. Leo wrote the sequence just like that—the pencils fall out of his pocket. I said, "You realize, Leo, pencils are only so big. The gantry of a studio is forty feet up. But I can do it all right." When he saw it, he said that it was one of the best shots in the picture, yet he never knew at the time. I asked the prop man to give me some dummy pencils and pens to drop in this sequence, over three feet long! And it worked.

TW: After making *The Earthsea Trilogy*, do you see yourself based in America permanently?

MP: No, I hope not. One of the things I hope to get together is a group of producers and then a studio like Pinewood. That's why Coppola and I were thinking of buying Pinewood. Also, I hear that a consortium in England would like to do the same thing. Good luck to them because it's no good having the dead hand of Rank over the whole thing. If Rank is not going to make pictures, then let them get cut. What isn't fair is to sit on the whole thing and say, "We're not going to make any more pictures." It has a dampening effect on the whole British film industry. I would like to get together a group of five or six clever producers—some of whom are over here making pictures—to guarantee Pinewood a certain number of pictures per year. That's how we did the old independent producers set-up when we went from Denham Studios to Pinewood with David Lean, Ronald Neame, Carol Reed, and that bunch. It's not too late to do it again.

Bibliography

Christie, Ian, and Andrew Moor, eds. *The Cinema of Michael Powell: International Perspectives on an English Film-Maker*. London: British Film Institute, 2005

Christie, Ian. *Arrows of Desire: The Films of Michael Powell and Emeric Pressburger*. Rev. ed. London: Faber and Faber, 1994.

Christie, Ian, ed. *Powell, Pressburger, and Others*. London: British Film Institute, 1978.

Gough-Yates, Kevin, ed. *Michael Powell in Collaboration with Emeric Pressburger*. London: British Film Institute, 1971.

Howard, James, *Michael Powell*. London: B. T. Batsford, 1996.

Powell, Michael. *Million-Dollar Movie*. London: Mandarin, 1993.

Powell, Michael. *A Life in Movies: An Autobiography*. London: Heinemann, 1986.

Salwolke, Scott. *The Films of Michael Powell and the Archers*. Lanham; Md.: Scarecrow Press, 1997.

"Carol Reed on Directing Orson Welles in *The Third Man*," by Charles Thomas Samuels, excerpted from his "Interview with Carol Reed, 1971" in Samuels' book *Encountering Directors* (New York: G. P. Putnam's Sons, 1972), 163-179.

Immediately after the Second World War, Carol Reed (1906-76) ascended to the front rank of British filmmakers with *Odd Man Out* (1947). This coincided with his becoming his own producer, and, for the next four years, everything he touched as a director turned to gold. *Odd Man Out* was a beautifully complex psychological thriller that overcame its grim subject—the final hours of a mortally wounded IRA gunman on the run—to become a critical and box-office success on both sides of the Atlantic. Along with Michael Powell and Emeric Pressburger, David Lean, and Frank Launder and Sidney Gilliat, Reed was part of that generation of British filmmakers whose movies transformed the British film industry

The success of *Odd Man Out* led to a contract with Alexander Korda, for whom Reed made five films, beginning with *The Fallen Idol* (1948). This was a superbly crafted thriller that turns on a child's misconception of adult emotional entanglements. It was followed in 1949 by the director's acknowledged masterpiece, *The Third Man*. This was Reed's second collaboration with Graham Greene and is the best *film noir* ever made in Great Britain. Like all the best of the genre, the film is deeply romantic, despite its surface cynicism, and it's this that has caused it to remain in the public memory for so long, together with the fact that *The Third Man* did not underestimate its audience's intelligence. The picture is set in a crumbling, depressed postwar Vienna, which, as beautifully shot by Robert Krasker in atmospheric black and white, seems almost to be a character in the story.

After his excellent but unjustly neglected *Outcast of the Islands* (1951), Reed found his critical reputation taking a somewhat downward turn in the 1950s and early '60s, when he turned out a number of more expensive but less meticulously crafted productions such as the Hollywood-made *Trapeze* (1958) and *The Agony and the Ecstasy* (1965). His fortunes revived with *Oliver!* (1968), an exuberant musical version of Dickens' *Oliver Twist*, which won six Academy Awards, including Best Picture and Best Director.

Charles Thomas Samuels: You've said that much of the excellence of *The Third Man* [1949] is due to location shooting. If you had your choice, would you shoot everything on location?

Carol Reed: Yes. I suffered a lot of opposition over going to Vienna with *The Third Man*. In those days, one didn't take actors on location. But here's an example of the way finance does dominate the business. If you've got five weeks on location, you know you've got to get all your shots in that period. We had a day and a night unit. The actors we used at night didn't work in the day and vice versa. We worked from eight p.m. to five a.m., then went to bed, got up at ten a.m., worked with the day unit until four, and then went back to bed until eight. That way we got double the work done in the same time. It's a bit of a rush, but it's better to rush than not get it all and have to match things in the studio.

CTS: Despite your expressed admiration for producers, you've often acted in that role yourself. Why?

CR: Because on those particular pictures I didn't need a producer, the money was set. But a producer can be very valuable.... I've never had problems with producers except when they've tried to rush me. Some producers are inclined to do that even when they know you're not behind because they hope to earn some time in case you fall back. When they do that to me, it has the reverse effect.

CTS: How much supervision do you give your editor?

CR: I edit as I go along—during the lunch break. I never take lunch in the studio; I don't like to sit down or see anyone else sitting down. I feel more lively when I stand. I go into the cutting room at one every day to see the previous day's rushes. Then each Saturday I work with the editor (if we're not shooting) so that the final cut only takes two days after shooting's done.

CTS: Your editing is very brisk.

CR: David Lean told me I cut too much.

CTS: He cuts too little. Tell me, why did you use Robert Bearing to edit so many of your films?

CR: I had no control. He was chief editor for all films made at Gainsborough. I didn't get on with him.

CTS: Could he change your work?

CR: It was such a different business then. Bob Bearing was inclined to resent directors. Very often I wasn't even invited to see the editing. But a director must work with his editor. Directing is conveying to actors what you had in mind while working with the author. After that, the editor must understand not only what you did on the floor, but what the author had in mind—a man the editor has never even met.

CTS: Let's move from technique to content for a minute. Although several of your films are outstanding, they rarely move outside traditional practices—except one in particular. You like unhappy endings (that's why I find *The Fallen Idol* [1948] case puzzling). Is this a conscious rebellion against commercial formulas?

CR: You must always do as you like, gambling on the possibility that what you like is also commercial. I used to be very much criticized for ending my films unhappily. At one time, it was thought that every picture must end with an embrace so that the audience could go out happy, but I don't think that's what it did. A picture should end as it has to. I don't think anything in life ends "right." The ending of *The Fallen Idol* is only partly happy. After all, the boy is now finished with the butler, although he used to adore him. In *The Third Man*, Graham Greene wanted Joseph Cotten to overtake Alida Valli in that car; then the film would finish with the couple walking down the road. I insisted that she pass him by. David Selznick had some money in the film (I think it took care of Cotten and Orson Welles's valet). I must say he was very nice and appreciative about the picture as soon as he saw it, but he said, "Jesus, couldn't we make a shot where the girl gets together with the fella?" "It was in the original script," I said, "But we chucked it out. I'm not sure if it was a good idea." But I mean, the whole point with the Valli character in that film is that she'd experienced a fatal love—and then along comes this silly American!

CTS: Whose idea was it to cast Orson Welles as Harry Lime?

CR: Mine. I was having dinner one night with Orson. I'd just gotten the synopsis from Graham Greene, which I thought was all right, so I told Orson that there was a wonderful part in it for him. He asked to read it, but I said, "Look, the script's not ready yet, but I'm sure you'll like it even though you don't come on until halfway through." "I'd much rather come in two-thirds of the way through," he replied. After a week, I got Greene's treatment, which I accepted. By this time David Selznick wanted me to do *Tess of the D'Urbervilles* [1891, Thomas Hardy], which I wasn't very keen on. He had a script, which we both thought was pretty bad, so I asked him to have work done to it and meanwhile let me go ahead with *The Third Man*, since it was something we could knock off quickly. I said I wanted Orson and Cotten, who I knew was under contract to Selznick, as was Valli. "Cotten and Valli you can have," he said, "but you can't have Orson." I asked why, knowing very well that Orson wasn't under contract to him and that he preferred me to use someone who was. Besides that, I think Orson one day had made a pass at Jennifer or something. Selznick was very strong on Noël Coward's playing Harry, but of course that would have been disastrous. It went on and on. When I started the film, Selznick was still going on about Noël. Alexander Korda, the producer, didn't care, however, so in the end I got Orson.

CTS: What was Welles like to work with?

CR: Wonderful! Marvelous!

CTS: He didn't try to direct himself?

CR: He was difficult only about the starting date, telling me how busy he was with this and that. So I said, "Look, we're going on location for five weeks. Any week—give us two days' notice—we'll be ready for you. And give me one week out of seven in the studio." He kept to it. He came straight off the train in Vienna one morning, and we did his first shot by nine o'clock. "Jeez," he said, "this *is* the way to make pictures!" He walked across the Prater, said two lines to Cotten, and then I said. "Go back to the hotel, have breakfast; we're going into the sewers, and we'll send for you." "Great! Wonderful!" He comes down into the sewers and says, "Carol, I can't play this part!" "What's the matter?" "I can't do it. I can't work in a sewer. I come from California! My throat! I'm so cold!" I said,

"Look, Orson, in the time it's taking us to talk about this, you can do the shot. All you do is stand there, look off and see some police after you, turn, and run away." "Carol," he said, "Get someone else to play this. I cannot work under such conditions." "Orson, Orson, we're lit for you. Just stand there." "All right, but do it quick!" Then he looks off, turns away, and runs off into the sewers. Then all of a sudden I hear a voice shouting, "Don't cut the cameras! Don't cut the cameras! I'm coming back." He runs back, through the whole river, stands underneath a cascade over his head (this out of camera range, mind you!), and does all sorts of things, so that he came away absolutely dripping. "How was that?" he asks. "Wonderful Marvelous!" I said. "Okay. I'll be back at the hotel. Call me when you need me." With Orson, you know, everything has to be a drama. But there were no arguments of any sort at all.

CTS: He improvised that scene! But surely not the famous hand coming through the grate!

CR: That was my hand; I did it on location before he arrived because I knew that Harry must try to escape the sewers. The shot immediately preceding that was done with Orson in the studio, because in Vienna there isn't any staircase leading directly up to a drain. . . . And the censors objected to Cotten's shooting Harry Lime (since it was a mercy killing). That's why Trevor Howard now shouts from off-camera, "If you see him, shoot." Cotten isn't killing a friend, you see, he's only following orders.

CTS: Who was responsible for the marvelous business in the introduction of Harry: the great idea of his being exposed by the cat?

CR: Oh, God, so many cats! That was all improvised.

CTS: How?

CR: I do happen to remember this. I was worried about finding Harry in that doorway; I didn't want Cotten just to pass by and see him because then the audience wouldn't know who the man in the doorway was. When Cotten brings Valli flowers, I placed a cat on her bed that Cotten tries to get to play with the string around the gift. But the cat just turns and jumps off.

CTS: Much as Valli won't respond.

CR: Exactly. Then the cat jumps through the window. Whilst Cotten had been trying to get the cat to play, I had him say, "Bad-tempered cat." Then I worked in the line for Valli: "He only liked Harry." We next look out the window, see a man come down the street, and watch him enter a doorway. So far as we know, it might be anyone. But by going over to him and playing with his shoelaces, the cat establishes that it's Harry.

CTS: Here's the director as author!

CR: It was a little trick, you know. But we used so many cats: one in Vienna, running down the street; another in the studio on the bed; another to play with the lace ... What was difficult was to get the cat to walk up to it.

CTS: How did you do that?

CR: Sardines! But how you bring it all back! The problem then was to get the cat to look up at Harry.

CTS: Let me search your instinct here. The devil is often shown accompanied by or in the shape of a cat. Is that what suggested this moment to you?

CR: No. I just liked the idea of a cat loving a villain—the charm of the man! Furthermore, I wanted Cotten to shout at Harry, although not knowing what the audience knew: who was in the doorway.

CTS: Another brilliant decision in the film is the zither music. How did you decide on Anton Karas?

CR: When we were on location, I used to store props in a studio outside the city. Whilst the boys were unloading, I'd go to a store to get carafes of wine for them. Nearby there was a tiny beer-and-sausage restaurant, with a courtyard in which this fellow played a zither for coins. I'd never heard a zither before, thought it was attractive, and wondered whether we could use a single instrument throughout the film, especially since the zither is so typical of Vienna. I got Karas to come back to my hotel one night, where he played for about twenty minutes. I then brought a recording of that back to the studio to see if the music fought against the dialogue—as some did—but a good deal of it worked well. Karas then came to London to live in that little cottage adjoining this house, which we used to own in those days. I had a moviola with a dupe of the film so we could match his playing against portions of the action. One night he asked me to come back and listen to a new tune he'd done, what came to be called "The Third Man Theme." "Why haven't you played that before?" I said. "I haven't played it for fifteen years," he answered, "because when you play in a café, nobody stops to listen; music is just background for talk and drinking and shouting. This tune takes a lot out of your fingers. I prefer playing 'Wien, Wien,' the sort of thing one can play all night while eating sausages at the same time." It turned out he'd composed the tune himself but had nearly forgotten it. What's driven other zither players mad (they can never figure out how it's done) is that he played the tune and then, with an earphone, re-recorded it, adding thirds. In the ordinary way, no zither player could do it.

CTS: Apart from the pleasantness of the music, there is the precise matching of musical phrases or chords and dialogue or action throughout the film. Did you tell Karas where things should go?

CR: Yes. For example, in the cat scene, I asked Karas to play a few sort of walking notes while the cat crossed the street and then, as it looked at Harry's shoe, ascending chords, which break into "The Third Man Theme" when it finally sees Harry and we hold on the cat's little face. That's the advantage of working with a single instrument. Usually, I talk to my composer, saying, "You know, we should have something amusing there, something romantic here." Then after three or four weeks, he comes to me, plays the piano, and says, "Here's what the drums are going to do," and then, "The strings are doing this." It doesn't mean a bloody thing to me. I just cross my fingers but don't know until we get to the first recording session, when it's too late to change.

CTS: Another notable feature of *The Third Man*, although one is already conscious of it in *Odd Man Out* [1947], is your penchant for off-angle shots. Was that a conscious effect?

CR: I hope it's not noticed by someone who's less familiar with pictures than you are. I intend it to make the audience uncomfortable.

CTS: So they'd think, "I don't know why, but this view of things is off."

CR: Exactly.

CTS: But you didn't use those shots before *Odd Man Out*, did you?

CR: I don't think so. I used it so much in *The Third Man*, however, that I remember William Wyler, after seeing the film, made me the gift of a spirit level. "Carol," he said, "next time you make a picture, just put it on top of the camera, will you!"

CTS: But from all the possible devices for disorienting the spectator, why did you choose this one?

CR: I shot most of the film with a wide-angle lens that distorted the buildings and emphasized the wet cobblestone streets (it cost a good deal to hose them down constantly) ... But the angle of vision was just to suggest that something crooked was going on; I don't think it's a very good idea. I haven't used it much since—only when I need to shoot someone standing behind another person who's sitting and I don't want to cut off his head.

Bibliography

Davies, Brenda. *Carol Reed*. London: British Film Institute, 1978.

Drazin, Charles. *In Search of the Third Man*. London: Limelight Editions, 1999.

Evans, Peter William. *Carol Reed*. Manchester, U.K.: Manchester University Press, 2005.

Moss, Robert F. *The Films of Carol Reed*. New York: Columbia University Press, 1987.

"'I'm a Picture Chap': David Lean on *A Passage to India*," by Harlan Kennedy. From *Film Comment*. 21.1 (Jan.-Feb. 1985): 28-32.

Spanning four decades, the movies of David Lean (1908-91) came ever more vastly built and budgeted, and with ever vaster breathing spaces between them. Five years each between *The Bridge on the River Kwai* (1957) and *Lawrence of Arabia* (1962), and three between *Lawrence* and *Doctor Zhivago* (1965). Five years between *Zhivago* and *Ryan's Daughter* (1970). Then fourteen years between *Ryan's Daughter* and *A Passage To India* (1984) [his final film].

In any event, the shade of E. M. Forster must have been casting sympathetic sighs Lean's way. The novelist's own travails in writing *A Passage To India* (over a ten-year period) were almost as momentous as Lean's in reaching the starting line on his longest, most cherished book-into-movie project. Yet, Sir David once insisted (knighted in the summer of 1984), "I would rather make one good picture in three years than make four others in the same time." Who could have doubted it? Who could have failed to be impressed by it? In a British cinema stuffed with oddball loners—Michael Powell with his hothouse romanticism, Robert Hamer with his gallows farce, the myth-seeking modernism of Nicolas Roeg and John Boorman—Lean's oddness was less *outré* but no less provocative.

One can describe almost in a straight line Lean's early, brisk rise from manning the clapperboard for Gaumont Pictures (he quit his father's accounting firm for films in 1927, aged nineteen) to becoming a writer-editor-commentator for Gaumont British newsreels to editing feature films (*As You Like It* [1937], *Pygmalion* [1938], *One of Our Aircraft Is Missing* [1942]) to his co-directing baptism on *In Which We Serve* (1942, sharing credit with Noël Coward) through to his own early movies, from the Coward and Dickens adaptations of the forties up to *Summertime* in 1955. But to understand Lean, you have to understand the principles of detonation in the British artistic temperament, a process unlike any other on earth. When frustrated British reticence reaches fission point, it turns straight into holocaust grandiloquence: the paintings of Francis Bacon, the films of Michael Powell, the magic moments in Laurence Olivier's acting.

It was after *Summertime* that Lean became, spectacularly, his own master. It's as if the repressed British artist had sensed release at the call of fifties blockbusterism, just as in *Summertime* skittering Katharine Hepburn sloughs spinsterhood at the mating call of Rosanno Brazzi. In adapting *A Passage to India*, Lean was keen to insure that Forster's own independent-minded women—the young Adela Quested (Judy Davis) and the older Mrs. Moore (Peggy Ashcroft)—didn't come over as "aggressive." Ironically, Lean's women, certainly in his early films and even (if more simplemindedly) in *Ryan's Daughter*, have often been the feistiest of independents: Jean Simmons' spitfire Estella in *Great Expectations* (1946), Hepburn yacking her way to late-blooming sexuality in *Summertime*, and, of course, Celia Johnson taking a gulp and throwing propriety to the winds in *Brief Encounter* (1945).

For the male artist—especially the British male artist—depicting the growth of passion and independence in a woman is a challenging task. Lean is often far more confident handling the absurdist agonies of the constipated British soul—Alec Guinness's Colonel Nicholson in *The Bridge on the River Kwai*, Peter O'Toole's pale, agonized Lawrence—than with plonking big, uncorseted emotions down on the screen. Yet so, in a way, was E. M. Forster—that miniaturist of the heart whose characters never quite trust their own emotions, even when they're most passionately gripped by them. Lean's challenge in *A Passage to India* was to marry his *gaucherie* of feeling with subtle insight into the novel's tragic collision of human value systems and cosmic nihilism, and to make the British movie about India "to which all others are trailers."

In 1985 at Hollywood's Bel Air Hotel, Harlan Kennedy interviewed Sir David Lean on the subject of *A Passage to India*.

Harlan Kennedy: When did you first read *A Passage to India*?

David Lean: You know, I cannot remember. It's a jolly hard book to read—it's tough. Have you been dipping in? *(Yes.)* I'll tell you a fascinating thing about it. Do you want me to go on and talk like this? *(Sure.)* I like a fairly strong narrative in a film and E. M. Forster—I don't think he's as concerned with narrative as a lot of people would claim. The trouble with making a film is that he keeps going off on the most wonderful sidetracks, and one is tempted to go down them with him. One writes pages of script and then thinks, "Well, wait a minute; I've gone off the story.

And then you have to cut, because it's a huge book. It was terribly difficult, because he's got a narrative there but it's awfully hard to find it. I used to sit myself down and think, "Now what is this section really about?" Now the end section—that's a fine kettle of fish. New characters popping up, a dying Rajah, and so on. Aziz letting his instruments rust.

HK: Obviously you had to collapse incidents, and a portion of the film totally invented by you, which does not derive from Forster, is the scene where Adela Quested (Judy Davis) goes cycling in the country and discovers an overgrown temple encrusted with marvelous erotic carvings of couples . . . well, coupling.

DL: That's totally mine, yes. You see the reason why?

HK: It depicts the sexual stirrings and awakening of desire within Adela.

DL: Correct. In the book and in the play particularly, I must tell you, Miss Quested was an absolute "stick," and I thought she was quite uninteresting. And when the idea is presented that Aziz had attempted whatever he attempted, in the caves, I thought, "What?" It didn't work. And I wanted to set it up so that you could argue afterwards, "Did he? Didn't he?" In the book and in the play Miss Quested was not a believable character on the whole, as far as her sexuality was concerned. I thought that I had to find a way that fills her out a little more, to let you see that she is beginning to awaken sexually . . . because India can do this, you know. There are two lots of people that go to India: Some get off the plane and want to get the next plane out; others want to stay for six months—and she obviously is one who wanted to stay for six months, and I wanted to catch a bit of that.

HK: Was the temple real or a construction?

DL: A couple of the long shots of the temple through trees are real; the rest is constructed in little bits and pieces cut together. It was all shot in different places, and I didn't know until I cut it if it would work—I went out on a limb. It does work, doesn't it?

HK: Indeed it does.

DL: Good. I meant it to be sort of sexually frightening—you know, her feelings, the roaring, and, my God, the monkeys going after her.

HK: Does this scene marry with a line—not in the book—at the trial in which she states that she did not love Ronny, her fiancé?

DL: "Seeing Chandrapore so far away, I realized I didn't love him." That's me. I was trying to make her go, as it were, almost into the past so that she's removed from the town, Ronny, just that. You know, it happens to people when they go down to the Mediterranean on holiday—Swedes, Finns, English people—go down to Spain and behave as they wouldn't normally. It's that sort of thing. And so the idea is that it's a sort of walk into old places, old mountains with that old ancient animal climbing up them.

HK: The mountain is fantastic.

DL: It's good, isn't it? It works. Because we went all over the place looking for that, and I found it. Nobody knew about it, because it's such a huge country. And it's about an hour out of Bangalore.

HK: There's a remarkable lack of music in the film. All the drama is in the voices and images. I also noticed that you were cutting on particular words. For example, someone would say, "Tomorrow we are in Ranjipur," and we cut to Ranjipur. Is this a purposeful technique you were using—opposed to dissolves?

DL: I rather *like* the technique. I haven't got many dissolves. In fact I've only got one fade-in, fade-out, which goes from the crocodile to the garden pasty. And there was a good reason for that, because I suddenly realized that to cut from the crocodile eating a body to "tea for two"... well, wiseacres would find that very funny. So I faded out and faded in, to separate them.

HK: In the trial scene you intercut between the earlier Judy Davis cave scene and the trial to illustrate her state of mind.

DL: Yes. When you have the court scene she says, "I lit a match," and I cut back to her in the cave looking out, and Aziz appears at the entrance of the cave; then I cut back to her in court looking at the cave. And you hear the voice, and it follows you. I was awfully pleased with that, and I thought it worked.

It's quite interesting the way you can cut and jump around in time in movies—I don't think it's been done too often—and there's enormous scope for it, as long as it's crystal clear so that you don't lose your audience and have them thinking, "What the hell is that?"

HK: Again in Forster, at the garden party (or the "bridge party," as he calls it) all the Indian men were dressed in European fashion, and it was very uncomfortable. But in the film it looks so nice that it doesn't look bad or uncomfortable—and the dialogue about "Why aren't we treating our guests . . ."

DL: Well, I thought it was bad enough to have the English characters all seated up on a raised part and the Indians standing below, just being totally ignored, looking up. I think Forster went a little bit overboard. I must tell you that one or two people objected that in the trial, which I practically rewrote and made a big scene of it, I put Mrs. Moore's death in the middle because I wanted Mrs. Moore to hang over the trial. I think it works.

One of the biggest scenes in the book is at the trial, when all the English take their seats and move up onto the platform until they're told by Das, the trial judge, to move down. I believe it would look really stupid if you're going to have a trial at which Aziz and eventually the girl are up against the English—they've got to be worthy opponents. And people moving their chairs up and down would be wrong. I'm glad I made that change, though many people said that Forster had them move up and down. . . . I know he did that but I refrained from doing it very purposefully in the same way I didn't "guy" the Indians with spats and awkward collars—I think it's a bit corny.

HK: How did you attempt to duplicate the mystical sound, the "ou-boum" Forster describes as a property of the caves? It was almost mocking—the eternal mocking the temporal.

DL: You know, it's very interesting, but "booms" were attacked like mad at the time by D. H. Lawrence, for instance. . . . But Forster said, and I think it's rather good, that the boom was a trick that he would have attempted nowhere else but in India. And it was, of course, a very worrying thing for me because if "BOOM" doesn't work, the whole cave incident doesn't work, and you've got everything falling in on you.

HK: Was Forster right about the British in India?

DL: Forster, oh dear, oh dear. I think he hated the English out there. And he was queer, and you can imagine how they must have disapproved of that—this damned Englishman working for a Maharajah. The dislike was mutual, but I've toned down a lot of that. It's all very well to criticize the English but just take a look at New Delhi, look at the railway system, look at the postal system—which works. We've left them all sorts of bad things, I suppose, but they also got some very good things.

HK: Do you feel that Forster's portrayal of the British woman in India was a fair one?

DL: I think that was more or less fair. In fact, I've made it rather worse, if anything. I've taken some of the worst stuff and put it onto the women, on to Mrs. Turton, the Collector's wife, rather than the men, because I don't think the men were all a lot of fools. It's awfully easy to sit back and say they were a lot of clowns. They weren't. But you can still meet these women in India today. Mrs. Turton would be retired and find herself, having had twelve servants, suddenly lucky that she has one. She doesn't know what hit her. It's rather sad, really. Because they lived a tremendous life out there—created their own towns.

HK: But the British of today have integrated themselves more fully into Indian life.

DL: Well, I'm quite a good example. I married one. I was married to her for several years.

HK: You can't get closer than that, I guess.

DL: Guess not.

HK: Now about the 1960 play *A Passage to India*, by Santha Rama Rau...

DL: I'll tell you a funny thing about that. I saw the play about twenty-five years ago, and it was a terrible thing because Norman Wooland—he was in Larry Olivier's *Hamlet* [1948]—played Fielding. He was awfully good, and I could not get his face out of my head. Whenever I thought of Fielding, I saw Norman Wooland up there superimposed over everything. The same thing happened with Zia Mohyeddin, who was very good as Aziz. (I gave him a small part as the guide to Peter O'Toole in *Lawrence of Arabia* [1962].) He was too old for Aziz now, and I believe it broke his heart because he wanted to be in it. And I just couldn't get *his* face out of my head. Now, I'm glad to say, they've been supplanted, but they're hovering there....

HK: Why do you keep working with Sir Alec Guinness?

DL: Well, Alec started his film career with me on *Great Expectations* [1946], then he did *Oliver Twist* [1948], *The Bridge on the River Kwai* [1957], and *Lawrence of Arabia*. It was rather a good working partnership. I like Alec. And I think he has the most difficult role in this film. It required a tremendously good character actor to bring it off, I think.

HK: Why is it the most difficult role in the film?

DL: You see, Godbole is everything. He's sort of first cousin to Mrs. Moore, he's got a sort of extrasensory perception—at least I gave him that; he's part mumbo-jumbo, part highly intelligent and cynical, part funny. It's a real bag of tricks to contain in one character.

HK: How do you prepare your films? Do you storyboard, do you do step-outs?

DL: I nearly always write the shooting script and imagine seeing it as a finished film on screen. I think that *this* might be good in a long shot, *that* in a close-up, *that* in a panning shot. And I try to write down the pictures that I see on an imaginary screen. I'm a picture chap, I like pictures, and when I go to the movies I go to see pictures. I think dialogue is nearly always secondary in a movie. It's awfully hard when you look back over the really great movies that you see in your life to remember a line of dialogue. You will not forget pictures.

HK: What films do you like?

DL: People ask me this, and so I'm wheeling out old answers. I remember when I first went to the movies, they hit me right in the eyeball. I'll never forget seeing *The Four Horsemen of the Apocalypse* [1921]. It had a wonderful sweep to it. And I saw it again only a few years ago, here in Los Angeles at FILMEX [Los Angeles International Film Exposition]. A new print and a forty-piece orchestra. Absolutely stunning, I thought. And I also like stars. It became a sort of thing to laugh at Valentino, Errol Flynn. For God's sake, they were both terrific—Douglas Fairbanks, too. Go and see *The Dawn Patrol* [1938], go and see *The Adventures of Robin Hood* [1938]: Flynn at his best. Wonderful! Wonderful man to watch!

I suppose it was those early moviemakers mostly I remember from my boyhood . . . getting out of the suburbs of London and into a really magic house . . . looking at that beam of light coming through the smoke. There were things on the screen that you thought you'd never ever see in real life, and I've been lucky enough to see a lot of them. I'll never forget seeing King Vidor's *The Big Parade* with John Gilbert and Renée Adorée saying "Goodbye" with the trucks going up to the "Front," and her left alone and everything moving against her. I've used it several times. I love that business with a single figure against moving people. . . . And then much later the shock of seeing *Citizen Kane* [1941] and the way Orson turned everything upside down. Wonderful, that dance he had with the girls in the newspaper office. Terrific! Hard to do that sort of thing.

HK: Have you seen Richard Attenborough's *Gandhi* [1982]?

DL: I have and I haven't. In India I saw a pirated tape that was a good half-hour short, and it was of appalling quality. So I can't really say that I've seen *Gandhi*.

HK: Why is there this sudden interest in India? Spielberg had a short sequence in *Close Encounters of the Third Kind* [1977], plus *Indiana Jones* [1984], *Gandhi*, two TV mini-series, *The Far Pavilions* [1984], and *The Jewel in the Crown* [1984]. And now Judith de Paul has just completed *Mountbatten: The Last Viceroy* [1986].

DL: People asked me that in India. They sort of approached me with a knowing smile: (*Lean in imitation of Indian speech.*) "I suppose you are cashing eeen on the present trend," or something like that. I think it's coincidence. I know we weren't trying to cash in on anything. . . . Kubrick did *2001: A Space Odyssey* [1968], and since then we've had a rash of space operas. Somebody will do a hit film about New Zealanders and everybody will rush off to New Zealand! That's movies.

Bibliography

Anderegg, Michael A. *David Lean*. Boston: Twayne, 1984.

Brownlow, Kevin. *David Lean: A Biography*. New York: St. Martin's Press, 1996.

Castelli, Louis P. *David Lean: A Guide to References and Resources*. Boston: G.K. Hall, 1980.

Maxford, Howard. *David Lean*. London: B. T. Batsford, 2001.

Phillips, Gene D. *Beyond the Epic: The Life and Films of David Lean*. Lexington: University Press of Kentucky, 2006.

Pratley, Gerald. *The Cinema of David Lean*. New York: A.S. Barnes, 1974.

Silver, Alain, and James Ursini. *David Lean and His Films*. 1974. Los Angeles: Silman-James Press, 1992.

Silverman, Stephen M. *David Lean*. New York: Harry N. Abrams, 1989.

Williams, Melanie. *David Lean*. Manchester, U.K.: Manchester University Press, 2017.

"Charles Crichton at Ealing Studios: An Interview," by Sidney Cole. For the British Film Institute (1987: previously unpublished in book or magazine form).

Director Charles Crichton (1910-99) began his career as an editor in 1935 with Alexander Korda's London Films, and in that capacity he worked on such productions as *Sanders of the River* (1935), *Things to Come* (1936) and *Elephant Boy* (1937). He soon left London Films for Ealing Studios and rose quickly through the ranks, making his directorial debut with *For Those in Peril* (1944).

Meticulous to the point of being referred to as a "perfectionist," Crichton came into his own at Ealing, a studio noted for its comedies, and among his best known are the quirky but charming *Titfield Thunderbolt* (1953) and the wildly popular *Lavender Hill Mob* (1951). He then tried his hand at drama—outside of Ealing—with *The Stranger in Between* (1952), starring Dirk Bogarde. When Ealing closed its doors in 1959, Crichton's film work petered off, and he turned more and more to television, becoming a prolific director of crime and adventure series. His occasional forays back into feature films were not particularly productive, and for the most part he remained in television, directing episodes of such popular shows as "Secret Agent" (1964), "The Avengers" (1961), and "Space: 1999" (1975).

In 1988, at the request of the star John Cleese, Crichton agreed to direct Cleese, Jamie Lee Curtis, and Kevin Kline in the offbeat comedy *A Fish Called Wanda*, which turned out to be a huge international hit. It was his biggest success, and also his last film. Charles Crichton died in London at 1999 at age the age of eighty-nine.

1. *Young Veteran*

Sidney Cole: What was the last picture before the outbreak of war that you worked on?

Charles Crichton: That was *The Thief of Bagdad* [1940].

SC: Yes, which wasn't completed so they took it away to America.

CC: It was nearly completed.

SC: So what happened to you now that there was a war on? How did it affect you?

CC: Well, I worked for a little while on a propaganda film at Denham Studios. You know, one was waiting to be called up. Then [Alberto] Cavalcanti wanted me to go and cut a little film called *Young Veteran* [1940] at Ealing, and apparently my work was satisfactory because they wanted me to go on and on. So I became a "reserved occupation" and I stayed at Ealing.

SC: Yes, those were "reserved occupation people"; if I remember rightly you had to be thirty years old and in certain grades in the industry that ACTT [Association of Cinematograph, Television, and Allied Technicians] had arranged with the government to be part of the war preparation. Did you know Cavalcanti before he asked you to work on this film?

CC: No, I'd never met him.

SC: He just knew you by reputation?

CC: I don't know. I just got a "please go and see him" and that was it.

SC: How did you get on with Cavalcanti?

CC: Very well, of course. In a funny kind of way he had the same sort of approach to things that Bill [William] Hornbeck did. Because, for instance on *Young Veteran*, which was meant to be about a young chap returning from Dunkirk, we would go and see a whole lot of newsreel material, including some from that French series, I can't remember what it was called, that they made before the Germans walked in. They got the negative over here, and he would select all sorts of things like troops skiing: everything that to me had nothing to do with his theme, but somehow or other he managed to find beautiful images to illustrate what he was getting at, if that makes any sense to you.

SC: It's a very creative way of editing, isn't it, binding different things together with a common theme?

2. *For Those in Peril*

CC: I began as an editor. Then I started to direct; the first film was a propaganda picture called *For Those In Peril* [1944], where we rushed around the English Channel in high speed motorboats, boats that were used for picking up crashed airmen and the like. It's a horrifying thing to say, but it was very exciting rushing around the Channel in high-speed motorboats. And that was the first picture Dougie [Douglas] Slocombe photographed, except he didn't photograph the interiors.

SC: Who did, Gordon Dines?

CC: No, Ernie [Ernest] Palmer.

SC: What were your particular problems on *For Those in Peril*? You say it was quite exciting and it wasn't dangerous, but you must have had some problems.

CC: Just hanging on to the boat. You know, we were warned beforehand that if a crash call came, they'd take no notice of us if anybody needed help. And we got a crash call once, and to accelerate from just idling along at five knots to something like forty-five knots in no time at all—I mean how we didn't go overboard, I don't know. Mind you, we rather enjoyed our predicament sometimes because the first time we went out, we really tied down the camera; it was a very narrow little boat. And we had Ted Lockhart, who was an old sailor, and we thought we were absolutely safe, the way everything was done. And we could see them all grinning in the wheelhouse, because we were up in the bow, and we came out of the harbor at considerable speed. Of course once we got past the jetty, we hit a wave and we all fell over. The camera went "blomb," you know; we had managed to strap ourselves, though, and we were careful enough to make sure we had ropes.

SC: What camera were you using, can you remember?

CC: Probably a Newman-Sinclair.

SC: It wasn't damaged?

CC: No.

SC: You said there was no danger, no aircraft?

CC: The big danger was Dougie Slocombe. [Laughter.] Because one day we went out and arranged all sort of things like Spitfires diving at us and actually firing on us. And it was an extremely rough day; in fact, all ships were confined to port except the film unit because film people were mad and expendable anyway. [Laughter.] So we were tossing about in the Channel, and these Spitfires were coming and we were trying to get the boats with machine-gun bullets to hit the water and so on. And Dougie was in the wheelhouse saying, "Can't you shoot a bit closer?" [Laughter.]

SC: And they did.

CC: They did, indeed. [Laughter.]

3. *Painted Boats*

CC: Then we made *Painted Boats* [1945], which was a more docile, peaceful experience.

SC: That was the one about canals, which I seem to remember because I was at Ealing at that time; you enjoyed it very much. Was Bill Blewitt on that one?

CC: Yes.

SC: Tell me about Bill Blewitt.

CC: Blewitt had been the postmaster at Mousehole in Cornwall. I think Harry Watt or Cavalcanti discovered him, I don't know—the documentary boys had used him quite a lot before the war. He was a natural actor, enjoyed his drink, was a rogue and a lovely person to talk to or in whose company to be. He would sit in the pub at the side of the canal and tell a fascinated audience long stories about his early days when he was a boy on the canal. Well, he'd never seen a canal before, but everyone would believe him, with absolutely rapt attention.

SC: I remember he was a great storyteller. I remember on one occasion at our local pub, the Red Lion, at Ealing, he persuaded people he wasn't Bill Blewitt, that he was his twin brother, inventing a whole history. He was, as you say, quite a natural actor.

4. *Dead of Night*

SC: So after that, your next picture there was one I was associated with, *Dead of Night* [1945].

CC: That's right. That's when we began to know each other, to our mutual advantage or disadvantage. [Laughter.]

SC: Tell me about *Dead of Night* from your point of view.

CC: I was just lucky to be given this comedy sequence to direct with Basil Radford and Naunton Wayne. And my first day's work was appallingly bad, actually. I was trying to slow them up in their delivery all the time; I was looking at it more from an editor's point of view, I think.

SC: I remember that first day's rushes. It takes me back and you will remember it, too, because the story as I heard it was, I saw the rushes with Mick [Michael Balcon] and we felt that it was the way you said: you slowed Naunton and Basil down, and then we came onto the floor. And as I heard it, certainly it must have been from you, Basil Radford saw Mick and me coming and he said, "Aha, here come the angry boys." So you re-shot that first day.

CC: Yes, that's right

SC: But that's the sort of thing one learns by doing, isn't it? You can be told a lot of things in theory, but you learn in fact by making your own mistakes.

CC: Absolutely.

5. *Hue and Cry*

SC: You did *Hue and Cry* [1947] after that, which is a very famous picture and was very enjoyable to make, I should think—certainly enjoyable to see.

CC: I think making any picture is a rather masochistic experience, but yes, it was fun, I suppose.

SC: Tell me about the famous shot where you and [Henry] Cornelius, who was producing, worked out how many kids you could get into one taxi cab.

CC: I didn't, that was Corny. I had always envisaged that the taxi would stop at a place where we could conceal a whole lot of boys, and we would open one door and boys would pour out and be re-fed into the cab. But Corny shot that shot. I was on the bombsite at the time, shooting other stuff, and then I saw him doing this shot. And the taxi came, and without stopping or anything—it obviously didn't stop at a pre-prepared position—he just crammed about fifty boys into one taxi! [Laughter.] To hell with what they felt about it.

SC: They probably enjoyed it. I remember it's a marvelous shot in the film, where this endless succession of small boys pile out of this one taxi.

CC: That's right. Very good shot.

SC: By the end of *Hue and Cry* you must have been beginning to feel very sure of yourself as a director.

CC: No, no, you're never sure. Quite honestly, the first time I ever had much confidence was after *The Lavender Hill Mob* [1951], when I began to feel it was all done by the associate producer, plus the cameraman and the operator, because they were good. Then I suddenly went to do a picture outside called *Hunted* [1952], without any of those people, and I found it was still successful and that gave me a lot of confidence, because I was now disassociated from all those people who had helped.

6. *Against the Wind*

SC: Could I revert for a moment to *Against the Wind* [1948]? We did a piece of casting on that film that we thought was rather ingenious at the time but rather misfired: Jack Warner.

CC: Yes, well, we chose him to play the main villain part, a double spy. We chose him because he was so charming, nobody could possibly believe he could be a double agent. And, as you remember, just a week before we were due to start shooting, Jack said, "This isn't going to work; people aren't going to believe that I can be a villain." But we talked him into staying with us and, as it turned out, we were quite wrong, because the whole thing misfired completely. Nobody could believe that dear Jack could be a villain.

SC: I remember we took it to a preview, do you remember, Charles? We couldn't tell much from the preview audience but we went with Jack into a pub after the preview, and there was a little man standing at the bar who looked at Jack and said, "You're Jack Warner, aren't you?", and Jack said, "Yes." And the little man said that he had been to the picture and it was all wrong and that had quite an effect, I think, on Jack. Although the intention was good, to surprise the audience possibly, Jack certainly had too pronounced a persona as what he was, a jolly nice chap, for it to really work.

CC: Mind you he played a villain in *Hue And Cry*, but that was comedy.

SC: Nevertheless, I think he played it well in *Against the Wind*.

CC: Oh, he played it brilliantly!

SC: Especially the scene between him and Simone Signoret when she hears that that's who it is. I suppose that sort of scene would probably work better these days, as audiences have got more sophisticated.

CC: Yes, I think so.

7. *Nine Men*

SC: I'd like to go back just a tickle in your career to a film that occurs to me as interesting, one called *Nine Men* [1943], on which you were the associate producer, I was supervising editor, and Harry Watt directed. That was quite an interesting picture.

CC: I didn't really produce it. I was credited, but all I did was manage to wangle the rights to the story from the poor author for an incredibly small amount of money. And he offered to bash me up when he found out the picture was so successful. But that credit was a mistake: I wasn't really creative on that picture at any level.

SC: Well, I think you were in on the editing; I seem to remember the combination. If I can put it modestly on behalf of both of us, Charles, we combined our editing talents—we would work alternately on sequences for that picture.

CC: Oh, yes, we worked together on it. But in the sense of working on the script or helping Harry Watt in any kind of way, I don't think I helped very much. The only thing I ever did to help him, it was during the war: the trains were terrible and he rang me up about half past nine one night saying that he was shooting in Wales, he was in terrible trouble, and would I catch a train immediately and come down? I said, "But Harry, it's only twenty minutes before the last train goes." He said, "You must come, you must come." So I put my clothes on over my pajamas and rushed out and managed to catch the train. I got to Paddington, I got one of those terrible night trains that was absolutely crammed with people, no seats or anything, and I sat in a bog all the way, the only place I could find a seat. The train engineer didn't know what he was doing. It was a nightmare journey, get to the hotel—won't go into that—piss pots under the bed and everything else, get some rest; clean myself up a bit in the morning, go down to the location about nine o'clock, then walk across the sand towards Harry, who looks at me in amazement and says, "What the fucking hell are you doing here?" [Laughter.]

SC: He'd completely forgotten. Had he had a few whiskies?

CC: He'd forgotten all about it.

SC: So you took the next train back.

CC: No, we stayed and did some second-unit work.

8. *Train of Events*

SC: I think the next picture was *Train of Events* [1949], another anthology film like *Dead of Night*.

CC: Which you produced entirely, didn't you?

SC: Which I produced, yes, that's right. Tell me about the sequence you did, the story you did in that. It had three stories.

CC: My story? Good God, I've almost forgotten it.

SC: It had Irina Baronova in it and John Clements.

CC: Well, the interesting thing was that we rehearsed it. There were Clements, as you know, Baronova, who was a ballerina, and Valerie Hobson, who was a cinema actress. One of the difficulties a director always has is in trying to get everybody's performance to gel at the same time. So here we were with these three people from different walks of life, as it were. John Clement's performance improved, improved, improved, improved all the way through rehearsals, and it improved on the floor as well. The ballerina, her performance was stuck; she got it as far as she was going to go and never changed. Valerie Hobson got worse and worse and worse the more we rehearsed, because she was a film artist and used to doing things instantly.

9. *The Lavender Hill Mob*

SC: A real peak film was the next one, wasn't it, *The Lavender Hill Mob*?

CC: I was sliding before *The Lavender Hill Mob*. It rescued me, I think. Because, you know, *Dance Hall* [1950] didn't do very well.

SC: And whose original idea was *The Lavender Hill Mob*? Tibby [T. E. B.] Clarke wrote it, didn't he?

CC: What happened was Tibby had just written a police story, *The Blue Lamp* [1950], and Mick [Michael Balcon] wanted to repeat the success of *The Blue Lamp*, so Tibby was sent off and he couldn't find an idea, but he did find this idea about the gold bars and the Eiffel Tower. And he sketched it out to Mick, who was doubtful about it by the way, but Mick sometimes would allow people to go their own way. So Tibby wrote a treatment that people liked very much. Michael Truman was the associate producer. Tibby's original story, after they had successfully turned all the gold bars into Eiffel Tower paperweights, followed what happened to each little Eiffel Tower, so that a whole lot of new characters were introduced. Michael Truman was the one who said this would be disastrous, you must follow through with the central characters and leave the rest. And eventually Tibby did find the solution. They made a mistake on the top of the Eiffel Tower about the bars, so we were able to follow just the main characters.

SC: Rather than the original subsidiary ones. That seems a very, very important contribution, indeed.

CC: And that's what associate producers used to do for you.

Bibliography

Barr, Charles. *Ealing Studios*. 1977. Moffat, Scot.: Cameron and Hollis, 1998.

Duguid, Mark. *Ealing Revisited*. London: British Film Institute, 2012.

Perry, George C. *Forever Ealing: A Celebration of the Great British Film Studio*. London: Michael Joseph/Pavilion Books, 1981.

Shail, Robert. *British Film Directors: A Critical Guide*. Edinburgh, U.K.: Edinburgh University Press, 2007.

"The Filmmaker and the Critic: An Interview with Lindsay Anderson" (1989), by Scott Stewart and Lester Friedman, from *Film Criticism*, 16.1-2 (Fall/Winter 1991-92): 4-17.

Lindsay Anderson (1923-94) was a British film critic and stage-and-film director. Anderson received a degree in English from Oxford University and in 1947 became a founding editor of the film magazine *Sequence*, which lasted until 1951. Subsequently he wrote for *Sight and Sound* and other journals. Anderson began directing in 1948, making documentaries for an industrial firm, and in 1955 he won an Academy Award for his short documentary *Thursday's Children*. In 1956 he coined the term Free Cinema to denote a movement in the British cinema inspired by John Osborne's play *Look Back in Anger* (1956). Anderson and other members of this documentary movement allied themselves with left-wing politics and took their themes from contemporary urban working-class life.

Anderson's first feature-length motion picture, *This Sporting Life* (1963), adapted by the English writer David Storey from his novel, is about a brutish miner who succeeds as a professional rugby player but who fails in love. The film is a classic of the British social-realist cinema of the 1960s. Anderson then directed productions at the Royal Court and other theaters before making his next film, *If . . .* (1968), in which three English students violently rebel against the conformity and social hypocrisy of their boarding school. Next he directed the premieres of Storey's plays *In Celebration* (1969), *The Contractor* (1969), *Home* (1970), and *The Changing Room* (1971). Anderson's subsequent films included *O Lucky Man!* (1973), *In Celebration* (1974), *Britannia Hospital* (1982), and *The Whales of August* (1987). Among his later stage productions was Storey's *March on Russia* (1989).

Scott Stewart & Lester Friedman: In your mind, what have been the important societal influences on British cinema during the past ten years?

Lindsay Anderson: By the end of the 1960s the radical impulse in British filmmaking was over. In particular, the rush to conformism that has characterized Britain during the last twenty years has deeply affected movie making here. On the positive side, television, and specifically the policy of Channel 4, has helped filmmakers in this country, since it has given some relief to the eternal economic problem. Yet, at the same time, there has been continual pressure to think of movies in terms of American distribution. The home market is not going to pay for film production, so there is the need to break into the American market. This desire has characterized British cinema since the 1930s, even though it has never been fully achieved. The idea that video sales would be a help to a smaller-budgeted picture also seems to be vanishing because video sales inevitably go to the big-budget pictures.

SS/LF: Earlier you mentioned what you characterized as "the rush to conformism" in Great Britain. What are the specific effects of this "rush to conformism"?

LA: Either it creates a bad atmosphere for artists or it can sometimes create a good atmosphere. By this I mean it gives them something to think about. I'm afraid at the moment there isn't much kick left in this country. We've yet to grieve over the loss of the socialist ideal—something that's happening across the world. The hardcore communist-socialists, particularly the people who haven't had to live under them, represent an ideal, a force that has more or less perished. If you think back into the thirties, you can't help envying the artists of the left, hard on the left. It's very different times now. It's really hard to be anyone. Either you go with the profit-making philosophy of Thatcher and Reagan, or you're left with a kind of anarchic despair—which is how you could characterize *Britannia Hospital* [1982]. The only substitution for a left ideal, I suppose, is the green ideal, which could take hold of the imagination of the people, the young particularly. It hasn't got the same force of conformism, of dedication to career and class position, of the acquisition of material goods, as other elements of British life. These forces have taken over.

SS/LF: How do you feel about the way in which contemporary British movies deal with class and race-related issues?

LA: By comparison with the traditional British cinema, today's movies demonstrate a much wider choice of subject area about almost all aspects of society; they also deal with them much more freely than directors in traditional British cinema ever would. But, of course, you've got to bring in television. One of the absurdities, really critical absurdities, is this silly division between the cinema of the theaters and films for television. Film critics, if they weren't so lazy, ought to review every new film made for television. Yet they prefer to live an easy and quiet life. There is also a journalistic hierarchy now. But one must see what's being shown on television every day because it is just as relevant as the movies in the theaters that the film critic writes about it. Critics enjoy being facetious at the expense of bad theater pictures, which is easy to do, rather than to cover a good film made for television. Don't forget that *My Beautiful Laundrette* [1985] was a film made for television and shot on 16mm. In fact, Stephen Frears was initially quite alarmed by the proposition that it was going to be shown in cinemas.

SS/LF: What do you feel about the exodus of so many talented British filmmakers to America and elsewhere?

LA: When you deal with the British cinema, you deal in quite a complicated subject. Economically, Britain can't support such an industry. There is also the plain fact that America represents, to many filmmakers, the chance to move beyond the barriers of class, since class is not much of a consideration in America. Ridley Scott, for example, also belongs to that generation that grew up making movies for television and is, therefore, interested in style and technique—and in little else.

I would also mention David Puttnam here. The difference between, say, Alan Parker and David Puttnam, who are friends, is that Puttnam is somebody who desperately wants to become somebody, who is part of the establishment. I mean he's a snob. The greatest joy for Puttnam would be to be Sir David Puttnam. He no doubt will get that title if he gives enough money to this charity and that cause. So Puttnam is very divided in his attitude toward America. He can't cope with it and failed terribly. It wasn't the first time. Remember this. Before he produced *Chariots of Fire* [1981], Puttnam spent two years in Los Angeles as the head of filmmaking for some record company. He failed. Then he accepted the Columbia job, taking on the American film industry like a complete idiot. He failed again. He's not like Parker. Parker has not made the same mistakes. Parker is a fully accredited American filmmaker now. He's not a British filmmaker anymore.

SS/LF: Many of your films deal with tradition and how Britons deal with it in their daily lives. Do you think English people, in particular, are torn between tradition and movement away from it?

LA: I have an ambivalent feeling towards tradition. I have a particularly strong suspicion towards tradition when it loses its vitality and truth, when it becomes simply a politician's cliché. When Margaret Thatcher talks about the Falklands, saying we're a *Great* Britain again, that appeal to a tradition of greatness is absurd—and bad. But it's a complicated question at the moment when a decision has to be made as to whether we were going to defend the Falklands. I don't necessarily think the wrong decision was made, so I don't join in the cry of Warmonger Thatcher. On the other hand, we should have never gotten to that stage. If it weren't for our ineptitude, it would never have happened. That's what was really wrong. Then she used the whole tragic action as a royal plum to feed people's patriotic fervor, which I find disgusting. You could say the boys in *If . . .* [1968] were traditionalists, which sounds paradoxical because all the apparatus of tradition appears to be on the side of authority, but that's not necessarily true. They are part of the tradition of independence, the rights of the individual, the right to question authority and to behave freely. When traditions become fossilized, and instances of reaction as well, then they have to be rebelled against. That act in itself is a tradition.

SS/LF: In *If . . .*, what did you have in mind when the headmaster went up in a puff of smoke?

LA: It may have been a mistake. I think it may be a mistake. I'll tell you two things about that. Very often while you're creating you have to make a quick decision. One thing I had in mind was I never ever wanted to be literal, just literal. I think that if the headmaster were just lying there it becomes just that episode, and I didn't want that. At the very end of *If . . .*, it's Mick [Malcolm McDowell] against the whole mass society, not just about the headmaster anymore. I was surprised that young people cheered that ending when it first came out. Perhaps they didn't look beyond the end, because it's very difficult for me to imagine that Mick is going to win.

SS/LF: David Sherwin (the film's scriptwriter) said that by the film's ending Mick has become a monster as bad as the system he fights against.

LA: That's idiotic. I don't know why he said that. I think that's completely untrue. Mick isn't as big a monster as the system. That's silly. He's actually not a monster at all. He's terrified, of course, although it's up to you to determine what you see on the screen. I think at the end of *If*... Mick is absolutely desperate. It's just him and this small band of followers. That's all he's got.

SS/LF: What was in your mind when Mick is getting his beating? You cut to the boys listening, but you end up with Peanuts [Philip Bagenal] looking into the microscope at what appears to be cell division.

LA: I think it's just another perspective. You know a lot of things are not always rational. It's a poetic suggestion. Make what you will of it. I think it's good to have a few things like that. I hope people will get something out of what the artist is not fully conscious of himself. By the way, David Sherwin and I are talking about doing a sequel to *If*... This would be a sequel taking place at the school with many of the same characters twenty years older.

SS/LF: Is Malcolm McDowell interested in doing this?

LA: Oh yes! He's a wonderful actor. It's just a shame Hollywood had no idea what to do with him. He's even wonderful in *Sunset* [1988] as the villain. Very, very bad. Embarrassing actually. He seems more of a personality than an actor. I read some reviews and there wasn't really any mention of Malcolm. His wife is a wonderful actress as well. Absolutely wonderful. I had the pleasure of doing a play with them both about eight months ago called *Holiday* [1928], by the American Philip Barry. She's a very excellent, intelligent, and charming actress.

SS/LF: What about the controversial "chaplain-in-the-drawer" sequence in *If*...? Do you expect us to take this literally?

LA: Of course not! It is a clear metaphor, and one of the elements that is designed to work towards the conclusion of the film. The film is not, in the end, literal. You see there were these expectations like, "Golly, you shouldn't have done that." They've got these idiots who are so systematic that have this sort of expectation. People need to have respect for the artist. They need to look at things with an open mind and wait a little bit before they exercise their superiority over the artist.

SS/LF: Your films seem to present a balance between education, and by that I mean attempting to make the audience active thinkers, and entertainment. Do you look for films balanced like your own when you choose to go see a film?

LA: I'm actually very lazy about going to see movies and, as you can see, I'd rather collect old movies and watch them at home. I'm really very bad. You'll realize how bad I am when I tell you I haven't seen *A Fish Called Wanda* [1988]. I doubt that I will. It's a very successful picture. But the tradition of English facetiousness is not one that I respond to. My taste in humor is more satirical.

SS/LF: What are your feelings about the films of Carol Reed?

LA: *The Fallen Idol* [1948] is better than *Odd Man Out* [1947]. I really think so. I think *Odd Man Out* probably is a little more pretentious. I mean it's interesting from that perspective, but I think that Reed is a very curious and sad case really. He's obviously a man of immense talent who somehow went astray. He ended up in *Oliver!* [1968] somewhere. It's very strange. But you should see *The Fallen Idol*—it's a very good film.

SS/LF: One critic once said about *Britannia Hospital*, in reference to its tone, that you had resorted to ranting instead of wit. What's your reaction?

LA: Rubbish! You know they really are all idiots! I think the movie is violent, extremely violent. We live in a very violent world. Another critic at the time said the movie was hopeless. Well, that's what it's likely to be at a time of disaster. I can't help the bourgeois critic who longs to be left alone, who needs assurance. They want to be reassured. The nearer you get to the terrifying truth, the more they want not just to evade it, but to discredit you as well. So, you go off to see *A Fish Called Wanda*.

SS/LF: How did you come to direct *The Whales of August* [1987]? It seems to be very different from anything else you've ever directed.

LA: Well it is, but anybody who wasn't chicken would accept the opportunity to direct Lillian Gish and Bette Davis. It is the least political of my motion pictures. But one can have different attitudes; one can make different choices for different reasons, as a theater director is likely to make different choices. I mean one might say why do you direct a play by Chekhov instead of a play with contemporary social implications like *The March on Russia*, which I have directed? The point is this isn't a conflict. I've made films that have strong social implications, but trying to be objective about my work, which is always difficult, I think my work has always shown an extremely strong humanistic attitude. That's the kind of film that *The Whales of August* is. So think that if anyone looked at my work through the years they would see elements of lyricism in those works and in *The Whales of August*. I believe *The Whales of August* has a more recognizable poetic style than *On Golden Pond* [1981]. It's more lyrical. Although that, of course, was a much more popular film because it's much more schmaltzy.

SS/LF: How did you find working with Bette Davis?

LA: It's very hard work because she's a very abrasive and destructive person. I imagine she always has been. Of course, she's much more difficult now because she's been ill. She's got a demon in her, whatever that demon is. She has become this sort of sad media figure—good for TV interviews because she'll say nasty things. By the way, I've spent the last year in Toronto making a mini-series for Home Box Office. It's called *Glory! Glory!* [1989]. I took that on because, amazingly, the script turned out to be quite good. I was very astonished by it actually. That does have some relevance to some of the things I have done. But I'd say that I've taken advantage of opportunities to make films outside of Britain, mainly because the possibilities of filmmaking in Britain for someone of my temperament are very difficult, very limited. That's what I said earlier about the present conformism in Britain. The violent rejection of my last British film, *Britannia Hospital*, is evidence of this.

SS/LF: Why do you think this was?

LA: We're accustomed, to put it pretentiously, to a film culture in which absurdly grotesque horror is part of a tradition. My film was so satirical that it demanded a sense of humor. Of course, the trouble is that people have begun to think in clichés. If they think they're going to see a satirical social film, then they're not prepared for the kind of extended satire present in *Britannia Hospital*. That in itself is actually relevant. It's satirical about the craziness of the progress of science. In the end of the film, you have this crazy doctor who is making absolute sense, but of course it's gone beyond his sense into further madness. By the end of the film, you have a film that's pessimistic about the possibility for human survival because we have science for science's sake and outside the realm of a human purpose. So the ending, of course, is extremely dark.

SS/LF: Do you think of yourself as a man of the theater or a man of the cinema?

LA: The answer is both really. I've been extremely lucky to have been able to alternate. After I've made a film, I haven't felt an overpowering need to make another one. In that way, I'm a lot like John Ford, who at one time said: "I'm not a career man." He had a fantastic career, except towards the end of course, but in this sense he was very fortunate. He never had to sit down to scheme and plan how to get a picture made, since pictures were being made all the time. I don't think he needed to keep a career going. Being a filmmaker today is a gift I don't really have. I'm not proud of that, but I'm simply not able to fly to Los Angeles, have meetings, sell stories—all those aspects of modern filmmaking. I'm absolutely hopeless at it. In that way, I'm not sure that I am a filmmaker. I mean I'm a filmmaker in the sense that I have done some films, but I'm amazed that I've managed to do even that.

Also, I never have compromised. I think this is why, at times, people hesitate to send me scripts. For one reason or another, I've turned down a lot of them. I don't think I've made anything that represents a compromise, so I haven't made very many films. But at least the ones I've made, I can stand by them. I think it's incredible to make a mini-series for HBO, incredibly lucky really, because I didn't even work on getting it.

SS/LF: How did *Glory! Glory!* happen?

LA: I think it happened because the producer, whose name is Bonnie Door, had this idea of a film or mini-series about evangelists on television. She had this notion long before the big scandals in recent years, which are indeed more farcical than the film we made. The people in *Glory! Glory!* all behave in a rather nefarious way from time to time, but there is a certain charm about them. They are much more charming than those people you see on American television.

When I came into the project it was late, and HBO was very scared. Although they put money into it, they didn't really know whether they wanted to go through with it or not. They told Bonnie Door that she must get a director who is not just any director; he must be special. They tried Nick Roeg and others. Finally the script arrived here, and I liked it. I said yes, it's delightful, and I went to Los Angeles. We met the HBO people there. I hadn't really realized that this was crucial, that what I said about the script would determine whether HBO would do it or not. I did quite a good sales pitch, and they went ahead. The script had been written before the writers' strike, which was then in progress, so I couldn't sit down and re-write it. Shooting had to be started and completed within two months. I thought this was great. For once I'm not going to go through this hell! I'll take this script as it is. We did have to make some minor changes, and we did have to cut, but essentially it was the first time I basically went with a script. It was incredible luck that this coincided with my temperament.

I do think, however, there were elements there that, if I had had time work on the script, I would have looked to develop more fully. Especially when you consider Jim and Tammy Faye. If you look at them, they're much more extreme, and more obnoxious, than anything in our movie. But I think it makes the film rather nice, really; it's different; it's not a satire of Tammy and Jim or anyone else. Who's that other horrible one? Jimmy Swaggart. There is nobody in it as awful as Swaggart, not even the old chap in the beginning. Oral Roberts is the one who inspired the series because Bonnie had done research on Oral Roberts several years ago. That gave her the idea, and she got Stan Daniels to write it. Stan Daniels is a very interesting chap and a very good writer. He worked on the "Mary Tyler Moore Show" and "Taxi." I think it's a superior script. It did well. It was very well received.

SS/LF: Could you elaborate on why you once called Humphrey Jennings the only "British poet"?

LA: You have to see his pictures. He's very important actually. Jennings was a very interesting filmmaker who didn't make a very large number of films. He started as a painter and had a very strong feeling for tradition. He came to maturity during the war, the ideal time for him to be able to make his films, which were very patriotic without any drumbeat in the background. Working in the medium of documentary cinema, he wasn't at all commercial. He didn't have any commercial pressures on him; therefore, he was freely able to express his strong, personal, patriotic feelings about his country. It's interesting that he didn't survive the war. He tried to go on, but he didn't make it. Somehow that particular time inspired him, and then very sadly he died young.

I guess that one could say what does one mean by the word "poetic"? We don't want to get into a long discussion about lyricism and all that. I would say Humphrey Jennings is a poet in a way that you could say David Lean is not a poet, in my view. I think he has a very, very personal style in his handling of a film, a poetic use of the medium. You should see Jennings' *Listen to Britain* [1942], *Fires Were Started* [1943], and *A Diary for Timothy* [1945]. That's all you need to see. The great confusion, of course, is between documentary cinema and journalism. Documentary through television has more or less become journalism. So what I call the "poetic documentary" is hardly made now. It's more or less dead today. I've made one or two. You know I often think of that remark about Jennings rather ruefully. I wrote that, oh God, twenty years or more ago. It always seems to be quoted, and I'm waiting, of course, for someone to ask the next logical question: does Anderson consider himself a poet?

SS/LF: Well, do you regard yourself as a poet?

LA: I would rather be regarded by others as a poet. When I do say poet in that sense, I mean something particularly personal, a lyrical feeling in cinema, consistency in personality with an integration of style and content. You get that with John Ford, of course; the way he uses the camera displays an easily recognizable style.

SS/LF: How do you feel Thatcherism has affected the films of contemporary British filmmakers like Stephen Frears and Derek Jarman?

LA: We unfortunately seem to have fallen completely for what we call the "auteurist" philosophy of filmmaking, that being the absurd notion that the director is responsible for the entire picture. This leads to errors, particularly in the case of someone like Stephen Frears. What you're thinking about are a couple of films written by Hanif Kureishi. Whatever you think of Hanif Kureishi—I don't like Hanif Kureishi myself—that's Hanif Kureishi and not Frears. The two films written by Hanif Kureishi that Stephen, being an intelligent fellow, took on don't imply any thought of anti-Thatcherite policy on the part of Stephen Frears. Before that, Stephen directed other things on television by Alan Bennett, who is not in any way a radical; he also directed *Gumshoe* in 1971, an Albert Finney film. That was the first thing he directed before he found his feet, so to speak. There's another film he made, *The Hit* [1984], and he's just directed *Dangerous Liaisons* [1988]. What do these films tell you about the personality of the director?

I think you'll find that Stephen chose *My Beautiful Launderette* because it's a lively kind of script, intelligently written. It was something contemporaneous. It had a visceral kick to it. It's not particularly anti-Thatcherite, is it? I never thought it so and, of course, *Prick Up Your Ears* [1987] has very little social content as well. So I'm really cautioning you not to be too journalistic in your thinking. A journalist will make a trend out of two pictures, and they do need more analyzing than that.

Derek Jarman. Again, there isn't any real consistency there. I don't know how you rate Derek Jarman's work: *The Last of England* [1988], *Caravaggio* [1986], *War Requiem* [1989]. There really is not a consistent attitude in any group of English filmmakers, British filmmakers, as to compare with, say, the group of the Free Cinema, a related group from the 1960s, and the films, in general, that were made in the first half of the sixties. Here you did have a fairly consistent social point of view, class point of view, and partly for that reason we were scorned and rejected by English middle-class critics and intellectuals, who all strongly resisted radical filmmaking. You will find, of course, isolated or lonely examples of people working from that viewpoint. I certainly didn't feel a part of any intellectual group. Also I must caution you, as happens when one gets older, you get lazy, you get less interested. Unfortunately, I don't religiously go to all these movies, and I don't go to movies the way I would if I were a critic.

SS/LF: One critic claimed, about Stephen Frears, that you can trust him to take a piece of work and not muck it up.

LA: Well that's a charming thing to say. By contrast, Stephen was being very kind to me while he was doing a five-part series based on Alan Bennett's books for television. He directed only two of them, and he very kindly got me to do one. I said to him and to Alan Bennett: "Look, this is tricky for me. As a film director I'm used to working on the scripts (and the script they showed me wasn't fully complete). I'd like to work on this with Alan, if he's prepared to, in a way one would work on a movie." Alan Bennett said, "I'd love to," and we actually worked on it together very happily. We made a one-hour television piece called "The Old Crowd" [1979]. This piece was extremely criticized. One critic even noted that I was the first director who's been able to make Alan Bennett unfunny. Now, in a sense, I take this as a compliment because what we produced was not just a very good transcription of an Alan Bennett script, but something else. It was more like a movie.

I'm not taking anything away from Stephen at all. He's been very, very clever, intelligent, and good in his selection of material; he's put it on the screen very, very well. The only thing I would say is that he has not yet, and perhaps he won't, develop into a director whose films belong to him rather than to the scriptwriter. There's no reason why he should. If it wasn't for the snobbism of the *auteur* theory, we wouldn't think twice about it because what actually matters is what is up there on the screen. Stephen can now do more or less what he wants to do. He is a very interesting case. He's very independent, very individual in his choices. But how far he wants personally to commit himself is another matter. He's been blessed and also been very intelligent. One of Stephen's qualities is intelligence and choosing to do good material.

SS/LF: You've done a lot of writing on John Ford. Yet he's certainly not a social critic, is he?

LA: No, no, no, he wasn't. But I would say that the conflict in Ford between traditionalism and individuality was extremely strong. The sense of the independence of the individual makes him an individualist and also a traditionalist. You see Ford was a great artist, but an artist about whom there is a great danger to intellectualize too much. Read some of the commentary by some of the latter-day, what you would call, *auteurists*. There is a book by Tag Gallagher with a lot of good research in it, but it's absolutely idiotic. It shows the need of the "intellectual" critic to try to construct some intellectual conception that will actually justify his existence, so he sits down and writes a paper about it and about the pessimism of Ford. *My Darling Clementine* [1946] is not a pessimistic film, nor is *She Wore a Yellow Ribbon* [1949]. This critic would try to make out, like Peter Bogdanovich, that there is a progression to pessimism.

What happened to Ford was that he got old and, of course, old age brings different insights. He got old in a world in which he felt increasingly alienated, but he was not a person who would ever discuss that in an interview. The only time he would be able to talk about something like that with someone was if he knew this person well enough to get drunk with him. Of course, he wasn't going to betray himself, and he was absolutely right. We're all interviewed absolutely too much, and it's a very dangerous mistake to be honest. Most interviews filmmakers give are going to be used one way or another for the films they have made. You have to be aware that you're making publicity at the same time. So a lot of these interviews you can't take too seriously.

There are only two books you should read about Ford. Mine, and John Ford's son's book called *Pappy* [1979, Dan Ford], which isn't an academic book. But it's good. I think the trouble is that, as a whole, the academic study of cinema has developed people who have to make jobs for themselves. So they fabricate. Academicians have to fabricate to justify the fact that you are paid so much a year to be a professor of cinema or something. None of these things should exist. They become an end in themselves. I don't think they enlighten people.

SS/LF: Do you think we should study the history of cinema?

LA: The history of cinema—that's a different matter. You see you slipped in that phrase there. I think the history of cinema is essential to study, but a history of cinema not nearly dealing so much with aesthetic differences. It should be much more involved with the social implications and the economic problems of cinema. There's a great deal to discuss before one gets on to deconstruction. Aesthetics doesn't have anything to do with the experience of art. It is an end in itself. To write about style is a tremendously difficult thing to do, but it's a very valuable thing to do if anybody did it right.

This is another reason why you ought to read my book about John Ford. It has much more to do with the experience of seeing John Ford's films than these theoretical books. I mean that idiotic thing by Peter Wollen, *Signs and Meanings* [*Signs and Meaning in the Cinema*, 1969] or some such thing. I don't know how anybody can really get through that stuff. You still find academic studies that seem to be totally infected by *auteurism*. I remember going to a seminar in Italy about John Ford and listening to all that academic nonsense. One contribution I made was to say you've got to understand that some of Ford's films were written by Dudley Nichols, some were written by Frank Nugent, and some he took on because he had nothing else to do. You have to make these differentiations. These are supposed to be academics, after all. Yet none of them were capable even of mentioning a writer. So most of what they were talking was rubbish, actually. They were constructing an image of this John Ford they found appropriate. That's why Ford, during one interview, told Peter Bogdanovich to shut up.

SS/LF: So how do you make an audience think?

LA: Now there's a fatal assumption. You can't make them all think, though I have tried to. I try not to satisfy an audience's expectations. Maybe that's the defect of a lot of filmmaking: that it's careful to remain within the audience's expectations in the hope of getting a distribution deal. I suppose if you want to become a professional filmmaker, it would be wise for you to adapt your work to your market. If you want to become what I call a film artist, you're apt to go the other way.

Bibliography

Anderson, Lindsay. *Making a Film*. New York: Garland, 1977.

Graham, Allison. *Lindsay Anderson*. Boston: Twayne, 1981.

Hedling, Erik. *Lindsay Anderson: Maverick Film Maker*. London: Cassell, 1998.

Izod, John. *Lindsay Anderson: Cinema Authorship*. Manchester, U.K.: Manchester University Press, 2012.

Lambert, Gavin. *Mainly About Lindsay Anderson*. London: Faber and Faber, 2000.

Silet, Charles L. P. *Lindsay Anderson: A Guide to References and Resources*. Boston: G. K. Hall.

Sussex, Elizabeth. *Lindsay Anderson*. London: Studio Vista, 1969.

"Novels, Screenplays, and Films: An Interview with Karel Reisz" (1998), by Carmen Pérez Ríu, from Literature/Film Quarterly, 31.2 (2003): 156-160.

Karel Reisz (1926-2002) was a Czech-born British film and stage director who made only eleven movies during his career but was instrumental in the creation of British New Wave cinema in the 1960s. After working on the film journal *Sequence* and authoring a book on film editing, Reisz began making documentaries about working-class life, among them *We Are the Lambeth Boys* (1958).

Reisz's first feature, *Saturday Night and Sunday Morning* (1960), the story of a jaded young factory worker, brought fame to him and his star, Albert Finney. It was followed, most notably, by *Morgan: A Suitable Case for Treatment* (1966). *Morgan*, adapted from a TV play by David Mercer, is a sporadically interesting fantasy about a young artist, reluctantly divorced from the wife he adores and prevented by a court injunction from approaching her, who dons a gorilla suit in order to exact a King Kong revenge on the society he blames for his predicament. *Isadora* (1968), a biography of dance pioneer Isadora Duncan, met with little success, however, and resulted in a hiatus in filmmaking for Reisz.

His Hollywood ventures included *The Gambler* (1974) and *The French Lieutenant's Woman* (1981). In the 1990s Reisz turned to the stage, collaborating with Harold Pinter and winning critical praise for his rendition of Terence Rattigan's drama *The Deep Blue Sea*.

Carmen Pérez Ríu: You started with the Free Cinema movement, which imparted a social and psychological stance to British film. This documentary movement attempted to get free from commercial restraints. I wonder if at this stage in your career you consider that you have followed a similar path and achieved what you wanted.

Karel Reisz: In the main, yes, but not completely. As the films get more expensive, you do get more constraints from the studios, yet on the whole my career has been quite unrestricted: no complaints.

CPR: Of the filmmakers like Lindsay Anderson and Tony Richardson who spearheaded British Free Cinema in the 1950s, you're the one who lasted. But you've been criticized both for your early ideological approach and then for your subsequent move to American subjects.

KR: So often the critics assume that one is the lackey of a corrupt system, but in fact a big element of what they regard as one's conformity is simply a desire to have an audience. It's a difficult thing to balance out—wanting to work and getting the work you want.

CPR: The first film you did that was not strictly British was *Isadora* [1968]. How did you become involved in this project?

KR: A French producer came and told me he wanted to make a film about Isadora Duncan. He'd just seen *Morgan* [1966], a film that I'd made with Vanessa Redgrave, and he said, "I'd like a film about Isadora Duncan starring Vanessa." And I myself was intrigued by Duncan.

Vanessa Redgrave is a quite remarkable actress; it's all intuitive with her. She doesn't "work out" a walk, "work out" a manner of speech or any other externals. Vanessa plays around with the character until it seems to come through to her, and then she just floats away and does it. She's very untheoretical. She just grabs things out of the air and has the ability to absorb them without their standing out as devices or gimmicks. It comes out of homework she's done, but this is the kind of homework that, with a more earnest or deliberate actor, could prove really embarrassing. With Redgrave, because everything is generated by emotion, it comes out fine.

CPR: You are reputed to be a director with a great interest in outcasts, in any event characters that fall out of the ordinary, like Isadora Duncan. Why is this? Why have you so often chosen this sort of character?

KR: It is very difficult to talk about one's own work in an analytical way. You know, what happens is: you read material, you talk, you live, and ... suddenly you find there is a subject that interests you. It isn't that you know in advance what your chief theme is going to be; you find a subject interesting, and then over the years you find that it has been the same subject every time. But this isn't intentional; there's no program. It's something inside you, and I think that from such a point of view the artist is unwise to pin down themes too much. I mean it's the critic's job to say: "Oh, yes, he's done that every time," or, "The artist should keep himself free to discover whatever it is that really obsesses him."

I think you are right that there is a common subject to my work, but, again, it is certainly not intentional. "Oh, I must make another film about a rebel"—you know, it doesn't work like that. You find yourself—I find myself, or I've found myself in the past—interested by subjects where the central character goes in some way against the grain of his world, and why that is so in my case you would have to ask my psychoanalyst. Not that I have one, but . . .

CPR: From a political perspective such as the one that inspired Free Cinema, do you think that art in general, and cinema in particular, can not only record reality but also help to bring about changes in society?

KR: Well, in a political way not very much: mainly the cinema reflects society rather than changes it. I think I would have to say there is not very much influence in this sense; I don't think the arts change society in the way you describe. You know, it's been tried: the Germans tried it, the Russians tried it. If the attempt to change the world through art is too overt, the audiences reject it because they think they're being lectured. So the answer to your question, to repeat, is a very qualified "no."

CPR: Why is the costume film still so healthy? Why does it appeal so much to directors and audiences? Is it a sort of escape from reality?

KR: No, I don't think it is necessarily an escape from reality at all. In fact, I think that working at arm's length in a different period in a different country makes it easier for one to identify meanings, because you're taken away from day-to-day reality.

I think *The French Lieutenant's Woman* [1969] itself, the novel, the Victorian story, treats a relatively traditional subject. I mean, it is not all that different from some of the Thomas Hardy novels. Except I think there is an element in it that almost makes it a Victorian novel used as a kind of science-fiction vehicle, since it posits the possibility of a woman with twentieth-century desires living in the nineteenth century and having therefore to live a normal life she wouldn't otherwise have wanted to live. Then there is a very strange thing that happens in the novel: about three-quarters of the way through, the woman changes completely. But we don't see the transition. At one point she is down in line and then there is the big scene and she runs away and disappears; the next time we see her, she's sort of become a twentieth-century woman, more or less emancipated. The psychology of the character here doesn't seem to interest the artist, John Fowles, at all; if he had been interested in that, we would have seen the transition, but he is interested instead in putting this woman into one world and then moving her into a more liberated world. And Fowles is able to do this because he has established this pattern of going away from the past to the present, and back to the past, from speculation about or general discussion of the past to the male character's actually traveling to America. So that when the leap comes whereby we must judge what the French lieutenant's woman is doing, we say: "Oh, I see! We're in a different world now"; she's joined the Pre-Raphaelite group, the morality of which is completely different from the morality of the Lyme Regis Society.

So there is a very strong intellectual, speculative element in the novel. It isn't really like a Hardy novel, which all takes place in one world; in Fowles, we jump around. And the speculative element is strong not only in the sense that the narrative keeps jumping about, but also in the particular plot device that changes this woman from one kind of person into another kind. There is, then, a rather elaborative pattern to *The French Lieutenant's Woman* as a piece of fiction.

CPR: The Victorian Age, in particular, is nowadays still very much on the minds of British intellectuals, writers, and filmmakers. Why do you think this is?

KR: The literature—also that of the pre-Victorians—is very, very strong: the quality of the work of Jane Austen, Hardy, and George Eliot is quite remarkable. It is not surprising that works of such quality remain in the public consciousness, but, you know, Shakespeare's plays are still performed all the time. Some of the French writers survive in the same way. I think it has to do with the romantic quality of the work, which is very much alive.

CPR: How would you define the relationship between the film of *The French Lieutenant's Woman* and the novel?

KR: Oh, I wouldn't try! I think if one does an adaptation of a novel, one has some obligation to be interested in the spirit of the novel—what it was basically trying to do—but one has absolutely no obligation to the letter of the novel, to its details. The two media are so completely different: the novel works by description, the cinema by demonstration, and these two processes are fundamentally different.... When you make a movie, you have an obligation to dramatize; you need to keep the flow of events going in such a way that the audience is held for two hours. I keep thinking that the problems of film are totally different from the ones a novelist encounters. You know, in the cinema you have no problems of description, for instance; but when a novelist introduces a character, he has to tell you what color her eyes are, how she looks, what her history is, what her clothes are, and what kind of person she is. In a movie, the person is simply *there*. On the other hand, the novel has the huge, different possibility of the author's commentary. In this case the presence of the author is something that is permitted and fascinating, and you can't do that in the cinema. You can't suddenly have somebody addressing the audience. So the means of the two media are completely different, and I think you don't do any novel a favor by being faithful to its details. You need to interpret them for the medium you are working in.

CPR: Harold Pinter's screenplay for *The French Lieutenant's Woman* concentrated on the relationship of the twentieth-century players with the film they were producing and with their own characters. This subplot helps to maintain the meta-textual statement of Fowles's novel, but it has been described as disruptive for some audiences. Do you think the film somehow depends too much on the novel because of this?

KR: Oh, the film is very dependent on the novel, yes. The events may be very similar but the details are completely different. You see, I think that the important thing about the two continuities is that they enable you to jump out of the story and comment on what fiction actually *does*. It's like a discussion of fiction, but I think that in the case of movies we're talking about a natural drawing of attention to the fact of filmmaking. And the problem is to keep the thrust of the narrative alive while pulling the carpet out from under the characters every now and then. Of course, it would have been easier to betray the novel and tell it all in one continuity, but that wasn't really an option.

I think the other thing that's very interesting in the book, is interesting in the film in a different way. In the novel, when Fowles jumps out of the story, he consciously uses the sort of sensibility that is vey much from the twentieth century—he talks about Henry Moore, and he talks about Freud and the modern. In the movie, we keep jumping to the twentieth-century sensibility of the *actors*: their whole sense of sexuality is different, their whole sense of loyalty is different, their moral and spiritual priorities are quite different. And the comments they make about the parts they are playing add to the paradox. So, of course, the film is a different artwork from the novel. But it's an equivalent, too, in that it's an attempt to retain the game begun by the novel. We haven't rejected the notion of the game, but we have changed the rules of the game.

CPR: How would you define the two styles that you created in both of the film's stories?

KR: They are very differently lit. One is lighted in a highly dramatic, direct way, and the other uses bounced light and no shadows. They look different. On the modern set there is an attempt to create a kind of patterned way of looking, whereas the Victorian stuff is dramatically lighted, with much sharper angles and much heavier shadows. It's got a different smell and feel.

CPR: I feel that Anna is a much more conventional character than Sarah in the sense that her responses are not quite as brave or as purposeful.

KR: Another way of saying this is that Anna is involved in an emotional relationship that isn't very important to her. What's important to her is the work, and when the film ends, there is no suggestion that the relationship she's created during the filming has got any weight or permanence in her life. Of course, there isn't time to dramatize the modern characters with the same depth as the others. But I think they are quite specific enough people and not just an actor and an actress. I think there is also an assumption of equality between the two of them, which contrasts very strongly with the relationship of the comparable Victorian characters.

CPR: Why did Pinter make Sarah a painter, an artist?

KR: What is she in the novel? Doesn't she keep a diary? You see, having a character keep a diary is a literary way of getting to the interior of the character. Drawing is a visual way to do the same thing, so we see drawings by Sarah.

CPR: Yes, there is a very powerful scene in which she is drawing her self-portrait.

KR: Well, as said, this is a cinematic equivalent of a confessional diary. If we had had a diary, Sarah would have had to read out of it, which is a very unfilmic device. This way we were able to achieve the same effect through imagery, by the nature of what she draws and the comparison she makes by looking into the mirror. It's another adaptive device—it's not a translation.

CPR: Pinter reduced the social statement about the Victorian period, didn't he? He concentrated more on the meta-textual than the social.

KR: I think the complexity, the number of points you can make, in the course of a long novel differs from what you can do in another art form. Also, as I said earlier, in a film you have the obligation to keep the thrust of the narrative moving forward in order to hold the audience, and this is a difficult enough task with all the temporal jumps in this picture that keep taking the viewer away. It is also true that we did shoot a long "social" sequence, the equivalent of the scene in the novel where the officer goes to see the prostitute; we did shoot that and found that it carried a very heavy commentative weight. So much so that the sequence unbalanced the story somehow—it seemed rather like a piece of sociology in the middle of a drama, and that's why we dropped it.

CPR: To what extent do you feel compelled to use novels as sources?

KR: I don't feel compelled at all. I mean I've made some films that have been derived from fiction sources, and some films that haven't been. There is no compulsion either way on my part. From the point of view of the film industry, it's easier to get money for a project from the financiers if there is another way that they can experience the film before you make it. Reading a screenplay is an extremely difficult thing—people don't do it well; the professionals don't do it well either, the money professionals. *The French Lieuten-*

ant's Woman was already a very popular book, so I think the money people just thought, "Yes, this is a good bet." But a short story or a newspaper article can be just as good a source. I don't think there is any rule about this.

CPR: Some directors, like Anthony Minghella and Sally Potter, have declared that after reading a book, they somehow "saw" it in their minds in cinematic images. Since you have made a number of adaptations, I was wondering if this was the case for you as well.

KR: That does happen, but it's not the only way. You know I made a movie called *The Gambler* [1974], which started when a young man came into my office and gave me sixty pages of autobiography. So you can't really make any rule about what stimulates the creative juices of the director—there are many things.

CPR: Which is the most important stage of film production for you as a director?

KR: All the stages are part of the same process. And they are all important. There is a huge jump between the original idea and the script; there is a huge jump between the script and the rehearsal; there is a huge jump between the rehearsal and the shooting; and there is a huge jump between the shooting and the interpretation of the filmed material in the cutting room. Then there is a minor jump when you put in the soundtrack. All of these are part of one big process. And pretending that one stage is more important than another is somehow to misunderstand the cinematic medium. What is important is to give relative autonomy to each of these stages in the process. I mean, once you start shooting the material, it changes from what it was in the script; it grows as other sensibilities become involved. And when you're in the cutting room, you must be careful that you're responding to the material you actually have, not to the material you thought you were going to get when you first read the script. So the whole thing is an organic process. And if you are a filmmaker, you have to be open to that.

Well, I'm talking about the way I work, but there are clearly many directors—and many good directors—who don't work like that. You know, Buñuel is on record as saying that the process of filming is boring, that he's all done after he's written the script. O.K., that's his way. My way, and I don't put it in opposition to anyone else's, is that I hope, for instance, that the actors will surprise me. Naturally I cast actors that I think are well suited to their roles, but I also hope that they will bring fresh colors that I didn't know were there.

CPR: Do you use improvisation?

KR: No, I don't use improvisation; I use rehearsal. You know, I don't change the dialogue, but of course making the dialogue live involves rehearsal, movement, timing, and a sense of rhythm, of presentation. So I don't use improvisation in the sense that the actors decide on their own what they say, not at all. But I do undertake rehearsal. I'm very, very slow in the morning, which means that sometimes we don't shoot until the afternoon. It takes a long time before I know what I want to do, and then I shoot very fast.

CPR: For my last question, I am going to describe the associations that critics have made of the cinema with other things, and perhaps you can tell me what you think. The cinema is a mirror.

KR: Well, no. No, it's much more like a painting, much more a re-invention.

CPR: The cinema is a dream.

KR: Yes, but it depends on the style. In dreams you jump from significant moment to significant moment; you don't open closed doors and that sort of thing. So in a sense there is a kind of emotional concentration to dreams that you find in the best of cinema, yes. However, there is a certain style of cinema that is very literal, very dependent on realistic detail, which the dream is not.

CPR: The cinema is a peephole.

KR: No, definitely not for me.

CPR: Finally, what is your next project?

KR: I'm working in the theater now. I'm going to New York to do a play, a Harold Pinter play called *Ashes to Ashes* [1996]. It's set to open in February of the coming year [1999] at the Roundabout. Do come see it.

Bibliography

Gardner, Colin. *Karel Reisz*. Manchester, U.K.: Manchester University Press, 2006.

Gaston, Georg M. A. *Karel Reisz*. Boston: Twayne, 1980.

Reisz, Karel. *The Technique of Film Editing*. London: Focal Press, 1953.

"A Kind of Filming: An Interview with John Schlesinger," by Leo Verswijver (1994: previously unpublished in book or magazine form).

As a major filmmaker from 1962 to 2000, John Schlesinger (1926-2003) directed some of his era's best films: *Darling* (1965), which earned his leading lady Julie Christie an Academy Award for Best Actress; the poetic masterpiece *Far From the Madding Crowd* (1967); and the controversial *Midnight Cowboy* (1969), the winner of three Oscars including Best Picture and Best Director. Schlesinger also had the privilege of directing such talented actresses as Glenda Jackson, Vanessa Redgrave, and Shirley MacLaine, in addition to Christie.

Schlesinger first worked as an actor in minor parts until 1958, then was a documentary filmmaker for the BBC (British Broadcasting Corporation) for the next three years, before turning to directing features in 1962 with a small and intimate masterpiece called *A Kind of Loving*: a low-key but effective exercise in the "kitchen-sink" school of drama that was grounded in working-class characters, industrial locales in northern England, naturalistic performances (Alan Bates starred), and gritty cinematography. Even more accomplished was *Billy Liar* (1963), based on a novel and play by Keith Waterhouse. This often very funny film follows the fortune of a young Yorkshire funeral-home worker (played by Tom Courtenay) who relies on his elaborate fantasy life to escape from the drudgery of his job. Other Schlesinger films of note include *Sunday Bloody Sunday* (1971), *The Day of the Locust* (1975), and *Marathon Man* (1976).

It was only in the 1990s that John Schlesinger began to find it difficult to make the movie projects he firmly believed in. *The Next Best Thing* (2000), starring Madonna, turned out to be his final effort as a filmmaker.

Leo Verswijver spoke with Schlesinger at his London home in May of 1994.

Leo Verswijver: Could you tell me something about *Dead Give Away*, which recently got cancelled? What happened exactly?

John Schlesinger: It's a story of what happens to movies now. It's the casting, you know: there are only so many bankable names that they are prepared to pay vast sums of money to, so they can guarantee a picture. These stars may open the picture, but they cannot guarantee its success. Otherwise, why do they not always have successful films with these highly paid stars? But, unfortunately, it's the only way to get a film off the ground these days. You have to come up with someone who's got the appeal, not only to the American distributors, but also to the overseas distributors. It's really tough.

LV: Could we go back to your début film, *A Kind of Loving* [1962], to me always one of the most intelligent, stylish, and beautiful pictures of the decade? It earned you four BAFTA nominations right away, and you also won the Silver Bear at the Berlin Film Festival. You made quite an entrance with this picture.

JS: Well, the film was very well received in Germany and Italy. The French wouldn't show it; they said, "Oh, *les amants anglais*, oh, oh!" They just said it was a silly film. But the film did very well overall; we didn't need France because in those days you could make a film with limited sources and still get quite a generous time period during which to shoot. It was possible back then to make a profit in *this* country alone—a very different system and a very different situation compared to now.

LV: Were you, in your early days, influenced by the Free Cinema movement?

JS: Free Cinema is something I had nothing to do with whatsoever. It is a name for a group of directors who made documentaries, people like Karel Reisz and Tony Richardson. At that time, I was working for television. They regarded me as a maverick, you know. Lindsay Anderson once said, "You must aim higher for television." Which of course I was doing, in my own way. So I'm not connected with Free Cinema. However, what it did, it opened some doors to a kind of naturalism that we perhaps needed in the British theater and subsequently film—*Look Back in Anger* [1956, filmed 1959], by John Osborne, that kind of thing. When the Free Cinema directors started making movies, they insisted on forming their own companies instead of selling away the rights to their work. So Richardson made his own films. That's what opened the doors, so I suppose this period was in a way very productive.

LV: Do you still watch your first movies, like *A Kind of Loving*, *Billy Liar* [1963], and *Darling* [1965], when they're shown on TV?

JS: No, I hate television. Once a film is on television, it's on the wrong-sized screen. I have seen these pictures at festivals where they have honorary retrospectives, but I don't watch the entire movies. *Darling* is even the least favorite movie that I've ever made. I think it's too pleased with itself: it's a bit knowing, a bit nudgy. There are scenes in it that I thought at the time were wonderful; I was boasting about what a good shoot I had had, and I liked Julie Christie an awful lot—she was amazing—but I think *Billy Liar*, my second film [also with Julie Christie], is a much better work. *Darling* had so much success in America that when we came back here for the opening, it got quite badly treated by the press. I was upset at the time, but I thought they were probably right. I know *Darling* was popular, but I don't look back thinking, "God, that was a good film."

LV: What about *Far From the Madding Crowd* [1967], your third film with Julie Christie?

JS: It was very beautiful to look at. I had a wonderful designer, Richard Macdonald, and it was my first film in color. He taught me a lot about controlling color. One of the reasons that color is dangerous is that black and white leaves so much more to the imagination. Take the famous shower sequence in Alfred Hitchcock's movie *Psycho* [1959]. If it had been in color, I think all the blood spatters and everything else would have been almost unbearable. But in black and white, something is left to the imagination. For *Midnight Cowboy* [1969], I used grayish color because so much in it was about neon lights, advertising, Times Square, and this kind of thing.

I was frightened of using color; I liked black and white very much, so I had to learn to use color until it was totally controlled. I haven't shot a black-and-white movie since *Far From the Madding Crowd*, although I have shot sequences in black and white. *Madding Crowd* had two things: it was derived from a well-known classic, which is a disadvantage because everybody had the classic in his head—the casting, the scripting, etc.; everybody has his view of the book because everybody knew it so well, that is, *if* they knew it. So that was a disadvantage, if I look back and think maybe we weren't quite free enough with the adaptation of the novel. It dealt mostly with man as dwarfed by the landscape, and he's not up to it: he's inadequate and struck down by some terrible disaster; he has to pick up the pieces, which is what life is about. So I'm drawn to this philosophy of Hardy, and the film was, again, wonderfully designed by Richard Macdonald, who unfortunately died last year; and it was lit by Nicolas Roeg, so I had a very good collaboration on *Far From the Madding Crowd*. It's not my favorite among my films, but I'm very proud of it.

LV: What are your favorite films among those you have made?

JS: I'm fond of my first two [*A Kind of Loving* and *Billy Liar*], and, from my middle period, I'm very fond of *Midnight Cowboy*, *Sunday Bloody Sunday* [1971]—with the superb Glenda Jackson!—and *The Day of the Locust* [1975].

LV: Don't you think that *The Day of the Locust* is probably your most underrated film?

JS: Yes, I think it is. It was poorly received. I think it was misjudged, but I think it's beginning to get appreciated now. I think it's a very good film, and, of all my failures, it's the one I'm most proud of. I regard the novel as probably the best piece of writing about Hollywood that's ever been produced. It was suggested to me as a film many years before I ever made it by a producer who brought it to me, but there was no way at the time that anybody was going to give me the break to do it. You need a great commercial success to be able to get the work, a movie or two afterwards, with which to hang yourself—if you know what I mean by that. I liked the idea of Nathanael West's 1939 book and then Warner Brothers asked me, after the success of *Midnight Cowboy*, "What would you like to do? Come make a film for us." I said that I'd like to do *The Day of the Locust*, so a day later they bought an option on it. We had a series of meetings, the screenwriter Waldo Salt was brought in, and we started to work on it.

Later on I got very disillusioned because Warner Brothers wanted to spend only a small amount of money on the picture, certainly not enough considering that there would be some big sequences in it. I had also gone through the experience—despite having won the Academy Award as Best Director that year [for *Midnight Cowboy*]—of having a film of mine cancelled, a project I was passionate to do. So I was in one of those negative work-moods, that kind of attitude, so I stopped laboring over the script of *The Day of the Locust*, and the then-producer said, "Look, I need help, and you helped me a lot on *Midnight Cowboy*. Please, don't desert me." I didn't see the point, so I told him to take his money and run because the film would not be made. It was the beginning of my eyes' being widely opened about the monstrosity of our profession in terms of what you have to deal with concerning front offers. Everybody has such stories and they will continue to have such stories—no matter who you are. So it's not just me, it's universal to the business that we're in. We're asking for vast sums of money with which to put our fantasy on the screen, and the producers in turn are spending vast sums of money on advertising and getting the product to the public. So they're looking at production with a different set of values from mine.

I remember that I finally agreed I needed to do some work on the script, so I did and started to get excited again. I adored Waldo Salt, a highly intelligent and very sensitive man who went through terrible problems during the McCarthy period [he had been blacklisted from 1951 to 1962]. But there had to be a way of working with him; he was very difficult to pin down. You really had to sit next to him and say, "Tomorrow, ten pages please." The script had to get made that way, rather than wait for Walt to finish it. The first draft of *The Day of the Locust* was a disaster; it was dreadful. He almost waited for D-day before we had to deliver—he then just dashed it off. It was only by sitting next to Walt, creating the pressure that he needed to write, that we ever got a screenplay that began to excite me. Then we changed producers and I felt I had a good partner who was strong, and we were able to convince Paramount to make the picture.

LV: Looking back now, after all this time, are you pleased with the casting of *The Day of the Locust*?

JS: I think we might have made a mistake. I remember the producer who first sent me the novel years before, he had said, "I think you need an woman older than the one in the novel." In the book she's seventeen and very difficult to handle with all her attitudes—you know, acting the role of the big star, which she tended to do in the story. I thought Karen Black was a wonderful actress, but, looking back, she's not attractive enough. The other problem is not to make her too attractive. We also read the script with Raquel Welch—one of the ideas in the casting—and we decided that she was just *too* beautiful to play the part. There was something offbeat about Karen Black, wanting to make it, her eyes too close together, things like that. I also thought we had found a big star with William Atherton, but he wasn't one. The best performances are from Donald Sutherland and Burgess Meredith.

LV: Where and how did you get the idea of casting silent-screen actress Madge Kennedy in *The Day of the Locust* and the following year also in *Marathon Man* [1976]?

JS: I was introduced to her by George Cukor. I loved Madge Kennedy, so I thought I had to cast her.

LV: Do you like silent films?

JS: I've made a study of them, but I'm not a film buff. I go to the movies, but in London it's not so easy, because you never know when the film starts; in Los Angeles, where I spend a lot of time going to the cinema, it is much easier. Besides, there are a lot of other things I'm interested in, like music, theater, opera. I go to see live performances as often as I can. I've been to an awful lot of them since I came back to London.

LV: You've also directed for the theater. What was that like?

JS: I did my first production in about 1964, a short play that had never been performed before—by a friend of mine, Peter Hall. He asked me to do it and I immediately agreed; then I did my first Shakespeare. I was very nervous, but I did it. Although I liked the pure way you work with actors in the theater, my head was really into movies. You know, in the theater you and the actors are just working with the dramatic text, you grow with the text. In the cinema, well, you have to work with and on everything, and I find that more exhilarating.

There was a time in my life, though, when I lost confidence in myself and I went back to the theater to do a Sam Shepard play, just with four actors, and it was such a great experience to do, because we were working with four very good actors. I had a very good time and that experience gave me my confidence back.

LV: How do you explain the success of *Midnight Cowboy*?

JS: If I knew that, I would never stop turning out successful movies. I didn't know it was going to be *that* successful; I chose to do it when a lot of my friends and advisors were saying, "Be very careful what you do after *Far From the Madding Crowd*." That was a flop and they said I shouldn't be doing this new picture. *Midnight Cowboy* was quite ahead of its time, and, when you look at it now—we just celebrated the 25th anniversary of its release—you realize that it couldn't be made today. No studio would touch it. It earned me an Academy Award, and it was nice to have won. It probably means more to me now than it did then.

LV: On *Marathon Man*, you worked again with Dustin Hoffman. Was that just a coincidence?

JS: I thought he was the right casting for it, but he didn't. He wanted us to write the script as if he were an adult, a teacher rather than a student. We tried that and decided it wasn't working, so I went back to him and said, "I know you are thirty-eight but mentally, in this film, you've got to think yourself as twenty-eight and as a graduate student. I can't make you a teacher, which is what you wanted." And this is exactly what we did and it worked out very well.

LV: Other films of yours, such as *The Believers* [1987] and *Pacific Heights* [1990], are also thrillers like *Marathon Man*. Are you a fan of the genre, or of Hitchcock?

JS: Yes, but I don't sit down and look at Hitchcock movies and then say, "Let's make ours and we'll use this and that from him." But I think Hitchcock used clever irony—because he's British, of course—horror, and suspense brilliantly. I'm afraid the Americans are not very big on irony. I do like the sharpness of thrillers, the possibilities that abound when you're playing games with the audience. I enjoy doing that. *The Believers* was dealing with an improbable, not totally believable story, you know: the idea that people can be sold, be taken in by a particular aspect of religion to the extent that they actually do something bad to themselves as a result. The film had some things that I liked very much; I like thrillers that are about things that I myself am frightened of: they're a way of getting back at myself. I'm quite frightened of the idea, for example, of spiders being pushed into the body, or that somebody can put a spell on you. I suppose some such things are possible, however, and I was attracted to the movie because of that.

LV: *Madame Sousatzka* [1988] is a totally different kind of movie.

JS: I think it has a very good heart. It's about art and commercialism. The commercial aspect is very central in many people's lives these days—how to survive it.

LV: Do you stay with a movie until the very end, the editing, including all the final finishing touches a film needs?

JS: Yes, absolutely.

LV: And you're always there from the very beginning as well?

JS: Yes, and that's a result of my television days when I did exactly the same. I remember when I was working for television, one of the films I made was a documentary about the Victoria Bus Station. I remember my first trip to Brussels to do a documentary about the World Expo in 1958. I enjoyed making these documentaries very much. When I started at the BBC, I got in because of a short documentary I had made about Hyde Park—"Sunday in the Park" [1956] it was called. It had the makings of something that attracted the attention of someone at the BBC, who was in a good position. He gave me the break and nurtured me along very well. That's what started it.

LV: Ever since your first film, you have been able to perform at a pretty high level for your profession.

JS: You think so? It was a struggle to get there for some years, doing commercials, documentaries, second-unit stuff, everything—you name it. Every time you're out there to make a film, you're wondering if it's going to work. I've never felt, by the way, that one of mine stayed all the time in a saleable position. I think it's quite wrong to think in that way; you have to challenge yourself as often as you can. I like making films but I hate the business. I absolutely despise the people I have to deal with most of the time.

LV: You are very modest about your own achievements, aren't you?

JS: No, I'm very pleased with some of my films, but I'm also very critical of some of what I've done. A few things I like very much, a few things I don't.

LV: There's this saying that you're only as good as your last movie. Is it true?

JS: I think so, now more than ever. I think my generation of filmmakers is having a tough time in making what we want to make. With the right mix of actors and people, I myself might still be bankable all the way. Recently, I've read two scripts that I liked but was unable to finance.

I saw Lindsay Anderson last night at a memorial concert for a composer friend; he, Karel Reisz, Richard Lester, and Arthur Penn—I'm talking about my contemporaries—all people that were really on the map in the sixties, these guys are having quite a tussle to get something made nowadays. It's very difficult; inevitably, younger people are coming up and you have to make room for them, you know.

LV: When you made your movies from the 1960s through the 1980s, did you have *carte blanche*?

JS: Let's just say that I like collaboration; I like working with writers and technicians and even good producers. Good father figures, I'm very happy with that. I recognize film as a collaborative medium, unless you write the script yourself—then you are really the sole author, but writer-directors are not so common. What is happening now is that you fight for the final cut, which I still have—that's the 11th commandment, thou shalt have the final cut—but there are all sorts of restrictions. The film has to be a certain length; if it exceeds that length and the producers and distributors can get their hands all over it . . . If you test a film and it doesn't test well, it's an awful business. If I had tested *Midnight Cowboy* or *Sunday Bloody Sunday*, if I had put those films before a public who then turned into critics for one night, of course they'd object to all sorts of things that were in those movies that had never been seen with any frequency before. We would have been in a terrible state. I'm convinced I hate previews or the system under which they're used now to iron a film out, to make it appeal to the lowest common denominator. This is what happens in the American cinema and to a certain extent the British, which is kind of connected to the American film industry. There is also still an international cinema, with people working in their own language who'd love to break into the American distribution system on a big scale; and there are certain quality foreign films that reach the United States but mostly remain on the art-house circuit.

LV: Did you ever think there was a difference between making a film in America compared to making one in England?

JS: I love working here in the U.K., but I don't want to make films that are too narrow. My greatest pleasure was in making two films for television about British spies; they were written by Alan Bennett, who is one of the wittiest screenwriters. I had a huge success with those pictures, but only on the small screen or on video. They were made-for-television. I had a very good time making those films, total freedom; I didn't have to worry, nobody wasn't looking over our shoulders trying to make us make a movie that would appeal to as many people as possible. I had hoped for that kind of situation for *Midnight Cowboy*.

I know that *Sunday Bloody Sunday* itself was a rather specialized film, and that it probably wouldn't get a very wide release and would offend people. The distributors were ashamed of it—they were frightened of it. Since I'm gay, I can say that the most normal thing for that doctor and that boy was to be lovers, to kiss, to be in bed. People walked out, saying this is not a film for nice people. Now, twenty years later, they make a film like *Philadelphia* [1993], which is certainly the first commercially big picture from America to deal with AIDS, but they cut out anything that *might* offend, stuff from the private life of the Tom Hanks character. I feel they could have risked more, but of course they pulled back and what's happened as a result? It's a commercial success. I wish it had risked more and had still made a commercial success! [Laughs.]

LV: That's the kind of movie you would have made, isn't it?

JS: Let me tell you, I have two scripts that deal with the gay-AIDS subject, and I don't know which one will go first; one of them I've been working on for six years. The script just isn't quite good enough—yet. And if you want to do something that's explosive, potentially, then it must be done very well.

LV: How would you describe your films? Do you think they share a common theme?

JS: I hope they're of good quality in any case, and I do think they all share the same theme, in a sense: very few have happy endings, many have question-mark endings. If I did provide a sort of happy ending, they'd accuse me of being sentimental. But all of my films are about people resisting compromise yet having to face it, people pushed into a corner who have to survive in some way, whatever their experiences may be—physical or emotional. I think my movies are about survival in very strange circumstances.

Darling was about a girl who could not make up her mind and always thought that something better might be around the next corner. Therefore she was unable to stick to something and take it wherever it would lead her. *Midnight Cowboy* was about a fantasy, doing the one thing Joe Buck does well, which is to screw with great satisfaction, but he ends up living with a friend and companion who needs him desperately, just as badly as Joe needs him. *Billy Liar* was about a boy who never took the risk of leaving the environment he's desperate to leave in order to realize his ambitions, who then meets someone who can take him there, but he doesn't have the courage to go and feels safer with his fantasy. *A Kind of Loving* was about a man who thinks he loves somebody and realizes he doesn't really, and has to make a difficult decision: do I stick with her or do I leave her? In those days people stayed with each other perhaps more than they do now. *Sunday Bloody Sunday* was about a man and a woman both in love with the same person, with different attitudes toward the liaison—the man feeling the triangular compromise was worth it, the woman not. Even *Marathon Man* is about someone who has to confront something—violence—though he's scared of it. There's also the Jewish theme in it, which was one of the reasons I did it. The Hoffman character is reluctant to get involved, yet in a way he's drawn into the situation and has to deal with it somehow, pushed as he is to the extreme.

The effort in making a film is so great that I've always said, "I don't want to make films just as entertainment," as that word is commonly understood. Yet entertainment can mean many things: it can mean getting the attention of the audience, moving them, making them angry, making them scared, making them *think*. To me, entertainment is grabbing someone's attention, so I hope the audience leaves a film of mine after having had a good experience of some kind that's special.

The thing that always angers me, coming from the people who write about the cinema, is that there must always be something that's absolutely recognizable in each of a director's films, the same thing over and over again. They don't regard you as a real filmmaker if that ingredient isn't there. I mean, Fred Zinnemann, like William Wyler, made many different kinds of movies, from musicals to whatever. *High Noon* [1952], *Julia* [1977], *Oklahoma!* [1955]—Zinnemann was a genuine moviemaker, but people don't consider you the real thing if you don't have what they call a "signature style." There's a lot of bullshit connected with this idea as promulgated by the *auteur* theorists, along with their idea, which I intimated earlier, that a film should be considered the product of a single author. Naturally, *Sight and Sound* and the British Film Institute are writing from a more intellectual point of view than the *auteurists*, but I'm not into that, either: I don't consider myself an intellectual.

Anyway, I've got a total of six films I'm working on whose screenplays I'm doing right now, because it's so uncertain as to which one I can get financed. To put all your eggs into one basket is impossible these days. Some of the scripts I've been working on for some time, some are newer ones. The one that I think I'm going to do next, for the BBC, is an adaptation of a very famous novel written in the thirties about a girl who wants to change everybody and everything. It has a lot of charm and humor and is a bit of a satire on D. H. Lawrence and Thomas Hardy. I don't know if we're going to get it done because it definitely needs more money. Anyway, I like the subject because it fits in with other subjects I've chosen.

LV: An entirely different question: have you ever considered going into politics?

JS: No! I hate politics; I'm not a political animal. I'm concerned about human beings and politics very often is concerned about conception, about ideas and not about human beings in the end. I'm a filmmaker, a maker of entertainment in one of its forms. I also like working in the opera house or in the theater with a play. I've done three operatic productions, one of them in Salzburg.

LV: What did you think when David Puttnam became the head of Columbia?

JS: Well, I think he was politically inept. I think he played his cards very badly. I think Puttnam should have made space for the old brigade and worked with them and used them and not antagonized a system that you can't beat. Instead, he thought, "I'm going to do it my way and get rid of these people," and it all backfired on him.

LV: Would you accept the offer of running a studio?

JS: No, I would hate it. I'm not an executive; I'm only a filmmaker. I would hate to do such a thing. I was asked to lead a course at the Royal College of Art, teaching movies—I don't want to do that either. I like the idea of influencing, helping younger filmmakers. I went to Sundance last year; it was a very rewarding experience to help people with their films and talk to them, to try to be helpful. But I don't want to produce other people's films—although there are certain people I would like to work with as a producer. Martin Scorsese sent me a book I like; if we can find a way to adapt it, although it would be very difficult to adapt . . . I like Scorsese's work, but I also like the work of the Coen brothers [Joel and Ethan], of the Taviani brothers [Paolo and Vittorio], and of course of the great, acknowledged masters like Luis Buñuel, Federico Fellini, Akira Kurosawa, Billy Wilder, and Stanley Kubrick, among others. And I think in the U.K. we've got a few young people now, like Stephen Frears, who sometimes hit the mark. In general, you know, I have great admiration for filmmakers.

Bibliography

Brooker-Bowers, Nancy. *John Schlesinger: A Guide to References and Resources*. Boston: G. K. Hall, 1978.

Mann, William J. *Edge of Midnight: The Life of John Schlesinger*. London: Hutchinson, 2004.

Phillips, Gene D. *John Schlesinger*. Boston: Twayne, 1981.

"The Movie Lover: An Interview with Ken Russell," by Gene D. Phillips. From *Film Comment*. 6.3 (Fall 1970): 10-17.

Ken Russell (1927-2011) was a British film director whose use of shock and sensationalism earned him both praise and reprehension from critics. After training as an electrician in the Royal Air Force for two years, he tried his hand at various genres of the arts, including acting, ballet, and photography. One of his early efforts in filmmaking drew the attention of the British Broadcasting Corporation (BBC), and Russell was offered a job as a director of documentary films. He continued his work there as the director of BBC television's *Monitor* and "Sunday Night Film" programs for a decade.

The two feature films *French Dressing* (1963) and *Billion Dollar Brain* (1967), which Russell completed while working for the BBC, were both successful, but it was *Women in Love* (1969), based on D. H. Lawrence's novel, that established his reputation as a major film director. The visual beauty of this film and its tasteful handling of erotic scenes won the approval of public and critics alike. His next picture, *The Music Lovers* (1970), portrayed the anguished life of Pyotr Ilyich Tchaikovsky in a flamboyant, sensational style that infuriated audiences. *The Devils* (1971), based in part on the Aldous Huxley novel *The Devils of Loudon*, aroused even more vehement criticism with its story of mass sexual hysteria in a convent. Russell then made *The Boy Friend* (1971) and *Savage Messiah* (1972) before he again achieved a commercial success with *Tommy* (1975), a film based on a rock opera. His later movies include *Lisztomania* (1975), *Altered States* (1980), *Crimes of Passion* (1984), *Whore* (1991), and the musical horror-comedy *The Fall of the Louse of Usher* (2002).

Gene D. Phillips interviewed Ken Russell in a London pub, near the place where the director was supervising the final editing of *The Music Lovers*, on the subject of Russell's career: past, present, and future.

Gene D. Phillips: Like John Schlesinger, you broke into films by way of television. How did you get into TV in the first place?

Ken Russell: In 1959 I got the chance to do some ten-minute segments for a TV series called *Monitor* [1958-65]. Huw Weldon, who is now managing director of BBC-TV, worked on the series too. After awhile I was allowed to make some longer documentary shorts for use on the program. I did one on the dance craze, the guitar craze, and one on pop artists called *Pop Goes the Easel* [1962]. My segment on photographers probably influenced Antonioni's *Blow-Up* [1966].

Finally I was asked to do some full-length biographies on the lives of great artists of the past: composers like Elgar, Debussy, Bartok, Prokofiev, and Delius; the poet Rossetti; and the dancer Isadora Duncan. Then I did a film in 1964 called *French Dressing*, a kind of seaside comedy, but it was an ill-conceived project from the start: the chemistry of the characters was wrong and the story never quite jelled. It was a flop, so I continued on in television.

GDP: Among all of the TV biographies that you have done, which ones are among your favorites?

KR: Three of the ones I most enjoyed doing are *Isadora, the Biggest Dancer in the World* [1966], *A Song of Summer* [1968], about the composer Delius, and *Dance of the Seven Veils* [1970], which was suggested by the life and music of Richard Strauss.

GDP: I have seen all of the ones you named; I admired Karel Reisz's subsequent film on Isadora Duncan very much, but I must say that I enjoyed your television version much more than Reisz's film.

KR: Reisz's film version used most of the incidents in Isadora's life that I used, but I managed to tell her story with a little more economy in about half the time that his picture runs.

GDP: This is partially due to the fact that you ran through the whole of Isadora's life in a kind of kaleidoscope-newsreel fashion at the beginning of your TV film (à la *Citizen Kane*), which gave the viewer a capsule view of her life that you could then easily expand as you went through the rest of the story.

KR: And Vivian Pickles, an excellent actress who had not done many important roles, was perfect as Isadora. Since Isadora's life was so pathetic *and* tragic, I tried to lighten the material at times.

For example, I used the old Betty Hutton recording of "The Sewing Machine" from the 1947 Hollywood film *The Perils of Pauline* on the soundtrack when Isadora was falling in love with Paris Singer, the sewing machine manufacturer.

GDP: Nevertheless, at certain points your *Isadora* has some darker tones than Reisz's film. For example, you showed that Isadora's Russian husband was an epileptic and a kleptomaniac and how this complicated their relationship, while the movie *Isadora* ignored these facts. With your interest in biographies of this kind, how did you wind up doing the film of *The Billion Dollar Brain* [1967]?

KR: I had a contract with Harry Saltzman to film the life of the Russian dancer Vaslav Nijinsky, with Rudolf Nureyev in the lead. Then Nureyev decided that he could not play the role of a dancer who was inferior to him, and the project was off. So I directed the spy film *The Billion Dollar Brain* for Saltzman, instead, since at that time he was doing a series of these films in the hope of making the Harry Palmer character played by Michael Caine as popular as the James Bond character.

GDP: I understand that Nureyev has at last decided to do the role of Nijinsky and that Tony Richardson is now going to make the film. At any rate, *The Billion Dollar Brain* flopped as your first film had done, and so it was back to television.

KR: One of the biographies that I did at this time was the aforementioned one of the composer Delius, who spent the last years of his life blind and crippled by syphilis while living in an English country cottage with his faithful wife and his amanuensis. It was a difficult TV film to make since I felt that I didn't know enough about Delius and his milieu, so I couldn't formulate just how I wanted to approach the material. I did not feel that way about D. H. Lawrence at all, incidentally. But I went ahead with the Delius biography anyhow, since making films is a voyage of discovery. I used a lot of location shots in the country, since Delius's music deals so often with nature and because he died there.

While working in TV I always shot outdoors as much as possible, since the indoor sets always seemed to me to look like sets: four blinking flats with pictures hung on them. I shot almost all of my television films outside a TV studio on location. In general I always disregarded the fact that I was doing them for television, although working in TV has made me partial to big close-ups, and I still use them often in motion pictures.

GDP: You said that you felt at home working on material from D. H. Lawrence when you filmed *Women in Love* [1969].

KR: I had immersed myself in the book and worked on the script, so that by the time I went on the floor to shoot the film I knew what I wanted. Nevertheless, I am a great believer in inventing things on the set. Working in TV you learn how to cut costs and prune down the project to essentials. When you work fast, moreover, you get a certain spontaneity from your cast and crew and they make suggestions about how to improve a scene during shooting.

GDP: I understand that Glenda Jackson, who worked for you both in *Women in Love* and in *The Music Lovers* [1970], is particularly good at suggesting things that you can use in a scene.

KR: Glenda Jackson is my kind of actress. Some actresses talk about the character they are playing incessantly—not Glenda; you have a preliminary discussion of the character with her and then she sticks to that throughout the filming. She makes a great many suggestions, and I usually accept about half of them. I only work with people who understand what I am trying to do because of the short time we have to work. In order to make a period picture on the same budget as a film in a contemporary setting you have to sacrifice something, and I sacrifice time. I assemble around myself a cast and crew that can intuit what I want and to whom, therefore, I have to say very little. Glenda is the prime example of the kind of person with whom I like to work.

GDP: Most of your work for television and motion pictures has had a period setting. Why are you drawn to the past for subject matter?

KR: I love period films: the possibility of opening a book into the past fascinates me. You don't have to worry that every last detail is historically accurate; a lack of total authenticity doesn't matter: in the end a little roughness is not a bad thing. I generally select period material because all the stories I do are about the relationships of people to their environment and to each other, and about other eternal questions that we are just as concerned about today as people were in the past. Topics of the moment pass and change; besides, one's feelings toward contemporary topics tend to distort one's presentation of them. We can be much more dispassionate and objective, and therefore more truthful, in dealing with the past. To see things of the past from the vantage point of the present is to be able to judge what effect they have had on the present.

GDP: You said that you worked on the script of *Women in Love*. Since so many critics commented on how faithful the film is to Lawrence's novel, could you tell me how much of this fidelity to Lawrence was due to you?

KR: The first script was done by an excellent screenwriter, but it had nothing to do with Lawrence. He had the old idea that unless you change something beyond recognition you are not being creative. This attitude is a terrible affront to the original author of the novel, especially if the author in question happens to be a writer like D. H. Lawrence.

A second version of the script was done by another screenwriter and it was appalling: at the final fadeout Alan Bates and Jennie Linden were to gallop off into the sunset. At this point 1 took a hand in writing the script. I used as much of Lawrence's dialogue as I possibly could. Nearly all of the conversation is verbatim from the novel. For the storyline, I pulled out of the novel's action the bits that would hang together as a narrative. So I suppose that I am as responsible as anyone for the film's fidelity to Lawrence.

GDP: Was the nude wrestling match between Alan Bates and Oliver Reed your idea, then?

KR: The wrestling match was in the novel and I wanted to use it in the same symbolic fashion that Lawrence had used it. At its conclusion Birkin [Bates] says to Gerald [Reed], "We are mentally and spiritually close. Therefore we should be physically close too." This is not a plea for a homosexual relationship between them. Birkin believes that two men can each get married and yet maintain an intimate relationship with each other that is different from, but which nevertheless complements, the heterosexual relationship that each has in marriage. Gerald could not commit himself to Birkin on this level not only because he thought such a relationship unconventional, but also because he really could not reveal himself or commit himself to anyone. I originally thought of a swimming context for the scene, since how else could you explain the two men stripping off for the match? But Oliver Reed said that that setting would be too poetic. He suggested that it should be more of a real physical confrontation between the two men locked in a room sweating and straining, and that is how we did it.

GDP: Since *Women in Love*, as frank as it is, was so well received, were you surprised at the dismay in England caused by your TV film on the life of Richard Strauss, *Dance of the Seven Veils*?

KR: I saw that television biographies were becoming filled with terrible clichés that had grown out of imitation of my TV films—deification of the artist is wrong; he should be presented as a human being who, despite his faults, managed to create lasting works of art. The telecast began with an announcement that what was to be presented was a harsh and violent personal interpretation of Strauss's life and work, but one that was nevertheless based on real events. This should have been a sufficient warning to those who might be offended by watching it.

Those who were offended by it took the film much too literally. It was meant to work on a deep symbolic level. For example, in order to get across the fact that Richard Strauss was uninterested in the Second World War because it didn't touch him personally, I presented a dream sequence in which Strauss is forced to watch his wife raped and his child murdered by the Nazis. Just as a Nazi holds a gun to Strauss's head, the image dissolves into that of his son with a toy gun and then the camera pulls back to show the Strauss family in a kind of *Sound of Music* [1965] Tyrolean setting completely removed from the realities of the war. This is the insulated atmosphere in which Strauss wrote his *Capriccio* [1942] and *Metamorphosen* [1944-45], as if the war didn't exist.

GDP: What about your treatment of Strauss's capitulation to the Nazi regime? That offended a lot of admirers of his work.

KR: Strauss was one of the most famous people in Germany at that time, and if he had taken a stand against the Nazis this would have had a tremendous effect. I was trying to shock people into a realization of their responsibilities. Strauss thought of himself as an ageless superman. He based his *Zarathustra* [1896]—which has since become identified with Kubrick's use of it in *2001: A Space Odyssey* [1968]—on Nietzsche's conception of the superman. Then in later years when he was out of favor with Hitler he wrote an obsequious letter to Hitler. At this point I have his wife put on him the mask of an old man, for Strauss has finally admitted his weakness and dependence on Hitler's favor. Later, after the war, when he is conducting the *Zarathustra* in London after he has been completely exonerated by the Allies of having endorsed the Nazi regime, the music swells to a crescendo and I have Strauss rip off the mask of the old man: he is still the crypto Nazi with the superman fantasy underneath the façade of the distinguished elderly composer.

GDP: The day alter the program was screened on BBC-TV, a motion was introduced in Parliament condemning your version of Strauss's life and music as vicious, savage, and brutal. Some TV critics suggested that you were trying to increase the limits of what is permissible on television.

KR: The BBC got an enormous number of phone calls after the film was televised, as many for as against. Members of the television audience are all asleep in their armchairs. It's a good thing to shake them up, even if it's only as far as the phone. Huw Weldon defended *Dance of the Seven Veils* when it was shown for fifty members of Parliament, and John Trevelyan, the British film censor, supported the film as well.

GDP: To me your *Dance of the Seven Veils* is the most visually brilliant piece of work you have done so far, especially in the fantasy scenes.

KR: In every film I have created the style has been dictated by the subject. *Song of Summer* was an austere, restrained film, mainly about three people in a bare, white room. That was the way to do that particular story. *Dance of the Seven Veils*, on the other hand, was a picture about a self-advertising, vulgar, commercial man. I took the keynote of the film from the music, a lot of which is bombastic. I also built up the portrait from the man himself; and 95% of what Strauss said in the film he actually said.

GDP: You even gave him a screen credit for contributing to the dialogue. You are undoubtedly in for more criticism from music lovers for presenting Tchaikovsky as a homosexual in *The Music Lovers*.

KR: There is a Russian version of Tchaikovsky's life coming out as well. When I went to United Artists with the idea of doing his life, they pointed this out to me and I replied that my approach to the composer's life was sure to be different from the Russian version. For one thing, the Russians have never admitted that Tchaikovsky was homosexual. I have been quoted as saying that my film is about a homosexual who marries a nymphomaniac. This is a flip way of putting it, but basically it boils down to this, and this is what the film explores. The film takes only two years in Tchaikovsky's life, the period when he was married. This was the turning point in his life.

Tchaikovsky himself said that his inner conflicts are there in his music and they are. His *Sixth Symphony* [1893] is tortured and terrible. In one scene in my film Tchaikovsky [Richard Chamberlain] is shown in bed with the rich Vladimir Shilovsky, whose possessiveness helped push Tchaikovsky into thoughts of marriage. Besides, he had always longed to have a family. In addition he believed that man was governed by fate. He had written an opera, *Eugene Onegin* [1879], in which a girl writes love letters to a man who turns her down and thereby ruins his own life as well as that of the girl. Tchaikovsky started getting letters from a girl, Antonina Milyukova [Glenda Jackson]; he decided the situation was too much of a coincidence with the story of his opera to be ignored, and so he met and married her. The marriage, of course, was a disaster.

As in my television lives of composers, I make a definite connection between the man's life and his music. The composer-conductor of the film's music, André Previn, has drawn on Tchaikovsky's music throughout the film, and there is not one piece of music that is present for its own sake. It's all there to reflect some aspect of Tchaikovsky's life and personality.

GDP: What future projects do you have in mind?

KR: I would like to do *The Devils* [Russell did, in 1971], and have done a script based on both Aldous Huxley's book [1952] and John Whiting's play [1961]. I also used the available documentation, but I had to thin it out since it is so vast. My script is based on the same historical incident that served as the basis of Jerzy Kawalerowicz's 1961 Polish film *Mother Joan of the Angels*, which I saw about five years ago. A frustrated mother superior in a convent, whom I hope will be played by Glenda Jackson, gets dreamy about a priest. Cardinal Richelieu does not like the priest and has evidence planted on him to discredit him. My version of the story will bring in more of the political background of the period than did the Polish film.

GDP: In defending you against the negative criticism of your TV film about Strauss, Huw Weldon said that you happen to be a Roman Catholic and would not set out to offend any religious group in your work. Do you feel that your background as a convert to Catholicism will be a help to you in making *The Devils*?

KR: Possibly. My Catholic background helps me to distinguish between normal religious practices and the bizarre things attributed to the nuns in *The Devils*. Since Kawalerowicz is not a Christian, the whole idea of convent life would seem bizarre to him. At any rate, I don't mind now if I am not able to make the film, since I have worked it out shot by shot in my imagination; I can run it in my head any time I want to. Although I must admit a finished film is often very different from the way one has initially pictured it in one's mind.

GDP: Do you intend to adapt any more novels for the screen?

KR: I am interested in Evelyn Waugh's 1934 novel *A Handful of Dust* [filmed in 1988 by Charles Sturridge], but I will not attempt to update it to the present, as did the recent film [1969, John Krish] of his 1928 novel *Decline and Fall*. Waugh's novels are relevant to the present, and they do not have to have the setting updated to prove it. I would also like to do Graham Greene's *A Burnt-Out Case* [1960], which is one of the few novels written by Greene that has yet to be filmed.

GDP: Greene, who has done some scripts himself, once told me that the initial script that he does from one of his novels usually has a great deal of the original dialogue from the novel in it; but he deletes most of this as he revises the script and in the end most of the original dialogue is gone. Yet you told me that most of the dialogue in *Women in Love* is directly from the book. Do you then disagree with Greene's approach to adapting a novel to the screen?

KR: Not really. If a man adapts his own novel to another medium, he feels that he's done it this way once; in the interim it has grown in his mind, since one's ideas about any subject change and grow over a period of time. But if I adapt something written by someone else to the screen, I am approaching it fresh and want to leave the thing the way it is as much as possible.

GDP: I understand that Lesley Hornby—alias Twiggy—has said that she will take out time from her modeling career to do a film with you if the right part turns up.

KR: Yes, and I hope the right part does turn up. If so, she will be the greatest thing to hit the screen since Marilyn Monroe.

GDP: I gather that you have achieved total artistic control over your films.

KR: While I was at the BBC I was my own boss, and after *Women in Love* I was ready to go back to television for good, since I was allowed to act as my own producer on all of my previous TV films. I find that when someone else is producing, I have a battle royal with him most of the time. After one has poured one's lifeblood into a project, it is difficult lo accept the fact that someone else is really controlling the project. Now that I do have the same artistic freedom in making feature films that I had in television, I think I will stick with films.

Bibliography

Atkins, Thomas R. *Ken Russell*. New York: Monarch Press, 1978.

Baxter, John. *An Appalling Talent: Ken Russell*. London: Michael Joseph, 1973.

Flanagan, Kevin M., ed. Ken Russell: *Re-Viewing England's Last Mannerist*. Lanham, Md.: Scarecrow Press, 2009.

Gomez, Joseph A. *Ken Russell: The Adaptor as Creator*. London: Frederick Muller, 1976.

Hanke, Ken. *Ken Russell's Films*. Metuchen, N.J.: Scarecrow Press, 1980.

Lanza, Joseph. *Phallic Frenzy: Ken Russell and His Films*. London: Aurum Press, 2007.

Phillips, Gene D. *Ken Russell*. Boston: Twayne, 1979.

Russell, Ken. *Directing Films: The Directors Art from Script to Cutting Room*. London: B. T. Batsford, 2001.

Russell, Ken. *The Lion Roars: Ken Russell on Film*. Boston: Faber and Faber, 1994.

Wilson, Colin. *Ken Russell, A Director in Search of a Hero*. London: Intergroup 1979.

"Money Matters/Movie Material: An Interview with Tony Richardson," by Colin Young. From *Film Quarterly*, 13.4 (Summer 1960): 10-15.

The novels and plays of the New Wave of young non-conformist, anti-establishment English writers had been providing literary and drama critics on both sides of the Atlantic with a large share of their copy in the late 1950s and early '60s. It was only a matter of time before some of this original material found its way onto the screen. In 1957, the Boulting brothers made a rather hapless version of Kingsley Amis's 1954 novel *Lucky Jim*, and Jack Clayton chose *Room at the Top* (1959, from John Braine's 1957 novel) as his first feature film. But the name most firmly associated with the new writers as sponsor, theater producer, and finally film producer-cum-director was Tony Richardson (1928-91), himself a young man in this thirties at the time.

Before he was taken on by George Devine, artistic director of the Royal Court Theatre, Richardson had been noticed for a production of a Chekhov one-act on English television and for various one-night-stand Sunday shows in theaters off the West End. During the same period, John Osborne was an unknown and largely unwanted writer. His play *Look Back in Anger* (1956) had been turned down by several London theatrical companies before it came to Richardson's attention; its success at the Royal Court established Osborne and Richardson in the London theater, and 1958 they formed a company, Woodfall, to produce the films of their choice. The first two were adapted from Osborne plays: *Look Back in Anger* and *The Entertainer* (1957). Although Richardson was not the sole author of his own material, his films were filled with disenchanted people whom he nonetheless treated sympathetically, as if they were important—which he obviously thought they are.

Richardson's first film, *Momma Don't Allow* (1955), was a short subject. His films dealing with the British urban working class include the screen adaptations of his stage successes *Look Back in*

Anger (1959), *The Entertainer* (1960), and *A Taste of Honey* (1961), as well as *The Loneliness of the Long Distance Runner* (1962), based on the novella by Alan Sillitoe. Richardson also produced Sillitoe's novel *Saturday Night and Sunday Morning* (1960), directed by Karel Reisz. One of his greatest successes came when in 1963 he directed Osborne's adaptation of Henry Fielding's novel *Tom Jones*, a rousing evocation of the crudeness and vigor of eighteenth-century English life. The film won Academy Awards for Best Picture, Best Director, Best Original Score, and Best Screen Adaptation. Among the films Richardson later directed are *The Loved One* (1965), *The Charge of the Light Brigade* (1968), *Ned Kelly* (1970), *A Delicate Balance* (1973), and *Joseph Andrews* (1977). He was married to the actress Vanessa Redgrave from 1962 to 1967.

At the invitation of Richard Zanuck of Twentieth Century-Fox, Tony Richardson came to Hollywood in 1960 to discuss Zanuck's suggestion that he film *Sanctuary* (1961), which was to be based on Faulkner's 1931 novel and also on his on his 1959 play *Requiem for a Nun*.

During Richardson's stay in Los Angeles, Colin Young conducted the following interview.

Colin Young: How does it come about that the films you direct and produce all happen to treat contemporary subjects?

Tony Richardson: I will always want to make films of this kind, about the world in which we live, films that are part of that world— I think this is the sort of thing that the cinema does best. So far it has been possible to finance these pictures, although there will always come a time when one can't, but up to now we have been very lucky. *The Entertainer* [1960], my latest, is completely finished: in fact I've just slightly re-edited it and re-dubbed one reel. Walter Reade will release the movie in the United States, the same people who released *Room at the Top* [1959] here. British Lion will release it in England.

The Entertainer was financed quite differently from *Look Back in Anger* [1959]. The earlier picture was financed completely by A.B.C., which is a subsidiary of Warner Brothers, who also put up some money for Richard Burton. *The Entertainer* was partly financed by Bryanston (a subsidiary of British Lion), partly by Walter Reade, and partly by the National Film Finance Corporation, all of them quite independent of any major movie company. Until recently, Harry Saltzman was associated with John Osborne and me in the company that has produced all my films—Woodfall. Bryanston has a more or less permanent relationship with Walter Reade, which put up 25% of the budget in return for the American distribution rights.

Look Back in Anger was made for about £250,000. *The Entertainer* cost just over £200,000, while the last film we made, *Saturday Night and Sunday Morning* [1958 novel by Alan Sillitoe, adapted to film in 1960 by Karl Reisz], cost £117,000. *Look Back in Anger* was more expensive—because the property was much more expensive, and so was the cast. Richard Burton is a very expensive actor; all the cast was expensive—none of them were on deferment of salary, and there was undoubtedly additional studio overhead. (The film was shot at Elstree.) In *The Entertainer*, Laurence Olivier, Osborne, and I all took deferments and, although it is a much more ambitious picture, it was made more cheaply. Deferments of salary are now quite common in the British film industry.

In Britain, of course, it is impossible to finance a film except through a distributor. The whole business of financing is difficult, perhaps more so in England than anywhere else in the world, because England is trying to live up to a scale of production that is quite unreal for so small a country. British films ought to cost the sort of money that films cost in France, but in fact England has half been caught up in a Hollywood tradition; and although British movies of course do not cost as much as American ones, they still cost far too much for the size of the country, and for the amount that they can take back. It ought to be possible to make a film, and especially the sort of film I want to make, for about £30,000-50,000, as you can do in France. But given the present financial and union setup, it is quite hopeless. All my pictures cost too much money.

CY: Can you explain the role of the unions? Is it exactly the same as in the United States?

TR: No. But the movie industry in Britain *is* heavily unionized and therefore it is not possible to operate with such a small crew as is used, say, in French New Wave films. Yet it isn't only a question of the unions: there are charges imposed on the producer in England that in America are laid against the distributor, which in the case of my films amounts to many thousands of pounds.

In Britain you can't do a movie outside the unions—nor would it be desirable to do so, because after all you have to have professional people working in every department. I don't want to sound anti-union, because I believe in unions, but it is necessary to concede that they are at present conceived in a way that is perhaps not right for a certain kind of small, commercially unambitious picture. And the union is the only source of technicians who can do professional work. There are no other sources in England, as there are in America—from the universities, among other places. If I did not go to the union, I would have no idea who could shoot a picture. Even the cinematographer Walter Lassally is a member of the union.

However, in the end, I have no desire to work outside the union; it is just that I wish the union people could at times be a little more imaginative. But a much more serious problem is the general system of financing and distributing motion pictures.

The whole tone of the movie business is to strive for technical perfection, but we all know that this doesn't matter so much—the film can be appalling in many ways technically yet still be a wonderful and marvelous work. Gloss guarantees nothing, whereas the cost of technical perfection hampers the movie industry.

We are going to shoot *A Taste of Honey* [1961] entirely on location. This is something I've wanted to do for a long time, and all the technicians in the unit also want to do this. I have a team of technicians now who want to work in this way, and we are going to try to work with a minimum number of people. We shall end up with a crew of about fifty: you need four on camera, any night exteriors require a lighting crew, and in fact to work efficiently you have to have a certain amount of lighting during day scenes also, and this all involves generators. Then you have the art department, assistant directors, make-up and hair and wardrobe, assorted production people, and the accountants—reduced to the minimum, around fifty people. Reducing the number beyond this makes for an inefficient operation.

There is a scene in Jean-Luc Godard's *Breathless* [1960] that goes on for twenty minutes, shot in a real room, and the setups are obviously very clumsy and awkward, and people have to climb over furniture to get any sort of a shot at all. Nevertheless, this *helps* the film. The thing I don't like about it is the final gesture the picture makes under its cloak—the contemporary French cynicism, the French shrug. But I also don't think you can go out and make movies with six people. Even in a unit of fifty, there would be no one *not* doing more than one man's job.

A Taste of Honey will be shot for three weeks in Manchester and five weeks in London. The action is no longer confined to the one house of Shelagh Delaney's play [1958]. Delaney and I have done the script. Nigel Kneale, who did the script of *Look Back in Anger*, did a first draft of *The Entertainer*, and then John Osborne and I went away and re-wrote it.

The Entertainer was shot during six weeks on location and for two weeks in the studio. Only the apartment scenes were shot in the studio. I hate studios; I no longer want to shoot even interiors in a studio. I would rather work under the limited conditions that a location imposes upon you. For the sort of realistic films I want to make, by improvising one's way out of the impossibilities of real conditions, you get something onto the screen that is more true, somehow, than something contrived on a studio set. It's a question of taste, really—you're on top of the people in real rooms, and you can't do a lot of camera movement, which isn't a thing I'm terribly interested in, anyway. I think a real set forces you to come to a simple kind of relationship with your people, to make a direct statement with the camera more than anything else, and more than you can do in studios. Because once you are inside a studio, you start taking walls out, you start thinking, "Wouldn't it be fun if we tracked from here to there, pan round there?" You know, you start thinking of doing a lot of fancy stuff, and when you do that, what you get in fact is less of the human reality.

Apart from two studio sets, then, *The Entertainer* was shot completely on location. The studio sets were treated differently in *The Entertainer* from the way they were treated in *Look Back in Anger*. In *Look Back in Anger*, the set, the apartment, was built for the action.

I think it worked, but it was utterly unlike the reality of a real room. In *The Entertainer*, I tried to set the thing in an absolutely real room, exactly as the room would be in real life, but I still don't think it's as good as reality. I think that once you go into a studio, you have to build a completely different sort of set. In any event, all the scenes in the apartment of *The Entertainer* were very difficult because they are essentially quartet or quintet scenes, which were really written according to theatrical convention—which means difficult to do on the screen.

However, the movie of *The Entertainer* is very unlike Osborne's play. For instance, the music-hall episodes served a different function in the play—they commented in an almost Brechtian fashion on the dramatic action. Although they were also for the most part realistic music-hall numbers, Archie Rice was commenting at the same time on his own situation—and with all sorts of political and social references. The minute you put him in a real location, on screen, everything changes. The theater can have this kind of juxtaposition: this is one of the great advantages of the theater.

But this is also why it is so difficult to translate an Osborne play to the screen, and why I think filmed plays in general are so impossible. In the theater you can do these "artificial" things, which are suggestive and atmospheric—like double time in Shakespeare. In *Othello*, for example, you can create the impression that Othello has been jealous for six weeks, whereas in fact he's only been in Cyprus for a day. But movies are specific and particular, and take place in a definite place and a time, so that Archie Rice becomes a character existing at a precise seaside town, doing particular numbers. And the numbers can no longer have this double significance—they have to be just the sort of numbers this dead-beat, third-rate music-hall artist would have. This means that you have to suggest the other values, the political and social commentary, in a different way. We do it through Archie's character—we get closer to his character, and implicit in it are all sorts of gestures and attitudes. But they are not externalized in the way they were in the music-hall numbers of the theater.

I started in film with *Look Back in Anger* and *The Entertainer* because I happen to have directed the plays on the stage, and I knew the subjects, and it became possible to use these works as a way of entering the movie business. I never again want to make a film of a play I have staged. I think the two media work in a completely different way, and once materials, stories, characters, and subjects are put in a particular mold, however much you try to translate them into a different mold, they are still a bit stuck in the place where they started—though I think this is much less so in *The Entertainer* than in *Look Back in Anger*. This is why I am glad to be doing *A Taste of Honey*, because I have *not* worked with it on the stage. Once you've staged a play, you have your favorite bits and you know how they work, and if you're doing the film version with the same actors, they have *their* bits, so that makes matters even worse.

Alan Sillitoe's novel *Saturday Night and Sunday Morning* had a limited success in England—it wasn't a bestseller but it earned the critics' esteem. I think novels are fine as sources for film; it's only plays that I think are difficult to adapt. After *A Taste of Honey*, I want to do an original script more than anything. There is really no shortage of ideas on my part. I also want to do a film on India—a four-hour epic sort of picture—about the freeing of India from the British. It will take me about four years to get the material together for it. I want to cover the period from 1911 on: the political evolution of the country. It's such a terrific subject because its references are so enormous; this is just about the only successful meeting of East and West, where people have got together and, in spite of the things that went wrong, the horrors and enormities that were committed, nevertheless in the end hammered out something very valuable. The subject is the sort of big-scale historical thing that I think I would love to tackle.

CY: You have said that you have a personal interest in the contemporary subject. You have also managed to finance one or two of these projects. Since no one else seems to do much of that, are we to assume that not many other people share your interest?

TR: I think that's true. You see, a very extraordinary thing has happened in England: everyone is writing *plays*; all the young creative talent is directed at the theater. There are at least twenty interesting dramatists in England at the moment in various stages of development, people who have written one good play or more, or who will obviously write a good play in the near future—writers similar to this New Wave of directors in France who want to make films, whereas there's no one in France under about fifty right now who is writing plays of any value. The generation of significant French theater consists of Sartre, Anouilh, Beckett, and so on, just as the important, original writing for the theater in America is still being done by Tennessee Williams and Arthur Miller, and there really hasn't been anyone major since these two.

You can't really precisely define these cultural breakthroughs, but when one occurs, as now in England, then a whole series of artistic people begin to think in the same way. It happened with the Elizabethan drama, and although this seems an overwhelming comparison, the same kind of thing has happened in the cinema in France and in the theater in England, just as it happened in Russia following the 1917 revolution—all sorts of people, from different circumstances, coming together to make movies or stage plays. I don't think there are many people yet in England who want to make the films I have been speaking of, but I think there will be. The cinema is a director's medium, and I don't think there are enough British directors at this point who understand this, who understand the difference between working in the theater and working on a film.

CY: Incidentally, when will we get to see *The Entertainer*?

TR: It will be released in the States at the end of August. You must also take note of *Saturday Night and Sunday Morning*, directed by Karl Reisz. He wanted to do it and had an idea about how to do so, and we set it up for him to do. Albert Finney plays the lead—he's quite marvelous and will surely be the next great actor. Shirley Enfield (who plays Olivier's girlfriend in *The Entertainer*), a very talented actress, is also in the film, and we have tried to keep a continuity of technical crew as far as possible—the whole unit will continue work on *A Taste of Honey*. They all have an attitude in common and work together in a certain way.

The subject of *Saturday Night and Sunday Morning* is, roughly, the release of the weekend. It is about a sort of rebel, a kind of anarchist, something of an anti-authoritarian boy living in this terrible, drab, ghastly town who has set himself up against the Establishment. He sleeps around on the weekend, gets drunk, creates wild scenes, and so on. Then he gradually matures and channels his rebelliousness into a more potent form. He works in a large bicycle factory as a machinist. The film's about work, in the end—the whole business of work in these English towns and the sort of tension it produces. My kind of picture.

Bibliography

Radovich, Don. *Tony Richardson: A Bio-Bibliography*. Westport, Conn.: Greenwood Press, 1995.

Richardson, Tony. *The Long-Distance Runner: An Autobiography*. New York: Morrow, 1993.

Shail, Robert. *Tony Richardson*. Manchester, U.K.: Manchester University Press, 2012.

Welsh, James, and John C. Tibbetts, eds. *The Cinema of Tony Richardson: Essays and Interviews*. Albany, N.Y.: State University of New York Press, 1999.

"'Who Would Have Believed It?': An Interview with Nicolas Roeg," by John Stezaker (2013: previously unpublished in book or magazine form).

Nicolas Roeg (born 1928) is one of the most inventive and influential film directors of the last century. In 1962, he worked as a second-unit cinematographer on David Lean's *Lawrence of Arabia*; in 1964, as cinematographer on Roger Corman's *The Masque of the Red Death*; and, in 1966, on François Truffaut's *Fahrenheit 451*. Since then, Roeg has directed thirteen feature films.

Roeg made his solo directorial debut with *Walkabout* (1971), which was filmed in the Australian outback and told the tale of two abandoned schoolchildren and the teenaged Aborigine who guides them through the wilderness. Roeg also performed cinematography duties on *Walkabout*, which is renowned for its stunning color-saturated visuals. He went on to direct many other films, including the psychedelic drama *Performance* (1970), starring Mick Jagger as a former pop superstar who is drawn into the criminal underworld of 1960s London; the erotic psychological thriller *Don't Look Now* (1973), which starred Julie Christie and was based on a short story by Daphne du Maurier; the science-fiction film *The Man Who Fell to Earth* (1976), featuring an otherworldly David Bowie; *Bad Timing* (1980), starring Art Garfunkel; and *The Witches* (1990), based on Roald Dahl's popular children's book of the same name. His last film, *Puffball*, was released in 2007.

In his memoir, *The World Is Ever Changing* (2013, Faber & Faber), Roeg reflects on over half a century of filmmaking, insisting that, as memory has "no continuity of time," the chapters can be read in any order. The book's title is a line from *The Man Who Fell to Earth*, in which David Bowie, playing a melancholy alien, murmurs: "The world is ever changing, Mr. Farnsworth, like the universe."

In the following interview, Nicolas Roeg talks to his friend, the artist John Stezaker, about collage, editing, and memory, and film's ability to "trap shadows."

John Stezaker: Let's get right into it: upon the release of *Performance* [1970], the critic of *Life* magazine described it as "the most completely worthless film I have ever seen since I began reviewing."

Nicolas Roeg: I've still got that somewhere. It's one of the few clippings I've ever kept. Warner Brothers threatened to sue me for not delivering the film they were expecting. That affected me very badly. It was difficult to hang onto self-belief. Self-belief needs a bit of camaraderie and there wasn't much of that about. What made it worst of all was that the people criticizing the film clearly didn't get it at all.

JS: Is *Performance* nonetheless a film you look back on with fondness and pride?

NR: I don't look back on any film I've done with fondness or pride. When I look back on my films, and on the past generally, I can only use the phrase, "Well, I'll be damned."

JS: After the *Performance* furor, the sensible thing might have been to play it safe—except that's not you're your style, is it?

NR: I've never tried just to enhance my reputation. Never moved upwards from one thing to another. That sort of thing is of no interest to me at all.

JS: Instead you collaborated with the playwright Edward Bond on a film about a brother and sister who get lost in the Australian outback: *Walkabout* [1971]. This is the movie in which your fondness for playing around with time really comes to the fore. In one sequence the boy—played by your son, Luc—sees a buffalo falling over and dying. You then run the film backwards so that the buffalo is seen getting back to its feet.

NR: It seemed perfectly natural to me that the boy should want to bring the animal back to life in his head.

JS: In all your films, you have tended to be pretty unsparing towards your actors. In *Performance*, James Fox was so disturbed by the experience that he became a Christian evangelist for almost ten years. On *Bad Timing* [1980]—a film that the boss of its distributors, Rank, called "a sick film made by sick people for sick people"—almost everyone threatened to walk off, including its star, Art Garfunkel. This was after you shot for twenty-four hours without a break. Do you think of yourself as a ruthless director? One who relishes taking actors to the brink?

NR: No. No, I don't think I'm like that at all. All I've ever tried to do is be truthful to the work I'm doing.

JS: You have worked with rock stars on three of your four best films. Why?

NR: Because they have a greater ability to light up the screen than regular actors. Indeed, during the filming of *The Man Who Fell to Earth* [1976], in which David Bowie played an extraterrestrial who goes by the name of Mr. Newton, I really came to believe that Bowie was a man who had come to earth from another galaxy. His actual social behavior was extraordinary—he hardly mixed with anyone at all. He seemed to be alone—which is what Newton is in the film, isolated and alone.

So many professional actors have lost their *intent*, their *beginnings*. They're no longer this traveling group of players among whom one performer one evening is a king, and another evening is a beggar. What I love about the other actors—the non-actors, the *singers*—is that they don't know who they are yet. And actors shouldn't know. I worked once with Peter Finch, an old friend. I knew Peter for years and years, ever since his arrival in England. He kept that traveling player quality, curiously enough. He was an "actor chappie." Others become—well—really sort of businessmen.

JS: As well as being obsessed by film, I know that you have had a lifelong interest in mysticism—something that's most apparent in *Don't Look Now* [1973].

NR: Once, I was visited by a medium who told me that she believed I had been her mother in a past life. What's more, the medium said, she had witnessed my giving birth to her in a vision. Far from being alarmed, I was intrigued. In that moment, my own sense of awareness seemed dislocated, and I was conscious of being in the presence of the scene she was describing, as though I were dreaming it.

JS: Does your belief, or partial belief, in past lives make you more sanguine about the thought of dying?

NR: No, no, I'm very anxious about it. But the other day an extraordinary thing happened. I was in here looking for a book and

I pulled a different one out by mistake. As I had it in my hands, a page fell to the floor. When I picked it up, I saw that one heading said "Mysteries of Life, Death, and Futurity. Things Not Generally Known." Then I saw that the book had my father's name written on the flyleaf. Now, that's just too mystical for me to think it's a coincidence.

My father was an extraordinary man. When my sister and I were very young, he used to tell us fairy stories that he'd made up. My mother was always telling him my father that he should write them down, but he would say, "Well, they've all been done before. There are so many blooming books in the world—why should I write another one?"

JS: It's tempting to think that this remark must have had a profound effect on you.

NR: It was pure chance that I ever got into the film business. There was a studio opposite my parents' house in Marylebone, and I got a casual job there after he left school. Even as a teenager, it was plain that I had a peculiar way of looking at the world. Early on in my career, when I was working on a film called *Tarzan's Greatest Adventure* [1959], I told the bemused producer that the title was a mistake because it was a superlative—leaving him no alternative but to call his next film "Tarzan's Disappointing Adventure"!

JS: You went on to become a highly distinguished lighting cameraman—most notably for David Lean, first on *Lawrence of Arabia* [1962] and then on *Doctor Zhivago* [1965]. However, you zeal for experimentation didn't go down well with Lean, did it?

NR: Matters came to a head when we were shooting a battle sequence in *Doctor Zhivago*. I remember David's turning to me and saying, "You think I'm old-fashioned, don't you?" I said "No, I don't—and actually I meant it. Even so, I knew that a curtain had come down. Shortly after, I was sacked.

I had no idea what sort of films I wanted to make when I became a director. Instead I fell into directing when Donald Cammell, who'd written the original script for *Performance*, needed someone with visual flair with whom to collaborate.

JS: Can you name a film by another director that was vital in your artistic development?

NR: *Last Year at Marienbad* [1961], with its wealth of spatial and temporal ambiguities. I saw it when it came out. I thought: "This is fantastic!" In the lobby, people were saying, "What was that about?" The same people eighteen months later would see nothing unusual in Alain Resnais's film. Same thing now, you see? I'm not out of time. They're out of time. This applies to critics, as well: there is so much going on in people's heads and this is why criticism is interesting to me. I'm not talking about whether someone says one of my films is good or bad; I mean that what the critic says reveals so much about the critic, about which area of life or thought he is trapped in. Who was it that said that the observation or criticism tells more about the observer or the critic?

To get back to *Marienbad*: Resnais's film helped me to arrive at the core of my own filmmaking: the supremacy of the image over the word, the eloquence of juxtaposition, the primal power of montage. I create images and tell stories on film, and if you're dealing with *thought* on film, then I think it's cheating to use literary means. My films have never been literary or linear—*life* isn't linear, it's sideways. I want people to read the *images* in my films. Thought can be transferred by the juxtaposition of images, and you mustn't be afraid that the audience at first will not understand. You can say things *visually, immediately*; film is not a pictorial example of a published work, it's transference of thought.

Time itself is fascinating, in life as in art. We have no concept of what time means. It has nothing to do with the Judaic calendar or the Chinese one. I think that the computer and the Internet will change our whole idea of time, just as much as the mechanical watch did. The watch changed the world terrifically, altered our entire consciousness of time. It changed everything; it even changed the imagination. So too will computers. It's a curious thing, this notion of time, isn't it? The present instantly becomes the past before you can even acknowledge it, and even the notions of how you and I consider the past—I'm a good deal older than you—are vastly different.

That was something I felt very connected to in *The Man Who Fell to Earth*: the concept of this person who was sort of stuck out of time. Mr. Newton was this freaky alien who came here with very advanced notions of science and space travel, then the minute the world caught up to him … he was nobody, just another person who felt alienated from the world, trapped in his own neuroses. And if you ever want to make a film that inadvertently charts the passage of time, just put the "latest" special effects in it. Nothing will date your movie quicker than those! [Laughs.]

JS: I have to say that your films, including *The Man Who Fell to Earth*, are never about what they seem to be about at first. *Don't Look Now* fascinates me for reasons I can't explain. It's both mainstream and an elegy to *film noir*, and I love it for that. *Insignificance* [1985] initially seems to be about a preposterous meeting between Albert Einstein and Marilyn Monroe, but some of its scenes don't seem to have anything to do with the main story. For example, Joe DiMaggio—what happens to him? He's wandering around, trying to catch up with things, but the plot is always just one step ahead of him. In some ways, he is narratively superfluous and yet his inability to get into the plot makes him central: he represents the viewer, or perhaps the director.

NR: There's a marvelous line in John Huston's *The Treasure of the Sierra Madre* [1948]: "You don't see the gold beneath your very feet." The prospectors, played by Humphrey Bogart and Tim Holt, don't think they've found any gold, but when their much older companion dances at the foot of the mountains, they glimpse it in the sand under his feet. It's like a premise to the film.

When I was very young, I began to suspect that what I was actually feeling I shouldn't be feeling. I became more conscious of my own emotions and reactions, and was sometimes ashamed of them, because they seemed to be stupid. I lived with that until I realized the only reason I thought certain things were stupid was because they were unfamiliar to me and they weren't readily recognized, and perhaps this was a gift. Of course, it also meant you might do something stupid in the very act of expressing yourself.

JS: Your films always contain these climactic moments, with no regret afterwards. In mainstream cinema, any loose narrative ends are neatly tied up, although perhaps if they're trying to be avant-garde they might leave one small question open, just to encourage a sequel.

NR: Very true.

JS: Whereas your films have so many loose ends that you'd need a hundred sequels to begin to work them out. On the other hand, you could say that each film by you is a sequel to the one before it. For example, the railway in *The Man Who Fell to Earth* becomes the model railway in *Track 29* [1988].

NR: That's something I was thinking about the other day; I like time*lessness*. You know, our idea of the future and the past is quite a recent one. We're now advancing at great speed in terms of understanding our tiny microcosm of the universe, but doors are still being opened to us all the time. We're living in an era that's very exciting because the pace of change is extraordinary. An era used to cover about 100 or 150 years, or three monarchical reigns, but now it lasts only about a decade and then you're completely out of date.

JS: Related to this idea of timelessness, your films are like dreams. Cinema for you seems to occupy dream-time. You allow things to fracture and separate into multiple realities, yet you use mainstream narrative strategies to draw people in. It's only after a while that it becomes clear something weird is happening. Unlike directors such as Ken Russell or Derek Jarman—the fantasy people—you're exploring the absolute hyper-reality of cinema, so the experience for the viewer becomes almost hallucinatory.

NR: I want to tell each person who sees my films something different: everyone gets a different whisper in their eyes and ears. I want to embrace people, whatever that means. Yet, I realize that there may be only three viewers who understand what the hell I'm talking about. Then a little time goes by, and perhaps those three people tell another three, then nine more people, and then there are fifteen people, all of whom say, "Let's have another look at this."

JS: I also think your films are very timely.

NR: Well, one of my films was called *Bad Timing*, after all. And *Eureka* [1983] was very bad timing. The early 1980s: Reagan and Thatcher were in, greed was good, and here was a film about the richest man in the world who still couldn't be happy. Politically and sociologically, it was out of step.

JS: I just screened *Track 29* for some students and they really responded to your combination of naturalism and hallucinatory unreality. You have talked about resisting universality but, in a sense, all your films have a universal story. The climactic moment comes about three-quarters of the way through the film, then there's a kind of weird aftermath effect that leaves the audience devastated. You know that experience of drinking heavily and waking up in the morning thinking, "What have I done?" There's always one of those moments in your films.

NR: I suppose it's because film has such an ability to trap shadows; the film is much more in charge of the process than anybody imposing anything on it: indeed, it's a total mystery. When something innovative takes place in the arts or sciences, initially there's a sense that the person doing it simply doesn't know how to do it "properly." But what is properly? Things that adhere to the conventional formula are much more inviting to audiences than those that try to push the formula in another direction, or invert it or make it more personal. I prefer the artist who doesn't respect convention. I love the story of Picasso's response to a Nazi who looked dismissively at his painting *Guernica* [1937] and asked him: "Did you do this?" To which Picasso apparently replied: "No, you did."

It's extraordinary, this sensation of: "Who would have believed it?" When I was about eighteen, I was in the army, and I was invited to a rather grand wedding. The bride went to change and didn't come back. She saw this man whom she didn't know him—he was just one of the guests—but they looked at each other, and she ran off with him. Fantastic! It's still in my mind; I could direct that scene exactly as it was. I can still see myself sitting at the wedding and the cake and the person I went with and where we went afterwards. I've got very little time for most memories, but the ones I do have are sharp and clear. They have a grading that makes me think: "Damn, has this all been a dream?"

JS: In a way, cinema is like a cleansing mechanism. Normally you go to see a film, you immerse yourself in this other world, and you come out feeling better, having vicariously experienced the excesses and extremes of the tragic mode and all the rest of it; everything is tied up nicely and you carry on with your life. Your films, by contrast, leave a kind of strange aftertaste that has something to do with something remembered. For example, I recently saw *Castaway*

[1986] for the first time, and I came away from it chiefly with the image of Oliver Reed turning a pebble in his mouth.

NR: Where did you see it?

JS: It's really hard to get hold of. I saw it on a video—I think it was a pirated copy: of very poor quality.

NR: Fantastic! Oliver Reed was so good in it. He was such a wonderfully nice person. He had great compassion and empathy, as well as being an extraordinary artist. He was an original, and he stayed original. Nobody could imitate him. I've never seen a story, a painting, or a poem that expresses anything of what I felt about him and what he projected.

JS: I feel that all cinema is about forgetting, but you interrupt the mechanism in some way in order to allow the viewer to remember. It's always about this effort to remember the details, like the red raincoat in *Don't Look Now*—sensations that are profoundly visual. The way you seem to create this effect is by cancelling, or estranging, the narrative flow. As in the mirror sequence in *Eureka* when the viewer is not sure whether Rutger Hauer's character is the killer or not, and he confesses but not in words—it's done visually. The image tells you the truth, or seems to tell you the truth, but the image is often somehow at odds with what you are being told narratively.

NR: Words have only the tiniest importance. Half of what we say we don't mean. I love that American expression: "Sure, I hear you. But what are you saying?"

I love what you just said about the red raincoat and that mirror sequence because I don't exactly plan anything; I can't look ahead, and therefore I always find myself excited by the surprise. Somehow it makes matters more human, more real, more truthful when I'm surprised by something we use on the set, something in the actor's behavior, or some reaction that isn't in the script. It's like a mystical tip-off.

It's not very British to embrace a sudden change in behavior or manners or thoughts—to run off with the bride, as it were. This is very much an American attitude. We all have those terrible moments in life, though, when we regret not having spontaneously done something and think: "I was so stupid."

JS: There's a line in T. S. Eliot's *Four Quartets* [1943] that really reminds me of your artistic work: "Footfalls echo in the memory, down the passage which we did not take." That's the atmosphere of *Don't Look Now* and *Track 29*. You use cinema to add to the real; cinema is about a kind of transparency, but you make it even more transparent and, in so doing, you create this mystery.

Is *Don't Look Now*, by the way, a film you're particularly proud of?

NR: I can't, I mustn't look back and think about things—just onward. I think with one's work it's who you are at the time, and what's done, and that can't be undone. Anyway, one's view of the past is quite different from what it actually was. You can't help inventing stuff. It's impossible not to.

Life is a mystery, in any event. What fascinates me is that criticisms of *Puffball* [2007] opened a door of understanding in me, not about changing anything but of not understanding it. I guess the difference between pretentious and corny is very slippery, and to my critics I'm pretentious. But the mystery of life is exciting to me because we know nothing about it.

JS: This is why, if I may say so, people find your films difficult: they're not prepared for you; there's something very uncomfortable in everything you do. That's part of the art and why it's as good as it is. But people can react to that and say: "I don't want to be uncomfortable. I don't want to see Oliver Reed all covered in mud and Amanda Donohoe in the nude." You know, it might irritate some people, but it stays with them, whereas other cinema doesn't.

NR: That covers it all. We live in mysterious times.

JS: To return to the *Four Quartets*, which explores the idea that you can stop time only within time—I was thinking of this in relation to the medium of cinema. "Only through time, time is conquered" could be your motto. "Before the beginning and after the end. And all is always now. Words strain, crack, and sometimes break, under the burden." This makes me think of *Walkabout*, and of the very essence of your films. The narrative breaks up; it does all sorts of strange things. It's before the beginning and after the end. There's a kind of reverberation with which you hold an image before it flows away. All cinema is a flowing away of ideas, but you've found a way of subverting the narrative, of stopping the flow—words strain, crack, break, whatever is happening. That's what you do.

NR: I recognize what you're saying. A lot of filmmaking, you know, can be linked to *prestidigitateur*—a shuffling of the cards. And that's a marvelous thing. But if you say, "Oooh, shall I show you how I did that?" then it kills the wonder of everything.

I remember the time an author approached me while writing a book on *Performance* screenwriter Donald Cammell. "It's all true," I told the author after reading his manuscript, and then I added, "But it wasn't like that."

JS: In *Track 29*, Gary Oldman's character, Martin, looks like a kind of British fashion victim stranded in middle America, but at the end—after the marvelous "shuffling of cards"—you realize that he's a blind man, Oedipus, and the whole film has been a sort of Oedipal drama. But he's also like the alien, the David Bowie character in *The Man Who Fell to Earth*, because he's come from nowhere. I can't help feeling that these outsiders are you: they're the film director; they come into the world and, almost without knowing what they're doing, they make everything happen around them.

NR: They're about all of us. We are all private people. We're all on our own. When people say, "Oh, someone has seen something that wasn't there," it's absolutely true. It can't get more pure or private than that. Yet what's extraordinary is that we make ourselves happy or we become happy through a situation and the person who was in it. This is what connects us to people's lives, their happiness, unhappiness, hope, or fear. In a sense, everything around us is making up our story in microscopic ways.

Certainly, when a situation becomes more forceful we can be swept up with it, or revolt against it. We have to be careful or else we're swept to even greater heights—or depths. Perhaps this is going too far in terms of what it is to be alive, but for me it's also connected to the idea that children's toys that have been kept in their original boxes, unplayed with, are the most valuable. Yet that seems so sad, since it means whoever owned the toys didn't play with them. I loved it when my boys played with their things. I have kept them in their broken state, and they now take me back to the time when they got broken.

JS: When you were making *Track 29*, your children would have been playing with trains. In a way, you made a child's total fantasy; you aligned yourself with what Gaston Bachelard calls "the magnifying gaze of childhood." You put the camera where the child's gaze was and made that gaze into an entire cinematic spectacle; that's the reason the visionary scene of the miniature railway is just so amazing to me, as is the scene where Oldman smashes it to pieces.

NR: The crew didn't want the railway to be broken; they couldn't watch.

JS: Recently, there was an exhibition of Ice Age art at the British Museum. One of the most extraordinary things about it was that, although the artists must have spent thousands of hours fashioning these tiny little figurines, almost all of them were smashed very soon after they were made. Why do we have this urge to destroy something the moment we create it or discover it?

NR: I don't know.

JS: It's just what a child would do.

NR: That's true. And it's wondrous.

JS: All the characters in *Track 29* are children in a way, aren't they? A beautiful touch in that film, which is reminiscent of Reed's pebble in *Castaway*, is the orthodontic brace that allowed Theresa Russell's character to become a woman at the end.

NR: The wife of the person from whom we were renting the house for the filming turned up. She was an air hostess with these amazing teeth, and I thought: "This is fantastic. I must have the braces." So, in a sense, they came with the house.

JS: A hundred years ago, when they began to use radium for the first time in X-rays, they thought they would be able to see through everything; they were going to render the world completely transparent, precisely in the manner of an imaging machine. Of course, cinema was central to that project, because it offered a way of visualizing all this. Ultimately, though, when you probe you find that—just as when you put those scans on top of real people in *Puffball*—it's like peeling away one layer only to find another underneath.

NR: The X-ray machine is the most extraordinary thing. Yet, if you dissect it, it's not very mysterious at all.

JS: X-raying is the most underestimated medium. I mean, enough books to fill a library have been written about the impact of photography or film on our conscious minds, but X-raying really touches our unconscious. We used to belong to the period of enlightenment, and now perhaps we belong to the period of "endarkening," where increasing knowledge only deepens life's mystery. I think your films are pivotal to this notion.

NR: These discoveries make you realize how little we know. I have begun to think completely differently about some matters: as if, for example, there is now reasonable proof that men and women were born together yet have broken apart.

JS: Yes, we have that myth, don't we? It's somehow embedded somewhere in us. It's in our parentage. We are the product of it but we can't grasp it in any substantial way. Recently, I was giving a lecture in Leeds and one of the students asked me why I like old images. I went into a long discourse about obsolescence and so on, and a professor, Griselda Pollock, shouted: "Nonsense, John, it's not old images in general, it's images from 1940 in particular. What you're trying to do is marry your mother and your father." She didn't know that only two days earlier I had visited my mother and she had given me my father's passport from the 1940s. In those days, women were added to their husband's passports once they got married, so when I opened it I found these two pictures I'd never seen before of my mother and father, a few years before I was born, on opposite pages of the passport. My mother gave me the passport as part of a process of dispossession that she is going through in her old age. I receive gifts like this on every visit now. But this one was particularly emotional. I could see myself in the combination of images; they looked as if they were waiting to be spliced into one. So, in a sense, Griselda hit the nail right on the head.

In your films, women themselves are central. Whether it's Julie Christie, Theresa Russell, or Jenny Agutter, you love them; you adore them. As viewers, we fall in love with each one of those characters every time we see them—not because we know them, but because we can't know them. They are completely untouchable.

NR: They belong to me in a way. They belong to me in a way that they don't know. "Belong" is not the best word to use, but the very fact of these characters, of their imaginative existence, is inspiring.

JS: They're muses. And you're an old-fashioned artist with a muse.

NR: If you say so ...

Bibliography

Feineman, Neil. *Nicolas Roeg*. Boston: Twayne, 1978.

Izod, John. *The Films of Nicolas Roeg: Myth and Mind*. Basingstoke, U.K.: Macmillan, 1992.

Lanza, Joseph. *Fragile Geometry: The Films, Philosophy, and Misadventures of Nicolas Roeg*. New York: Performing Arts Journal Publications, 1989.

Roeg, Nicolas. *The World Is Ever Changing*. London: Faber and Faber, 2013.

Salwolke, Scott. *Nicolas Roeg, Film By Film*. Jefferson, N.C.: McFarland, 1993.

Sinyard, Neil. *The Films of Nicolas Roeg*. London: Letts, 1991.

"'It's Not Just about Me': Ken Loach and the Cinema of Social Conscience: An Interview" (2009), by R. J. Cardullo, from *The Minnesota Review*, no. 76 (Spring 2011): 81-96.

Ken Loach, unquestionably one of Britain's most important filmmakers, is best known for his gritty and compassionate portrayals of working-class life. Early in his career, a series of socially conscious BBC (British Broadcasting Corporation) films established the fact that Loach was both a skillful artist and a crusading social critic. *Cathy Come Home* (1966), an accomplished blend of fictional and documentary techniques, was one of his most successful—and controversial—early efforts. Although Loach occasionally returned to television (the even more controversial *Days of Hope* [1975] was a landmark BBC mini-series), he subsequently moved on to feature films, most notably *Kes* (1969), *Family Life* (1971), and *Ladybird, Ladybird* (1994), which are justly regarded as milestones of British social realism.

Loach's films can be divided, however roughly, into two broad categories—intimate family dramas that illuminate the politics of everyday life and more militant films determined to skewer both the forces of reaction and the reformist wing of the labor movement. The first category is best personified by the now classic *Kes*, a moving account of how a young boy's alienation from the rigors of school and the demands of a dysfunctional family is temporarily assuaged by his devotion to a pet falcon. *The Big Flame* (1969), a stirring chronicle of a group of dockers whose experiment in workers' self-management is eventually sabotaged by the union bosses, typifies the more didactic strand in Loach's work, which is often labeled Trotskyist but is equally amenable to positions espoused by anti-Leninist Marxists and anarcho-syndicalists. Historically-based films by Loach such as *The Big Flame*, *Days of Hope*, and *Hidden Agenda* (1990) were condemned as subversive by conservatives and chided for supposed "ultra-leftism" by orthodox radicals, but they remain some of the few cinematic examples of bona fide anti-Stalinist leftism to reach mainstream audiences.

With his no-frills visual style and lean, sequential narratives, Loach is not out to impress anyone with technique. In fact, it is his bug-like dedication to the task at hand—concentrating on nailing down one moment without glamorizing it, but forgetting this accomplishment as soon as it has been passed—that makes his films so unerringly lifelike and effective. Another defining trait in Loach's oeuvre is that he often casts unknowns and non-professionals for leading roles. Crissy Rock's heart-wrenching turn in *Ladybird, Ladybird*, for instance, about a volatile woman's fight to wrest custody of her children from Social Services, is a quintessential example of Loach's gift for drawing gutsy, memorable performances out of unseasoned players. Throughout his work, Loach immerses us in human problems or conflicts—addiction (*My Name Is Joe* [1998]), mental illness (*Family Life*), poverty and street life (*Cathy Come Home*, *Poor Cow* [1967]), the travails of labor organizers and immigrants (*Days of Hope*, *Bread and Roses* [2000]), political struggle (*Carla's Song* [1996], *Land and Freedom* [1995])—that are noticeably from the "real world" and populated with characters who appear to inhabit, with grit and integrity, the same fraught universe as we do.

Ironically enough, the Thatcher-Major era, usually considered the most dismal epoch of the twentieth century by British radicals, engendered Loach's most productive and artistically satisfying period, during which he produced a series of award-winning feature films that firmly established him in the pantheon of great European directors. (His films have always been more popular in mainland Europe than in his native country or the United States.) *Hidden Agenda*, for example—a drama about the conflict in Northern Ireland—won the Special Jury Prize at the 1990 Cannes Film Festival. *Riff-Raff* (1990) won the Felix Award for Best European Film; *Raining Stones* (1993) won the Cannes Special Jury Prize; and *Land and Freedom* won the FIPRESCI International Critics' Prize and the Ecumenical Jury Prize at the 1995 Cannes Film Festival. It was also a substantial box-office hit in Spain, where it sparked intense debate about its subject matter, the Spanish Civil War. *My Name Is Joe* won numerous accolades, including three British Academy

Awards and Best Actor at Cannes for star Peter Mullan. Cannes jurors went on to award the Palme d'Or to *The Wind That Shakes the Barley* (2006), Loach's militant, stirring drama of the Anglo-Irish War (1919–21).

Loach's more recent output has proved uneven, even though *Land and Freedom*, *Carla's Song*, and *My Name Is Joe* are all peppered with vibrant, privileged moments. *Land and Freedom* is probably the closest approximation of the revolutionary fervor of the Spanish Revolution of the 1930s that will ever be committed to film. Before *Carla's Song* becomes bogged down by an unwieldy romance set against the backdrop of the Nicaraguan Revolution, it itself is enlivened by a spirited romp through the streets of Glasgow in which Robert Carlyle shines in the role of an antiauthoritarian bus conductor. The focus of *My Name Is Joe* on drugs and crime frequently recalls genre movies that have mined similar material with more panache, but the plucky hero's humor and perseverance nearly make us forget the film's convoluted, overly schematic plot.

The following interview with Ken Loach took place in July 2009 at his home in Bath, England, shortly after the release of *Looking for Eric*—perhaps his most popular, or accessible, film. Subsequent to it, his most notable work has been in *I, Daniel Blake* (2016)—about a widowed denied unemployment benefits and support allowance despite his doctor's finding him unfit to work—which won the Palme d'Or at the Cannes Film Festival.

R. J. Cardullo: In interviews, sometimes, you express a lot of optimism about the power of cinema to change hearts. At other times, though, you express cynicism about the very same potential of movies to do anything other than reassure and entertain. If that's true, why choose this medium for consciousness-raising? You seemed discouraged at the time, for example, by the response to *Cathy Come Home* [1966], since it promoted piecemeal reform rather than radical transformation.

Ken Loach: That film portrayed an injustice but, of course, homelessness is worse now then when that film was made. With *Cathy Come Home*, we were adopted by people with whom we really didn't feel we had much in common. I think that was influential in pushing our little group to the left; we were social democrats when we made that film and would-be Marxists when we finished it. We realized the inability of social democrats to do anything constructive.

Just to judge in more general terms, if the cinema is any kind of force for social change, then it's a force for the bad, because most films are about one guy with a gun solving a problem. The ideology of the cinema, of mainstream films, is a very right-wing ideology. One hopes to God that such a cinema can have no effect whatsoever, because, if it does, we're all screwed! Of course, maybe my films can have a small sort of impact with one or two people, now and then. That's all I can do, really: make films and hope they have some impact. Some people are writers, some people are poets and painters. Filmmaking is all I can do—I couldn't really do anything else. But also, films are more than wanting to set out to make a political statement. I hope filmmaking is much more than that. It's more about how people live together and what families are about, and all the things that make drama, not just something you can put in a slogan.

We shouldn't have any illusions about what film can do. I mean, it's just a film, and when all is said and done, everybody gets up and walks out of the cinema. So, the best thing you can do is to leave people with a question or to leave people with a sense of disquiet—in the case of *My Name Is Joe* [1998], for example, a sense of solidarity with the characters, a sense of "that's my world, I'm part of it, they're part of me." It's not about some other people, it's about the world I am a part of and a world I am responsible for. And in a way, that knowledge is responsibility, I think. You can't know about that and then walk away from it—at least I hope not. The only old-fashioned word I can think of in this regard is, again, solidarity.

RJC: Still, there is a political conviction embedded in your work. There's a very palpable progressive current running through your *oeuvre*, from beginning to end, and I wonder if you don't ever feel that it's a sort of Sisyphean task to tell the truth about a historical situation or the way people live.

KL: Well, I never see my work in such all-embracing terms. Also, I always work with a writer, and there's a producer, and we all put our heads together and try to make the film. It's not just about me.

I suppose that, in the end, all you can do is make a little contribution to the general noise in the world and say, look, maybe you should look at things in this way, or did you know what happened here? "Just consider this for a moment," or "Look at these few people"—and hope such a question or exhortation hangs around in your mind a minute or two after you leave the cinema. You can't do more than that, I believe.

RJC: What's the difference, do you think, between making a film which is politically charged and a film that's propaganda?

KL: I don't know. I suppose what you try to do—I'm not saying you always succeed—is just to be a sympathetic observer. And also you show that the filmic action exists in a context, not in a vacuum, and you just observe it in a kind of cool yet engaged way, without winding up in melodrama. That's the aim, anyway.

RJC: A follow-up question, connected to the debasing of culture as a result of its commercialization in a market economy. At present one can observe a homogenization of culture: cities become more and more alike, people all over the world listen to the same music, watch the same soap operas on television, buy the same brands of consumer goods, etc. It has been argued that this phenomenon is directly related to the liberalization and deregulation of markets and its by-product, i.e., globalization, which in turn has led to the monopolization of the production and distribution networks by American, privately-owned conglomerates and to the trivialization and debasement of world cultures. How has globalization affected the cinema and the work of cinema directors? And do you think that this cultural homogenization is reversible within the framework of the internationalized market economy?

KL: I do not think that cultural homogenization is reversible within the framework of the global market economy, no. The laws of the market are inexorable. They lead to monopoly, a continuous search for profits where new technology has to be constantly harnessed to cut labor costs in order to increase production. We find ourselves in this spiral that is actually actively pursued by politicians who try to increase the growth rate. In doing so, they increase the spiral of exploitation and overproduction, reducing profit margins at the same time as they reduce wages, and so on. I think that if this is the system in which you find yourself, its laws are inexorable. So, I do not think it is possible to reverse it. In the cinema, people can act as artistic eccentricities around the margins but the central thrust in cinema, as in everything else, is driven by economics and investment.

As far as the world of cinema is concerned, the pressure from the United States is unrelenting. They make occasional concessions, or they talk about concessions, to the Europeans and to the rest of the industry. However, they are dominant and they are pushing for more and more free trade, which means more and more access for them to European cinemas. Even the small subsidies that the French are giving to their own cinema are under threat from the United States, especially in its pursuit of the MAI [Multilateral Agreement on Investment] proposal, which, among other things, aims to increase free trade in the film industry. According to this agreement, the subsidies given by the French have to be granted to everybody, such that it would further weaken European cinema. Against that, you have very weak European politicians who engage in a rhetoric of safeguarding European cinema but in practice, apart from the French, do very little. So, the Italian cinema has more or less been wiped out, the Spanish cinema is battling hard, the British cinema for a long time was wiped out and is just now struggling back, but without much help from the state. Although there is a continuous effort from people who care to rescue some kind of cinema other than the one that the American industrial model produces, this is constantly being knocked back and all the pressure from the United States is for unrestricted access to all markets for U.S. films. Interestingly, in cinema, where the United States is dominant, the Americans talk about free trade, but in other industries where the U.S. is not so dominant they are protectionist—as, for instance, in some sections of the computer industry. They are very protectionist when they want to defend their own domestic industries, but when they think they can dominate someone else's they become very liberal.

RJC: Do you still believe in the possibility of progressive social change, considering this hyper-capitalistic mode of production in which we find ourselves?

KL: I think the choice is going to be thrust upon us quite soon because obviously we're destroying the planet at a pretty fast rate. And I don't think this mode of production can accommodate the changes that have to be made to stop the using of the world's resources so fast. The big corporations have to show a profit, they have to find cheap raw materials, they've got to find ever-growing markets, they've got to expand. That's the dynamic of their method. The earth is finite, and they're rapidly using it up. So the mode of production is on a collision course with the raw materials with which they've got to work. And sooner or later the situation has to change. Now it may not change, it may end in disaster, or they may make minimal changes and then totter on a little bit longer. But sooner or later the conflict has got to be resolved. And the only way I can see its being resolved satisfactorily is with a planned economy, where production is for what people need, not for private profit; we plan how we use the earth's resources and how we deal with it. That's got to be faced, or it may not be, in which case we all blow up. I have no idea. People say we're in a very extreme period of right-wing political hegemony. Well, we are, but we can't go on like that forever.

RJC: I think, nonetheless that you may feel optimistic about the future, because very often in your films there's an element that makes you think things could get better. Is that by chance?

KL: I mean, when you look at statistics—I think there was a UN report in a recent edition of *The Guardian* that said there were 225 people who own and control the same resources as 2.7 billion people, which is 40% of humanity. And when you look at those figures, it's quite hard to imagine the resulting level of inequality, and the amount of human suffering. But then you look at the ideological debate that's on the news and the radio and the two things don't really mesh or coincide. So I think there's sometimes a disconnect, and I think that's the great challenge. Many, many people create the language of "flexibility" and globalization and modernization, and it's designed to make everyone else give up and be hopeless.

Still, I'm always reminded of those wonderful words of Woody Guthrie, who said, "All a human being is, anyway, is just a hoping machine." I think there are the possibilities now of great progress.

Fifteen years ago people who talked about global warming were seen as cranks and idiots. So I don't think anything is impossible or, by contrast, inevitable. I think it depends on our making decisions and organizing; I think we have to be massively creative and look for opportunities and work together. If we lose faith in that notion of collective effort, I think we are sunk. You know, people like Angie [in *It's a Free World* (2007)] have lost hope and say, well, nobody gives a shit out there. Our experience of working out there with so many people in different parts of the world is that they do give a shit. And we have to maintain ourselves and encourage ourselves and do what we can within the conditions in which we work.

RJC: Some people *do* see your films as depressing, I have to say. And I think it's in the interest of people who don't like your films to portray them that way.

KL: I hope they're not depressing. People always fight back, and that's the thing which gives you hope. I hope I've indicated that from time to time. The most depressing thing is the political slogan "there is no alternative." But there is. History hasn't ended, contrary to what Francis Fukuyama once said. It's always a dynamic situation.

RJC: Over the course of your career, you seem to have found two modes of storytelling. One is a focus on contemporary stories about the struggles of marginal or oppressed people, and they're very personal dramas. The others, like *Land and Freedom* [1995], *Carla's Song* [1996], and *The Wind That Shakes the Barley* [2006], grapple with historical events. If it's our duty to criticize our leaders and illuminate the present by looking to the past, do you ever feel that you want to make a movie, through such "telescoping," about the war on terror or the Blair-and-Bush era?

KL: Yes. In a way, they're huge subjects. I think often it's easier to take a story from the past, the immediate past, because the essential elements of the story emerge much more clearly. And that will comment on what Bush and Blair were doing, maybe as forcefully as if you were to do a contemporary story. Staying contemporary is like trying to see the landscape when you're at ground level, and from there you can't see very far. The clutter of detail is very difficult to see beyond. If you're a bit above the landscape, then you see the contours. It's a bit like that when you do a historical subject—you can see the contours of the event more clearly.

I'm sure there are many films that could be made about Iraq or Afghanistan, for example. Maybe when you're working on such a contemporary subject, one way to tackle it is through documentary. The danger is, if you're doing a contemporary subject, you're chasing the headlines. Something might happen next year that, if you're telling the whole story, you'd want to include. And we don't know what the end of this story is yet. But when you do a story about Ireland in the 1920s, you know what the whole story is—and the taste it leaves, and what it left in its wake. And that then determines what is retrospectively important. You see what I mean? It's easier to get a handle on the whole thing.

RJC: You tend to cast a lot of non-professional and unknown actors alongside better-known actors in your films. Why?

KL: Well, you just try to find the best person for the part and whom the audience will believe. If somebody is a hugely well-known face, and you put that person in a film where you want the audience to think they're watching something as it's happening, when the well-known face pops in, it's disorienting. It can introduce new developments. On the other hand, you just want to find the best person for the part, whoever that person may finally be.

RJC: How do you direct non-professional actors?

KL: The same as anybody else.

RJC: Tell me about that, if you would.

KL: Well, I don't direct people in the sense of telling them how to do things. You just put them in a situation with the dialogue and make certain that everything around the scene propels the actors onto a certain path. I would never say to them, "I want you to say it like this." We might talk about it a little bit, but the direction should be self-evident without analyzing it. Directing should be completely hidden, as I see it.

RJC: In order to direct that way, you must have to spend hours and hours getting to know your actors.

KL: Not really. The audition process takes care of that. You usually see people six or seven times before you cast them, so by the end of that time you know them quite well. But talking about directing and acting in a self-conscious way is very destructive, I think.

RJC: What do you take into consideration when casting a non-professional such as David Bradley, the young boy in *Kes* [1969], or Crissy Rock in *Ladybird, Ladybird* [1994], who had worked as a stand-up comedian but not as an actress?

KL: First, as I suggested a little while ago, you don't want to treat them any differently than professionals. In casting, it's best to try little things out, do little improvisations, see who you think is going to touch an audience. A kind of natural eloquence is quite important. Some people will speak and the words don't take off—they've become very pedestrian. Again, it's a class thing. Working-class men and women will often speak with a remarkable eloquence and rhythm and Crissy absolutely has that. She can just turn a phrase brilliantly, and in a way that she's totally unaware of.

RJC: You always cast from the locale where your film is set. For the sake of argument, what would be wrong about hiring a really excellent RADA [Royal Academy of Dramatic Art] actor who did a great Mancunian accent?

KL: Some actors who have been to RADA are good and have retained their identity, but I think the reason to get someone who really is from, in this case, Manchester—or Glasgow, where I've done a lot of work—is that they don't have to think about how they speak; it is actually part of them, since you learn the rhythm of language where you grew up. It isn't just a question of phonetics, of the sound of words. It's how the language is used, the rhythm of the language and the way of thinking that the language dictates. Speaking is much more than imitating the sound. The language is part of the culture of the place and so, being from there, and knowing that, and not having to consider how you're speaking—all those are much better than having to self-consciously try to make the right sound.

RJC: So you don't iron out regional accents, which tend to be obliterated in mainstream British and American films. *Riff-Raff* [1990] was even subtitled in the United States.

KL: Yes, that's right. If you ask people to speak differently, you lose more than the voice. Everything about them changes. If I asked you not to speak with an American accent, your whole personality would change. That's how you are. My hunch is that it's better to use subtitles than not, even if that limits the films to an art-house circuit.

RJC: When people talk about "the craft of acting," then, and spending many years studying the Method, do you just think, "What a bunch of nonsense"?

KL: No, not at all. This is film acting of a particular kind I'm talking about. If you want to work in the theater, then you do need some training and you need to discover how an actor works, because in the theater you need to work out with everyone else the line of the performance and the triggers to the different emotional moments and the changes of mood of the character. You've got to work that out in rehearsal with the text, so that you can play the whole thing from beginning to end in one evening and then do it again the same the next night and the night after that. In film you don't have to do that. It's certainly not the way we work. You just have to make one moment absolutely credible and believe in it totally, and you don't need the theater technique to do that.

RJC: But what about the kind of technique that Robert De Niro or someone like that would use?

KL: Well, I think there's a germ of truth in it, but it's often caricatured and turned into something else.

RJC: Related to this, all of your films have an improvisational quality. How much dialogue is scripted and how much is improvised?

KL: We work around the script, but the script is always the key. The lines give the actors the tools they need, but then you've got to make it spontaneous. If you look at the script before we've finished the film, and then afterwards, you'll find that we stick pretty close to the original dialogue.

RJC: I know you withhold scripts and play tricks on actors, as it were, to generate a certain sort of immediate or spontaneous response. I wonder how actors generally respond to this kind of improvisation.

KL: Well, by the time we've cast them, they know that's how we're going to do it, and if they didn't want to respond in that way, we wouldn't cast them. And—touch wood—I haven't yet had a bad experience. I do think it's important that people play things for the moment, or in the moment; you should play a scene so that you don't anticipate what's going to happen. I quite like the actors just to get though the *experience* of the film. So you perhaps give them the script in sections, just what they need to know at that particular time.

RJC: They don't ever feel tricked in any way?

KL: No, no. Because that's just built into the process and we've talked about that before we do it, as I said. You've got to find people who will enjoy that. I mean most people do. I can't remember the last time somebody ducked out on us. They might have done so thirty years ago, a kind of older actor might not have responded to it, but now everybody just enjoys it really. At least, they are kind enough to say they do. After all, one of the whole points of acting is listening, isn't it? It's reacting. If you've rehearsed it all beforehand, and the people in the scene know what's going to be said, in the end it's very difficult to listen after a bit, because you know what's coming. So part of the trick is to make it so that you have to listen because what will be said to you will be framed differently, and you've got to reframe it so it actually has to go through your mind all the time. And that's really important. I mean it doesn't always work, but the situation is akin to that of a painter when he's painting a house or painting a wall. You always have an open edge and the paint is always wet for your next brush stroke, and I think acting has to be like that. There has to be an openness about it, kind of an uncertainty, a sense of danger, because once it's sealed off and everybody knows what he is doing, when he is going to flick the ash off the cigarette, things die really. And what's crucial here is the cameraman who can catch all that. That again is where other collaborations and other partnerships come in.

RJC: Did you withhold the script from the actors on *Cathy Come Home*, for example?

KL: I think we did, yes. We certainly did on *Kes*. The kestrel is killed in this film and we smuggled a dead kestrel into the scene where David Bradley, who played Billy, would find it and he didn't know it was going to be there. I think surprise is the hardest thing to act—something like the police raid in *Looking for Eric* [2009], which the actors didn't know was going to take place.

RJC: Could you tell me a bit more about how you work with actors on the set?

KL: The key thing is finding the right people. Finding people who will just go straight of their own volition. I mean the key thing is to tell the story in sequence so that it unfolds with them and they go through it so that the work they do today is the rehearsal for the work they are going to do tomorrow. When I started, we would do things like read-throughs—you go to a television show and you would do a read-through on the first day—and usually that was the best performance we got. It was often downhill from then on, because the director—which was me in that case—would come in and start asking daft questions, would give the moves, the actors would rehearse it for two weeks, and by the time they got to the end of the second week, they were bored to tears; they had lost that intuition, that impulse, they had lost their sense of instinct about how to say a line. You know we would even, God help us, talk about vocal inflection, which is death—the moment you start talking about that, you should pack your bags and go. The important thing from my point of view is to keep the performer in touch with his or her instinct, because that's really precious; you live off that for the two or three hours that it takes to do a scene. So good directing is just protecting the actors' instinct, I think.

RJC: How has your process developed over the years?

KL: It's just learning by mistakes. You look at what you're recording and then say, "Well, that isn't as good as it could have been. What would make it better?"

RJC: Do you feel an affinity for any filmmakers working now who, like you, have a bit of a political inflection to their work, like John Sayles?

KL: Yes, John Sayles has done some very good films. I think we probably work in different ways, but I believe his *Matewan* [1987] was a good film. I very much approve of his general view of the world, and I always look forward to his films.

RJC: Are there any other filmmakers working at the moment with whom you feel a connection? Or just admire?

KL: I like the Dardenne brothers' films. I think there are a few others, but I'm not good at remembering names. I am friends with quite a lot of filmmakers—Mike Leigh, for example. But we do very different work.

RJC: Do you argue about film technique with Mike Leigh?

KL: No, no, no. You might gossip, but you would never challenge each other. Because everybody's got his own process, his own way, and things that interest him and things he wants to express, and that's how it should be, really.

RJC: Are you committed to the realist mode of storytelling?

KL: I think it's more interesting than fantasy. It's more exciting. That style of performance is more interesting to me. You might cut stuff together in a nonlinear way—there are all kinds of ways of breaking the storyline up—but I think advances in most art forms come when people just try to get close to the bone of what is really going on in life, the core of our experience. I think art gets decadent when it becomes obsessed with form and style and all the rest. Just to give a crude example, when the impressionists started painting light instead of objects, they were actually just trying to get closer to the process of looking at something. In a rather more humble way, that's what I am trying to do.

RJC: How do you feel when you're called a realist director? Do you feel comfortable with that term?

KL: I don't know. I don't think about it, really, and it doesn't enter into my process of working. You just start by trying to find a good story and figuring out how you're going to tell it. I suppose I'm not a non-realistic director or an anti-realist, but, as for the rest, I couldn't care less.

RJC: Were you impressed by the Italian neorealist films when you first saw them?

KL: Oh, yes. They were very important for me. Not so much at the time, but thinking back, I realize that they made quite an impression on me—films like De Sica's *Bicycle Thieves* [1948] and Rossellini's *Open City* [1945], certainly.

There were also other important influences. When I was at the BBC and we started to do 16mm, handheld stuff in the streets, what we had in mind were documentaries. There was also a very famous theater director in Britain, not so well-known now I guess, called Joan Littlewood. She had a whole tradition of working-class theater and her work was a big influence. Not directly, because it's not cinema, but the idea that drama didn't have to be about middle-class people suffering among each other. Littlewood had the idea that drama could stem from the lives of ordinary working people. There's also a venerable literary tradition along that line, including Dickens and Zola—you could even go back to Shakespeare for some of this inspiration.

RJC: How important is Barry Ackroyd's contribution to your work?

KL: Barry's a great cameraman. We've worked together a long time. His great attribute is that he will be able to capture the essence of a scene, judging the moment exactly when to pan from one person to another or when to catch a movement on the wing. To me, he lights well, but his greatest attribute is his operating of the camera.

RJC: Can we look at your beginnings for a moment? Your father was an electrician who went on to be a foreman at a machine-tool factory. How did you get into film?

KL: Well, I don't know. It was through luck, really. It was a familiar pattern: those who remember the fifties will remember the secondary moderns and the grammar schools, and if you were lucky, you got to the grammar school. And the town I'm from was a town of some 75,000 people, and only sixty boys a year, from the age of eleven, had the possibility of going on to further education and moving on. For 90% of the kids born in that town, at the age of eleven, that was it: they were going to be manual laborers, clerical workers, or whatever. So, I mean, I was lucky. I did what many people did: got the scholarship, did national service, and then I went to university. I was fortunate enough to be part of the first generation that could be awarded a grant to study at university. That was a huge breakthrough for us; it was like being a kid in a sweetshop, just wonderful. It was very beguiling, like walking into paradise, going from being a kid in an industrial town to being at Oxford. A number of us there had done our national service first, so we were around twenty or twenty-one and had gotten over the idea of being in school. We just wanted to have a great time. Work was the last thing you thought about. I had secretly harbored the idea of being an actor, so that's how I got started doing theater. I spent too much time doing acting, nearly got thrown out of university, hung on, got a job in the theater, and from there got a job at the BBC—which I thought was stepping down a bit, really, because the theater was really where the art was and television was selling your soul. But television at that time was very much theater photographed electronically, so that there would be stage sets around the studio and three cameras poking in and it was a very theatrical affair. And what we tried to do in a reaction against that was to get 16mm cameras and make fiction in the streets and, in a way, my career just moved on from there.

RJC: When, in your lifetime, were you first struck by social injustice? Where did your political ideology find its beginnings?

KL: I got involved in the 1960s, I suppose, when I was working with writers who were looking at the important issues of the day. When I worked at the BBC in the mid-'60s, there was a whole group of us who became political together through the process of our work. We did a series called "The Wednesday Play" [1964-70], which was on right after the news. The point of the series was to do contemporary fiction. But, again, we wanted to switch from shooting things on a set indoors, which was more theatrical, to shooting with 16mm handheld cameras on the street. And that was the whole politicizing process, really, because that's when the "new left" was really born, a child much more of Trotsky than the Communist party was. A lot of the writers we worked with were older and I learned a lot from them. Those were very heady days for me and others like me.

It was a very political time: we had a Labour government after a long period of Conservative rule. We helped deliver leaflets for Harold Wilson. And there was a sense that things would change, but of course they didn't. And that process of seeing things not changing and realizing what the Labour Party was and what social democratic politics were was very instructive for us. It was a time when the working class's organizations were stronger and there was a discussion of politics in the air in a way that there isn't now. So I just began to read books about what we were seeing around us.

It very quickly became apparent that if you wanted to see change, then you had to push the Labour Party to one side and say, well, there's another analysis. And of course once you are hooked you are hooked. It would be great not to carry that burden around, but what choice do you have when confronted by someone like Margaret Thatcher, whose way of rescuing the economy was to make the working class pay.

RJC: Are you a cinema buff?

KL: No, I don't go very often. I think when you've been doing it a long time, it's the films you saw when you were young that stay with you. It's the same with everything—music, everything. It's the music you heard when you were a kid that stays with you. For me it was the music of the '60s. Aside from the Italian neorealist cinema, the Czech films of the 1960s were what I really found most exciting: the Czech films of the Prague Spring, films that are just very humanistic, that just enjoy people, that respect them, and where you feel some kind of warmth. I don't see it in the cinema now, which is sad.

RJC: Do you ever go to see big, glossy Hollywood films?

KL: No! I just get irritated by them. Maybe that's my loss, but I don't go to see them or much of anything else. If you win at football, if your team wins, that does keep you going to the next game; it really does. And I can't remember the last time I had that feeling in a cinema. I remember enjoying films, but not feeling that sense of exhilaration.

RJC: What about the escapist aspect of popular cinema that lets you get away from your everyday life? Any virtue there?

KL: Yes, well I guess that works. But I think, personally, I get that from music more. I think cinema can do it; I just don't think it does do it very often in a satisfying way. It doesn't for me.

RJC: Especially now, during a recession, it seems relevant to ask whether the role of cinema in bad times is to give an escape to people.

KL: I think that such a role trivializes the cinema. Of course, that depends if you take cinema seriously. If you take it seriously like a novel, poetry, or the visual arts, the point of cinema, or one of the points of cinema, can be to reflect on why things are bad.

They are not acts of God. You want to be able to understand why things are bad because then you go out strengthened, with some sense of an understanding. Understanding gives you strength. If you're just bemused by why things are bad, all that the cinema does is distract your attention, and then it's a pretty useless medium. You might as well have a lobotomy, really. What's the difference? I think that cinema should, that cinema can, give you an insight into why things are bad. What you do with that insight or understanding is another matter.

RJC: One of the things that people compliment you on is your consistency, the fact that you're still making films about the same sorts of people and subjects after all these years. I wonder if you consider it an achievement that you never decamped to Hollywood. Did you ever even feel any temptation to do so?

KL: I think Hollywood is boring, really; the little I know of the American industry makes it sound like the last place where I'd want to go and work. I just don't find it attractive. I don't find the work they do interesting; I find it predictable. If you're interested in food, by analogy, you wouldn't go to a hamburger chain. I just find mainstream Hollywood production uninteresting. And nobody's waved a lot of money in my face, anyway! I did shoot *Bread and Roses* [2000] in Los Angeles—which was surrealist enough!—but that is hardly a Hollywood film and did not have American money behind it.

RJC: How would you describe the popular perception of Ken Loach films, particularly the perception of people who haven't seen any of your movies?

KL: I don't know. I'm not sure there is a perception, actually. I have no idea. I think the trouble is that sometimes reviewers and film critics overuse certain words. I mean, I'll be truly pleased never to read the word "gritty" again as it is applied to my work. Such an adjective doesn't help perception. You want an audience to come in without preconceptions and just enjoy what's there, without being prejudiced by a stereotypical image.

RJC: Does it worry you that because you're seen as a left-wing film director, all the people who go to see your films will agree with you and you'll end up preaching to the converted?

KL: Well, I mean if they all do, then we'd probably be doing rather better politically than we are doing, wouldn't we? The thing is that the people who tend to go see independent films or non-mainstream Hollywood films like mine will tend to be more radical anyway, so it's almost a self-selecting group.

RJC: Are you interested in getting your stuff on TV and to a wider audience for that reason?

KL: Yes. I began in television and all films are seen on television anyway at some point; even if it's through DVD, you see the films on the set. It's all one industry, in the end.

RJC: One of the things I always get from your films is the idea that apparently insignificant lives are important enough and interesting enough to be on screen, just as much as any other ones.

KL: It pleases me very much to hear you say that. If that is true, then to some extent I have succeeded, artistically as well as politically.

RJC: In several of your films from the 1990s, such as *Raining Stones* [1993] and *Riff-Raff*, you moved into comedy, which is still on display in your latest picture, *Looking for Eric*. What prompted this shift?

KL: I've always done bits of comedy; it's very false to remove it. You can't be in this particular hotel and not have a sense of comedy. You might as well put your head in a gas oven otherwise. Comedy is everywhere. I feel it's always been there in my work, although sometimes you work with writers who have a stronger sense of comedy than others. The guy who wrote *Riff-Raff*, Bill Jesse, was a very funny man—as is Barry Hines, who wrote that film we did ages ago, *Kes*.

RJC: Nonetheless, *Kes* seems quite sober in comparison with *Riff-Raff*. There seem to be links between the early films, though they are not necessarily comic ones—in *Kes*, for instance, the boy's fate is completely determined by the school and family, while a film like *Family Life* [1971] doubtless presents the family as an entirely malevolent force.

KL: Different families, of course. In *Kes*, there was also an older brother with his own problems, whereas in *Family Life* there's this whole oppressive set of familial relationships. The parents have such a clear idea of what the daughter is going to be, such that, in the final analysis, she doesn't have a chance.

RJC: Why are families so important in your films?

KL: Because the family is where most drama happens in our lives, isn't it? That's where we learn everything. All of the tension, drama, and comedy contained in those familial relationships are incredible. A lot of classic dramas center on the family; it's the raw material for drama quite often. Even though families are the springboard for everything we do—or maybe I should say *because* families are such a springboard—we could say that families are at the same time political entities. Of course, they're not precise mirrors of the world outside, but they do launch you into the world and form you, so you can't imagine a character without a family. Before I start making a film, I and my actors work out a little family plan for everybody, because then you know what's projected you into a particular situation or onto a particular path.

In *Raining Stones*, for example, to make the family function we did little improvisations. The family of actors went to church together or they went on an outing to a McDonald's restaurant together. They just got to relate to each other and it was better than a performer's going cold into the first day of filming, thinking, "Christ, you're supposed to be my wife. How do I talk to you?" That sort of thing should be in place before you start on the first day.

RJC: Like *Raining Stones*, many of your films take place in the north of England—a region that can be considered somewhat marginalized, the periphery as opposed to the center.

KL: Yes. I myself am from the Midlands, which is closer to the north than it is to the metropolis. When I was young, we always used to go to seaside places in the north and we were familiar with the northern comic sensibility. There's a humor there, but there's also a humor in working-class London. I think it's a class thing, not a regional thing. But it's particularly strong in the north, where there's a whole tradition of stand-up comedy there that I enjoy very much.

RJC: Beneath the surface, it's possible to notice a very consistent set of concerns in your work. Just as alcoholism is not really the subject of *My Name Is Joe*, domestic violence is not really the subject of *Ladybird, Ladybird*. It's merely part of the female protagonist's background, the symptom under which lies a much larger cause.

KL: Yes. That's really a film about grief and how it can leave a person very damaged, and about someone who was damaged as a child. When do you start blaming people for their actions? When they're young, clearly they have our pity and understanding. Suddenly, they become the villain, but what made some people the villain should engender our ambivalence toward them.

RJC: In *Ladybird, Ladybird* you're ambivalent toward both the protagonist and the social services bureaucracy.

KL: Yes, it's a very difficult situation. That was a great film to work on, not least because the actress, Crissy Rock, would just take your breath away during the filming.

RJC: Through her character, you don't necessarily portray the working class as heroic; above all, you seem interested in exploring the complexity of its dilemmas.

KL: There's a kind of fun about working-class characters, you know, and their stories work on a very primal level. Working-class experience is where drama, the raw material of drama, exists. But there's also a political reason to focus on the working class in art: if change is to come, that's the progressive element which will provide it. That's where the engine for change will originate. It won't be brought to us as a gift from above, but through the work of people from below.

RJC: The rapport with your screenwriters—themselves all from the working class—seems crucial, whether it's with Jim Allen on *The Big Flame* [1969], Barry Hines on *Kes*, or Bill Jesse on *Riff-Raff*.

KL: It's really central, yes. Good films begin with their scripts.

RJC: Do you have any advice for first-time directors?

KL: Don't take advice. You have to make up your own mind as to what to do from the very beginning. Don't follow the industry ritual; the industry practice, I think, is very damaging, very sterile. Follow your own voice and get on with it.

Bibliography

Cranston, Ros. *Ken Loach*. London: British Film Institute, 1997.

Hayward, Anthony. *Which Side Are You On?: Ken Loach and His Films*. London: Bloomsbury, 2004.

Hill, John. *Ken Loach: The Politics of Film and Television*. Basingstoke, U.K.: Palgrave Macmillan, 2011.

Leigh, Jacob. *The Cinema of Ken Loach: Art in the Service of the People*. London: Wallflower Press, 2002.

McKnight, George, ed. *Agent of Challenge and Defiance: The Films of Ken Loach*. Westport, Conn.: Greenwood Press, 1997.

Oliver, James. *English with English Subtitles: The Films of Ken Loach*. Suffolk, U.K.: Screen Press, 2003.

"The Complexities of Cultural Change: An Interview with Stephen Frears," by Cynthia Lucia, from *Cineaste*, 28.4 (Fall 2003): 8-15.

Stephen Frears is a director whose films resist easy classification. He has worked in both his native England and in Hollywood, and both within and outside established genres. Indeed, to study Frears is to crash headlong into those *auteurist* limitations film theorists have debated for decades. Perhaps because he himself pays genuine respect to the collaborative nature of film as an art form—above all acknowledging the primacy of writers who create source novels and screenplays—Frears appears to "tiptoe" into his own work through the "back door," unlike, say, Hitchcock and Welles, who unambiguously "occupy" their work—often quite literally. While it is difficult to say just what constitutes "a Stephen Frears film," it is possible to find Frears in the sensibility surrounding character and in the films' attitudes and interests. First and foremost, Frears devotes careful attention to the way people live, how they think (often given greater prominence than *what* they think), and how they react within their social environments, often on the precipice of irreversible change.

Having gotten his start in the BBC (British Broadcasting Corporation) during the late 1960s, it is no wonder that Frears grounds his films in social-realist themes—even when refusing the overtly political stance adopted by his former BBC colleagues Ken Loach and Mike Leigh. Frears's films examine self-interest in the context of community and the needs of smaller ethnic or marginalized groups in the context of a dominant culture, whose rules are designed to inhibit and exploit those "others" living on its periphery. Like Jean Renoir, Frears seems intrigued by the dialectical interplay of rules and games, and infuses his work with a humor rooted in a keen awareness of human struggle.

Though he may not always admit it, Frears is also meticulous in his attention to visual style. Whether the world is downbeat and gritty, as in his *noir*-inflected *The Hit* (1984); stylized and elegant, as in *Dangerous Liaisons* (1988); or wide and expansive as in his western, *The Hi-Lo Country* (1998), Frears tends to favor the longer take over more rapid cutting, with shot composition inviting viewers to contemplate the characters in the context of their environment.

After the appearance of Frears's first film, *Gumshoe* (1971), an engaging revisionist detective film starring Albert Finney, more than a decade elapsed before he made his second film, *The Hit*, preferring instead to work in British television. Then Frears won international acclaim in 1985 with *My Beautiful Laundrette*, a film also originally created for television. Made in collaboration with the British-Pakistani writer Hanif Kureishi, *Laundrette* focuses on London's Pakistani community, as does *Sammy and Rosie Get Laid* (1987), a second collaborative effort with Kureishi, which delves even more deeply into a new London about to explode with racism, class division, poverty, and homelessness. A harsh indictment of the Thatcher government, the film also acknowledges an international political climate of class inequities and abuses, infusing not only the local but also the personal worlds of its characters. The peaceful, picturesque London of the past is alive here only in the romantic yearnings of an older generation.

Frears's attention to sexual politics in *My Beautiful Laundrette* and *Sammy and Rosie* also finds expression in *Prick Up Your Ears* (1987), based on John Lahr's biography of the British playwright Joe Orton, who was hammered to death by his lover Kenneth Halliwell, a would-be writer who became increasingly abusive as his younger lover won greater acclaim. As in *Laundrette*, the gay relationship in *Prick Up Your Ears* never draws attention to itself as a novel cinematic subject, which it most certainly was at the time.

Dangerous Liaisons, Frears's first Hollywood film, starring Glenn Close, John Malkovich, and Michelle Pfeiffer, won three Oscars: for art direction, costume design, and adapted screenplay. Explaining why he cast "big" American stars, Frears says that he didn't want to make "a sort of 'respectable' period film," but rather "a film about passion." Decidedly less successful than *Liaisons* were Frears's other "big" Hollywood films—*Hero* (1992), starring Dustin Hoffman, and *Mary Reilly* (1996), starring Julia Roberts. Frears acknowledges his greater comfort in directing more modest Hollywood films like

The Grifters (1990) and *High Fidelity* (2000), both starring John Cusack and both successful pictures.

Continuing to move between Hollywood and Britain, Frears skillfully employed leavening humor in such films as *The Snapper* (1993)—originally made for British television—and *The Van* (1996), both based on Roddy Doyle's "Barrytown Trilogy" of novels. He also directed *Liam* for British television in 2000. Based on Joseph McKeown's novel *The Back Crack Boy* (1978), the semi-autobiographical screenplay written by Jimmy McGovern returns Frears to multicultural themes—this time, however, in 1930s Depression-era Liverpool, where a Catholic working-class father begins attending fascist rallies upon losing his job and noticing that the Jewish families in town have a much easier time of it than he does. One of the achievements of the film is in its adopting the perspective of the seven-year-old son Liam (Anthony Burrows), who suffers from a debilitating stutter. The moving performance of the young Burrows is testimony to Frears's skill in working with actors, also evident in *Dirty Pretty Things* (2002), with its international cast of performers, many of whom speak no English and were therefore heavily dependent upon a dialogue coach.

The setting is contemporary multicultural London, where immigrants, some legal and others illegal, seek refuge. A Nigerian doctor, Okwe, is hunted by his government and flees, leaving behind his seven-year-old daughter. Driving a taxi by day and manning a hotel desk by night, Okwe sleeps little, napping on the couch of a hotel housekeeper, Senay, a Turkish immigrant granted asylum in England. In their shared vulnerability, living on society's margins, Okwe and Senay seek comfort in a growing friendship, and perhaps a growing infatuation on Senay's part.

Cineaste met with Stephen Frears twice—once in April 2002, at the Istanbul Film Festival, where he was honored with a lifetime achievement award, and again recently in New York, when *Dirty Pretty Things* had its American premiere. In his engagingly self-deprecating manner, Frears spoke with *Cineaste* about his filmmaking career spanning more than three decades—and continuing into the twenty-first century with such titles as *The Queen* (2006), *Philomena* (2013), and *Florence Foster Jenkins* (2016).

Cynthia Lucia: In *Dirty Pretty Things* [2002], you're looking at immigrants in London, as you were in *My Beautiful Laundrette* [1985], and *Sammy and Rosie Get Laid* [1987]. Those earlier films were set in Thatcherite London of the mid-1980s. In what sense have things changed, or what sorts of changes were you attempting to pick up on in this new movie, set in London in the twenty-first century?

Stephen Frears: The situations in the films are not remotely comparable. The influx of the migrants has all happened in the last ten years. Asylum is a huge political issue and the government doesn't handle it very well. In multicultural London it's O.K., but the government sort of whips up the fears in the rest of England, as though these people have two heads or something. There's no attempt made to explain the problem, to explain that these people are serious. It's just assumed that they're crooks or terrorists or somehow feckless; whereas, it seems to me that crossing the world to get a decent living for your family is not something you do casually.

If I think about it, and I promise you I haven't thought about this before, there may be a connection between something that happened to me in the 1970s and the fact that, at the end of that decade, I stopped making films about the England that I grew up in. What happened was that, in my mid-twenties, I discovered that I was Jewish, that my mother was Jewish, which had been concealed from me. It's hard to make the connection between what goes on in your psychology and what happens fifteen years later when you're making a film about a multicultural society. In the late seventies, I was still working with Alan Bennett, who was a very English writer, and I was still making films about Anglo-Saxon people, but around that time I stopped, and the characters became people more on the margin. I haven't really made one of those English films in twenty years—with the exception of *Liam* [2000]—and other people also stopped making those kinds of films.

CL: Is it mainly because that England no longer exists?

SF: I would have thought not, I would have thought it was a more complicated working of my unconscious. I've made a lot of films about the England I grew up in, but I just ran out of steam. When the queen mother died, that was the England I grew up in—

entirely familiar. *Enigma* [2001] is about the England I grew up in, but the Hugh Grant films aren't. There are people who say that my work with Alan Bennett is the best stuff I've ever done. If they're right, it would be a rather sad view of my life.

Then I met Hanif Kureishi, and after that I went to America. So in my middle age I found two new subjects—I found America and I found non-English subjects.

CL: So you think this is more a response to internal conditions than to external circumstances?

SF: It's in response to external circumstances that Hanif wrote *My Beautiful Laundrette*. But my response to it was internal.

CL: Why was your Jewish background concealed from you?

SF: I don't know. My mother died before I could get a straight answer out of her. It would have been the late 1930s. My aunt, her sister, always denies it. I think it might have been a form of rebellion against her parents. I've no idea. I was brought up, I went to church rigorously, bored out of my mind for years. I'd also grown up to be a rather secretive person. If I think about it, since secrets were being kept from me, I'm not surprised. It's quite a common experience—Christopher Hitchens, for example, had his Jewishness concealed from him. I can't just say it was anti-Semitism—that would be too glib.

CL: Have you ever had the desire to take on a Jewish subject?

SF: *Liam*! That's the first time. And I got into terrible trouble with people who said the film is anti-Semitic.

CL: Why do you think people were saying that?

SF: Because the Jews were either a rich shipping family or they were the rent collectors. I can see what they're saying, but I suspect English society was like that, and I wanted to show it. I was insistent on casting Jewish actors. I wouldn't cast non-Jews to play Jews. Maybe that is a sort of anti-Semitism, I don't know; but I got into trouble. It seemed to be rather an interesting argument, which I clearly haven't thought through—I haven't prepared my defenses and worked it out. It wasn't the response in the United States, but I remember that a critic in Toronto was the first person to say it is an anti-Semitic film. If you ask one of my friends, who is Israeli, he describes having seen the film with his wife, who herself said the film is anti-Semitic. But it also seems to me that if you're making a film about anti-Semitism, you would have, by definition, to make it anti-Semitic.

CL: *Liam* was made for the BBC. How would you compare your earlier experience at the BBC when you started out as a filmmaker with your experience in working on *Liam*?

SF: *Liam* was an attempt to turn the clock back. A lot of films like *Liam* were made in the sixties and seventies. The world has changed. At the time there was a thing called public-service broadcasting. The BBC was a very middle-class place when I was working there. It had just taken on the responsibility of new writing, and the best English writers were working there. It was a sort of new medium, and it dealt with a new subject, which was what Britain was really like. It was just a wonderful place to be. In those days the BBC was financed in this rather eccentric way. It was the voice of the Establishment, yet it tolerated dissent from people like me, Ken Loach, and Mike Leigh. Now it's much more conscious of audiences, worrying about ratings and about competing with Rupert Murdoch and all of that. While it isn't like PBS in the States, it's becoming more like PBS. The BBC is caught—it can't decide whether it should be trying to maintain the rather high standards of the past or compete for an audience.

CL: It would seem that *Liam* was, to some degree, caught in that same conflict at the BBC.

SF: Yes. When I read *Liam*, I said, "Look, this is a good piece of writing and it should be made. It has no commercial value whatsoever." Because the writer Jimmy McGovern was a very successful television scenarist and, to a certain extent, because of me, we were somehow able to force the BBC to make it. They preferred to make the film as a commercial enterprise so, almost against my will, it became a part of the commercial cinema, where it has no place at all. I had it written in my contract that *Liam* could be shown only on television, but then, in one way or another, they're able to maneuver you into agreeing that it go into the cinema, which gave me no pleasure at all. Although the cinema gives me enormous pleasure, I didn't set out to do *Liam* for the cinema. I've done it before—*My Beautiful Laundrette* and *The Snapper* [1993] were made for television, and both films ended up very successfully in the cinema. But the fact that *Liam* ended up in the cinema is a sort tragic irony.

CL: The timing of its release, so close to that of *Angela's Ashes* [1999], was also a bit strange or maybe unfortunate.

SF: I wasn't concerned about that. When they showed *Liam* on British television, it was very, very successful. You release it in another country, and you wonder why people would be interested in the film. It is about a very narrow part of English social history that people of my age remember, so it has a sort of nostalgic value. You don't pretend to make a film like *Liam* for a world cinema audience.

CL: Do you consider it a political film?

SF: McGovern is really a historian of the working class, so it's actually a rather accurate piece of history. It also contains an autobiographical element interwoven with political matters. That's the kind of work we were doing back in the seventies, and the kind of work Ken Loach has gone on doing.

CL: When you have a child as a central figure, there's always the danger that the presence of the child onscreen, while powerful, will sentimentalize the material.

SF: I hope it doesn't do that, but it's hard for me to say. I never had the sense of its being a sentimental film. As far as I can see, *Billy Elliot* [2000] is a sentimental film, so I would distinguish entirely between that kind of writing and the writing in *Liam*.

CL: You have spoken about having hit upon the "magic formula" with *My Beautiful Laundrette*. What was that formula?

SF: Well, it's hard not to use words like that. I was given a script that I thought was very good. I made it for television because I thought what it said was important and would hit a large audience and clearly would be striking. The idea that it would become a cinema hit around the world was nowhere in our minds. My career became successful—so did the careers of Daniel Day-Lewis and producer Tim Bevan. Afterwards you think, "Oh, I see, if you're going to bring about a revolution—because it did cause a revolution—you have to have Dan, an actor about to become a star; you have to have a producer who's going to end up being one of the most successful producers in Britain." You suddenly think, "Oh, yes, we got all the skittles in a row—without even knowing it." So that's the kind of magic I'm referring to. And, in the end, it happens because a writer wrote about something that people recognized when they saw it, but five minutes before, they didn't know it existed. When they see it, they say, "Oh, yes, of course!"

CL: But it's also your manner of presenting it. When you look back on it, is there anything about the aesthetic choices you made as director that also accounts for the film's power and success?

SF: No. It was very cheap and made in a very carefree way. It was subversive. It entirely suited my temperament, and the subject matter was so interesting. I didn't know anything about Pakistani culture. And it was funny—it was just sort of how life should be, really. But you can't plan it—you can only try to read it intelligently. I had to have it all explained to me. I was just doing what I'd done before. Of course, I was very experienced: I'd been making films for fifteen years.

CL: But there was something about the way you worked with the actors and the way you photographed Daniel Day-Lewis, for example.

SF: I came down to the location on a Friday night, and Dan was standing under a lamppost that was a little bit raised, and I said, "Oh, you're playing it like Marlene Dietrich." I don't know why he stood there, but he looked like Marlene, even with his dirty blonde hair. So that is how I photographed Dan, because he "told" me to do it by standing there.

CL: You noticed it.

SF: If you ask Catherine Deneuve what Truffaut did, she says he did nothing, he just happened to notice what you were doing. I don't know why Dan went and stood there, but I did think, "Marlene Dietrich."

CL: Mike Leigh speaks about the very complex and intimate manner in which he works with actors. Do you have any particular approach?

SF: No. Observation. Choose them well and give them freedom.

CL: Can you comment on your collaboration with Kureishi in both *My Beautiful Laundrette* and *Sammy and Rosie Get Laid*?

SF: Before I worked with Hanif, I did a lot of work with Alan Bennett, as I mentioned. Alan educated me, and Hanif clearly turned me upside down. All I can say is "thank you" to Hanif for taking on somebody older than himself. And I congratulate myself for being open enough to listen to him.

CL: You almost speak about your films as if they're not your films, as if they should be credited mostly to the writers.

SF: I do come second. I don't invent the films. I have a clear sense of that. What the writer has done, I admire. Maybe it has become less like that in recent years. Maybe it's a completely dishonest position. For all I know, it may just be entirely an act of self-concealment on my part. Other people say it is. I made a little joke about being imperialist and colonizing writers' ideas. I remember the comment of one writer I worked with in television: "Well, you somehow absorb it, and you regurgitate it in some way," and it's been gone through in my intestines in some complicated manner that I don't fully understand. But maybe I'm just hiding. That's also involved in the equation. I wouldn't want to pretend I can't see that. But that may be necessary, or that may be what I have to do. The truth is, it's the actors who expose and reveal themselves.

CL: But obviously you bring something very specific to the films you direct.

SF: I just prefer to read the script and make my own decisions. If you're asking what I think I can do, I think I can bring things to life, which seems to me, far and away, the most profound thing you can do. In giving life, you dramatize the story. Generally, I go in and when I shoot, it's as though there's a sort of path through the woods, and it's the most interesting way through. Often people don't see that, and I show them the path. Then I can say to the editor, you can go and cut it now because I've shown you the secret passage.

CL: Do you become a part of the writing process?

SF: I question—which is part of my function in all parts of the filmmaking process: Why are you doing that? Why are you playing it that way? You conduct an intelligent conversation with everybody. That's different from saying, this is what you should do or this is what you should write. So it's hard to claim credit. In fact, Jimmy McGovern talked about that in an interview. On one particular section of *Liam*, he thought I was able to give him a really good idea, and all I said was, "It's not good enough. Write something better." I didn't know what he should write, but he did go away and write something much more interesting. So you're really there in a rather destructive way, while at the same time encouraging the writer to be adventurous, to have the confidence to go somewhere. It's trying to make sense of what they're offering.

CL: As it seems you did with Steven Knight, the screenwriter of *Dirty Pretty Things*.

SF: Yes.

CL: You said that one of the things you're very good at doing is "introducing the frivolous into the serious." What larger dimension does it contribute?

SF: All I mean is that humor is a good way of telling a story; it makes difficult things acceptable. You point to various jokes in a film like *Dirty Pretty Things*, and they're a way of making the film more human—and making people enjoy it and understand what you're trying to say. The alternative would be to give lectures, which would be appalling.

CL: You seem to do what a very good teacher does, one who doesn't give the answers but who is able to reveal the questions.

SF: Yes. The questions are what's interesting. Once you find out what the questions are, the answers are pretty simple.

CL: What were the questions in *Dirty Pretty Things*?

SF: It's always the same: Who are these people? What are they doing? Why is this story interesting? What is the story telling or teaching you?

CL: What do you think it's teaching you?

SF: I suppose it's to do with tolerance and understanding other people. And that if you encourage these people and bring them to life in their conflict, they'll tell a story that's entertaining and interesting. But the story has been laid out by the writer, so I really don't have to worry about that. What I worry about is the business of bringing it to life.

CL: *Dirty Pretty Things* deals with a situation in which the British government grants asylum, while at the same time it forbids immigrants to work, placing them in a rather difficult situation.

SF: Senay, the Audrey Tautou character, is applying for asylum. The law is that they give you forty pounds a week, which is about sixty dollars, and you can't take a job and you can't rent or sublet an apartment. The people granted asylum are given money, but they're not given enough to live on, so of course they all take jobs illegally. They're immediately open to being exploited in sweatshops and hotels and places like that.

CL: What promise does England hold for people like Senay, whose dream ultimately is to move to New York? What greater promise does America hold?

SF: America has always been the dream that people want to realize, but at a certain point people realize it is a dream, an illusion, as Senay does. But the Statue of Liberty is there welcoming people. I imagine the people who landed on Ellis Island didn't have very nice lives, but their children have grown up to be film directors and doctors. England has always done very well out by its immigrants. That's the mysterious thing—the Asians, for example, are very, very hardworking and have brought considerable prosperity to Britain. I think the reason people want to come to England is that we don't have identity cards. In Europe they have identity cards, so it's that much harder. Also, in the nicest possible sense, there is a tradition of tolerance in England. Somehow we are thought to be this very tolerant country and probably, in many respects, we are rather tolerant. At the same time we're very unwelcoming to people.

CL: It would seem that the socialized system of health care in England—far more developed than anything in the States—would be more attractive to immigrants.

SF: For illegal immigrants, it's more complicated. They don't want to have anything to do with the system; they're terrified by the system, so they just keep away. You have to deal with the immigrants' fears.

CL: In England it seems there's a strong tension between a socialist impulse and capitalist pressure, or perhaps necessity.

SF: In a way, that's what all the arguments are about in England—the sort of contract that was worked out after the war that Mrs. Thatcher tore up. That's what people like me were complaining about.

CL: That tension is beautifully and humorously presented in *Dirty Pretty Things* in the scene shot in the hotel kitchen, where the porter Ivan prepares a room-service sandwich, adding a sprig of parsley while saying, "It's the little touches that make a difference—that's capitalism!"

SF: I like all those jokes, but it's ironic, isn't it?

CL: Are those "little touches" corrupting for immigrants who seek a better way of life?

SF: Well, they have come to a capitalist country. The truth is, nowhere is there a utopia.

CL: The characters seem to have a genuine innocence.

SF: Yes, that's a very traditional approach—you show their innocence, then put them against the perils of the world.

CL: What have they learned?

SF: Ivan has learned a sort of cynicism that will get you through. If you understand all these things, you can keep your head down and survive. The other two, Okwe and Senay, get trapped by it all, though I suppose they learn that they'd rather operate on Sneaky, the Sergi Lopez character, than get operated on themselves. They've turned the tables on the system. Of course, it would be much better if it weren't necessary for them to do that.

CL: Do they become tainted by their experience?

SF: No. They're strong people who can deal with it, but the fact that Senay doesn't break down and crack, doesn't mean that something awful hasn't happened.

CL: Do you believe that Sneaky has raped Senay, when he has prepared her passport in exchange for her kidney but also demands sex as the "deal breaker," tearing up her passport application when she initially refuses?

SF: Well, the fact that she agrees under duress, to me, is rape—because she's in a position where she can't say no. I remember thinking that something awful has happened to this girl and you have to sort of deal with that, but also you want the plot to keep moving, so I didn't want the film to stop and become a story about a girl being raped. But you have to respect the fact that something so violent has happened. You have to work out a way of dealing with that without allowing the film to be somehow "kidnapped."

CL: Rape does become metaphorical in the film, both sexual and surgical, as well as spiritual.

SF: Yes, that level of exploitation seems so appalling.

CL: Sergi Lopez is such a fine actor, however, that even after the rape, he somehow remains engaging. The audience still chuckles when—with his swaggering manner—he appears, amazed, at the hotel room properly prepared for a surgical procedure.

SF: Yes, it's terrible. Life would be so much easier if the villains didn't have these enjoyable sides.

CL: Was this deliberate or simply a testimony to Lopez's acting and powerful screen presence?

SF: The most horrible people are also entertaining. They are in their own way human. I knew his character was about to face the terrible punishment of having his kidney removed. It didn't seem to me that you have to lay it on very thick, because the plot was about to be very violent towards him.

CL: What about the character of Okwe, as played by Chiwetel Ejiofor? In some ways he seems too good.

SF: First of all, the writer was interested in writing about a good man, and secondly, in a way he's trying to retain his dignity, his integrity. If he becomes as bad as the people exploiting him, then, in a sense, he'd have lost. He still has to look at himself in the mirror. Even though he performs the surgery—on Sneaky rather than Senay—he's still very attentive to the man who's being looked after.

CL: The performance of Ejiofor puts me in mind of Sidney Poitier in his early roles in 1960s America, when the rare African-American protagonist had to be almost excessively noble in order to be accepted by white audiences.

SF: That's a very perceptive thing to say, and I was very, very aware of it. Ejiofor very much reminded me of Sidney Poitier. I could see it historically. Only when Sidney Poitier appeared were African-Americans allowed to play leading roles. Now, of course, they play people with faults, people who are human. At the time, though, you could see that Poitier was the first "acceptable" heroic black actor. I was quite aware of that and thought there was wisdom in drawing upon that, because, so far as I know, *Dirty Pretty Things* is the first film of substance made in Britain that's featured an African actor in a starring role. There hasn't been a film about an African. The world hasn't become that wonderful all of a sudden.

CL: Yes, the world hasn't "improved," as the character Guo Yi, played by Benedict Wong, points out. He's a wonderful character who is, in a sense, "living with the dead." He's both practical and aware of the world, yet somehow removed from the world. Is his philosophical distance a result of his "living" in the morgue as a hospital worker?

SF: It's a result of his being in exile. That's the best job he can get. You get the impression that he's a highly educated man who's doing work beneath him. I love the idea that he's living in the morgue, and especially the scene where he sews up the jacket pockets on the corpse.

CL: Okwe chews "khat" to stay awake.

SF: Yes. If he goes to sleep he'll dream, and he'll remember the mess he's come from.

CL: You have spoken about your interest in making *Dirty Pretty Things* stylistically different from your earlier films, referring to the style of Wong Kar-wai. But it strikes me that his films—*Happy Together* [1997] and *In the Mood for Love* [2000], for instance—take very different stylistic approaches. Which of his films did you have in mind as a model when you were shooting *Dirty Pretty Things*?

SF: I only know *Chungking Express* [1994] and *In the Mood for Love*, both of which reflect such a good, modern style. I just admire Wong Kar-wai—he's such a young filmmaker. It wasn't that I felt certain elements of this script worked in that style so much as feeling that his work had a kind of modern quality, and I was trying to make a modern film. But the cinematographer Chris Menges and I are the same age. We were too old—some of our other crew members were young and confident; I was old and terrified!

CL: You spoke about wanting to create a somewhat happy ending.

SF: Yes, as happy as I could reasonably get away with.

CL: Is Okwe's mouthing the words "I love you" to Senay perhaps going too far in that direction? It doesn't seem entirely true to his character.

SF: That might well be right—perhaps it's too sentimental. You can see, in that, the struggle I was going through—I was trying to make as happy or as romantic an ending as I could find.

CL: Why?

SF: Oh, I don't know, because I was being soppy. It's such a delicate line you're treading. I could tell you there were as many people who wanted a happier ending. You create characters that people care about, and it seems to me that to just sort of chuck them away is being too brutal with the audience. You kind of find a way of telling the audience that these people are going to be all right. It seems to me a good fault. The larger issue is reduced in the end to something as small as that—does he say the words or does he not say the words? Suddenly that becomes a metaphor for the larger struggle you're going through as a director.

CL: While all of your films are political, some are more overtly so than others—*Sammy and Rosie Get Laid* and *My Beautiful Laundrette*, both based on Kureishi's work, for instance. But it seems that politics enters through the back door in other films of yours. *High Fidelity* [2000], for instance, takes on a political dimension in Rob's insistence on remaining a kind of adolescent.

SF: Yes, of course, it's a feminist film. It's a cry for men to grow up.

CL: And that's feminist?

SF: In my experience, yes. I have mainly been told to grow up by women, so I think of it as feminist. The people who have most stopped me from behaving like a child in my life have been women. It seems to me *High Fidelity* is about a man dealing with that. So I think of it as political—it's been politicized.

CL: Is economics a part of it, too? Rob seems to feel insecure because Laura is a lawyer.

SF: It has never occurred to him to be with a woman more successful than he is, so he's threatened sexually by her economic freedom, by her moving up in the world. It's about sexual politics, isn't it?

CL: One review of *High Fidelity* talked about the fact that in some ways women seem very much beside the point.

SF: That's an absolutely absurd thing to say. On page one she leaves him, and he spends the whole film wanting to get her back. How could women be beside the point?

CL: They are the point, but as characters they aren't all that fully developed beyond his desire for them.

SF: That's the limitation of the writing.

CL: But it occurs to me that while the film does marginalize women to a certain extent, it does, at the same time, make a statement about marginalizing women. It's not entirely a flaw in the film but rather could be seen as part of the film's strategy.

SF: I think it's about the immaturity of men, but the immaturity of men would include marginalizing women. It's not in Rob's interest to mature because men can get away with being immature—up to a certain point, and then the trouble starts. In my experience women always deal with life much better than men. Even in the case of actors, the women are endlessly impressive—they know their lines; they know why they're there; they know they have to look pretty; they're very stoical; they're very dignified about it; they don't make a fuss. It's always the men who make a fuss.

CL: Why is that?

SF: They would say because it's harder to be a man than a woman. My assumption is that women somehow aren't given the choice to be immature. In the end, things like babies mean that women don't have a choice, do they? Once they have a baby, the baby has to be fed. That's kind of the end of it. So the idea of a woman standing around saying, "I don't want to feed my baby," is ridiculous, I think. I can see it because I come from the privileged middle classes—I can see that working-class people who have to struggle more in their lives are better equipped to deal with life. In my experience, hardship is a great educator. I've been very, very lucky. I am aware of how people who have to struggle have learned how to deal with things and are very impressive. I'm full of admiration for them.

CL: You cast a black actor, Lisa Bonet, in *High Fidelity*, while in the novel the character she plays is a white American singer.

SF: My thinking was that for an Englishman to end up in bed with an American singer would be very, very exotic, like going to bed with a movie star—it would be exciting and quite startling. As you know, the novel was set in England, so it seemed to me, you'd have to do something comparable in an American setting. I didn't actually think we should get a black woman. I just saw Bonet in a film on a plane and thought she was wonderful. It seemed to me, it would have to be kind of special in that rather sort of adolescent way.

CL: You've worked twice with the actor John Cusack—in *High Fidelity* and earlier in *The Grifters* [1990]. He also co-wrote the screenplay for *High Fidelity*.

SF: The real work on that screenplay was done by D. V. Vincentis, who's just a really clever, bright guy.

CL: Cusack's narration is handled well. The device is made all the more interesting through its sustained use and the constant, graceful movement in and out of his direct address to the camera. Was this the idea of the screenwriter?

SF: It's possible I suggested that. I read the book when it was first published, and when I was asked to make the film, I read the book again, and I thought it had these wonderful bits. The original script I read used voice-over, and in slowly working with D.V., one of us said, "Oh, why doesn't he just talk to the camera." I thought he should be sitting in his room telling his story, and then D.V. wrote it as direct address. The best thing in the book, apart from the writing of the character Jack Black played, is the stream of consciousness, so actually it was an entirely pragmatic response to what was good in the material. Everyone was much more nervous about it than I was, especially John Cusack.

CL: *The Hi-Lo Country* [1998] also makes use of narration, but it functions more conventionally in that film as voice-over.

SF: You only put voice-over in when you need to tell things that you can't find another way of expressing.

CL: What are the rewards of working in a genre such as the western? Do you find yourself entering into a "dialogue" with the genre in an attempt to do something a little bit different with it?

SF: I really liked the rather unconventional novel by Max Evans on which *The Hi-Lo Country* is based, and I said, "I really like this book, but I don't know how you make films like this, so someone's going to have to teach me." Then Walon Green appeared and wrote the screenplay, and, indeed, he did teach me how to make it. I said, "Oh, I see, I'm making a western! There's a cattle drive in it! Oh, I see, it's like *Red River* [1948]." Well, I found all that very, very interesting. Not only did I then have to learn about the American west, but I had to learn about western films—why they're shot where they're shot. There's a book in which an Italian photographer had himself photographed at various locations where John Ford had shot his films, and, as you look at it, you slowly start to understand why Ford chose the locations he did and photographed them in the way that he did. So I found learning about the west and about westerns doubly interesting.

CL: How did you choose the particular locations in *The Hi-Lo Country*?

SF: A lot of it comes out of economic necessity. In fact, it was rather interesting because we went to Santa Fe—it's a New Mexico story—where there's a ranch near a western town, a location where other films were shot. But actually the film is set further north, right along the Colorado border. You can't stay there because there aren't any hotels, so to get to the country where I wanted to make the film is very difficult. Eventually I discovered a place called Las Vegas, New Mexico, which was just reachable and was much closer to the landscape that I wanted, so we filmed it there. Accepting the economic limitations—that the crew has to stay in hotels and all of that—I slowly started moving the film toward a much bleaker and more inhospitable landscape, which was nearer to what Max was writing about.

CL: It would seem you collaborated wonderfully with your cinematographer, Oliver Stapleton. The look of the film is very unlike that of the classic western, where the landscape is spread out before the characters, conveying a kind of endless possibility mingled with an underlying danger. In *The Hi-Lo Country*, you get a sense that the characters are enclosed by this landscape, even though it's expansive.

SF: That's what the novel is about. It's a Freudian novel.

CL: I felt the visual influence of Terrence Malick's *Days of Heaven* [1978] or *Badlands* [1973].

SF: Well, it's interesting that you say that, because actually the designer [Patricia Norris] had worked on *Days of Heaven*. So we were both engaged in working the area of rather old-fashioned characters.

CL: To me, *The Hi-Lo Country* and *High Fidelity* converge in interesting ways, especially in the characters of Big Boy and Rob, since both are hanging on to . . .

SF: . . . old fashioned values.

CL: Well…

SF: …something in themselves.

CL: But the external world defines that "something" for Big Boy in *The Hi-Lo Country*…

SF: …and Rob is obviously hanging on to his 'records' in *High Fidelity*. It's odd what happened to young iconoclasts when Mrs. Thatcher came along in England. We were the ones defending decency, honor, the BBC. I was the one saying to the BBC, "Look, you had these really good values, go back and honor those values." It's all daft. So, to your surprise, you think in your head you remain iconoclastic. But actually, it simply means that as the world has progressed, you've sort of diverged from it, and you find yourself actually deeply conservative. It's rather shocking. Ken Loach is a completely conservative filmmaker.

CL: Why do you say that?

SF: Because he doesn't approve of the changes that have taken place in society. He wishes that society could return to the way it was. In my book, that's called being a conservative. At the same time, he's also a social critic: "Society has changed in this way, and I don't approve of it; it was better when it had these values." In other words, change is a good thing and a bad thing—change is complicated. And both *The Hi-Lo Country* and *High Fidelity* are about change.

CL: You've spoken about happy endings—and *High Fidelity* certainly has one—but typically your happy endings aren't Hollywood happy endings.

SF: Well, you can't get "caught" having a happy ending, can you? I remember with *My Beautiful Laundrette*, saying that this film has to have a happy ending. In the last ten seconds, they flick water at each other. That's all that people wanted—that the characters get to laugh again and get to be friends again.

CL: You don't attempt to suggest that all problems are neatly resolved.

SF: There's a sort of moment where warmth reasserts itself. Or else the characters somehow transcend themselves, as in the ending of *The Grifters*, where they just shift to a sort of different scale.

CL: I wonder if it has something to do with what you've called "honoring your ignorance," which is a wonderful thing to say, because as long as one does that, one will always be curious and will, to some degree, escape cynicism.

SF: I survive on curiosity. I'm here [in Istanbul] because I've never been here before. I've remained curious. Orson Welles used to talk about remaining innocent.

CL: That's hard to do.

SF: Well, it's hard to do in Hollywood because the place is so cynical and so corrupt—it's wonderful! It's incredible! It's the most interesting place in the world! If you go to Hollywood, it's so incredibly interesting that, in an odd sort of way, you retain your innocence. Like Ulysses, who went past the Sirens and had himself tied to the mast so he couldn't get into the water himself, but still could hear the song. [Laughter.] I like to hear the Sirens' song. I'm glad I've been to Hollywood. You're with the most exciting grownups in the world! The world there is very wicked and exciting. I love all that. I can't get enough of it.

CL: You have the advantage of both being there and being professionally grounded elsewhere.

SF: It's easier for me.

CL: Earlier, you equated Hollywood films with expensive films, but there are those directors outside Hollywood, like Woody Allen, who manage to make small, relatively inexpensive films.

SF: That's what I've ended up doing. I made two big films, *Hero* [1992] and *Mary Reilly* [1996], which didn't work, and *Dangerous Liaisons* [1988], which did. Then I made three small films. I had a good time.

CL: *High Fidelity* was a small-scale Hollywood film . . .

SF: Yes, *The Grifters* itself was cheap; *The Hi-Lo Country* was cheap. So you learn your lessons—I can do this and I can't do that. It was while making studio films that I learned this, which is really odd because I thought I'd be really good at them. But I hadn't a clue.

CL: What was it that had happened or that surprised you?

SF: I don't know. I can't really talk about those films. I admired Dustin Hoffman in *Hero* and Julia Roberts in *Mary Reilly* enormously. I don't know what happened, in truth. But I realized there are things you have here that I don't understand, that I just don't know about. To me, Dustin and Julia were very good actors, but the audience had complicated histories with them and expectations, which I had no capacity to fulfill at all. When you turn out a Daniel Day-Lewis in *My Beautiful Laundrette*—well, nobody knew who he was until that moment. Once you deal with an audience who regularly see these actors, it's a completely different game. I couldn't fault either Dustin or Julia. There were things going on that were beyond my comprehension, and I was literally out of my depth. The people I admire are the people who do it week after week—bringing in big audiences. They're tremendous; they're really clever; they can do something I can't do.

CL: The Valerie Martin novel on which *Mary Reilly* is based presents a fascinating psychological study of the characters. Mary Reilly is a young servant, abused by her father, a man who is linked with Mr. Hyde in the story. She finds herself drawn to and falls in love with her master, Dr. Jekyll, whose struggles are not entirely different from her own and who likewise is drawn to Mary's innocence and her honesty.

SF: The situation is so interesting. I remember asking Valerie Martin what she would like the audience to think after reading the book, and she said, "Well, maybe that she'd be not quite as good a maid." It's such a wonderful idea, and then I think she got scared. She created a situation that she couldn't quite get hold of.

CL: But she created it.

SF: Yes, well, Robert Louis Stephenson created it.

CL: It's a film I think you should remake—just as Hitchcock remade *The Man Who Knew Too Much* [1956].

SF: I should remake it very, very cheaply. It should have been a very cheap film. I thought this situation is the most interesting thing in the world. I don't know what happened.

CL: You've spoken about the directors Lindsay Anderson and Karel Reisz as your mentors.

SF: I worked with them and both, in their ways, were remarkable. In a way, what they taught me most about was life—how to express ideas, that there was a connection between your work and your life.

CL: In a sense, you could almost place your various films in juxtaposition and see a tapestry (perhaps not visually, since you work in a variety of genres) revealing the social and political landscape of the late twentieth and early twenty-first centuries in England and America.

SF: I began by saying that the BBC took the responsibility of giving an account of what it was like to be alive in England at a certain time, and that's how we grew up making films. That there are consistency and coherence in my work doesn't surprise me at all. The fact that the films are set in New Mexico or Ireland or anywhere else is just incidental.

CL: Many of your characters behave with a level of cynicism, yet the films themselves never become cynical.

SF: Well, Mrs. Thatcher used to talk about cynicism. It always seemed to me that she was a real cynic. She was a completely cynical woman about the world—and we were rather naïve in her presence—but she would take every opportunity to describe other people as cynical. Now, the truth is, like everybody in the world, I find cynical characters enormously entertaining, and they're a source of tremendous drama, but that doesn't mean you endorse what they do. Finally, in *Dangerous Liaisons*, John Malkovich falls in love, which I'd say is rather naïve and touching and sort of adolescent, like something out of *Grease* [1978].

CL: But at the same time it doesn't seem simplistic or forced.

SF: That seems to me what the world is like. The world is very complicated, so you deal with the complexity of the world, and at the same time there are rather simple things. In my films—it's very hard for me to talk about this—I think life is generally shown to be quite difficult. And for some reason, the films that are successful are those in which people win, and the films that are unsuccessful are those in which they're defeated. I'm not sure, but I think that's what I formulated about a week ago! [Laughs.]

Don't you find life tough? I do. And I'm very fortunate, so if I find life difficult, what about other people? So, yes, I think the world is a tough place and living with other people is a difficult thing and living in families is a difficult thing and growing up is a difficult thing and getting a job is a difficult thing, and not running out and shooting people is difficult—it's very difficult not to run amok. So I find life very difficult. At the same time, I'm astonished that people keep going. I'm astonished that *I* keep going. I don't plan it—I'm just endlessly amazed.

Bibliography

Barr, Charles, and Stephen Frears. *Typically British: A Personal History of British Cinema*. London: British Film Institute, 1995.

Brill, Lesley. *The Ironic Filmmaking of Stephen Frears*. New York: Bloomsbury, 2016.

Geraghty, Christine. *My Beautiful Laundrette*: The British Film Guide. London: I. B. Tauris, 2005.

Hacker, Jonathan, and David Price. *Take 10: Contemporary British Film Directors*. Oxford, U.K.: Oxford University Press, 1991.

Kureishi, Hanif. *Sammy and Rosie Get Laid*. London: Penguin, 1988.

Michael Powell

Peeping Tom

The Life and Death of Colonel Blimp

Carol Reed

The Third Man

The Third Man

David Lean

A Passage to India

A Passage to India

Charles Crichton

The Lavender Hill Mob

Hue and Cry

Lindsay Anderson

If . . .

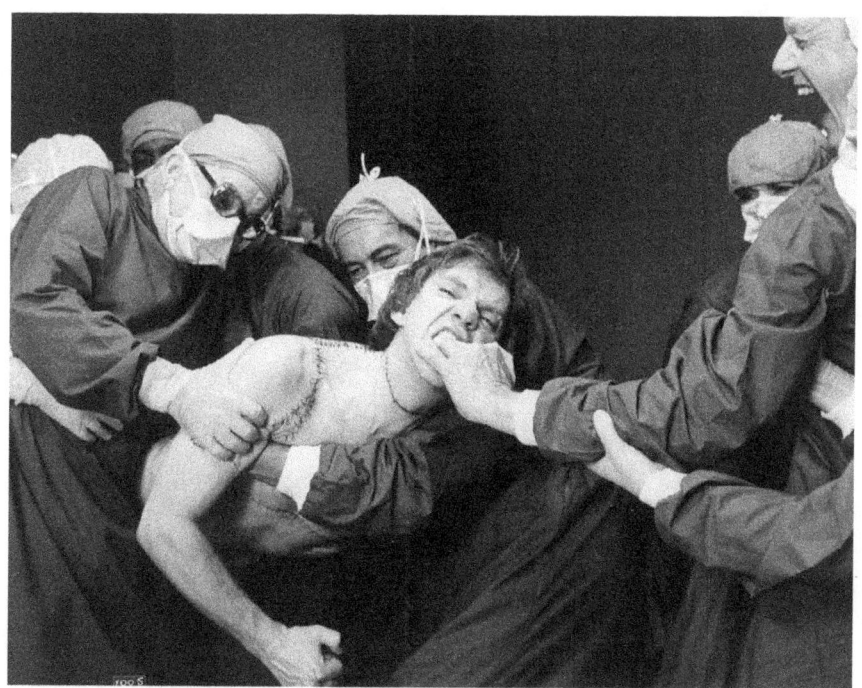
Britannia Hospital

Karel Reisz

The French Lieutenant's Woman

Saturday Night and Sunday Morning

John Schlesinger

A Kind of Loving

Far From the Madding Crowd

Ken Russell

Women in Love

The Music Lovers

Tony Richardson

The Entertainer

A Taste of Honey

Nicolas Roeg

Performance

Walkabout

Ken Loach

Kes

Riff-Raff

Stephen Frears

My Beautiful Laundrette

Dirty Pretty Things

Peter Greenaway

The Cook, The Thief, His Wife, and Her Lover

The Tulse Luper Suitcases

Mike Leigh

Secrets and Lies

Bleak Moments

Terence Davies

Distant Voices, Still Lives

The Long Day Closes

Pawel Pawlikowski

My Summer of Love

Last Resort

Kenneth Branagh

Henry V

Hamlet

Joseph Losey

The Servant

The Go-Between

James Ivory

Howards End

Howards End

Richard Lester

A Hard Day's Night

The Knack

"Peter Greenaway Holds Court: An Interview at the Venice Film Festival," by Karin Badt. From *Film Criticism*. 29.2 (Winter 2004-05): 53-66.

Peter Greenaway, by some accounts, represents outmoded filmmaking, and yet he holds forth, to all who will listen—much in the style of Gloria Swanson's famous line, "I'm big, it's the pictures that have gotten small"—that cinema today is outmoded: it has become, he argues, mere illustration of text and does not explore its visual potential as a peculiar seventh art. Digital filmmaking, however, as exemplified by his own most recent film, *The Tulse Luper Suitcases* (2004), allows for experiments in time, sequence, and action, and calls into question "storytelling" as only the variegated technology of contemporary cinema can.

Since the beginning of his career in the 1960s, Greenaway has been obsessed with storytelling. All of his films, from his short experimental meditation *Intervals* (1969) to the celebrated *Draughtsman's Contract* (1982) to the video-*glitz Pillow Book* (1996), have summoned viewers' attention to the artifice of the story, using tricks such as numbers, maps, and taxonomy to order sequences arbitrarily. Lately, though, the erstwhile painter has taken this directive to the nth degree. *The Tulse Luper Suitcases*, the third and final episode of a three-part "story," seems to overthrow master narrative altogether, at the risk of alienating those audiences who may long for a modicum of narrative convention. *The Tulse Luper Suitcases* is the open narrative of one man from the 1920s onward, as he examines the contents of ninety-two suitcases. A *tour-de-force* of superimposed images, split screens, and frames-within-the-frame, it literally leaves the story up for grabs.

This pronounced theoretical pertinacity may be the reason why Greenaway is no longer the feted wonder among movie critics, who otherwise begrudgingly admire his genius. Greenaway's masterpiece, *The Cook, The Thief, His Wife, and Her Lover* (1989), the film that launched his international success, did have a structuring story.

While playing with arbitrary narrative codes—the plot was structured as eight sections of a menu; the settings were color-coordinated like squares on a gameboard; and the pastiche of eras gripped the eye as a patchwork of costume, painting, and furniture—the film ultimately held the viewer with conventional emotional identification. We wondered about the wife and her lover, and what the thief would do to both. The story even satisfied our Western urge for epic narrative by ending with an actual cannibalistic sacrifice, at once a Girardian catharsis of story and history.

But now with *The Tulse Luper Suitcases*, Greenaway's most experimental film to date, it is virtually impossible for a spectator to identify with any one story, as no story—and there are dozens told—is ever completed. All begin, and none end, and at the conclusion we find out that Tulse Luper, the protagonist, does not even exist: he is a figment of the imagination. Greenaway has even engineered a website for the movie to be played as a game, where viewers can enter in and out at will, using the full potential of cinema to create a dialogue between image-maker and image-consumer. "Who ultimately is the creator, or the created? says Greenaway. Or, to cite Greenaway's favorite metaphor: "Who is the prisoner and who the prison keeper?"

A more market-oriented question is: who will play? Does this postmodern enterprise hold any allure for today's viewer, intellectual or not, at a time when—as a quick review of favored films reveals—we long for more stories, more characters, more grounding, more realism (or illusions thereof); at a time when documentaries and "mastered" attempts at truth (à la Michael Moore) are doing almost as well as Hollywood fictions or political campaigns, and when we ask not for language games and self-consciousness but for values, direction, and character? Even Greenaway's cohorts in experimental narrative—David Cronenberg and Todd Solondz, for example—keep conventions such as character at the fore to allow the illusion of a meaningful experience. Greenaway seems to be one of the few experimentalists continuing the Hollis Frampton ideals of the 1960s, pure to form.

And yet Greenaway and his poststructuralist enterprise may not be as out of the loop as it might seem. The contemporary viewer—

the consumer of story, not storytelling—may be impelled to play this newest clever language game, the hodgepodge of video frames that is *The Tulse Luper Suitcases*, once he or she knows that Tulse Luper is indeed a real character after all: he is Peter Greenaway himself. *The Tulse Luper Suitcases* is Greenaway's own story—in the making and the unmaking—as well as the history of his own films: a history, the postmodern director can be pressed to admit, that has even more than some truth to it.

Karin Badt conducted this interview on the terrace of the Excelsior Hotel in Lido, Italy, on September 10, 2004, following the Venice Film Festival screening of *The Tulse Luper Suitcases* (whose three parts were condensed into a single version in 2005, and which itself was succeeded by such Greenaway films as *Nightwatching* [2007], about Rembrandt, and *Eisenstein in Guanajuato* [2015], about the noted Soviet filmmaker).

Karin Badt: *The Tulse Luper Suitcases* [2004] plays with macrohistories: the history of the twentieth century around the world. But it also touches on your own history, with allusions to your own films, such as *The Belly of an Architect* [1987], *The Cook, The Thief, His Wife, and Her Lover* [1989], and an early film of yours like *Intervals* [1969]. Are you telling your own story as well?

Peter Greenaway: Yes, you are right: there are pieces of quite open autobiography in this film. Some of those life experiences in the film—such as ten-year-old Tulse jumping over a garden wall to write his name, making a stain on the wall to prove he has been there, in a small town in the southwest of the U.K.—that's me, it really happened to me. There are other pieces of autobiographical apparatus that are buried so deep that I almost can't see them anymore. But it's a professional autobiography, too. I'm crediting Tulse Luper with movies that are of course mine as well. So I've used that as an apparatus to make a review of all my work: about 400 films, a great number of films to get into seven hours. There are references to practically everything I've ever made, in terms of expositions and books. Also, we are devising this as an interactive CD-DVD activity; you can use the DVD to get the whole of *The Belly of an Architect* or to get the whole of the twenty-five short films that I have made.

So in a sense, the film as you saw it is the beginning of a DVD apparatus, in which can circulate all the other material.

KB: Does Tulse go through an evolution himself in the story, or are these just fragments of stories?

PG: There is a continuum. It's maybe that Don Quixote journey, that sort of James Joyce *Ulysses* journey, and that's not only a physical and geographical journey; it's also a journey to wisdom, which is so much a part of the cinema experience, like most tales from nineteenth-century literature. We have constructed sixteen episodes, but ideally since my numerological fetish is ninety-two—because ninety-two is the atomic number of uranium, and these are the Uranium years, the years in which one element affected the world like no other element—Tulse will live ninety-two years, and ideally when we finish this project, there will be ninety-two episodes. For example, the year 1960 is not yet represented. We have deliberately created a structure whereby even after the final film, we can still put more bricks in the wall.

My film is very obsessive about storytelling. It ends up as a parallel to the notion of the most famous storyteller of all time, Scheherazade, who had to tell stories in order to live. Maybe this is the definition of a filmmaker, of course, as well. So I try to tell you a story—story, story, story, story—on a one-to-one basis, dramatized, text to the screen.

One of my big anxieties is that I feel we should have an image-based cinema, and we basically have a text-based cinema. We have seen a cinema that demands a very low denominator of human experience between audience and screen. The two big box-office success stories are *Harry Potter* [series starting in 2001] and *Lord of the Rings* [series starting in 2001], but they are really books: they are illustrated texts. Essentially it's recorded theater; it's not cinema, cinema. So on this notion that if it itches, you should scratch it, and it worries me, I throw text at you all the time, all the time, to make a demonstration of how we have a text-based situation in education in our culture.

The first film of *The Tulse Luper Staircases* was very much about actors, auditions; the second one was about locations, giving you places; the third one is about storytelling. These are the three pillars of cinema, are they not—the actor, the location, and the story? This final film is like a snake eating its own tail, like two bookends that are the same, and you end up with the terrible, awful truth that what you have been watching for seven hours is a total fiction, because it never ever existed, which is a typical postmodern notion of the author as liar, the author as fabulist, the author as magician, the author as the great pretender.

And there are other things. There is no such thing as history; there are only historians. When is a jailer a prisoner, and when is a prisoner a jailer? We're also all jailers, and we are also all prisoners. Do we need the prisons? Probably we do, because otherwise we'll fall off the edge and never know where we are.

KB: When you become very conceptual about using storytelling to tell stories that ultimately have multiple meanings that refer back to the storyteller—the history, as recounted by the historian, then doesn't exist—the concepts themselves risk imploding, becoming valueless. But in another interview, you said you are actually obsessed with eros and death—with real topics. Death is a very present reality, an obsession, in your movies. So I was wondering, outside of your movies, what do you really think about death?

PG: Once upon a time you could have said that the only two non-negotiable events are sex and death. We can abrogate our sexual choices much more in the twenty-first century than we have ever been able to do before, and with things like contraception, we can make decisions about sexual activity that our fathers and forefathers could not have done. I suppose in some ways that death is negotiable with medicine, that there is a way in which you can keep people alive longer artificially, so some of the areas are becoming a bit grayer. But ultimately eros and thanatos, the beginning and end, are the most important things. I would argue that there are really only two interesting subject matters: one is sex, and the other is death.

KB: And the word "immortality": what does it mean to you?

PG: Well, I am a Darwinist. I have no belief in afterlife, no belief in reincarnation; I have no belief in moral systems about good and evil. We are basically Darwinian animals, so these are all moral constructs we invent for our own comfort and convenience. I suppose cultural immortality, is that possible? We can live on in our work. Picasso very famously said that we all need to leave a stain on the wall. And how does Tulse Luper begin, by writing his name: I have been here. So it's that gesture that every cultural practitioner wants to perform.

KB: What about sensuality? Your words are very sensual, in your texts for example, as in your *Pillow Book* [1996]. How does sensuality fit into your code? You have this idea of knowledge. But sensuality is a different order of things from knowledge and catalogues.

PG: Well, you know, I am interested in the physical world. I was trained as a painter, as a landscape painter, and I take great delight in the physical world, and I enjoy making the construct. I am very, very happy indeed when I am allowed to express ideas in images; those images could be on a canvas, or on a stage, or on an opera stage. There is just a great delight in the simple phenomenology of what we are capable of, what we are capable of looking at. And we live in a deeply sensuous world, and I think if we respect cinema we should let cinema be part of that phenomenon.

KB: You once talked about the importance of perspective in the Renaissance. What do you think your recent films add to perspective? What do they actually make us see? How do they change our vision? They ask us to see, but what do we see? How does it change what we see, the way you make your films?

PG: If I can take one example: cubism was invented by Picasso, Braque, and Klee, probably in the 1910s, in the south of France, and in a way it's been a great problem to jump over the concept of cubism. Most people are happy with impressionism, but suddenly in cubism they get lost. Cubism is a philosophical concept, which means you can see both sides of the wall at the same time. Now we are developing technologies where, in a curious way, that can happen. My use of multiple frames, for example: I give you the wide shot. a medium shot, and a close-up all the time. I give you the past and the present and the future simultaneously. Sometimes you notice that we have the actors giving you the performance twice over, and sometimes you can hear two different voices, giving a slightly different opinion about the notions of what I want to tell you about. For I am aiming after a multifarious cinema that gets away from a single event and a single time, with a single opinion. I am taking cubism out of the rather rarefied climate of the painting from the 1910s and am now making it part of a public medium like cinema.

KB: I still ask: why? For example, when I am looking at a double frame of two people in bed on the bottom and two people in bed on the top, and we're talking about different times as well, it provokes me to think about different times and different perspectives—but after that, I ask where do I go from there?

PG: Well, again it underlies what we have been saying. First of all, non-simultaneity of activity. I give two versions, done by two different actors, with basically the same dialogue, and how do they interpret it? Do they behave as lovers, or as eighteen-year-long married couples with great problems about childbearing? And so there's no singular truth, there are multiple truths. I'd like to give you four visions, or ten versions, but again there is a limit on the screen to what you can take in. So again in my answer to your question: multiplicity, non-singularity of event.

KB: Does digital cinema help your multiplicity of image?

PG: Absolutely. In the old-fashioned cellular cinema, it's not impossible to do, but it's very clumsy. I would have had to make two films and join them in a laboratory, and they would never have had that hands-on capacity—how I can use one image to echo another, so you get one character saying a word, and almost immediately it's seconded by another one. I could never do that before. I couldn't have made this film ten years ago, because the technology did not exist.

If you take the problem of language, we have the problem of translation; people used to say that cinema is an international medium, but it's not true, it's just not true. As soon as you use text, whether it's spoken or written, you come into areas of ambiguity and doublethink and in this film what was quite amusing, is we have invented a translator who can't translate, so we have to translate for him, so you get multiple lines of meaning and, often, a deep misunderstanding. Have you read Umberto Eco's work on translation, that there is no such thing as translation: everything is a negotiated half-truth, an act of betrayal? So again my film is a dissertation about the problems of translation.

KB: So your multiplicity of images is also a form of translation?

PG: What is a film itself? It is again a form of translation of human experiences, again very subjectively organized. We put the animation with the talking head with the television film with the drama, old-fashioned drama and new drama, so you bring all types of ways to tell stories all together, so what is actually happening in content is manifested by its own form and metaphor.

KB: Isn't your film ultimately a meditation on creativity, on Icarus playing with games, with creating meaning from a multiplicity of cultural references?

PG: I suppose so. I have to whisper this because it is so ambitious; it's my attempt to cinematically make James Joyce's *Ulysses* [1922]. Joyce collected all the narrative tropes that were known in the Western world and put them all together in one book. In order to make them really work, to understand the problems of translation and communication, he had to invent a whole brand-new language.

KB: Yet Joyce had a religious concept of grace that you would not agree with . . .

PG: A lot of my characters have the initials LB, which is referring to the major figure of James Joyce's *Ulysses*. Although *Ulysses* may be the least read novel of the twentieth century, it is probably the most important.

KB: But you also said that your own movie is a voyage towards wisdom. Is there a concrete wisdom beyond the joy and creativity of playing with culturally encyclopedic possibilities? Is there a wisdom or an ethics? A point to your films?

PG: Outside my house in Amsterdam, I have a statue of Descartes, who is supposed to be a Frenchman although he spent thirty years in Holland, so in some ways he is very, very Dutch, and the Dutch are very, very practical people, and Descartes famously said "Know thyself." And I think that is the point of the notion of wisdom. And Tulse Luper eventually accepts entirely the prison he has bought into. We are all imprisoned, not necessarily in a prison of locked doors, but a prison of ambition, of lust, of money, of desire to make a board game. But like children, we all need boundaries and edges, because chaos is impossible to deal with. And the most problematic phenomenon is liberty. Most people don't know how to use liberty at all, so it is quite wise of us sometimes, to put ourselves in prison. I often meet people who say, "if only I were in prison, wouldn't it do me good because I could really write that novel I always promised myself to write?"

KB: A few more questions about your evolution. You had the idea for *Tulse Luper* thirty years ago, I think, in one of your short films called *Vertical Lists* [1976]. What was it then?

PG: A long, long time ago, I was interested in polyglot figures, people like John Cage and Marcel Duchamp and Buckminster Fuller, who somehow managed to be generalists and not specialists, and put all the imagery together. So I simply invented this man to be in some sense an alter ego, in that sense of how small children create a companion in order to interact with the world, the small child who invents a friend at the breakfast table. And eventually, this man was Tulse Luper. I tried to find a name that had never been heard before, but was very English, for as soon as you name a character, it comes with baggage. Then I invented his wife, and his mistress and his friends, and his academic enemies, and we made a big movie called *The Falls* [1980], three-and-one-half hours long, and there are ninety-two people—we're back to ninety-two—and they have all been picked out of a directory, and all their names begin with FA double-LL. And the film discusses their predicament in face of a phenomenon called the VUE, a pun on view, which stands for the Violent Unknown Event.

This was made in the late 1970s, so theories of the end of the world and notions of deterrents and the dropping of the bomb were very much in the air. So the picture consisted of ninety-two different ways the world could end. But it was also interested in the Icarus theme, the great desire of all societies to fly; the famous one is the Greek version, but I think every society in the world historically and geographically has had a mythology of personalized flight. So the film had to do with that desire to fly, which is never going to happen—we are never going to sprout wings. And the fact is that helicopters, Concordes, and jets are never going to satisfy this desire. So this was a big encyclopedic movie about people who wanted to fly who were punished for the arrogance of wanting to fly. But it was also ninety-two different ways to make a movie, and ninety-two different ways the world would end. And that's really when this family of people came together, and then I left them and became interested in other concerns: for example, baroque imagery and notions of Catholicism and ideas about the representation of history. But now I have come back to the subject of *The Falls* again.

KB: Why ninety-two, the element of uranium? Is this about the nuclear age?

PG: I am a uranium baby. All my political and social life has been predicated on the threat of the bomb: I was born in 1942, and three years later they dropped the bomb on Hiroshima. And politically, as we all were when we were much younger, I was anti-Vietnam, ban the bomb, all that sort of phenomenon, so my social and political history has run parallel to the age of uranium: Hiroshima, to the Cold War, to the bringing down of the Berlin Wall. So the whole *Tulse Luper* project is sort of a reworked autobiography. Then there are all these quite big subject matters we talk about: the Holocaust and anti-Semitism, and racism and fascism and totalitarianism, because again these make up the big history of the twentieth century.

KB: And your politics? I noted a subtle critique of the bourgeoisie in *The Cook, The Thief, His Wife, and Her Lover*, and perhaps even of the England of that time.

PG: It was very anti-Thatcher: Mrs. Thatcher believed that things had a value only if you could ring them up on a cash register. There is a very significant moment in *The Cook, The Thief, His Wife, and Her Lover* when a man picks up a book and says, "Can this book make money," as if there were only currency, which is an absurd and ridiculous situation. But that was an era of great philistinism and cultural vulgarity, so I deliberately put all those pretensions together in that restaurant.

KB: And the French Revolution: how does that work into the fabric?

PG: Well again, that revolution is the great beginning of modern history, an incredibly volatile political examination of swinging from left to right—an exemplum of that kind of violence, which again in some sense in a European context came back again in the 1980s, that includes a violent polarization of political opinion.

KB: And politics now?

PG: Well, now there has been a curiously ... maybe I ought to be careful, because since 9/11, there has been a new politicization, which again for me is too narrowly based and deeply hypocritical. I suppose throughout the 1990s, we had a deeply apolitical generation, where people just weren't interested; they were interested in bourgeois pursuits and making lots of money and paying the mortgage. I think re-politicization, certainly of young people, is very important. But I am interested in aesthetics now and not politics.

KB: Do you connect aesthetics with ethical action?

PG: Absolutely. All the philosophers of the last fifty years in France have said that politics and ethics and aesthetics are all closely connected.

KB: So how do you want to affect your viewers?

PG: My cinema is a celebration of the world. I want to celebrate and make representations that are positive. I want to engage in all the dialogues of representation, which are now part of the cinematic phenomenon.

This film and my entire cinema are an enormous celebration of life—its events, its materials, its colors, its numerical systems, its scientific hypotheses. Some people think that my subject matter is very negative because I talk about death, about putrefaction, about female sexual humiliation, but in the end I am making no judgment because I don't believe in good and evil. Again, I am a Darwinist; I believe in the idea that we are animals with invented moral codes that are only there for our own convenience, historically and geographically. But I think all my films celebrate the sheer multiplicity and excitement of simply being alive. That's the base line.

KB: A personal question. Wasn't your father an ornithologist?

PG: He was, yes.

KB: Does that affect your way of filming?

PG: I'm sure it does. I'm not always sure, however, that psychological investigation will tell you everything about the truth.

KB: This is not psychological.

PG: No, but I'm dubious, because I can explain the relationship with my father in a classic Oedipal, antagonistic sense. I am the oldest son. And he was an ornithologist. He came from a background of naturalists and horticulturalists with a great love for—I don't think you can use the word ecology, a contemporary word—but I learned a lot about natural history from him, and the subject of his main interest, his focus in natural history, was ornithology. And I grew up as a small boy thinking that everybody could tell the difference between a greater black back stripe and a red shank, and I found that nobody could. It's a very obscure thing. But then again, I could never tell the difference between a Rolls Royce and a Bugatti, so it's all about specialized knowledge. And just as I came of an age that is classic—to be able to open a dialogue with my father, whom I could never speak to—he died. So I think my first four or five films are all my attempt to conduct a dialogue with my absent father.

KB: For example, which film?

PG: Well, for instance, if you take *The Falls*, which I have just talked about, or *A Walk Through H* [1978], which is about the reincarnation of an ornithologist, I wanted to try to provide my father with a series of ornithological maps so that he could go wherever he wanted to go. He was dead, of course, so it was irrelevant; it was my attempt to reconstruct his life. And if you have seen *The Cook, The Thief, His Wife, and Her Lover*, the actor played by Michael Gambon is the black side of who my father was, with his philistinism, his anti-Semitism, and all those other things. I loved my dad, but he had terrible political opinions, so I still had to grope with that.

KB: So the movie dialogues with him as a character ...

PG: Yes. And if you've ever seen *The Draughtsman's Contract* [1982], that was the positive but arrogantly innocent side of him, so there is often a revisiting of that unspoken dialogue that I should have had with my father.

KB: In terms of the great narratives of the twentieth century, such as psychoanalysis—well, you don't have that one in your films. You have great themes—such as eros and death—and Biblical narratives, with apples, but you don't have issues with Freud.

PG: Well, not directly, but if you think of the subject matter, *The Cook, The Thief, His Wife, and Her Lover* is about cannibalism: eat thyself, take me, this is my body, and that is Freudian ...

KB: Yes, Freud's *Totem and Taboo* [1913].

PG: And if you take things like *Drowning by Numbers* [1988], it's very Jungian, this examination of male potency and female impotency; the film's about gender preferences; it's about childhood memories that go pre-Freud, back to Wordsworth: give me the child and I'll give you the man. So I think all those things are, if not at the top of my agenda, then they at least flesh out the soup and make it thicker.

KB: What about anthropology and the idea of sacrifice?

PG: Again, cannibalism is part of that phenomenon. I am a profound Darwinian, as I've said, and I think Darwin is the most important scientist that the world has ever known.

KB: Why?

PG: Because he finally made us humble. All religions try to give us enormous amounts of vanity: they prop us up; they find excuses for our bad behavior. But Darwin finally said, look, we are animals; we have evolved over deep time; and if you think a zebra has a soul, how dare you?

KB: But Darwin doesn't account for mystery.

PG: Nothing does, though. Nothing can. There are the unanswerable three questions: Why are we here, where are we going, and what's it all about? Nobody has ever answered them. Darwin gets the closest possible to understanding why we are here, and how we got here. But even Darwin ultimately can't answer those three questions.

KB: So you never turned to the mystics?

PG: I find that mysticism is a sloppy way to do business. I am deeply rationalist. I am very Apollonian. I believe in scientific inquiry. I hate anything to do with the notion of Russian mysticism; I am against mysticism.

KB: And the movie directors you like?

PG: They would be rationalists. They would be people like Godard. I grew up with these people. I went over to Paris to see their movies as they came out. My great French hero would be the intellectual of the group, Alain Resnais. But after that, I would turn to American underground directors, probably people you've never heard of, such as Hollis Frampton, a really superb intellectual of the movement who made some truly profound statements about cinema...

KB: And space.

PG: And about space and all those sorts of notions. My cinema lies somewhere between Alain Resnais and Hollis Frampton.

KB: What about people today, young directors such as David Cronenberg?

PG: David Cronenberg has degenerated into a maker of sensationalist, illustrated novels. His fascinations are superficial. I do have an admiration for the fact that he attempts to hunt down difficult subject matter. I admire and respect David Lynch because he somehow beat the system, and his movies are of great fascination to me. But I don't think he is interested in movie form and language as I am. He has become a pasticher and hasn't developed. Lynch basically makes the same movies over and over again. I would love to have made *Blue Velvet* [1986], however, which I thought was an extraordinary movie.

It would be difficult to find anybody else who's interested in the same sort of things as I am. Can you think of anybody else who is interested in film language *per se*? That is important for me, because they say that in the twenty-first century, content has atrophied. To wit: who is Potiphar's wife? I am sure you won't be able to tell me.

KB: Who?

PG: Exactly. Rembrandt painted Potiphar's wife thirty-two times, I believe, from the 1630s to the 1650s. The content is gone. It doesn't mean we don't understand Rembrandt, but the content is gone, so we are left with the language. So the language becomes the content.

KB: There was an experimental film shown here at the festival, by Todd Solondz, with one character played by six different people.

PG: That's right, and I think Bill Viola has ventured into that area as well, so there is a way in which the language has now become content. And I think this is very, very important, for we need to deal with the tropes and paradigms of the language before we can understand the content.

KB: In terms of writers, novelists today, are there any you admire?

PG: I grew up with Jorge Luis Borges and all his disciples, Italo Calvino, etc. I am not very interested in the parochial English novel, which I think is boring and too narrow and local. All the great

American writers of the 1960s and 1970s are part of my formative background. A lot of what used to be called colonial English writing I still think is interesting. But there's nobody in particular, I think, who really stands out. You tend to travel along with the cultural baggage of your formative years—I think we all do that. Painting and photography are probably very influential on me.

KB: And architecture too?

PG: Architecture, certainly. I think architecture is the big success story of the post-Second World War period.

KB: Apropos of architecture: you once said that symmetrical frames in film are appalling for an audience. Do you use them on purpose?

PG: It's to draw attention to the artificiality of the image. The Bellinis—Gentile and Giovanni Bellini lived not so very far from here—were the masters of the secular *conversazioni*: the notion of the central image and the symmetry of the picture plane. And all these tropes are very important to me because I want to show you that you're only watching a film.

KB: But is it you who said that there is no such thing as symmetry in nature?

PG: Indeed.

KB: Is that true? When I look at an image, I can see it symmetrically if I choose to.

PG: Yes, but you'll find that the asymmetry is more important than the symmetry. Take the example of the human face: one side of the human face is not a mirror of the other.

KB: One of my students, when asked to pick his favorite movie from our class, picked yours, saying, "I didn't think you could do that in movies."

PG: Well, that's nice, because I am a great believer in legitimizers. And legitimizers are so important. You know, it was Alain Resnais who told me that you can be an intellectual in the cinema; he legitimized that. And Duchamp said that you can utilize the negative in art, so *he* legitimized *that*. And I am grateful to be a legitimizer for somebody else. Thank you.

Bibliography

Denham, Laura. *The Films of Peter Greenaway*. London: Minerva, 1993.

Elliott, Bridget, and Anthony Purdy. *Peter Greenaway: Architecture and Allegory*. Chichester, U.K.: Academy Editions, 1997.

Keesey, Douglas. *The Films of Peter Greenaway: Sex, Death, and Provocation*. Jefferson, N.C.: McFarland, 2006.

Lawrence, Amy. *The Films of Peter Greenaway*. New York: Cambridge University Press, 1997.

Willoquet-Maricondi, Paula, and Mary Alemany-Galway. *Peter Greenaway's Postmodern/Poststructuralist Cinema*. Rev. ed. Lanham, Md.: Scarecrow Press, 2008.

Woods, Alan. *Being Naked, Playing Dead: The Art of Peter Greenaway*. Manchester, U.K.: Manchester University Press, 1996.

"'Making People Think Is What It's All About': Mike Leigh and the Cinema of Subversion: An Interview" (2007-08), by R. J. Cardullo. From *Cinema Journal*, 50.1 (Fall 2010): 1-18; and from *Literature/Film Quarterly*, 39.1 (2011): 14-29.

Born in 1943 in Salford, Lancashire, Mike Leigh began his career as an actor, theater director, and playwright before moving into television and, eventually, film. After more than a decade of writing and directing for British television (*Nuts in May* [1976], *Abigail's Party* [1977], *Four Days in July* [1985], and other works), he became known to a wide international audience with *Life Is Sweet* (1990). Now, after more than three decades and over twenty films, Leigh has earned himself an international reputation for his bracing, bittersweet dramas about quotidian British life. In a generally bleak artistic landscape, he stands out importantly as someone who has attempted to make complicated and sensitive—and socially engaged—films about middle- and working-class England. Moreover, despite their perpetually gray English skies, pasty-skinned protagonists, and often minimalist plotlines, his movies appeal to a broad audience.

Leigh's greatest box office success to date has been *Secrets and Lies* (1996), the story of a white woman who comes face to face with the half-black daughter she gave up for adoption years earlier. *Naked* (1993) exposes the destitute and painful realities of urban life with its tale about a mixed-up drifter's misadventures in London, while the early *Bleak Moments* (1971) concerns the financial struggles of—and awkward relationships among—a group of young, socially isolated city-dwellers. In *Topsy-Turvy* (2000), the filmmaker examined the artistic-theatrical process in a work about the Victorian lyricist-composer team of Gilbert and Sullivan. In *Vera Drake* (2004), he treated the problem of illegal abortions in the 1950s. And Leigh's next film was the perennially optimistic *Happy-Go-Lucky* (2008), about a woman who sees the bright side of life even when presented with darkness. He followed this picture with the similarly comic-dramatic *Another Year* (2010), then turned to the artistic process once again with the biopic *Mr. Turner* (2014), about the British painter J. M. W. Turner.

Instead of coming to rehearse and shoot a film with a prewritten script, Leigh works closely and intensively with all his actors—from the main roles to bit parts—developing characters, scenarios, and dialogue over months of solo and group improvisations to build a finalized screenplay. Actors seem to love the director's way of involving them so integrally in the process. "I first worked with Mike Leigh in 1980," Brenda Blethyn of *Secrets and Lies* has said. "He likes you to invent the whole history of the character, and I've done it ever since." His process has been the constant approach that has allowed Leigh to craft some of the most extraordinary and seminal films of British cinema.

A vociferous supporter of the British film industry, the director, unlike many of his British filmmaking colleagues, hasn't been lured to Hollywood. "Given the choice of Hollywood or poking steel pins in my eyes, I'd prefer steel pins," Leigh once remarked. He continues to make movies in the U.K., and, in recent years, has started writing for the stage again. *Two Thousand Years* (2005), a play exploring Leigh's Jewish roots, received its world première at London's National Theatre. What makes Mike Leigh's films unique, even in Britain, is his gift for constructing an often humorously bleak and desperate world filled with characters whose comic behavior springs from their essence as human beings. The comedy connects to their genuine agony and joy, and therefore the films almost never contain scenes designed to just to get easy laughs. Indeed, Leigh's trademark is his almost preternatural gift for capturing, with emotional honesty, complex behavior.

As Leigh likes to note, he is anything but a naturalist. He refers to his love of circus, vaudeville, and the music hall. His films do not imitate everyday human activity, nor do his characters repeat ordinary conversation. The events and dialogue are deliberately heightened, as part of an effort to get behind the reality of day-to-day life. The exaggerated, sometimes grotesquely exaggerated, goings-on take their place in a certain British tradition, however. André

Breton once said something to the effect that there was no need for a surrealist movement in England because life and art there were already surreal enough. Just so, one of Leigh's most interesting features as a film writer and director has been his willingness to bite into reality at a somewhat different angle from both the British "neorealists" of the early 1960s and the director Ken Loach, with his working-class portrayals along the lines of "docudrama" and the "kitchen sink" school.

That Leigh's film career has had its share of ups and downs, veering occasionally toward sentimentality and occasionally toward condescension, owes much to the unfavorable climate in which he has had to work. The Thatcherite counteroffensive against the working class and the protracted rightward lurch of the Labour Party, as well as the British trade unions, have framed the past several decades. The systematic dismantling of the welfare state, the destruction of entire industries and even communities, the attempt to eradicate social solidarity in favor of ruthless individualism—all of these have made their impact felt. And in a traditional society such as Britain's, the traumatizing consequences have been particularly severe. More than he perhaps suspects or has intended, Leigh—a socialist and a proponent of social equality—has registered and often critiqued these developments.

The following interview took place at Leigh's London office in January 2007 and June 2008. With Leigh's permission, the two parts have been combined here into a unified whole.

R. J. Cardullo: When did you begin to get interested in the cinema?
Mike Leigh: I was seventeen in 1960 and it was then that I left Manchester and came to London. Prior to that moment, I had never seen a film that wasn't in English. You didn't see world cinema in those days; you saw Hollywood movies and British movies. About the only film I recall having seen was *Le Ballon rouge* [1956], the sentimental French film. However, when I hit London as a student, that was exactly the time of Jean-Luc Godard's *À bout de souffle* [1960] and the French New Wave, plus I discovered the rest of world cinema. What were my feelings about all that? I was

completely blown away by everything. This was also the time of the parallel British "New Wave."

RJC: That was what I was going to ask about next: the films of Tony Richardson, Karel Reisz, Lindsay Anderson, and others.

ML: I personally felt that the purest, most important, and most organic of those British films wasn't actually made till the late 1960s, and that was Anderson's *If...* [1968]. And it was not a film about working-class life, like a number of the British social-realist pictures—that was Lindsay digging into his own upper-middle class, public-school experience. About the so-called British New Wave films, good as many of them were and inspirational, because they were looking at working-class life, the fact is that none of them, without exception, was an original movie: every single one was an adaptation of a play or a novel. And although it's true that François Truffaut's wonderful *Jules et Jim* [1962] was also an adaptation of a novel, nevertheless, the inspiration for me was that *À bout de souffle*, Godard's *Vivre sa vie* [1962], and Truffaut's *Les Quatre cents coups* [1959] were original films that actually used film, as painting uses painting, to investigate something in a direct and original way.

RJC: There's no question that there is something to those British films of the early 1960s, but there are also problems.

ML: They're script-bound, as I've just suggested. The truth of it is, though, that there was great integrity to this cinema. Karel Reisz's *Saturday Night and Sunday Morning* [1960], Tony Richardson's *A Taste of Honey* [1961], Lindsay Anderson's *This Sporting Life* [1963]: these were serious works of art, that's not in question.

Curiously and importantly, the first film that did what those films did was really outside the fold; it was *Room at the Top* [1959], directed by Jack Clayton. The real revolution, in a way—which I didn't pick up at the time, because I didn't watch television—was what producer Tony Garnett and director Ken Loach did, which was to say, "Why don't we get away from this terrible studio-bound convention of doing what amounts to plays? Let's get out on the streets with lightweight cameras and newsreel equipment," as the French were doing. That was the revolution, and, a few years after it started, Tony Garnett himself got me into the BBC (British Broadcasting Corporation).

RJC: There was a certain occupational hazard, so to speak, in the British cinema at the time. To work in a country with such an immense literary tradition, including Shakespeare and Dickens—it must have been like having a very powerful father, and a certain parochialism and insularity seem to have resulted, in the theater as well as the cinema. I am thinking of the provinciality of so much kitchen-sink drama.

ML: Yes, I agree, but let's not throw out the baby with the bath water. For me, the natural influence, the early influence, was not so much British literature but the theater, vaudeville, circus, and pantomime, together with the British New Wave films; the Marx Brothers, Laurel and Hardy, Chaplin, and Keaton. This is one of the things that make me different from Ken Loach. There's also no question that a major influence is the time I spent as a youth in a socialist-Zionist movement. But the fact of the matter is that the heightened, theatrical, almost vaudevillian aspect of what goes on in my films is as important as my hard, socially realistic way of looking at the world. Those two elements are absolutely and mutually inseparable.

RJC: You've been making films for well over thirty years now. Why do you think they caught on in the United States only in the late 1980s or early 1990s?

ML: I don't know the answer to that. I suppose if you stick with anything long enough [Laughs.] . . . It's partly because I made a feature film in 1971 called *Bleak Moments*, which was quite successful in a very limited way, though it had no real commercial life. It won a couple of prizes in international festivals. And between that and 1988, which was seventeen years, I, like a huge number of British filmmakers, didn't get to make feature films, but made feature-length films for television. And it wasn't until *High Hopes*, in 1988, that I made my first proper, albeit low budget, theatrical film since *Bleak Moments*. And it's really only since then that the possibility has been there to have any international profile.

RJC: What enabled you to make the jump from television to features after all those years?

ML: There was a change in the circumstances in the U.K. They simply changed the rules. They changed the approach to television films, and did what we all had been talking about for years, which is to say, make the films on 35mm film, give them a theatrical life, and show them on television two or three years later.

RJC: Your films have proven quite popular in America, yet they're distinctly British in subject matter. What do you think American audiences see in them?

ML: I don't know. I just do these films. They are not in any way exclusively English or British or London films. They are in that milieu, obviously, but the issues in the films are issues that I intend to and expect to cross any barriers. As to why they're popular specifically in the United States insofar as they are, because they're only popular in Los Angeles, New York, Seattle, and a few other cities—maybe it's because they're good.

RJC: Unlike many Hollywood films, they're about real people in real situations.

ML: I feel that's entirely true, implicitly. Every film I make is implicitly an anti-Hollywood statement.

RJC: Stephen Frears, who also got his start on British television, has become a successful Hollywood filmmaker. Could you ever make that jump?

ML: No. I think it is neither desirable, nor attractive, nor feasible. Stephen Frears does so, and he does it very well, and I admire him for it. But he's a different kind of filmmaker. What defines what I do as opposed to what he does is not a question of budget or scale; it's that I make very personal, idiosyncratic films of a particular kind, of which I am author. He is, in the best possible sense, an eclectic, craftsman-like, jobbing, versatile director. He can take any kind of screenplay and make it work. I can't do that, and I'm not interested in doing that. It's not my job. I'm an authorial filmmaker. I plough this particular, slightly mad, lone furrow. So there's no logic to my going to Hollywood to do what I do. If Hollywood wanted to hand over the money with no strings attached for me to do the films that I do, fine. That is what they should do, actually. But they won't do that. They can't do that. They're pathologically incapable! But it's not an issue for me, really, provided I can keep getting the money from elsewhere to carry on developing my own particular rantings and ravings.

RJC: Your films are developed in a unique way. Can you discuss that?

ML: It boils down to, essentially, that I start with no script. I do a brief of the film for myself, which is usually pretty fluid. Then I work with the actors for an extensive period creating the characters, through conversation, research, and improvisation. Then we go out and invent the film on location, and structure it and shoot it as we go. To me, that's what it's all about. It's about using film as a medium in its own right, not as a way of including the decisions of various committees.

RJC: Can you elaborate on the process of improvising with actors?

ML: In essence, the main thing to understand is that when I make these films I say: "Come and be in my film. Can't tell you what it's about. I can't tell you what your character is. We'll invent that as part of the process. And you will never know any more than your character knows." That makes it possible to do long and detailed improvisations that investigate the years and years of people's lives in a spontaneous way. I don't get people together and tell them, "This is the theme. Let's all get together and improvise." It is a much more painstaking process of people getting together and growing. It's a way of building up a world like the real world, with all those tensions. We move out of that and distill things into a structured film. Always it has to work for me dramatically and from a literary point of view, but it also has to work from each actor's point of view of the character. I would never say to an actor, "You have to say that whether you feel it's right or not, and I don't care if you think he or she would say that—just do it." That's never happened, ever, and I wouldn't do that. Because by the time I get to that stage, I've been on this long journey with each actor such that I really understand the actor and the character and the actor understands his or her character totally. On the journey, one of the many jobs we do is to decide, and to work on, how the character talks and thinks; we determine the kind of language the character uses, the sort of ideas in the person's head, etc. It's a very precise process but also very much a harmonious collaboration. It is quite precise, indeed, down to whether there's a full-stop or a semi-colon at the end of a main clause!

RJC: O.K., so your process is very different from that of most other directors: you ask actors to go along with you on an intense journey during which they will spend months doing improvisations to develop their characters before anything gets set in stone. Because you arrive at defining the characters and storyline only after months of workshops with the actors, you are unable to tell them much about the roles they'll be playing at the start of the process. So how do your actors learn to trust you at the very start?

ML: In the first place, I'm pretty careful about whom I choose. I instinctively look for the kind of actor who *is* going to be trusting. There are all kinds of insecure people out there called actors; and some deeply untrusting actors—the kind that need to know exactly what's what at all times—might be quite good within the parameters of a certain sort of acting. But I can't work with such people. On the whole, I get people for whom not always knowing what's what isn't a problem.

RJC: How do you find out that this isn't going to be a problem?

ML: It's an instinctual thing on my part: I have a feeling about an actor when I meet him or her for the first time during our initial interview.

RJC: Is the interview a "twenty-minute get-to-know-you" chat?

ML: Yes, precisely. We're sitting in a room and there's nobody else there but the actor and me. We talk about the actor's life. Then if I feel the relationship's going to move forward, I call that person back in and we do some work for a while. At this point I'm just trying to get a sense of person and the performer. The actors with whom I collaborate tend to be confident in the best sense of the word: relaxed, cool, together, focused, open, intelligent, and they have a sense of humor.

My job apart, from anything else, is to build an ensemble composed of actors who all come from such a secure place that they can work together to make a film—my film. So on the whole, frankly, trust is not much of an issue. What I don't do is throw actors instantly into a dangerous situation. The actors I select for my projects sit and chew the fat with me for ages before we gradually get the characters going. And by the time they get to the bit that's dangerous, they've spent a lot of time sorting things out without any pressure. We're careful and slow. The reason my films work is that every actor on set is very secure; that makes them able to fly.

RJC: But there's still a sense of danger in your films. I'm thinking of the rape scene in *Naked* [1993], or the scene in *Life Is Sweet* [1990] where a young Jane Horrocks has her body smeared in chocolate.

ML: Sure. But it takes work to arrive at the stage where you can tackle those things on screen. Here's a bit of truth: very, very occasionally I hire an actor and get it wrong. The actor just doesn't trust the process or me as fully as I thought he would. But such a lack of trust has nothing to do with me or the process: it has to do with the actor himself.

RJC: In the United States, the actors I've seen seem to fall into two camps: you get the ones that work very much with their heads, or in their heads; they tend to be very literate and extremely intelligent. And then there's the other sort—the emotional, feeling actor who doesn't really read anything and has little idea of what's going on in the world, but nevertheless creates a performance from some apparently deeper or more instinctual place. When I watch your films, I feel that there's cohesion between these two different approaches.

ML: I couldn't agree more. I'm very familiar with both these sorts of American actors; I know exactly what you mean. The second category of actor you mention comes as a result of the so-called Method. The notion that acting is simply about intuitively responding to situations in the way you "feel" them couldn't be farther away from how I ask actors to work. On the other hand, the kind of acting that's wholly literary or cerebral is also wrong. It's useless for me to have actors so much in their heads that they can't be organic or whole.

What it all comes down to, really, is having actors who are totally able to think deeply about their characters while at the same time—once we have developed those characters—they can respond emotionally, and organically, to anything that comes their way. For actors to be able to differentiate between themselves and the characters they're playing while simultaneously remaining in character and spontaneous requires a sophisticated combination of skills and spirit. The bottom line is this: for those that can do it, it's a natural combination and they don't think twice about it. For those who can't do it, they can bang their heads against a brick wall from now till kingdom come and they still won't get there.

RJC: Do you think that the English actor-training system prepares actors to be people with whom you'd want to work? Or does the kind of actor you're looking for flourish in any kind of educational or cultural environment?

ML: There's a wider issue at stake here. It would be wrong to overlook the fact that I make films within an English context with actors who come from the same social environment as I do. There's something about the whole environment in which we all come together that makes my projects work. The success is further bound up with being committed, caring, and emotionally connected to the project while at the same time being detached from it and even humorous about it. This is what makes my work idiosyncratic and something that no one else does. But that's a whole other discussion. As to the training, I myself was trained as an actor. I trained at the Royal Academy of Dramatic Art (RADA) in London and began my career with the Royal Shakespeare Company (RSC). But the training, I have to say, was very old-fashioned and prescriptive.

RJC: What, just Shakespearean monologues?

ML: We didn't just do Shakespearean monologues, but the approach to acting in general was very mechanical. You learned the lines and the moves; you didn't discuss the play or improvise. Since then, the culture of drama schools has completely changed. Improvisation—the cornerstone of my process as a director—is now a standard part of actor training. Once upon a time when I was auditioning actors, a large proportion would come in and say, "I've never improvised. What do you mean there's no script?" Today, that's no longer the case. If I'm meeting actors under the age of forty, very rarely will I encounter this attitude; they all take improvising for granted. This is great for me because I wind up getting actors who are ready to hit the ground running. Then again, the way an actor is trained in the end doesn't ultimately have much bearing on my work. I'm interested in the actor as artist.

RJC: In the commentary for the DVD of *Naked*, one of those artists, David Thewlis, talked about rehearsing a scene between his character—the protagonist in the film, Johnny—and the young Scottish homeless character, Archie, played by Ewen Bremner. Thewlis talked about how the actors were so immersed in their roles that their characters got into a fight during an extended improvisational sequence and the police had to be called. Thewlis said that you had to intervene, imploring him and Bremner to step out of character in order to keep them from being arrested. Comically enough, Thewlis then said that he kind of wished he and Bremner *had* been arrested because the court would have been faced with trying a couple of fictional characters. You're so clear about the actor's being separate from the character, and yet this incredible visceral reality you create makes it hard, especially for the actors, to accept that it's all just fiction. What are your thoughts about this tension between performer and role?

ML: The delineation between the actor and his part is a practical matter. When the camera runs, you want the actor to *be* the character. But from a practical point of view—and this relates back to the second category of American actor that we discussed earlier—I can't negotiate and collaborate with a *character* in the creating of a distilled dramatic investigation of the raw material. I need to work with an *actor*. That stuff about actors who stay in character all the time is nonsense. It's bad for them. The thing is that when you work on a character over time, it gets to you; after all, you spend day in, day out, week in, week out with the character. I'm just pretty strict about making sure that when an actor goes into character, he or she comes out of character eventually, too. I like to be objective about what happens. For example, I never allow actors to talk about their character in the first person, as "I." This helps us remember the fact that we really are creating a fictitious person and that the actor is— and always will be—the actor.

RJC: Does asking the actor to be a key collaborator in defining the character sometimes cause problems? For example, I've heard that actors sometimes come back at you and say things like, "My character wouldn't rape this other character." How do you deal with that?

ML: That's true. It happened with *Vera Drake* [2004]. Understandably, this kind of issue has to be gently negotiated. I knew that the character in question could perfectly well be a rapist. And so did the actor, when it came right down to it.

RJC: But he was in denial for a bit?

ML: Yes, in some way he was, and fair enough. In that particular case—unusual, for one of my projects—the rape was a prerequisite. Normally I don't set plot points in stone. Another instance: there was a moment during the making of *Secrets and Lies* [1996] where Claire Rushbrook, who plays Roxanne, just buggered off in the middle of a massive improvisation. She disappeared and we had to go and find her. She left at a point that was effectively in the structure of the sequence I'd put together, but the final proof hadn't come out. I knew there was more to flesh out. But after I located Rushbrook, the actress said, "There's no way that Roxanne would go back." She knew that I wanted her to go back, but I can't just say to an actor, "Let's go back," because the action has to be organic and motivated. Then we discovered that if her boyfriend, as he does in the finished movie, says, "Actually, I think you should go back," she would do as he says, because she's getting fed up with his being a wimp and wants to validate any assertiveness he shows.

So these things have to be thought through and gently negotiated. Sometimes I have to say to an actor, "Is it plausible or impossible for the character to do this?" I do this because my job—and this is what all artists do whatever the medium, since all art is based on improvisation *and* order—is to start something that grows all over the place and then figure out how to shape it into something that's coherent.

RJC: Considering that this monologue is going on in your head all the time, when do *you* get to step out of character? Do you ever get to switch off? Do you sleep?

ML: What, while the film is happening? No. What do you want me to do? Go to Bermuda? It's a privilege to get to work on something that's so completely absorbing. It's terrifying, too. I have to get out of bed every day to make something happen. I wonder if I would have been capable of producing anything had I worked in a more conventional way with a prewritten script, because I'm of the procrastinator class. I could see myself waking up and saying things like, "Today I'll just have a reading day, tomorrow I can write," "I think I need to see a movie today," "I'll do the shopping first," or "I'll just make another cup of coffee." But because of the way I work, once the film goes into rehearsal, I have to be out of bed and on site by nine o'clock every single day—there's no point in hanging around, because the writing won't get done at home. When the project does take off, it becomes immensely stimulating. The whole thing is a powerful, gregarious, collaborative process. And I'm the one who has to make it all work for the actor.

RJC: You put actors at the center of your process, I gather.

ML: I'm asking actors to be creative collaborators.

RJC: For the uninitiated, how would you differentiate between improvisation and collaboration?

ML: What you're really asking me has to do with the general assumption that in a Mike Leigh film, we are looking at actors improvising on camera. Which we're not: that's not how they collaborate with me. We spend a great deal of time, six months or so, bringing the world of the characters into existence: that's the collaboration, which also involves improvisation. So that when it comes time to shoot, everything has been worked on, scene by scene and location by location; it's all been made very precise, before it's been shot. That's because the dialogue and the action have come organically: the actors have worked with me to create them from the ground up. What you don't get on my set is the sort of random line reading you get from take to take on a film where the dialogue is just thought of as lines on a page. It's never lines on a page in my films; my actors never see a script.

RJC: Who ultimately writes the script? You?

ML: No, I don't go away and write it by myself. I write it by working with the actors as they improvise. I then organize it and make suggestions. I put things in and take things out. It's a complicated process, as we explore the situations that are going to be the actual scenes in the film, then gradually deconstruct relations and reconstruct them, experiment with them, pin them down, fix dialogue, change things around here and there, cut and paste, until we arrive at something coherent and pithy that works. The final film is scripted sequence by sequence during the shoot. And that is only made possible by my having created the whole premise of the film previously and, implicit in that, the whole network of relationships. There is not so much a story at the beginning as a feeling and conception. As soon as I can, I share with the cinematographer what the general spirit of the film is. The production designer and the costume designer then tune in to what's going on and start to find out about the characters, and work with the actors so that everyone's on the case. I have constant conversations with the production designer in particular about possible images and locations and the reason behind things. So we gradually talk the thing into existence, making the film up as we go along. I do set down a kind of structure before we start shooting, but there are always elements that creep in; indeed, I very often don't know what the end is going to be. The journey of making the film is a journey of discovery about what the film is. I only do what all other writers, painters, and novelists do. All art is a synthesis of improvisation and order. You put something down and then you work with it. You discover what it is by interacting with it.

RJC: Does the process of discovering a film get any easier for you?

ML: I can only say what any artist would say, and that is that some things come easy and some things are tough, depending on a whole variety of factors.

RJC: That's certainly a different method of filmmaking than what other filmmakers, especially those in Hollywood, employ. How did you arrive at it?

ML: Maybe I'm wrong, but to me it's entirely logical. How I arrived at it—that's like asking Alexander Graham Bell how he invented the telephone.

RJC: Is it the way you made *Bleak Moments*?

ML: Oh yeah, I started developing it in 1965, in some plays. The difference is, it got more sophisticated. It was born in the first place (and this is still what defines it) from a desire to write and a desire to direct, and a fascination with actors. There are directors who are not interested in actors and acting, and I obviously am. I've tried to advance the whole possibility and scope of what acting can do. I found at a very early age that I was inherently bored by directing scripts that already existed. I also found it inherently arid to sit in a room, writing. So add all these things together and you've got the way I work.

Look, what we're talking about is fine, but it's not really the substance of my style of filmmaking. It's all about what happens creatively with the camera, with the cinematographer, with the editor, with the people on location. Everything that goes on with the actors is very important, but only by way of background and preparation. In the end, it's a complete process that grows organically and involves everyone.

RJC: Do you have a specific target audience, or are you aiming for a general audience with your films?

ML: A general one. The battle, really, is to get the films across to a popular audience. The problems in making films like mine are exclusively problems of distribution and exhibition. The battle is to try and make films like mine be perceived as commercial films for a wide audience. Because I don't think audiences are stupid. I don't think audiences are congenital idiots and children who need to be pandered to. I think anyone can get *Naked*. My assumption about my audience is that they are an infinite-sized group of people who are at least as intelligent as I am. I think I make populist entertainment films. But that doesn't necessarily mean soufflés and trifles.

RJC: So many people go to movies for escapism and light entertainment. Do you really think a film as dark as, say, *Naked* can reach a mass audience?

ML: Yes, I do. I think the only barriers are the prejudice of the exhibitors and distributors about what a film is. I think it would be ridiculous if every single film was a *Naked*. Just as I think it would be ridiculous if all someone ate was steak. You've got to have a mixture in your diet. I think films like *Naked* should sit alongside other kinds of films.

RJC: Would you rank *Naked* among your better works?

ML: Well, it's very hard to talk about better or worse. I don't know. I'm very close to these films. There are filmmakers who, very legitimately, have relationships for better or worse with their films depending on, say, whether the picture is too close to the book it's adapted from or taken from an original screenplay, whether they were hired into a project that already existed or were part of the project from day one, etc. None of those things apply to me. I'm as close to all of my films, each and every one of them.

RJC: Do you watch them?

ML: I do, and I like them. I mean, I'm not Gloria Swanson in *Sunset Boulevard* [1950], sitting there every night watching my own movies. But I do watch them, and I particularly love watching them with audiences. Some filmmakers say, "I can't watch my films; I can't stand them." My feeling, rather piously, is that if *you* don't like your films, how the hell can you expect anybody else to like them?

RJC: Your films can be quite pessimistic, I have to say. Are you a pessimist?

ML: Yes, I suppose I am a pessimist, as well as being an optimist. I'm pessimistic about some things; and I find it very difficult to be very optimistic about many aspects of the future given the way the world is today. As a parent, I worry about what the future will be like in ten or twenty years' time. About those things I'm a pessimist. About humanity, on the whole I'm an optimist, which is based on my belief about how people *can* behave toward each other. So all my films, in the end, contain a balance between the comic and the pathetic.

RJC: But wouldn't you agree that *Happy-Go-Lucky* [2008], on the whole, has a more festive and sanguine tone?

ML: Well, maybe you're right, because one reviewer wrote, "Can this be true, Mike Leigh has made a comedy?" Does it surprise me? No, not at all.

RJC: There's a real brightness to this film, isn't there? There are splashes of color in the set design, the costumes, and the very film stock that you used.

ML: At the point where I got a sense of what the film should be, and I was able to share that with Dick Pope—the cinematographer who's shot all my films since *Life Is Sweet* in 1990—and also my various designers, I immediately began talking about Poppy. I said that this is going to be a vivacious, positive, intelligent, bright woman with a great sense of humor and buzzing with energy, and the film really needs to take its cue from her character: i.e., the film itself should burst with energy and color. At this point, we decided to shoot *Happy-Go-Lucky* in widescreen—it's the first film

I've made that's been widescreen. And we set about shooting tests, just to work out what stocks to use, how to treat them, how to find the palette, etc. Curiously, at that precise moment—that week in fact—Fuji announced this new film stock called Vivid, which we used. And it's an absolute delight, which made possible this wonderful, rich, succulent color experience in the final film.

RJC: As for *All or Nothing* [2002], as opposed to *Happy-Go-Lucky*, there appear to be contrasting views. Some people think it's your bleakest film ever and some say it's the most optimistic.

ML: Well, some people have said that it has bleak moments—which is what my first film did. I feel that this film is entirely about redemption. It's about connecting. I don't think it arrives at completely comfortable conclusions. You certainly don't walk away from it thinking that everything is all tied up and fine. But I do feel that the spirit of the film points toward hopeful possibilities. I feel that *All or Nothing* is a film about potential, really; it's about possible fulfillment.

RJC: What interests you most as a cinematic subject?

ML: People relating to each other and the relationships between men and children and work.

RJC: British people, right?

ML: Again, I have to say that I don't personally see my films as being about London, England, Britain, or English things. Obviously, the milieu, the territory, or the landscape is that, but I am more concerned with the emotional landscape, as I have always been when the chips are down. Although it may sound pretentious to say so, I guess I think my work is about something more universal than just the U.K. I don't really see it as so nation-based.

RJC: Where did you shoot *All or Nothing*?

ML: On an estate right in the middle of Greenwich, with 340 flats and nobody in it. It was great. We had this whole place to ourselves. I could control everything that you could see and it helped to inform the general atmosphere of the film. It could have been an estate that was boring to look at but it was a really interesting place.

The whole thing about making films, in an organic film on location, is that it's not only about characters, relationships, and themes, it's also about place and the poetry of place. It's about the spirit of what you find, the accidents that you stumble across. It was great to find this place that had these qualities.

RJC: For about two-thirds of *All or Nothing*, your attitude toward the characters seemed a bit smug and self-satisfied. It smacked to me of emphasizing the stupidity of the characters—almost to the point that they were being laughed at. How do you respond to that?

ML: I have nothing to say to that. To me, it doesn't sound like the kind of film that I've made. I can't really respond to that, I'm afraid.

RJC: Do you agree that poverty has a strong fascination?

ML: No, because, so far as I understand what you're saying, that would suggest that poverty has a kind of fascination by itself. I think that it's important to look at in the sense that it affects a very large proportion of the world in one way or another. Do you mean that it has some sort of voyeuristic fascination for me?

RJC: Yes, because you've talked about the bleak emotional landscape in such a way that it appears to have poverty as the driving force behind it.

ML: I suppose that the implication of your question would be to suggest that maybe people who didn't suffer from poverty couldn't have the emotional problems that *All or Nothing* deals with. But I don't think that's the case. I don't think that these kinds of emotional experiences or breakdowns of communication are the prerogative of the poverty-stricken or the working classes. That would be absurd. However, the fact is that this film deals with these people.

There is no question in my mind that, although one could tell stories about other kinds of people, and I'm very comfortable doing that, this film is what it is. And, looking at people as I do, whose life is in some way stripped down nearly to its basics—not absolutely all the way, because that's not what I'm dealing with here—this film relates to the rawness of their emotions. But poverty as a subject is not inevitable. It just happens to be part of the whole combination of elements that *All or Nothing* deals with, but it's not what I would call an exclusive preoccupation or riff of mine.

RJC: On the other hand, most of your films have characters who are more or less at the end of their tether, a condition caused by poverty or social deprivation or something like that. And this one certainly has that. Poverty is inescapably part of it.

ML: I don't arrive at those portraits, though. It is not motivated by a particular kind of fascination with a certain sort of imagery. Huge numbers of people do live these sorts of lives, and I am drawn to deal with them because that's what life is about for a good many people.

RJC: Do you think the kind of people that the film is about would appreciate the humor in the film?

ML: It's not a matter of my opinion because I know it to be the case. I know the kind of people who have seen the film. It's always the case that the people who the film's about love it. Hitchcock famously said that the kind of woman who spends all day washing up and doing the housework does not want to go to the cinema to see a film about someone who spends all day washing up and doing the housework. And Hitchcock, on this thing and many others, was a million miles from the truth. He didn't know what he was talking about.

It is definitely and consistently the case that people love to see a film that reflects their own lives. Because you don't usually see that in the movies. They think it's an absolute gas. They relate to it and they are moved by it. It's very good news for them. In the 1970s and the 1980s, as I've noted, I didn't make films for cinema but for the television, along with many other filmmakers who were lucky enough to get the opportunity. We did films called "Play for Today" [1970-84] on Monday and Wednesday evenings. People loved them. They had huge viewing figures. They were these kinds of films. People were up for it.

RJC: I think you once said that movies should aspire to the condition of documentary, and I immediately thought of movies like *Armageddon* [1998] and *The Matrix* [1999], and wondered if you would do away with those if you had absolute power?

ML: No, no, I wouldn't do away with anything if I had absolute power because I'm in no way that kind of a fascist. So that's to start with, but I certainly wouldn't do that. I didn't actually say that movies *should* aspire to the condition of documentary. What I actually said is that in making a film, one wants—what one thinks when one actually shoots—to aspire to the condition of documentary in the sense that you want to make it happen so that it's completely three-dimensional in front of the camera.

RJC: To get back to *All or Nothing*, this picture seems to take quite a negative view of the white British male. And it seems to emphasize the strengths of white British women. Can you comment on that?

ML: It certainly isn't an objective of the film to discredit the white British man as such. I don't really know how to answer that question. Obviously, whatever you see in the film comes from the creative process of making it. It can't come from anywhere else. There are unsympathetic characters in the film. Clearly the most unsympathetic character is Jason, the boyfriend. But I would hope that, for example, Phil comes out at the end of the film beyond being merely discredited. It's not a one-note film. There are a lot of things going on in it. You can only talk about the strengths of women and the weaknesses of men by looking at them together. I don't know how to answer your question. It demands isolating out of the film some kind of national thematic strand which I don't think is really there. It wasn't my conscious objective to discredit the white British man.

RJC: I guess the women in the film are stronger than the men. They seem to have more inner resources ultimately in this particular film.

ML: You can say that's true of Maureen. But you can only talk about the central relationship between Penny and Phil in terms of a symbiotic relationship. It's not about stronger women and weaker men. I don't think that theory stands up in terms of what the film is about or what happens in it.

RJC: Do you feel that you have trouble with upper-middle-class characters? They seem to be rather stereotyped in films like *High Hopes*.

ML: I think *High Hopes* has a satirical element to it. But that's not what I normally do. Satire is not my natural tendency. I think *High Hopes* contained that in a very specific way. That results in the satirical portrayal of the upper-middle-class characters. I think all of my films up to and including *Life Is Sweet* had broader comic elements. From *Naked* onwards, I moved on to a different kind of feel and relationship to the characters. I don't find any characters more difficult than any others. *Topsy-Turvy* [2000] was full of middle-class characters and I had no trouble with them. They were Victorian in that film. They weren't even twenty-first-century figures. But I can understand if you found yourself at odds with my broader comic style in those films.

RJC: How conscious are you of exploring themes in your films?

ML: Jean Renoir famously said that all filmmakers make the same film over and over again. The truth is that I know that I return endlessly to certain preoccupations, but you're not necessarily aware that you do. If you look at all of my films, you'll find an undeniable preoccupation with pregnancies, being parents, being children, whether to have children. That comes out of a life-preoccupation really.

What I try to do is not to worry about that, because I realize that that is the sort of work I do. The important thing is to try to make a different sort of film within the genre and to tell a different kind of story within the overall parameters of the discipline—to confront different things and to deal with different issues, although the underlying themes remain constant.

You like to think that you're getting closer to something, if only because you get older—I'm past sixty now. As to the fatuous notion that I'm arriving at "the truth," I feel that that would be somewhat optimistic.

RJC: Did any Hollywood stars, after the success of *Secrets and Lies*, express an interest in working with you?

ML: Yes, they did. And I dealt with it with extraordinary diplomacy and subtlety. There are some people, like Jennifer Jason-Leigh, Willem Defoe, and Steve Buscemi, whom I know and like and are the "American version" of the sort of actors I work with here, who are feasible candidates to work with on the right project. There are bigger stars than they whom it would be ludicrous to contemplate having anything to do with for a split second.

RJC: Speaking of Hollywood, do awards mean anything to you?

ML: Of course they do. I mean, I'm in the movie business. It's important. I don't want to be an obscure name in the middle of the index of some esoteric tome about European cinema. So anything that happens that is part of all that and helps a film along, is good news, and I enjoy it, I embrace it, I encourage it, and I want it. No problem. Give me more of it. If any film of mine is nominated for an Oscar, I am thrilled. But the only thing that would help totally would be a film that was a runaway commercial success, and I haven't made such a film. I can get money but there is a ceiling beyond which people won't take a risk. But that's fine because we make the films we do below that ceiling.

RJC: What are your views about filmmaking in the United States, and about *Americans'* views of your films?

ML: First of all, most of us, myself not least, grew up on Hollywood movies—specifically, the great Hollywood movies of the Golden Age. Some of my favorite movies are Hollywood movies; Hollywood is obviously a large part of the cinematic spectrum. I nurture a healthy love-hate relationship toward the place. Of course, there's been a bit of American money in some of my films—*Topsy-Turvy*, for example—though not a lot. The important thing is for the funding to come without classic Hollywood-style interference.

RJC: Yes, because you don't create "packages," and everything in Hollywood has to be "packaged."

ML: The main problem is that the Hollywood system has already made the film before the director shoots a single frame. But to get back to your original question: in the seventeen or so years between *Bleak Moments* and *High Hopes*, I talked to people in Hollywood who might have backed my films on a number of occasions. And one of the things I always heard was, "The trouble with your films is that they will never work in the States. People won't get them." At the time, I thought there might be some truth to this. Then, when I came to the United States in 1986, for the first time—the San Francisco International Film Festival brought me out to the West Coast and screened all six of my films to date—audiences over there started to know about me and it turned out that the prediction about how American audiences would receive my films was wrong. The American audience, or a part of the American audience, really likes my films. On the one hand, I am very happy to be part of European and world cinema as a British filmmaker. But on the other, it's also very stimulating and rewarding to come to the San Francisco International Film Festival or the Oscars (which I've done three times) with these low-budget, foreign, offbeat, quirky, real-life, uncompromising films and be a bit of a Trojan horse. I enjoy the subversion of it all. Curiously enough, I've done industry screenings in Los Angeles with huge audiences and industry insiders. They say things like, "Wow, this is fantastic. Why can't we do this here?" And I think, "Well, actually, with all the resources you've got kicking around here, you could do anything you wanted."

RJC: But the Hollywood system stymies them.

ML: Yes. But the other thing I want to say is that there is a great tradition of independent filmmaking in the United States that I absolutely respect. There's some wonderful stuff that comes out of America against all the odds, like Steve Buscemi's *Trees Lounge* [1996]. Independent American filmmaking has always been there and it's not to be forgotten. Also, it would be ludicrous to suggest that nothing good comes out of Hollywood, because that's not the case. Sometimes really truthful, organic stuff surfaces by those who managed to stick it to the man and just got on, and away, with it.

RJC: There's been quite a migration of directors from the U.K. to Hollywood, from Sam Mendes to Phyllida Lloyd and, of course, Stephen Frears, whom I mentioned earlier.

ML: There always has been. What about Hitchcock? The Brits have always drifted over and that's fine. It's a complex issue. One of the reasons that I'm resistant to making films in the United States has nothing to do with *not* doing a film in Hollywood, but rather to do with what I'm committed to doing in the U.K. I feel very committed to the British film industry and its infrastructure.

RJC: How would you describe the film industry in the U.K. right now? Some people are very critical of it.

ML: The problem with the British film industry is its nervousness or insecurity about—and genuflection toward—Los Angeles. All those Hollywood grandfathers like Irving Thalberg and Louis B. Mayer have got a lot to answer for, because they invented a monster that is a curse to filmmaking: the interfering producer. Such insecurity leads to things within the U.K. film industry like wheeling in an American actor to play a part that should plainly be played by a Brit—Renée Zellweger playing Bridget Jones, for one stellar example.

RJC: How much does commercial success matter at this point in your career, anyway? You've now got a body of work that speaks for itself, so does commerce matter as much as it might have done in the past?

ML: That's always mattered. First of all, I make these films to be seen. There's no virtue in a film that nobody sees or very few people see. But unconventional as my films may seem to be, they're perfectly conventional in the sense that they are narrative films; they're movies that tell stories. They're not alternative or experimental films that we shoot for no money at all with a little camera. They're proper movies and they have to be funded, and although the budgets are tight, the money has to come from people who back films. And if you've made films that are not commercially successful, people don't want to hear from you. And they especially don't want to hear from filmmakers such as myself, someone who doesn't have a script, who can't tell the backer what it's going to be about, and who will not enter into any discussion about having Hollywood stars involved. The main thing is, I'm not a Trappist monk up in the mountains. I'm in the movie business, and I want people to see my films. Also, if there's any money made, it simply goes back into things. My most successful film commercially was *Secrets and Lies*, partly because it got the Palme d'Or at Cannes, partly because it was nominated for five Oscars. But as much as anything, it was because at the time of its release, to trace your birth mother—which is what the film is about—was illegal. And it remains illegal today in many countries, including all of South America and many of the Catholic countries in Europe as well as almost all the states in the USA. So there was enormous interest in the film. And because the film was, relatively speaking, commercially successful, it enabled us to raise rather more money than we normally would have done to make *Topsy-Turvy*. So the short answer to your question is that commercial success is very important, indeed.

RJC: Do you ever get frustrated when your films are shown only at selected cinemas?

ML: I am totally frustrated by that. That's never the intention. The idea that any film I have ever made should be dumped in what are regarded as art-house cinemas isn't acceptable to me. I am not concerned with making esoteric, obscure kinds of films. My films can speak to anybody about real things.

RJC: Let me address the representation of these "real things" on the screen by asking whether color is very important to you.

ML: That is the case. What you see in *All or Nothing*, for example, *Topsy-Turvy*, and all our films in fact—I say our films because Dick Pope has shot all my movies since *Life Is Sweet*, and my designers are Alison Chitty, who designed my earlier pictures, and Eve Stewart, who does them now. We work very cautiously and in great detail to create the palette of a film, the color and visual spirit of a film in relation to its feeling and what we feel we want to pull out of it. The most extreme investigation occurred in *Naked*, for which we used a process called bleached bypass where you don't complete the process in the laboratory. The palette was very restrained. There was no reds, no bright colors at all; it was very muted. In one way or another, that's the kind of thing we've experimented with in all my films.

With *All or Nothing*, we had this sense of people in this gray environment. And it is reflected in the work of the costume designer, Jacqueline Durran, who had worked as the assistant designer to Lindy Hemming on *Topsy-Turvy*. She was therefore very familiar with my approach to working.

With *Topsy-Turvy*, although we made the picture for peanuts given what you saw on the screen, the costumes were quite elaborate and relatively expensive to make. Jacqueline managed to costume *All or Nothing* for next to nothing. She hit the charity shops everywhere. She would go out to get one sweater and come back with 200 of them. She worked in a room adjacent to where we were preparing the film. You would go in and she would have dozens and dozens of variations of the same garment in subtly different shades of gray. She was really on top of the quite sophisticated job of squaring the color and palette requirements with the character requirements. In those terms, the harmony of all the different visual elements with the dramatic and character-motivated aspects of the film is very successful indeed.

RJC: What about the *mise-en-scène* in your work?

ML: In *All or Nothing*, for instance, there are lots of shots of people in this particular housing estate. There are choices as to whether you're looking at a big, empty *space* with somebody in it or *somebody* in a space. When my cinematographer and I were discussing how to shoot certain scenes, we would ask: "Is it a man in a room, or is it a room with a man in it?" Those are two different things. It has to do with the idea of what the image means. But we're not talking about a kind of symbolism that can be decoded and translated. That is, there are all kinds off symbolism in *All or Nothing*, but symbolism isn't really the right word. It has to do with a visual language that is organic to what is going on. Occasionally there are things that have some sense of external reference, but that's not what it's about because that's not what I'm concerned with in telling this kind of story in one of my films. These are not characters in an abstract void; they are in a physical world, interacting with each other and their environment. These things that happen are not random choices—these things become the imagery of the film.

RJC: To stay with *All or Nothing* for a moment, how did you edit the film? Did much end up on the cutting-room floor?

ML: Our editing is fairly conventional. What we shot was fairly precise, and therefore what we took to the cutting room was fairly disciplined. No more ended up on the cutting-room floor than does in any feature film one way or another. I do go through and pare down anything that is repetitious, as you do with any film. For example, what happened with the French woman Cecile and the vase—we saw her getting into the car with this vase rather fussily, with the antiques dealer hanging around. But when we stuck it all together it was clear that the scene was redundant. It didn't say anything interesting, and it made the whole thing take longer than it needed to. The scene outside the antiques shop would have telegraphed to you too obviously that she was going to be important.

RJC: What is the relationship between your theater work and your film work? How does the theater influence the films you have made?

ML: As I said earlier, I trained as an actor. I also went to film school. I developed my sense of drama in the theater because it was cheap. Movies by definition cost money. They are more elusive, or used to be until the invention of new technology. My film work has been influenced by my theater work in some sense. The convention of rehearsing a film for six months, which is what I do now, comes from the theater. And, of course, I wrote plays for the theater before I wrote screenplays. But there is nothing about filmmaking that I don't love—it is a great experience. It is something I am happy to do endlessly and can't get enough of. I love theater less than I love films, that's for sure; for every film that I've ever walked out on—which is not very many—I have walked out on about a thousand plays.

Film always seems so grown-up compared with theater. There is something rather insular and claustrophobic about people locked away in an airless, lightless building. I prefer getting out into the open air and real places with a whole gang of people: it is more enlivening. I love working with actors, I love working with technicians, and I love the family thing that is created on every film. And it really is a family—on my films, the atmosphere is very, very harmonious, always. Because if it weren't, you couldn't do this sort of work. You just couldn't: people really have to commit, on either side of the camera. Aside from that, I love the medium itself. I love the whole idea of what making a film means—you know, taking that little machine out and capturing the world with it. I love to shoot in places, on location. And I love the rhythm of filmmaking, what you can do with time. I even like the actual feel of celluloid. The post-production process itself is great, because that's when you really make the film.

RJC: Could you elaborate on what you find insular about the theater? Because it seems, for one thing, that theater actors thrive on the daily contact they have with the audience.

ML: Well, I think, from an actor's point of view, that is true. And certainly there is something very inspiriting about live performance. Yes. But there's something very insular about the *institution* of theater, whereas film gets you out into the street, and you're out there in the world and somehow there's something kind of healthy about the whole process of filmmaking, which I find isn't the case with theater.

RJC: Would you like to do something for television now? Or are you happy in cinema?

ML: So far as television is concerned, apart from a few televised studio plays—which have gone out of fashion—all I ever did was make films for telly, as we discussed earlier. They were films. The fact that they were shown on TV was a technicality, although obviously making films for the cinema means that you can work to motion-picture standards. It's good to work on a big screen. Going back to television wouldn't mean anything to me, especially not the television of today. Television in the 1970s was a very liberal outlet compared to nowadays. Nowadays you hear all these stories about neurotic, nervous bureaucracy. There never used to be this concern about ratings or the commercial element. In the context of today, television has no attraction to me at all. That said, some of my films are backed by Film4, which is effectively television money, and they will, as part of their journey, get seen on one of the Channel 4 outlets.

RJC: It seems to me that more and more highly-touted young directors today are working in a more cinematic, visceral, myth-focused, violent, overtly stylish manner, rather than what you call a "humanist" vein, especially in American independent cinema. How do you feel about that?

ML: The only way to approach thinking about this is to look at where various kinds of cinema come from, what are the motivating forces behind them and the prevailing conditions under which they are created. The fact is that there is a great tradition, which exists in Europe and plenty of other places, not least of all Japan, of making films about real life, uncluttered and unfettered and uninterfered with by the kind of disease that you can—broadly speaking—diagnose as Hollywood.

This tradition goes back a very long way. It is entirely possible for a filmmaker to go out and listen to the world and sense the world and savor the world and experience the joy and pain of the world, and express it in a completely pure, honest, interesting, and very cinematic way. There's no question about that, ranging from Satyajit Ray's first film *Pather Panchali* [1955]—which he made absolutely on a shoestring, with no film industry backing at all, and yet it remains a classic—to films that are made just as independently but within a film-industry context.

In most countries, even to some extent in Britain, the film industry has been a system that serves the needs of filmmakers in an organic way. But once you get a film industry that becomes more important than the organic needs of films that look at life, once it becomes a creature unto itself and grows out of all proportion to human scale, which is what Hollywood is, then it becomes impossible.

The fascinating thing for me about coming to the States and endlessly talking to filmmakers is that it appears that it's quite simply impossible for people to make independent films in your country. The films that are made in most parts of the world aren't "independent" films, they're just films, really. Here "independent" films means films made in spite of Hollywood. And some get made, but it's tough. Even when there's no interference from Hollywood, there are still too many people meddling with young filmmakers. I think artists need to be given the latitude and freedom and trust to get out there and really explore—and, to some extent, this is happening because of the new, relatively cheap technology.

All good cinema, and indeed all cinema in some shape or form, is concerned with style, is concerned with being cinematic, is concerned with form and content and the rest of it. But because Hollywood is so dinosaur-like in its overweighted industrialization, that whole weight squeezes the humanity out of it all. People are left talking about style and being stylistic, formalistic, and self-consciously cinematic, because that's what people have to hang onto. Instead of real integrity, real truthfulness, real getting out there and telling the stories that are out there.

It's not as if you have to walk very far from a studio in Los Angeles to find real life going on. There are still people living lives. But the scale of Hollywood means that everything becomes a commodity, including style. We're all concerned with style. I make very stylistic films indeed, but style doesn't become a substitute for truth and reality. It's an integral, organic part of the whole thing.

RJC: Sometimes independent filmmakers try to make movies outside the Hollywood system and about "real life" and "real people," but so often their efforts fall flat. Frequently the impediment seems to be that they feel they need to teach something or have a message.

ML: On your general point, I agree with you. This is the debate about agenda-driven art or ideas. My films are full of ideas, lots of different ones—things working on all kinds of different levels. For me, making a film is an exploration into what we feel. I'm not concerned with making films that are conclusive or prescriptive, and certainly not propaganda. I make films where either rationally or emotionally I tend to ask more questions than give answers. I feel that the audience should have something to work with when the film's over, something to discuss and argue about. But really what I'm talking about is the actual world out there—getting that on the screen. And you're right, somehow that doesn't happen very much in American films. Yet it's not as if the concept is absent from American literature. Although we have to pay—I say this with a note of irony—some of our respects to Robert Altman, who does go as far as anybody there in getting that.

RJC: Do you have a Marxist or leftist background?

ML: I don't have a Marxist background. It was, broadly speaking, leftish, liberal, with a quite unavoidable strain of anarchy. I have never been politically involved in any real sense at all. And, unlike my compatriot Ken Loach, I don't make films that have any clear agenda. Certainly you never walk away from a film of mine having a clear political view, because I haven't got one. So, to suggest that my background is Marxist would be undeserved. Of course I have socialism in my background—in my film *High Hopes* I deal with it in an inconclusive way. It's about how difficult it is to face up to the fact that you may call yourself a socialist, but what are you doing about it? Are we all sitting on the fence? And that's a personal statement, my expression of that sense of my own wooliness at the time that film was made.

RJC: Let me put my question in another way: do you have a sense of advocacy? Do you feel any sense of advocacy, on behalf of your audience, about how to cope with this world we're all messing up?

ML: I think there are different ways of advocating, to use your word. I would suggest that some films talk to you emotionally and not necessarily with a clear, rational slogan; they simply leave you with a feeling that may in some way inform the way you look at the world. Whereas other films may work through your emotions and the way you feel about the world, and the way human life is and the way society organizes itself, at the same time that they make a very specific, if implicit statement, about one sociopolitical subject or another. My natural instinct is to see society as a society that works because of the nature of the individuality of its individuals. I can't look at a crowd without seeing a thousand individuals. What's fascinating to me is that each of us is different. So in each of my films, each of the characters, large or small, is properly and organically and thoroughly, in a three-dimensional way, at the center of his or her universe. Such that, even though there may be a clear objective or point that I'm moving toward, you nevertheless get multiple perspectives, because the characters aren't ciphers. They're people, and the details of their humanity are what it's all about in the end.

RJC: As opposed to what you find in overtly political filmmaking, yours are genuinely, spontaneously created human beings. And that's not an easy thing to do.

ML: No, although in my view, Mike Leigh films are political in the sense that they are concerned with investigating, and reflecting on, how we lead our lives. But I would challenge anybody to say that they've walked out of a film of mine with one single, clear notion as to what I was telling them to think, because that's not what I'm up to. I want you to walk away with things to argue about and ponder over and reflect on and procrastinate about and, you know, supply for yourselves.

RJC: We have been living through difficult times for the past several decades, as a result of the culture of wealth and greed. But the present economic crisis is going to put an end to that cult, one way or another. Can you imagine a resulting, new political environment that would affect your own work?

ML: I suppose the answer to that question, at a fundamental level—it's a dodgy thing to discuss, because nothing is ever black and white—would have to be no. I think that I make films about how we are, although that's a pompous thing to say in a universal sense. Although my milieu is always specific, the actual things that happen, at a fundamental level, are endemic to what human life is about. You know, I've been to screenings of my work—in particular, *Meantime* [1983]—in London and Sydney where people stood up and harangued me for having the tools to make a film about the manning of the barricades . . . and not making it, not dealing with those issues. I accept the criticism because that is not what I'm concerned to do; I'm concerned to do other things. Were a revolution to come, the job for me, in fundamental terms, would still be to take the human temperature, as I always do; to look at people in terms of their needs and emotions, of how men and women function, what it is to be a parent and child, how to survive in the world as we know it. Having said that, I must also say that nothing makes sense to me except a world in which there is real equality. I can't believe, for example, that I live in a country where, after more than a decade of a so-called "socialist" government, we still have a railway system, an educational system, a healthcare system, and a steel industry which are riddled with the curse or disease of privatization.

RJC: We all know that no individual book or film changes the world, yet books and films, as an aggregate, do change the world. Do you have any thoughts about the relationship between art and social change, a long-term, indirect, complex, often subterranean relationship?

ML: Look, this goes back to something that has already more or less been said during this conversation. If I make films to which people genuinely respond, whatever their response, I feel that I'm justified in thinking that, in some minuscule way, I'm making a contribution to that person's life, or to individual people's ideas. I call my films subversive. I think it's subversive to tell the truth about things—not the obvious political truths, but about how ordinary people get on with their lives. That's what I do.

RJC: Have you ever considered shooting in a foreign country, apart from the United States, with a completely different crew and getting away from all that's familiar?

ML: It seems natural to work in a context that one understands. I think the most important thing is to work here in England with teams of people on both sides of the camera that are completely in tune with everything you need to make these great films with their very specific roots. The instrument is totally tuned and we can play anything on it, so to speak, within the parameters of the sort of film that I make. To go, for example, and make a film that isn't in English, where English isn't the first language—because specifics are so much a part of what I do, and language is so very important—it would be very difficult under such circumstances to play the instrument properly.

RJC: I don't mean necessarily to use foreign actors, but to be in a foreign place, a different environment, a different context.

ML: I must admit, I have done it twice. I made a film, the last BBC television film I made, *Four Days in July* [1985], which was set in Belfast, and which took a year to do. This is not a joke, for it was very much a case of making a film in a very "other" place. It was in English, but tapping into a whole different world, in the same language that was at the same time a different language—this was in 1984. Also, at the end of the 1980s, I went to Australia, where I created a play called *Greek Tragedy* [1989], which was actually about Greek Australians and all the actors were from a Greek-Australian background; and that was again a very specific investigation into a world that I didn't actually know very much about. So I've experimented with a "foreign context" to that extent. The only thing I would say in addition to this is that it remains a frustrated aspiration of mine to make a film with a much bigger budget, which would allow us to get out and about more, and such a film might involve what you're talking about. But if I wasn't allowed to take my regular crew along, where we all speak the same language and have a real rapport, I think it would be very difficult. I certainly don't see any inherent virtue in doing what you've posited just for the sake of doing it.

RJC: Larger budgets and foreign contexts aside, do you regret not having explored your Jewishness on film, which you have done in the theater?

ML: I don't regret it, and should I wish to do it, I will.

RJC: What exactly is it, then, that makes your movies different from others depicting ordinary English people—ordinary *people*—Christian, Jewish, or otherwise?

ML: What you're really asking is: Why is it that things that purport to be about real people fail to be actually real. My answer to that would be that the filmmaker is not aspiring to the condition of documentary; that is to say, they have caused something to happen in front of the camera which is not really researched and doesn't have a reality about it. It isn't three-dimensional; it wouldn't be able to go on if the camera weren't there.

Also, they don't understand it, they don't know who these people *are* really; they haven't asked questions about where they come from, what they had for breakfast, et cetera. I'd say that what I do is work very, very thoroughly indeed and get the actors involved from the word go to create a world that really does exist, whether we point a camera at it or not. Huge amounts of what we do, during our five-to-six-month rehearsal periods, never sees the light of day in tangible terms, as action in front of the camera. But we really know who these people are. We know everything there is to know about them socially, economically, and in every detail of their lives. And it all informs what happens. So it begins to do what it seems to me the job is. Which is, putting it at its crudest, to reproduce the real world with some kind of semblance of reality.

And not only that, but in looking at it and deciding how to shoot it and what it is I'm trying to say, I actually understand the world. I actually have taken the time and the patience and gone through the pain of the research to know what it is that we're dealing with. I suspect that it boils down to no more than that in the end. If you look at any of the great films from around the world—whether you look at Buñuel's *Los olvidados* [1950], showing those kids on the streets, or at one of Ozu's family dramas—there's no question whether these guys know what they're filming. They know the world, they know the culture, they know who the people are. This other style you're talking about is people making films in a culturally and professionally infantile, naïve, and ultimately presumptuous manner.

RJC: It seems that what *you* try to do is capture a reality that you actually believe in, as opposed to directors—many of them American—who want to make movies about regular people but depict their world the way they think it *should* be.

ML: And the question is: What is the source and nature of that notion of the world as they think it should be—the idealized world? It's like the debates over *Naked*, for example. Obviously, the assertions that it was a misogynist film are ridiculous and not even worth talking about. That criticism comes from the kind of quarters where "political correctness" in its worst manifestation is rife. It's this kind of naïve notion of how we should be in an unrealistic and altogether unhealthily over-wholesome way.

The decisions one would make about any character, whoever she is when we make her up, are implicitly political. In many a movie you've got a character that nobody's ever stopped to think twice about, it's just a character, a woman. But I do. I can't get to it until we've done all that, until these questions are really addressed, and have become the life force of the thing.

And the questions that are asked and the decisions that are made are political in the sense that by placing everybody in their social, economic, cultural, historic context, we create—in a distilled and dramatic and cinematic and therefore metaphoric way—a world that will contribute something to the way the audience lives their lives. And as far as I'm concerned, that is a political act. As distinct from making a film where you actually stand up at the end, walk straight out of the cinema, and shoot the first policeman you see and man the barricades, which may or may not be a good thing. Making my kind of film is a political act because life is about how you live it in the smallest way from moment to moment as well as in the great movements, which are actually easy to talk about.

RJC: To some extent, you combine politics and race in *Secrets and Lies*. Yet the intriguing aspect about race in this film is that it seems as if it's going to be a big issue at the start, but it winds up being less important as the narrative wears on.

ML: As you get to know Hortense, you simply forget that she's black because you get to know her and it ceases to be an issue. And that's what happens to the characters, too. When it comes to the crunch, on the whole, the thing that worries anybody least is the fact that she's black.

Again the idiots in some quarters came out waving their flags and saying, "Well, the film shirks its responsibility, and why aren't they intolerant towards her, why didn't they behave negatively"—as though everybody in the world would be racist, which was not the case in 1996, when the film was made. I knew—and this is built into the structure of the film—that a lot of people would make the assumption that Hortense was going to be reacted to in a racist way. But, finally, we made what is a very unequivocal political statement, which is: "We are all people." It seems incredibly obvious to have said that in 1996. It's not a very sophisticated thing to say, and maybe it's sort of a wishy-washy liberal thing to say, but actually that is what the film is all about: that, actually, other things transcend this and that is as it should be. In that sense, you could argue that I am presenting something as I think it should be. That's how people should behave.

RJC: Compared to *Secrets and Lies*, *Life Is Sweet*, and even *High Hopes*, a film like *Naked* has a very distinct quality to it. In the other three pictures, it seems as if all the people could almost live in the same neighborhood.

ML: You could look at it on another level; you might say that all of my films with the exception of *Naked* are about family, but I would disagree with that because I think all of my films, including *Naked*, are about family. The fact that there isn't a family in it doesn't stop it from being a film about people who have a need for family, who are constantly talking about family, yet who are constantly in retreat from their roots. All of that is what the film is about. So, in a sense, the actual difference that you identify isn't really such a difference at all. You could, for example, take a male character out of three of these films and line them up alongside each other and find some extraordinary similarities. Most obviously Cyril in *High Hopes*, Johnny in *Naked*, and Morris the photographer in *Secrets and Lies* are all very similar, and are characters that I would identify with in some way. All are guys with a passionate idea of an ideal world and how we should all be. The first guy, in *High Hopes*, has kind of given up on it and doesn't know what to do, is inert. The second guy is so angry with everything, the failure, that he's turned in on himself, and the third guy deals with it in the opposite way and carries on beings as positive as he can. But all of those things relate to each other. I think it's too easy to pull *Naked* out as being different, when in actual fact it comes from the same preoccupations, it's fished from the same sea.

RJC: Still, *Naked* explores "badness," and it does so with a destructive character who is simultaneously attractive—even charismatic.

ML: Yes, there was an element in that film that was entirely evil. It was a film about badness as much as anything else. Who wants to make a film about goodness? There are people around who can't do enough to be positive, and I wanted to deal with the opposite, which is also important. And I would suggest that what you see in *Naked*, and in my films generally, you mostly don't see in the movies. As a kid in the 1940s and 1950s, I would sit in movies endlessly—and that's mostly Hollywood and British films, because we didn't see any other films—and think wouldn't it be great if you could see people in films like people actually are.

RJC: That's unusual, since most people go to the movies to get away from reality.

ML: People say, "Ah, yes, but audiences just want to escape." I think that if people see a film like *Secrets and Lies*, where the stuff that's going on relates to things that they really care about, then it's more of an escape. They answer, "Well, yes, but then the audience worries about real-life things," but this is fulfilling, it's enriching, it's not like just eating candy for an hour and three quarters. It's actually really communing with something and feeling like you've been through something that comes out making you feel better able to go back and worry about the specific things that are your problems.

So I think people are very dumb, very mindless, about escapism and entertainment and all that. They say, "Ah yes, but we're in the entertainment business." Excuse me; I am also in the entertainment business and I make no bones about it. If my movie ever was not entertaining, it's a turkey as far as I'm concerned. My aim is to entertain, meaning, literally, what the word means. People forget what that word means. It means to make you stay here, to keep you in your seat. One of the things that drive me mad about watching films in the States is that nobody can sit still for two minutes—everyone's in and out, like bloody monkeys in a cage, eating and talking. The attention span is dreadful because, well, the films are boring, basically.

RJC: Unlike *Vera Drake*. As you know, I have my reservations about it, as I did about *All or Nothing*. But we're not here to talk about my film criticism. . . . Is this the most intense subject you've ever tackled?

ML: It's different, I'll say that. *Secrets and Lies* was about someone who brings up a child who doesn't know she has a half-sibling somewhere: secrets, after all, are how we live our lives. *Vera Drake* is darker because she's doing something she knows is criminal on a certain level. The film poses a moral dilemma that asks questions of you and asks you to see an essentially good person cast in the societal role of a criminal. In the current, immediate context of the fact that the law may be changed in the United States, people should be aware that if you change the law, we will retreat to where we were and go back to the situation that the film portrays.

RJC: What made you tackle abortion?

ML: This film isn't a sudden leap into a new subject, if that's what you mean. I have a basic preoccupation with life and how we live our lives. This is the film where I decided to deal with it directly. I remember what it was like before the law was changed in 1967. When I was a child I knew many women who had been to prison and you weren't sure for what, but you found out later. But mostly it's about an issue we have to concern ourselves with; at least I do, as a parent and as a member of society. The population of the world has increased since the beginning of this conversation by rather more babies than you could get into the top floor of this building, and not all of them are born into loving environments. That has to be confronted in this chaotic society. So I'm only concerned, in the film, to ask questions and to raise them, which is why I hope I haven't made a picture that is polemical and crudely propagandist and bludgeons you about the head.

RJC: What was your film stock for *Vera Drake*?

ML: Super-16. We shot it on Super-16 to save money. It was a tough budget of just under $9 million. Super-16 here doesn't look like that because of the brilliant cinematography, and also because Kodak developed an amazing Super-16 stock. It's got a great grain quality for blowing up to 35mm.

RJC: How much research did you do for this film?

ML: I did it in all sorts of ways. I talked to medical and legal people and historical people and people with sociological backgrounds. You name it, I did it. But that's what I always do. That's part of the job, and the joy, of creating a total reality.

RJC: Given that the abortion law changed in 1967, you set the film in 1950. Why did you choose this period?

ML: Well, first of all it has to be before 1967. I could have set the film in 1966, but the truth is that I think I chose 1950 because it's still in that postwar period, when there's still that sense of the trauma of the war hanging in the recent air, in recent memory. It's still in that functional utilitarian world of rationing, but there's a sense of togetherness as well; there's a sense of putting things back together again, and all of that's in the film. There's almost a kind of innocence or wholesomeness. If the film takes place a moment after 1956, then rock and roll has happened and therefore it's a different world—that's my perception of it. And so the time period felt right, because it's just on the cusp of things. It's still an old world, but the second half of the twentieth century lies just before it. It just felt right, really, given what has to happen to this family, ultimately, in the story. And remember, this particular 1950s world still exists in many countries where the law remains such that abortion is outlawed.

RJC: Do you think you made Vera *too* good a person, too angelic?

ML: No, I reject that premise. I don't think it's true at all. She's a perfectly real person of the kind—and we all know them—who are simply disposed to be helpful. Vera is a *good* person, a good person criminalized by society, such that the film in the end is about good and evil, the good and the bad.

RJC: Do you think she would have been able to carry out the abortions if she had admitted that's what they actually were, as opposed to just helping out young girls?

ML: She absolutely doesn't think that it's a criminal activity. To put this matter in its social and historic and universal context, the fact is—whether anybody likes it or not—that there have always been, in all societies, at all times, people, mostly women, who have been there, in your family or in the next street or in the next town, and who know how to deal with this problem. We may not like that but that is a reality.

RJC: That's not really an answer to my question. Vera may not view herself as an abortionist, may never even use the term. But she's not a stupid woman, and therefore she would surely know that, with each abortion, she was snuffing out a human life—or at least the possibility of one. I agree with you that *Vera Drake* in the end is about good and evil, but I see some of that evil in Vera herself.

ML: And I don't. Denial, yes; evil, no.

RJC: Even the police in this film are "good," sensitive and nonjudgmental.

ML: The decision to make the police, basically—especially the detective inspector and the policewoman—good guys and not bad cops was an entirely thematic and dramatic decision on my part, because I felt that to have bad cops come in and just beat her up and give her a hard time wouldn't . . . we'd learn nothing from that. Just as we'd learn nothing if she was a hard, extortionist abortionist. There'd be nothing to learn—there'd be no moral dilemma involved.

RJC: But, again, Vera's moral dilemma has to do only with her desire to continue her "helpful" work at the same time that she knows what will happen to her family if she gets caught. The aborted fetus is left out of the picture. Had you chosen to have Vera meet Lilly, her procurer, face to face, perhaps somehow, implicitly, this subject could have been raised. After all, Lilly is the one making money off Vera's abortions, not Vera.

ML: Oh, I see. That's interesting. That, what you're particularly referring to, that moment of their seeing each other, it never occurred to me. The truth is that whilst Lilly the procurer certainly could have been prosecuted under the law, the tendency was to prosecute the abortionists rather than the procurers. And for that reason I don't pursue the Lilly-strand. But also, dramatically, to be perfectly honest, I felt that to deal with what happens to Lilly, at the trial-stage of the film, would be cumbersome and in a way something of a red herring. But what you're saying is something else which is quite interesting, which is the notion of their actually, at some point in time, confronting each other, or of Lilly's being confronted by Vera. Well, such a scene is not in the finished film, but I am happy to leave it as one of the many things for audiences to ponder. And, though we disagree about some matters concerning this picture, ponder you have. So, from my authorial perspective, that makes *Vera Drake* a success in a way that I hope all my movies are successful. Making people think is what it's all about, isn't it?

Bibliography

Cardinale-Powell, Bryan, and Marc DiPaolo, eds. *Devised and Directed by Mike Leigh*. London: Bloomsbury, 2013.

Carney, Raymond, and Leonard Quart. *The Films of Mike Leigh: Embracing the World*. New York: Cambridge University Press, 2000.

Clements, Paul. *The Improvised Play: The Work of Mike Leigh*. London: Methuen, 1983.

Coveney, Michael. *The World According to Mike Leigh*. New York: HarperCollins, 1996.

Jones, Edward Trostle. *All or Nothing: The Cinema of Mike Leigh*. New York: Peter Lang, 2004.

Leigh, Mike. *"Naked" and Other Screenplays*. London: Faber and Faber, 1995.

Leigh, Mike. *Secrets and Lies*. London: Faber and Faber, 1997.

Leigh, Mike. *All or Nothing*. London: Faber and Faber, 2002.

Leigh, Mike. *Vera Drake*. London: Faber and Faber, 2010.

O'Sullivan, Sean. *Mike Leigh*. Urbana: University of Illinois Press, 2011.

Watson, Garry. *The Cinema of Mike Leigh: A Sense of the Real*. London: Wallflower Press, 2004.

Whitehead, Tony. *Mike Leigh*. Manchester, U.K.: Manchester University Press, 2008.

"Of Time, Memory, and the Movies: Talking to Terence Davies," by R. J. Cardullo (2012: previously unpublished in book or magazine form).

Terence Davies was born in the city of Liverpool in 1945 and raised in a working-class family. After leaving school at sixteen, he worked as a clerk until his mid-twenties before attending Coventry Drama School and later the prestigious National School of Film and Television. He began his career as part of a generation of British Film Institute-sponsored directors that included Peter Greenaway and Sally Potter; however, while his contemporaries have largely lapsed into self-indulgence, Davies is today regularly fêted as one of Britain's better living filmmakers. He first established himself with three celebrated shorts, known collectively as *The Terence Davies Trilogy* (1984; "Children," 1976; "Madonna and Child," 1980, and "Death and Transfiguration," 1983), which was followed by the features *Distant Voices, Still Lives* (1988) and *The Long Day Closes* (1992).

At this stage of his career, Davies' work was highly autobiographical, focusing on his childhood in Liverpool, and drew acclaim for its meticulous attention to detail as well as its sensitive yet often harrowing portrayal of emotional hardship and endurance. Two literary adaptations set in America followed: John Kennedy Toole's *The Neon Bible* (1995) and Edith Wharton's *The House Of Mirth* (2000), Davies' biggest commercial success to date. Returning to autobiography with *Of Time and The City* (2008), a documentary about his beloved Liverpool, Davies switched back to adaptation in his last film, *The Deep Blue Sea* (2011), based on Terence Rattigan's 1952 play.

Despite worldwide acclaim and a number of awards, Davies has often struggled to finance his films, and his unwillingness to kowtow and compromise his art has left him with long periods of inactivity. The result is that he has produced only five features, one documentary, and three shorts in a career that spans three decades.

R. J. Cardullo met Terence Davies at the British Film Institute in London in early 2012 to discuss his work, his influences, and the struggles of being an independent filmmaker. He had just finished a script about Emily Dickinson, but it was not to be filmed until 2016, as *A Quiet Passion*; this film was preceded in Davies' *oeuvre* by *Sunset Song* (2015), an adaptation of Lewis Grassic Gibbon's novel of the same name, about the daughter of a Scottish farmer who comes of age in the early 1900s.

R. J. Cardullo: What did cinema mean to you as a child, and how did it influence your decision to become a filmmaker?

Terence Davies: I was taken to the movies when I was seven by my father. There were eight cinemas within walking distance of my house, and then eight in town—there were sixteen, so you were never lost for anything to see. What was important at the time were the British comedies, which that time were better than the American ones. We had fabulous people in them like Alastair Sim and Margaret Rutherford . . . the list was endless.

When you're a child you're not aware of influence, you absorb—you absorb the world. And I suppose I absorbed film language because I was seeing it and I thought it was true. I didn't understand what a cut was; I didn't understand what a dissolve was, or a close-up. I just looked at it and I felt. I thought it was real. You're not aware that what you're seeing was shot on a sound stage, but you are affected very deeply by it nonetheless. For me it was magic, it really was magic.

A great influence on me came from poetry, not cinema: it was *Four Quartets* [1943], by T. S. Eliot. When we first got our television set in 1960, I watched Alec Guinness read them over four nights. I still read them now, once a month. I think that they're one of the greatest achievements of poetry in England. They're about the nature of memory and time, the nature of mortality—the terror and ecstasy of just being alive—and the nature of seeing. How by seeing something very small you can become changed by it, or perhaps it changes you. Eliot writes: "What we call the beginning is often the end / And to make an end is to make a beginning." Did the end precede the beginning or was the beginning always there before the end? That's such a wonderful description of the nature of time and experience and that particular passage always reminds me of that middle passage in the speech by Richard II when he says, "How sour sweet music is / When time is broke and no proportion kept. / So it is in the music of men's lives / And here I have the daintiness of ear / To check time in a disordered string; / But for the concord of my state and time / Had not an ear to hear my true time broke. / I wasted time, and now doth time waste me."

RJC: What did you learn at film school?

TD: I learned a lot at film school, particularly about structure—I made my first film at drama school in fact. I did it naturally, but I did it very clumsily because I'd never made a film before; I didn't know how you did it. There were certain things I did instinctively, and I didn't know why—I just felt it would be right. I didn't know whether it was right or not . . . I was never told it was right or wrong. I just trusted my instincts. I mean there are lots and lots of things wrong with the first part of the *Trilogy* [1984], for example: it's far too long and far too slow . . . but you learn by doing, that's the only way. What was a revelation at film school was to be able to see a film on the screen and analyze it—actually breaking down a scene into its component parts.

RJC: When you were making the *Trilogy*, were you trying to stay away from social realism?

TD: Not really, that wasn't conscious. I suppose in a way it is socially realistic to a degree because that is the tradition that had dominated British cinema since the late 1950s. But I knew I didn't want it to be realistic in the sense that "This happens, then that happens as a result, and then this happens . . ." That's not interesting. What I was more interested in was "What happens emotionally?" Which may not be the next thing . . . it might be a flashback or a flash-forward, but it doesn't matter; it had to be true to how I saw it. I didn't know why I saw it like that, and if somebody said, "Justify it," I couldn't. I could just say, "It felt right."

RJC: Time and memory are important themes in your work. What attracted you to these subjects and how did you develop them cinematically?

TD: Well, I think they developed emotionally within me, naturally. I then had to find a way of putting them in the order that felt right because memory is cyclical and not linear—that's what fascinates me about it.

There's nothing wrong, mind you, with a film's being a linear narrative if that linear narrative is well done. A lot of films have been made with a linear narrative that are great films. It's when the narrative is *grinding* it out, and you know what the dénouement is going to be, that there's nothing interesting happening. But if you take the attitude of being subjective toward what you're looking at or what you're feeling, then things arise—not as a result of plot point or narrative point, but they according to what is emotionally right as the next thing.

The problem with film is that it's always in the eternal present. When you cut, you always read it as "this is the next thing that happened." What do you do if you dissolve? Or if you cut and then dissolve? What does that mean? It begins to change the nature of how we perceive time. But film is closest, I think, to music. You don't have to be a musician to follow a symphonic argument; if you love the music, you'll follow it. My great musical love is Anton Bruckner. There's a wonderful moment in the *Seventh Symphony* [1885] where there's a huge climax to this wonderful tune, and then there's a pause, and then the tune returns on first violins, like a long, long echo of what we've just heard. Your inner ear has been waiting for some kind of resolution, but it wasn't waiting for *that*. It's devastating. It's so moving and so beautiful, and I think you can do that with film. You can deny expectation, but you've always got to imply that expectations are going to be fulfilled—but not necessarily in the way that you were expecting it. That's what makes things interesting.

For example, I can't watch films on an airplane. But I was once sitting in one and I got bored or I couldn't read and had no other form of escape. This film was on about a young girl living in an apartment who loses her job and she doesn't get on with her next-door neighbor. As soon as you see the next-door neighbor—he opens the door and he's just got jeans on and you see he's been to the gym—you just know exactly what the dénouement's going to be. You can start calling out the shots. Why waste ninety-eight minutes? We know they're going to get together and they're going to fall in love and they're going to be happy ever after. *Nauseating*! Because there's no ambiguity, there's no drama, and you don't care. You simply do not care. What would have been interesting is if the next-door neighbor had been an ordinary bloke. Just ordinary and they didn't particularly get on and they weren't particularly friendly.

We long to see somebody ordinary because these beautiful young actors all look the same. I can't tell the difference. The really depressing thing is you can then work out the story for yourself and you can actually call out the shots. There's nothing interesting in that. Why bother making such a film? What's it telling us? Nothing. Or what it's telling us is that the subtext is so shallow: only beautiful people get together and live happily ever after. They live in fabulous apartments. They don't seem to do any work at all. They eat junk food and yet she never puts weight on and his body is always gym-toned. Do you really expect audiences to swallow this? Presumably they do. Presumably the film made money. That depresses me because there's no feel for either a decent narrative and people you can believe in, or proper—not just pretty—images, which have meaning. You can shoot a film about a knife and fork, but if it's got subtextual meaning it could turn out to be beautiful. That seems to be becoming more and more rare. I want to try to get that feeling of what it's like when the curtains open and you see the opening credits and you see the first shot and you think, "I want to go on this journey." You've *got* to want to go on the journey!

RJC: Yet critics have said that your films have no storylines—interesting, unexpected, or otherwise. What are your thoughts on this?

TD: There are stories in my films, but the stories are very simple. They are not complicated. And there I suppose my template is Chekhov. What happens in Chekhov? Not a lot. He's talking about the human condition, which is interesting enough. And when you're talking about time and memory, that is fascinating in itself. So all you need is a very simple story, and all the best stories actually are. Is drama about lots of things happening? Well, actually it's not . . . Real drama is about something much more elemental—and gripping.

RJC: The simple stories in your films explore certain feelings—desire, misery, elation, self-pity—in a way that might be described as un-English, and yet repression, silence, and self-control are a component of them.

TD: Not only did I grow up in a time when "repression, silence, and self-control" were normal, but my mother was particularly stoic: "These are the cards I've been dealt, now I'll get on with it." And she did get on with it and that is, I think, rather heroic. Now everyone has to write a book or have a documentary made about his or her experience. Back then, those avenues were closed. There was a time when people did behave in a way that was considered seemly.

RJC: As you write your "seemly" scripts, how closely do you structure a movie?

TD: I write down everything as I hear and see it in my mind—every track, pan, dissolve, crane, piece of music. Everything is in the screenplay. I know every shot, but the order will change. So the script becomes an aide-mémoire, which is why I never do a storyboard. But content dictates form, so I'm not conscious of how or why I structure certain things in a certain way. Mahler said, "One does not compose, one is composed." And that's what happens with a film: it will tell its story in the way it wants to be told. And, you know, you want to tell it in the most succinct way, because that's always much more powerful. You learn how long to hold a shot, for instance—and how long not to hold one. There's a two-minute take with a static camera in my *Trilogy*, the boy's bus journey with his mother, which I always call my Angora-sweater shot, because by the time it's over you could have knitted one. There is a point, though, where a shot dies.

RJC: Do you decide ahead of shooting on a specific style for a film, an aesthetic?

TD: If there was an aesthetic, say, in *Distant Voices, Still Lives* [1988], it was that I wanted to show life the way it was back then. It was much more gentle and polite; there was much more of a sense of community. England is very philistine today. Also, I wanted to show real people. The working classes of that time have always been used for comic turns, on the stage or in films like David Lean's *Brief Encounter* [1945]. Noël Coward himself couldn't tell the difference between compassion and condescension. It's the same in Lean's *This Happy Breed* [1944]—chirpy cockneys, you know, with a chirpy cockney voice: "We've survived the war!" It's about as relevant and as real as the Man in the Moon.

And so I had a specific idea of how I wanted the cast to act. I didn't want them to act; I wanted them to be. And I said to all of them, you must see the *Trilogy* first and you must not act. You'll get the script a week before shooting. Just read it twice, once for sense and once for character, and then don't read it again. Learn the scenes we're going to shoot only the night before. We'll rehearse for ten minutes before we start, and then we'll do it in under ten takes. Because after ten they get repetitive. And very often we got it in three.

RJC: Do you look at paintings for inspiration?

TD: I know nothing about art. I've never gone and looked at pictures in a museum; I have no vocabulary to discuss them. Obviously, there are painters I like. I like the French impressionists and Seurat; I like Modigliani. I think Turner's paintings of Venice are stunning. But I don't like Picasso, for instance. I can't respond to some triangular woman with her tits on the side of her body. It may be great art, but it doesn't mean anything to me.

RJC: Do you shape the visual sequences to the music in your films, or vice versa?

TD: You never cut a picture to the music. That's the mistake I made with the two-minute shot in the *Trilogy*. If a scene is visually right, then you can use just a snatch of a song and it's enough.

My great passion in music is the symphonic tradition. I can't sing or play an instrument, but I can recognize a symphonic argument, particularly in Mahler, Bruckner, or Shostakovich. And so that really strong idea of how something should be organic, coupled with popular American music, which I was brought up with—that curious combination has been very, very helpful to me. Because the thing one has to steer clear of is sentimentality. You can get away with it in America, for the simple reason that Americans aren't the least bit embarrassed by sentimentality: that's because they're as hard as nails. The English are terribly embarrassed by it—because the British people are the most sentimental people in the world.

Yet they think sentimentality is vulgar. Like passion, they think it's vulgar. What you do is find ways to use a song or music that negates the sentimentality.

RJC: Why is passion vulgar in England?

TD: Because we're a very odd nation. There is this innate reserve. There is this intrinsic feeling that you have to have some kind of restraint. As we've discussed, I grew up in a world where the British were known for their restraint. Passion was disdained and it still is now because everyone wants to be cool, as though they feel nothing about anything. I was talking about this to a friend, and she said something I think is true: that the reason we're such a philistine country now, and a lot of the people are so horrible and the place is so dirty, is that we're no longer a colonial power and we've turned our colonialism in on ourselves.

We befoul our own nest because we've got nowhere else to do it. I think, too, that the British think passion is a badge of insincerity, that it's something only "they" do, the "dagos" abroad. It's the same as the eighteenth-century ideal of the "gifted amateur." To be professional is really rather vulgar. And our disdain for passion is exacerbated by our caste system, which is as rigid as anything in India or Japan.

RJC: It sounds as if America is the place for you.

TD: Well, you get welcomed in America, whatever class you come from. I remember when the *Trilogy* was going to be shown at the New York Film Festival, a young woman asked me when I was coming over. I told her, and she said, "Come and stay in my flat; I'll be away then." And it was No. 1, Fifth Avenue, and there were real Matisses on the wall. Extraordinary hospitality.

But the thing I don't like about America is that in Britain you can fail, and fail honorably, but you can't over there. There's a cruel, competitive edge. I remember the first time I went to Chicago, I was in a restaurant sitting in one of those half-moon open booths. And I overheard the people in the next booth, who were talking loudly, and I thought they were planning a murder. I was literally on the verge of saying to the waiter, "Look, I think you'd better call the police." By the time my food came, it transpired that they were opening a graphics office in the next state. I find the cutthroat attitude quite awful.

RJC: What films have influenced you?

TD: I can't say that particular films have influenced me. There are films that I've been absolutely knocked out by. When I was eighteen, I saw De Sica's *Bicycle Thieves* [1948]. And then there was Visconti's *Rocco and His Brothers* [1960]. Of course they were revelatory at age eighteen—one had never seen anything like them. And then I discovered Bergman and Kurosawa and Ozu, Truffaut's *The 400 Blows* [1959], and things like that. But I can't really say, "Oh, well, I saw Donald O'Connor in *Francis the Talking Mule* [1950] and it changed my life." [Laughs.]

I love American musicals, though I don't know how much they influence me; they once gave me the most enormous pleasure I've ever had. When I play the soundtracks now, I can remember where I saw the pictures. And seeing them again re-creates my childhood. Every time I watch *Singin' in the Rain* [1952], I cry. Because I remember being taken to see it as a child and seeing this perfect world. Because that's what the Hollywood musical created. When you grew up in a Liverpool slum and you saw these films, that's what you thought America was like. Everyone was rich, everyone was beautiful. There was no want, no poverty; it was always summer. That's very potent. It's as potent as religion. In fact, for me it's very much become a religion.

RJC: Are you part of the British cinema tradition?

TD: Well, I don't feel part of a British tradition, because I don't think there is one. I think every once in a while we produce good films in spite of our lack of film tradition, like those of Powell and Pressburger or the Ealing comedies or Nicolas Roeg's *Bad Timing* [1980]. But one problem is, we share a common language with the Americans, and they've always made films better than we have. They see film as film; they see the way it works. Our culture is centered on the spoken word, and the theater has always had more prestige here. We've produced great theater actors, but we cannot produce good cinema actors. The same with writers. What you get, when your writers come from theater and television, is a record of the spoken event. And that's not cinema.

RJC: How do you feel about films, about your films, as works of art?

TD: Look, at the end of the day most people don't give a toss whether a movie is a beautifully made piece of cinema. They don't care. So you can pour your soul into something, and yes, some people care, but most people don't. It'd be very nice just to be doing *Rambo 27*, because then you'd make a lot of money and materially you'd have a very nice life. But (a), I haven't got the talent, and (b), I haven't got the inclination. I'm very puritanical; I want my films to be good films, cinematically. But, again, at the end of the day does anyone really care? I remember reading an article about the scherzo in Mahler's *Sixth Symphony* [1906], which is a miracle of the sonata form. But think of all the people in the world who've never heard of Mahler and don't even want to.

You know, I was constantly asked at film school, "What is your audience?" I said, "I don't know." I make my films because I need to make them. I know that what I want from film is what I want from music: to be emotionally moved and intellectually stimulated. And I think all great art does that. Which is why one constantly returns to the late string quartets of Shostakovich, the symphonies of Bruckner and Mahler, to Welles's *Citizen Kane* [1941]. You go back and you rediscover something every time. And that's a joy.

RJC: You are not an explicitly political director, but . . .

TD: I am an intense republican, and I see the British monarchy as callously living off the people's money. The Catholic Church itself did me a great deal of damage. For somebody like me, who discovered at puberty that he was gay (it was then a criminal offense in Britain), the church offered no succor. I felt then that if I prayed and was really good, God would make me like everybody else. Those years when I prayed until my knees bled were awful. I finally realized that religion was a con, a lie, and that priests were just men in frocks, and I dropped the church when I was twenty-two. I was so angry. I'm still very angry about it, because it wasted a lot of my emotional time. It left a deep emotional hole in me—a sense of chaos.

RJC: Was this just an emotional rejection? Or do you think Catholicism is logically and intellectually flawed as well?

TD: Well, for me it's flawed because it starts from the premise that we're all sinners. I don't accept that. I think original sin is a monstrous idea. I don't believe most people are evil, though some undoubtedly are. The majority of people are basically good; they don't go around killing six million people. But it's all a question of belief or disbelief. If you look at it quite dispassionately, Catholicism is as remote, as unmeaning, as the Egyptian *Book of the Dead*. It's that remote to me now, and it's as exotic, as theatrical. The Catholic Church, if nothing else, has a great sense of theater. In a sense it's like watching a film. After two minutes—if you believe, then that's fine. If you don't believe, forget it. No matter how *good* it might be.

RJC: Your Catholic background seems to have left one mark on *Distant Voices, Still Lives*: its two parts are structured like altarpieces. Why is the movie in two separate parts?

TD: Well, I feel they complement one another. All of my terrible family history is packed into *Distant Voices*, which is about the nature of time and memory. But in Part 2—*Still Lives*—life has reached an even keel. I wanted to make something interesting out of our lives as stasis. The first part throws the second part into relief. And in Part 2 we see the chains that bind this family together beginning to loosen and the family drifting apart. Imperceptibly: they don't realize it. And that's why at the end, one by one, they go into the dark, which is a kind of metaphorical death.

RJC: How does *The Long Day Closes* [1992] fit into this scheme?

TD: *The Long Day Closes* makes my story, as chronicled in the *Trilogy* and *Distant Voices, Still Lives*, come full circle. It's more about the children who've not been explored, my younger brothers and sisters. It takes place during the three years between the time my father died and when I left primary school. Those three years were just ecstatically happy.

RJC: It might be presumed that such autobiographical or personal stories would have difficulty finding a universal appeal. Do you think that's the case or does one lead to the other?

TD: I think if it's done properly then one thing leads to the other because those things that are specific are usually universal. Chekhov, again, is universal but he's specific to Russia. *Kind Hearts and Coronets* [1949], one of the great films that have been made in the

U.K., couldn't have been made anywhere but in England; it's got a universal truth to it yet it could have been made nowhere but here. Just as *The Last Picture Show* [1971] couldn't have been made anywhere other than America but look how universal it is. Of all American films it's the most Chekhovian, yet it's so specific to Texas. And that doesn't matter.

RJC: Do you have a constant struggle with financing your projects and scripts?

TD: Yes, that's why I didn't work for eight years, between *The House of Mirth* in 2000 and the documentary *Of Time and the City* in 2008. It is really difficult if you are not in the mainstream as represented by Hollywood. We British are really enthralled with America, and not just politically but culturally. Why make films that they do better, anyway? What's worst of all is that you get twenty-five year olds who know nothing, saying, "You've got to have a climax on page 60." Well, who said so? Who made the story consultant or screenwriting instructor God? Or they'll say, "Every character has got to have a background story. . ." That would make the film four hours long! Are you going to fund a film that is four hours long? Silence. In *Singin' in the Rain*, for example, what background story has Debbie Reynolds' character got? She's actually got none. And we are still watching it over sixty years later. Funny that! And they show you the door.

And the worst of all is this idea that there is no difference between television and cinema. There is! And it is a very simple one. In cinema you go on a journey. In television they tell you where you are going before you leave. That's the difference. A lot of people in the film industry simply do not know the difference, and that's what's really shocking.

RJC: A lot of money does seem to get wasted on British films that try to copy the Hollywood formula.

TD: You could have the worst script imaginable, but put in a big star and it'll make twenty-five million. If you have a good script and you're not relatively well known, they're not interested. "We'd like to see this film, but not with my money"—that's the attitude. And it perpetuates with re-makes instead of something original, and they'll put the same old faces in because people will go. That does nothing for me, and it does nothing for an indigenous British cinema or any other national cinema—in fact, it does it a great deal of damage.

RJC: Speaking of Hollywood influence, you once described your first American-based film, *The Neon Bible* [1996]—based on John Kennedy Toole's early novel, set in 1940s Georgia—as "a film that doesn't work." Can you elaborate on this?

TD: It's holding onto images for far too long and not covering them properly. Like all transitional works it has got good things in it but it doesn't work as a whole. I was glad to have made it and made those mistakes, because I wouldn't make them again. I will not make them again! [Laughs.] And I couldn't have made the subsequent *House of Mirth* without having made that.

RJC: I consider *The House of Mirth*—also American-based, of course—almost your most "experimental" film because it's different from your other pictures: it's so classical. You worked on it with some well-known actors such as Dan Aykroyd, Laura Linney, and Gillian Anderson. What attracted you to the material?

TD: Well I love the book, you see. I was influenced by classic Hollywood films such as *Letter From an Unknown Woman* [1948], *The Heiress* [1949], and things like that. It was daunting—I mean some of those American directors have made more movies than I've had hot dinners. It was wonderful trying to realize a book that I really loved, and I think *The House of Mirth* [1905] is Edith Wharton's best novel, although I also loved *The Age of Innocence* [1920]. *The House of Mirth* is about the discovery of having moral integrity in a society that doesn't have any ... and God knows that is relevant today, because that's the kind of society we've got now.

RJC: What prompted you, after *The House of Mirth*, to make a documentary film for the first time—namely, *Of Time and the City*?

TD: I had waited a long time to work again. My previous film, *The House of Mirth*, was made eight years before, as I've noted. What happened was that there was a contest to make a documentary designed to mark Liverpool's brief period as European Capital of Culture. A lot of people applied for that money—157 to be exact—and I thought, "Why would they give money to someone like me who's never done a documentary before?" But they gave me the modest sum of £250,000 to make the film. I didn't have great expectations, so when it took off, it came as a surprise. Now eighty-seven film festivals want it! I also felt I'd completed making fictional films about Liverpool, and I didn't want to retread the same ground. So the documentary form would provide the opportunity for a fresh look at the past. But I insisted on making, not a strict documentary, but one based on my emotional memories—a subjective essay, which I discovered after completion was my farewell to Liverpool. My template for the film was Humphrey Jennings' nineteen-minute-long *Listen to Britain* [1942].

RJC: Given that your portrait of Liverpool is a subjective and poetic one, are you wary that you may have distorted the nature of the city in some way?

TD: The Liverpool I knew has disappeared. I've re-created a city that is no longer there. The last cinema in my old neighborhood, the Odeon, has been torn down. The city is now a mythical city for me, because memory is myth. I love the city of Liverpool, but have no illusions that there isn't a great deal wrong with it.

RJC: The passage of time plays a profound role in the film.

TD: We are at the mercy of time, but it's also an abstract idea. In my film I try to create a sense of the randomness of time by depicting it as moving from emotional moment to emotional moment, instead of in a linear fashion, by recording in sequence what literally happened over time.

RJC: Do you see Liverpool as a world you had to escape?

TD: The environment I grew up in was tiny. It consisted of house, church, street, and the movies. I felt I had to leave. I wanted a creative life, and I got one—through the movies.

RJC: Your most recent film, an adaptation of *The Deep Blue Sea* [2011], was a commissioned piece to commemorate Terence Rattigan's centenary. What was it that spoke to you in this particular play?

TD: At first, I struggled to find what the subtextual story was because the actual surface story is rather unremarkable. It *is*. But once I realized that the subtext was about love, I thought I would do it from the point of view of the female character, Hester Collyer. The play is also about a *ménage à trois* where they all wanted a love that the other person couldn't give. None of them are villains; they're all trying to do the honorable thing. Once I knew the subtextual meaning, I knew I could do it. Once I knew it was about love, which is the strangest of human emotions—it can be destructive, but it can be sublime—especially the true love of someone who is otherwise very ordinary. Hester's landlady tells her, "This is what it's like. A lot of rubbish is talked about it. But you wipe someone's arse and you keep their dignity so you can both go on. Suicide? No one's worth it." And she's right.

I remember that someone in my family tried to commit suicide in a sort of half-hearted way and one of my brothers-in-law (who is dead now) was a very blunt man, and I can remember him standing at the bed saying, "No one's worth it." I thought, "Yeah, you're right. No one is. No one." But to be driven to that state must be dreadful. Even in my worst despair, I've never wanted to kill myself. I couldn't do it. Suicide is an act of bravery. But *true* love is an admixture of all the things you've seen in life and one's own subjective idea of love. There's a wonderful quote from *Four Quartets* on this point: "Love is most nearly itself when the here and now cease to matter." That's fabulous.

Anyway, that's what prompted me to adapt this play; but it's also not just that. I grew up in the days of the women's pictures where the central protagonists were always women and they were always strong. I grew up when Douglas Sirk was at his height—with *All That Heaven Allows* [1955] and *Magnificent Obsession* [1954], for instance—and then I discovered on television Max Ophüls's *Letter From an Unknown Woman* [1948]. I also grew up with later work of Joan Crawford and Bette Davis, but then I discovered their earlier stuff. They were both very powerful in one way or another. So it seemed completely natural to me to make a women's picture, but what I didn't want was that the woman in it should be a villain, because none of the characters in women's pictures are.

RJC: How familiar were you with Terence Rattigan's work before this film?

TD: I'd never seen the plays on stage, and I'd never even seen the 1955 film version of *The Deep Blue Sea*, directed by Anatole Litvak and starring Vivien Leigh and Kenneth More. But I had seen, on television many years ago, the 1952 Anthony Asquith film of *The Browning Version*, which I think is the best because it's got that wonderful performance by Michael Redgrave. And I remembered going to see *Separate Tables* [1958], with Burt Lancaster and Rita Hayworth, which I think is really good. So I said I couldn't do either of those because I've seen the films and they would inhibit me. I said, "What I'll do is read the entire canon and see which I think I can do the best." And *The Deep Blue Sea* was the one I responded to the most.

I hadn't adapted a play before and was very worried about it, I can tell you. They told me my first draft was tentative and I said, "I know it is, because I'm very frightened of the material—i.e., can I do it from Hester's point of view?" In all his plays, Rattigan makes the first act about exposition—what happened before the curtain went up—and that's not terribly interesting: if you can show something, you don't need someone to tell you about it. Once I knew I could write the script from Hester's point of view, I knew I could get rid of a lot of the exposition by opening up her consciousness and letting her drift in and out memory as she waits for Freddie to come home. Basically, then, the first act is collapsed into ten minutes with the Samuel Barber *Violin Concerto*. You see two men and this woman and there must be some sort of relationship among the three. And then you explore what that relationship is and how she came to be where she is and what decisions she made. It's a very simple structure, really.

RJC: *The Deep Blue Sea* is a narrative of love as—to a certain extent—all your films are narratives of love. And you spoke earlier about how many contemporary movies flaunt predictable and false happy endings. What then is the responsibility of the filmmaker in presenting love to an audience? I ask because, as you know, false images of love as embodied in the cinema can be damaging. I speak from experience. I grew up as a boy who believed that the love I had to have in my life was meant to be a cinematic love, and this belief brought me much unhappiness and ultimately failed me. I had to unlearn such a desire.

TD: All the films from the period 1941 to 1959 give you a false, almost pernicious, attitude that you'll eventually meet Miss or Mr. Right, marry, have a few problems, and live happily ever after. Trying to actually unpick that emotionality from yourself is very hard.

RJC: Looking back on your career, you well know that you've received many critical plaudits. Do you feel that these have vindicated you as a filmmaker?

TD: Because of my personality, I get worried when I get a lot of praise. I become frightened. I'm an atheist now, but as soon as I start to think, "This is lovely," the Catholic in me says, "Beware the sin of pride." I get frightened. I mean, I read one bad review and I'll think they're right. I'm completely neurotic—that's all I can say! [Laughs.]

RJC: Do you have any projects that you are working on now?

TD: I've just written a script about Emily Dickinson [filmed in 2016 as *A Quiet Passion*], who is your greatest poet, I think. She was lucky. She could afford retirement because her father was a senator. But even then she had sonly even poems published in her lifetime, and then they altered the punctuation in them. One man who published her says to her in my screenplay, "But I've published you," and she says, "Yes, for which I'm grateful, but you altered my punctuation." He says, "Oh, what's a colon here or a semi-colon there?" She says, "To the reader, nothing. To the artist, it's an *attack*."

Bibliography

Davies, Terence. *A Modest Pageant: Six Screenplays with an Introduction*. London: Faber and Faber, 1992.

Everett, Wendy E. *Terence Davies*. Manchester, U.K.: Manchester University Press, 2004.

Farley, Paul. *Distant Voices, Still Lives*. London: British Film Institute, 2006.

Koresky, Michael. *Terence Davies*. Urbana: University of Illinois Press, 2014.

"'Girls Are the New Men': An Interview with Pawel Pawlikowski," by R. J. Cardullo (2004; previously unpublished in book or magazine form).

After cutting his teeth as a filmmaker with a series of acclaimed documentaries for the BBC (British Broadcasting Corporation) during the 1990s, Pawel Pawlikowski (born 1957) was named Most Promising Newcomer by BAFTA (British Academy of Film and Television Arts) for his 2000 feature début *Last Resort*; the follow-up, *My Summer of Love* (2004), won the BAFTA award for Best British Film of the Year. But neither picture felt obviously British, since each reflected a border-zone existence (literal or figurative) in a sometimes beautiful, sometimes horrific country. Indeed, both of these films are imbued with the sometimes wry, often sardonic spirit of the Czech New Wave of the 1960s; accordingly, each is less a convoluted narrative than a fable-like character study more preoccupied with the "unrepeatable" moments offered by idiosyncratic actors than with the idolization of glamorous stars.

Nor was the director of *Last Resort* and *My Summer of Love* "obviously British." Born in Warsaw, Pawlikowski first visited Britain in 1971 at the age of fourteen, then lived in several European cities before settling in the U.K. with his Russian wife and two children. His wife's sudden illness and death in 2007 put his professional life on hold while he focused on raising his children, with whom he now lives in Paris. Pawlikowski thus seems to have been an exile since he was an adolescent, always observing from the outside. And his films show it, from *Last Resort* and *My Summer of Love* to the more recent *The Woman in the Fifth* (2011)—a thriller about a troubled American writer living in Paris—and *Ida* (2013)—Pawlikowski's first film set in his native Poland, about a novitiate nun in the 1960s who must examine the nature of her own religious identity as well as the issue of her country's wartime past.

Insistent about not being pigeonholed, Pawlikowski is one of the most distinctive voices in contemporary British cinema—a director who refuses to churn out films that conform to predictable trends and generic prescriptions. Given the usual critical tendency to formulate Manichean divisions between escapist commercial fluff and committed political cinema, Pawlikowski is noteworthy for steering clear of both formulaic genre film and the heavy-handed didacticism that sometimes mars well-intentioned socially realistic pictures. While his movies occasionally evoke the acute observational prowess of Ken Loach, his willingness to collaborate with his actors before cementing a final shooting script is reminiscent of some aspects of Mike Leigh's working method.

R. J. Cardullo spoke with Pawel Pawlikowski after the North American premiere of *My Summer of Love* at the Toronto International Film Festival in September 2004.

R. J. Cardullo: How, for you, do the disciplines of documentary and fiction-feature filmmaking interact?

Pawel Pawlikowski: I don't think I was ever a proper documentary filmmaker. I've always been a bit of a hybrid. My documentaries tended to be quite oblique and constructed and often rather personal or subjective. I had little to do with the *cinéma vérité* tradition, where you stick a wide-angle lens on your camera and just follow your subject, or with the other type of documentary, where you just juxtapose moody or atmospheric shots with talking heads or voice-over commentary. My ambition as a documentarian was to look at real-life stories, situations, and characters cinematically. I tried to distill them into strong scenes and images and to put them in some unexpected order that amounted to a cinematic vision—particularly in a film I did in Bosnia, *Serbian Epics* [1992], which became rather famous. I didn't want to spoon-feed my audience. But this sort of lyrical, ironic filmmaking demanded a degree of mental participation from the viewers that many apparently did not have or want to give. So around 1995, I realized that it was getting more and more difficult to raise money for these films, even though I had won the Prix d'Italia, the Grierson Award, and so on. In a word, such documentaries became unfinanceable.

For me, the jump to fiction was not such a radical break at all. *All* filmmaking is about creating a world through photography, editing, and sound, and most good films feed off reality in some way. So although, as a documentarian, I was photographing things and stories that were real, I always tried to show them creatively or against the grain, as ambiguous and strange. Then and now, I'm always on the lookout for original stories, characters, situations, and places, and I always keep my ears open for good bits of "found" dialogue.

The fun part in filmmaking—both documentary and fiction—is exploring and finding things out about people, including yourself; it's getting under the skin of someone or something and finding the film. Of course in the usual sort of feature-film script, you get it all laid out—the characters are set, and they do what they do to move the plot forward; it all sort of adds up in the end, but there's no mystery, nothing to be discovered, nothing for the filmmaker to do, really. Directing that sort of thing is more or less like plumbing. Naturally if the script is a real work of art and the writer has genuine vision and has done some serious exploring of his own—as in Robert Towne and Roman Polanski's *Chinatown* [1974], let us say—then that's a different proposition. But such scripts never land on my desk.

RJC: I feel that there is very little "fat" in your finished films, documentary or fiction.

PP: Yes, the end result may seem "fat-free," but the process is more complicated: it's full of digression and waste. What usually happens is this. First, I need to get really excited about something: a character, a theme, a story. And this is the most difficult part. I am extremely lazy, so I really need to get worked up about something to want to get out of bed early every morning for a year or two. Once I've stoked up this fire inside myself, I start throwing all sorts of things into it—personal stuff, memories, people I knew, characters from favorite books, photographs, strange stories from the newspapers, material from my previous films, and all kinds of terrible, pretentious ideas and motifs. I also start driving around looking for landscapes, meeting people, taking pictures, and writing notes. Once I've amassed all this stuff, I try to sketch out the story outline and see what fits and what doesn't. I keep trying the different versions of the outline on people—a good friend, my producer, whoever will stay with me in the room and listen. It's trial and error. A good writing partner would help, of course—someone like-minded who could bring stuff to the table and spur me on in some way. I'm still looking for that person, in a long-term sense.

Once the outline and the characters are broadly there, the paring down begins. It's mainly a matter of finding the balance between character and plot, between the unexpected and the believable, between information and the image. So you start stripping away all your bad ideas, clever motifs, weak narrative lines, excess exposition, and blatant obviousness. What can help in this process is casting and screen-testing. Even meeting actors who are wrong for the part can help you focus. And when you finally meet someone who is right, that's a huge step forward.

So I keep trying things out, distilling, and slowly the characters firm up and the hidden shape of the film emerges. This can last right up to the first day of filming and sometimes, I am afraid to say, even beyond it. The main thing is not to tread water, not to rely on clichés. Sometimes you can't avoid them, of course, but what you want is to get to the heart of something. You just have to make sure there is a heart to begin with. The key thing is the initial impulse and where it comes from.

When it comes to the actual directing, I also try to keep things simple. I try to stay close to my characters, so the visual perspective tends to be limited. Of course, as for big, wide landscape shots, with interesting light and framing—that's a different matter. You need them to create the universe; you can never have enough of these. But otherwise I keep it small. I always feel that there is just one good angle from which to photograph a scene and there's no need for what's known as coverage. Unless you're really struggling, which sometimes happens.

I generally avoid tracking or crane shots. It's partly because I don't work with big budgets and these sorts of things take time to set up. But also I find that very few filmmakers know how to use such shots well. Usually these operations seem to be there just to draw attention to the fact that the director is directing. In fact, what they actually draw attention to is the fact that the film is missing a heart or some other vital organ. I remember on *My Summer of Love* [2004] we came up with some complicated shot for a very simple scene. We had the track laid and lit it, then I looked through the viewfinder and said to my cinematographer, "God, this is beginning to look like some … movie." Which was an anathema. We axed the shot immediately.

RJC: I know that you don't really start any project with a finished script, but instead with a shooting document. How does that affect your approach, and perhaps your ability to gain financial support as well?

PP: Well, it's difficult. It's more difficult than anything to work in this way, because it cements your (bad) reputation with the money people and reduces your possibilities as you advance—or try to—in your career. But for me, the script is just a jumping-off point. I love well-written scripts, but, you know, you need to look at the hidden life in scripts. You can't just look at the surface of things. I always look at the stuff that shows potential for making the movie. And I think a lot of the filmmakers that I respond to, work in a similar way: I mean directors like Wong Kar-wai and Terrence Malick. Do they have scripts? I don't know. Very often, though, it's good to have a script. Because it's a good disciplinary device, and it takes you into areas that are useful to explore and that enrich the whole process. The main thing is, you try to create these conditions under which you can put all the elements together and sculpt with them until you reach the desired end.

RJC: As a filmmaker, how do you decide what to reveal to the audience, and what not to reveal?

PP: It's a sort of balancing act between what you reveal and what you don't reveal—you know, how much help you give to the audience. I mean, I'm just learning as I go along, but my feeling is that if you create enough scenes that define the characters, and if you create enough characters who are believable and have a life rather than just a function in driving the plot, then people will get drawn in, forget they're watching a movie, and just follow the story. I love films where I'm not just being dragged around by excess exposition. And I know there must be more people out there like me.

RJC: So it's your style to be resolutely non-explanatory.

PP: I want each scene to stand on its own, to have a life of its own, and for the film to grow one step at a time, in such a way that you can't see the strings being pulled. My aim is to distill reality through ambiguous situations. Because life does have its mystery. Stories or narratives involve reinterpretation, to be sure, but, in reality, everything is ambiguous or slippery in the final analysis.

RJC: How did you end up making films, anyway?

PP: Film was my escape from everything. In Warsaw I used to go to the cinema all the time. It was very cheap and I'd go and see everything that was on. Hence film always meant something to me, but I couldn't imagine myself directing because I didn't know what it involved.

And then, when I became a pretentious teenager, literature was my main interest. I wanted to be a poet. I wanted to write serious, timeless poetry. Then I realized I had no talent, no language, nothing to talk about, so I gave up. When I was at university, I started making films in a workshop and suddenly I felt that this was it. I'm a guy who likes to walk around and observe; I like feeding off reality and transforming it in a kind of literary way. Even my documentaries were not really an empirical record, as I suggested earlier—they were more about what was going on in my head. Film became the medium for me.

RJC: So literature was a big influence on your work?

PP: The literary scene in Poland was actually much stronger and more dynamic—and people were much keener to hear about it—when artistic expression was a political problem, when you couldn't talk freely. It became the one authentic way of communicating. Everyday language was bizarre, contaminated by this communist phraseology, so any kind of authentic speech was cherished. And people knew the works of great poets like Adam Mickiewicz really well. Even if you couldn't buy them in a shop, you could hear them somehow and that meant a lot.

RJC: What was it like growing up in Warsaw?

PP: Strangely, as a kid—in this otherwise pretty tough police state—you had a lot of freedom because no one paid any attention to you. They were busy keeping control of the society, so you could do anything. You had the freedom of the town. I used to go all over Warsaw with my gang, skipping school and riding around on bicycles. It was quite an interesting street life. Nowadays you go into these squares and locales that we frequented and they've been turned into parking lots. There are not enough street kids roaming around. They're too busy studying and learning English, preparing for nothing in particular. There is no sense of future, no sense of career.

The world of teenagerdom was largely left to its own devices during this time. Comically enough, Poland was the freest of the eastern European countries. There were a lot of rock bands. Polish rock music was big all over the Eastern Bloc and there were bigger leaks from the West in Poland than elsewhere. I can remember buying "Lazy Sunday Afternoon" by the Small Faces—it was one of my first records. There were leaks to Poland all the time. It was a kind of cargo cult. We were absorbing anything that came from the West. This was the start of globalization, which is a nefarious process, but at the time it seemed innocent and sweet so I was all for it.

RJC: Warsaw seems to be changing fast these days.

PP: Warsaw is a city that has always had a very strong identity—before the war it had folklore and street life, and of course there was an aristocratic life and a middle-class life and a Jewish life. After the war there was zero population in Warsaw, but when they decided to make it the capital again people started swarming in. And, above all, people on the make came to Warsaw. If you wanted to make it you came to the capital, because the city itself was starting from scratch and you could too. There were no rules—apart from the Communist Party rules! Warsaw is a city of contrast, of overlapping layers. The city is always looking for its face because it keeps getting destroyed and re-created again. But all these different layers co-exist and there is so much vitality. It's a lively community and it's always changing. You can't call Warsaw beautiful, but it's definitely textured.

RJC: What do you think of contemporary Polish and European films?

PP: Polish films no longer interest people; in fact, they no longer interest Poles. In England, something similar is happening. Local audiences don't go to theaters to see England on the big screen—they get enough of that on television—so they go to the movies to see anything but. In France, there are always interesting films giving voice to particular views or visions, but, in my view, European cinema these days is best represented by independent American filmmakers (Paul Thomas Anderson, Jim Jarmusch) or by the new generation of Argentinian directors.

RJC: Since both *Last Resort* [2000] and *My Summer of Love* deal with disparate outsiders, do you think that, coming from eastern Europe and being something of an outsider yourself, you can look at British life with a certain amount of detachment?

PP: Yes, I think so. I tend to be an outsider in most places. Once I left Poland in my teens, I was put in that position—looking from the outside and looking at things without understanding what people are saying, and seeing life without being inside the flow of life. Not anymore, but for a period.

Even if I had stayed in Poland, though, my perspective would have been that of an outsider. As a teenager, my favorite books were novels like J. D. Salinger's *The Catcher in the Rye* [1951]. After the age of fourteen or fifteen, I spent a lot of time in different countries—not just England, but Italy and Germany, where I couldn't speak the language. This instilled in me a certain tendency to stare and observe—a kind of documentary obsession. And I didn't take anything for granted, since I was slightly removed from the status quo. So this theme of the individual at odds with his society is always appealing to me. Of course, if I had been making movies in Poland, I wouldn't have had to strain to abstract that reality as much as I do in my current films.

The kind of cinema I grew up loving included Italian neorealism and especially the Czech New Wave. Milos Forman's *Loves of a Blonde* [1965] was the film that showed me what cinema was capable of. Making a realistic film (although obviously in a stylized form) like that was a very radical gesture in a culture where free speech was limited. Nowadays, with Reality TV and everyone filming themselves, things are quite different. In any event, I like the cinema I like. And I am not a great fan of British cinema at the moment, the films of the last thirty years or so.

RJC: Why is that—for the last thirty years?

PP: Well, there are some—*Trainspotting* [1996] was tremendous, but generally it's not my sort of cinema. No, I loved the socially realistic British films of the 1960s. When my mother was a lecturer in English at Warsaw University, she had a free pass to the British Council, so I used to go to see all the British films without understanding a word of them: *Billy Liar* [1963], *The Charge Of the Light Brigade* [1968], kitchen-sink movies like *A Taste of Honey* [1961]. I couldn't figure out anything in these films but the images did stay with me (more so than did those from the other movies I was seeing)—and with them some kind of abstract idea of England. I had a privileged education in British cinema, then, without ever speaking a word of English.

So I was a great fan of British cinema, but for my own fiction features I was trying not to think in terms of sociology. British cinema was, and is, drowning in sociology: how people speak, how they behave; everyone is so self-conscious. In *My Summer of Love* these distinctions are clear: one girl is from the working class, one isn't. That goes without saying, and it's no big deal. There's no need to make a big deal out of class, especially since there are many English films that deal with nothing but class. Let's now concentrate on the story and the psychology; let's make it universal and slightly abstract. Every good film is a bit like a dream, when you come away from it. That's what a filmmaker should aspire to, rather than try to create some kind of social document. I want to create a little imaginative world that will stay with the audience.

RJC: *My Summer of Love*—despite certain documentary-like elements—is certainly much more concerned with the inner and imaginative lives of its protagonists. And you seem to retain from Italian neorealism the idea that it's interesting to work either with nonprofessional actors or professionals who don't have that much experience.

PP: Yes, I'm looking for actors that stimulate me and photograph interestingly, who also can provide me some sort of believable inner life filled with paradoxes—who are a bit mysterious, in other words, and who are not types. Most cinema is heavy with "types" who just serve the purposes of the plot. In landscape as well as actors, I'm always looking for something contradictory that reminds me both of my past and of good literature.

RJC: Just as "types" permeate films, the industry is also—at least from a marketing point of view—driven by genres. Perhaps some people will therefore try to pigeonhole *My Summer of Love* as a "lesbian" or "coming out" film, although it's not at all typical of that genre.

PP: I'm glad you said that. The film was very well reviewed last month in Britain, although a couple of critics did exactly what you—and I—feared they would. I wasn't interested in tackling the "lesbian movie" genre. I was just looking for an interesting pair of characters. I wanted to give the characters a certain autonomy in the narrative and make them a bit mysterious or complicated. Since you don't quite know what they're going to do or say, there's an air of discovery about every scene. You don't think that a scene is just there to lead to another bloody scene. Very often you're just sucked in by the ambience, and the film takes you where it takes you.

RJC: In many respects, the character of Tamsin, played by Emily Blunt, is like a character from literature—a charismatic figure who functions as something of a catalyst. Were you particularly interested in the collusion between a very flamboyant character and one who is much more vulnerable?

PP: Very much so. On the one hand, there's this girl with a lot of imagination and a lot of acquired knowledge—and great vulnerability as well—who ensnares another person and concocts various schemes. And then there's the other girl who doesn't have the same cultural baggage. Although she doesn't have any tools to understand the first person, she has spirit, wit, and a kind of generosity. In the end, she's less vulnerable than the posh girl. I like this sort of clash of characters and England is good at providing it. The trick was just to make it part of the story and not to get bogged down in questions of class.

RJC: Yes, that aspect of the film made an impression on me, since of course a director like Ken Loach would have handled this dynamic quite differently.

PP: These were existential, not sociological, questions for me. Part of the problem is that while, in commercial films, characters are functions of the genre or plot, this is even true in some noncommercial films, where characters can also be reduced to types. My previous picture, *Last Resort*, was about a Russian refugee—a young Russian woman. A lot of films about refugees just treat the characters as innocent victims; these characters have no autonomy.

This might be a socially conscious approach, but it's not interesting. Refugees can be as bad as anybody. They're just people, yet it's very difficult these days to give such characters an independent life and not reduce them to types.

RJC: This refusal to reduce characters to types is particularly interesting with reference to the character of the evangelical Christian in *My Summer of Love*, Phil, played by Paddy Considine. In an American film, there would be a temptation to portray him as a simple-minded fanatic and demonize him, whereas in your film he's treated with considerable empathy.

PP: In the United States, the evangelical Christians are much more "hands-on." In England, evangelical Christianity is characterized by a purer form of spirituality that is less political or connected to wealth and power. So we tried not to demonize the character of Phil or make him comic. The Brits, you know, tend to ridicule anyone who puts himself on the line and to crucify anyone who seems vulnerable or absurd. And it was very difficult to make this guy, on the one hand, believable and normal and, on the other hand, expressive and dangerous. This is a fine line and for a long time I couldn't get him right: he was either too bland or too demonic. I didn't solve that problem until the first few days of filming.

RJC: Did you feel that, making a film about young women, you had to be careful about how you shot it, that there was a danger of being voyeuristic?

PP: Yes, especially when it came to the scenes that enter intimate territory, we had to tread very carefully. We were aware that it was a danger area, that what we finally did could be misrepresented or misused somehow. But my general theory is that if you get the characters right, if you get into their heads, then there's no danger of exploitation. The real exploitation comes when you use characters in a film as pawns for the sake of some plot—or politics—and that's one thing I don't like. If you manage to get into the heads of people and see the world slightly against the grain, then I think you're engaging in a very moral exercise. I think that's the best that cinema can do these days—to immortalize interesting or even compelling characters, people who are not average, who are not media constructs. If you are truthful and try to cultivate the authentic, you'll be fine.

RJC: The landscape helps you in this respect: it really contributes to the overall tone of *My Summer of Love*.

PP: I really like the ambiguous landscape you get in that part of Yorkshire, where nature and post-industrial decay overlap. But I wanted to shoot this very English landscape in a new way. Because of the kind of light you get in Britain, most films tend to capture the landscape in greens, browns, and grays. But I wanted strong, saturated color, no half-tones. We went for reds and pinks that would contrast with the green, and we tried to shoot everything in an afternoon light, to try and sculpt the objects a little bit more—trying to bring out the familiar in them at the same time as we made it somewhat foreign. I wanted the landscape to be elemental, more down-to-earth and passion-driven, and thus more in keeping with the story and characters. For that we needed the sun. To everyone's horror, the place I'd set my mind on happens to be in the rainiest part of England, so it was a huge gamble. But we got away with it.

RJC: You used the same cinematographer on *My Summer of Love* as you did on *Last Resort*, didn't you?

PP: Yes, Ryszard Lenczewski, who is a good friend as much as anything else; he also shot my subsequent two films, *The Woman in the Fifth* [2011] and *Ida* [2013]. I think we are good for each other. We have very similar tastes and we always spur each other on. When we do have the odd quarrel, it's never anything personal: it's always for the good of the film. Ryszard is rather special. He is an old hand who knows all the tricks of the trade, but he's also never lost the enthusiast and the artist in himself. He was the closest person to me on these films. I think your work with the cinematographer should be as intimate and direct as your work with the actors. You have to be able to cut to the chase and keep trying things out until you succeed. I want to work with people who are genuine, open, and brave, people who'll get excited, who'll challenge me. Such people are rare. Most tend to hide behind their supposed professionalism or their status or their agents.

RJC: In *My Summer of Love*, why did you again make a film with women as the main characters, even as the main character of *Last Resort* was female?

PP: It's difficult to explain, but women represent something that is not—but at the same time is—me. There's a tension there, a perversity that I really feel we have in common, and also a conscience that goes in circles and in the end destroys itself. The world is not divided up into men and women, but rather into those whose conscience is enhanced by fantasy—who are seeking and who require transcendence in art or religion—and the consumers who are satisfied with the world as it is. That said, it's so hard to find a big man, a man's man nowadays, in life as in art. This is one of the reasons I did *My Summer of Love* after *Last Resort*: girls are the new men.

RJC: What was the inspiration, by the way, for *Last Resort*? Was the premise based on your own research?

PP: It was actually based on my own life. That was the starting point, anyway. But this sort of thing didn't happen to me, although my mother did bring me to England. She became a lecturer in English literature at a university there and married an English guy. For me, *Last Resort* is about a mother and her son. But I resented that everyone thought that the film was a plea for refugees. The character in the film is obviously a bogus refugee. If anything, she should have been sent back immediately for being a fake! Oddly enough, after the film's release, I began to be invited to all of these humanitarian events in support of refugees. This proves that journalists need a handle on any film they cover and that other people don't watch films properly.

RJC: *Last Resort*, from my point of view, is imbued with humanism and artistic integrity.

PP: I'd like to think such things are within me. I've always liked films where humans are at odds with the system, ordinary people who have some anarchy or poetry about them. I'm interested in characters trapped in a particular environment—characters with an intriguing dynamic that splits between their intellect and their emotions. I love to fall in love with such characters, and all the films that remain important to me are the ones where I've really fallen for the characters and have wanted to be up there on the screen with them.

RJC: In other words, you're not interested in making didactic films, where falling in love with the characters on screen is not the point.

PP: Well, I have a kind of internal debate about this subject, since I'm obsessed with politics. At the moment, history is being tackled by the spin industry. For this reason, I believe that making a film in which the characters are not stooges is in itself a political gesture. Once again, I'm just trying to go against the grain slightly.

Although *My Summer of Love* does not strike any political notes, I'm not dealing in staple characters and am going against the grain of the enormous media saturation that you find in Britain today. Young people these days are swamped with media images of all kinds, but my characters are not listening to any particular kind of music or using iPods or paying attention to pop culture. This itself was a political gesture of sorts, even if it was a negative gesture. It would be dishonest to make a political film like Michael Winterbottom's *Welcome to Sarajevo* [1997], which is a shallow and stupid piece of work. If you can't make a good political film—which is a neat trick—don't. Listen to Wittgenstein.

RJC: The critical acclaim *Last Resort* achieved was phenomenal. Did this create added pressure for you?

PP: Not really. Remember, I'd been around for a quite a long time before *Last Resort*. I'd already had my ups and downs. There was a time in the early '90s where I couldn't go wrong; every documentary I made seemed to come off just fine and I kept getting awards, great reviews, acclaim at festivals. Then the times changed and I had a lean period. I lost the commissioning editors, I sort of lost my audience, and I lost confidence. But I recovered.

Probably the biggest pressure is the one you put on yourself, knowing that whatever film you do next, you will have to live with it for at least a year and a half in the making. And if it's bad it's going to haunt you for many years to come. Also, as I said, I am really lazy and I can't understand directors who simply enjoy making films, especially those who keep churning them out year after year without having anything much to say.

The critical hype around *Last Resort* didn't affect me that much. I mean the film was what it was. I liked it, but it seemed to me that some critics who professed to love the film, hadn't actually seen it. The film was this rather personal story about a mother and son thrown into a strange, scary world that, again, was slightly abstract. My "political" contribution was mainly to show two foreigners with a degree of empathy, from inside, as interesting people, and not in the way they're usually shown in English-speaking films, as reprehensible gangsters or incomprehensible victims to be pitied. But despite what was there on the screen, these critics just went on about the film's gritty realism, about its being a searing indictment of the asylum system. And then, rather comically, a pompous right-wing critic was spurred into action and declared—for the very same reasons—that the film was a piece of shit.

The same sort of thing could well happen to *My Summer of Love*, so one shouldn't get carried away either way. What was great, though, was to see the audiences in Edinburgh and Toronto and at other screenings. They just went with the film and seemed to genuinely like it. As for critics, I have a pretty good guess what some of them will write. "After bravely confronting the issue of immigration in his uncompromising *Last Resort*, with its echoes of Frears's *Dirty Pretty Things* [2002] and Winterbottom's *In This World* [2002] (plus any other films involving immigrants they can think of), Pawlikowski has now tackled the genre of the lesbian coming-of-age movie, paying homage in the process to (and here they reel off a number of 'similar' films that I don't particularly like or haven't even seen)."

Yes, there are a lot of tone-deaf people out there, and they are not seeing the same films that I am seeing—or making.

Bibliography

Baker, Maxine. "Pawel Pawlikowski: Eastern European Analysis." In Baker's *Documentary in the Digital Age*. New York: Focal Press, 2015. 78-101.

Bardan, Alice. "'Welcome to Dreamland': The Realist Impulse in Pawel Pawlikowski's *Last Resort*." *New Cinemas: Journal of Contemporary Film*, 6.1 (2008): 47-63.

Helff, Sissy. "Fragile Balance: Imaginary Europes, Transcultural Aesthetics, and Discourses of European Identity in Pawel Pawlikowski's *Last Resort*." *Journal of Postcolonial Writing*, 51.2 (2015): 132-143.

Kristensen, Lars. "Mapping Pawel Pawlikowski and *Last Resort*." *Studies in Eastern European Cinema*, 3.1 (2012): 41-52.

Monaghan, Whitney. "On Boredom, Love, and the Queer Girl: *My Summer of Love*." In Monaghan's *Queer Girls, Temporality, and Screen Media: Not 'Just a Phase'*. London: Palgrave Macmillan, 2016. 101-126.

Monk, Claire. "Pawel Pawlikowski's Resistant Poetic Realism." *Journal of British Cinema and Television*, 9.3 (2012): 480-501.

Pulver, Andrew. "Pawel Pawlikowski." *Projections* (London), no. 12 (2002): 265-282.

Rydzewska, Joanna. "Beyond the Nation State: 'New Europe' and Discourses of British Identity in Pawel Pawlikowski's *Last Resort*." *Journal of Contemporary European Studies*, 17.1 (2009): 91-107.

Winter, Jessica. "Pawel Pawlikowski: Dreaming All My Life." In *Exile Cinema: Filmmakers at Work Beyond Hollywood*. Ed. Michael Atkinson. Albany: State University of New York Press, 2008. 63-72.

Wooley, Agnes. "Screening Asylum: Pawel Pawlikowski's *Last Resort*." In Wooley's *Contemporary Asylum Narratives: Representing Refugees in the Twenty-First Century*. Basingstoke, U.K.: Palgrave Macmillan, 2014. 75-91.

"Sharing an Enthusiasm for Shakespeare: An Interview with Kenneth Branagh," by Gary Crowdus. from *Cineaste,* 24.1 (1998): 34-41.

If any one filmmaker can be said to be responsible for the current renaissance of Shakespearean film production, it is Kenneth Branagh. In 1984, only three years after graduating from England's Royal Academy of Dramatic Art, Branagh became, at the age of twenty-four, the youngest actor in the history of the Royal Shakespeare Company to perform the title role in *Henry V*. He first came to the attention of international movie audiences with the 1989 release of his film version of *Henry V*, for which he wrote the screenplay, directed, and again played the title role. It received widespread critical acclaim, with many critics favorably comparing the film's darker, grittier, post-Falklands portrayal of England's military invasion of France and Branagh's more complex portrayal of the youthful, untested ruler, to Laurence Olivier's classic but more simplistic and patriotically inspirational, World War II-era production.

In addition to writing, directing, and/or acting in numerous other films in recent years, Branagh has produced three other Shakespeare or Shakespeare-related films, including *Much Ado about Nothing* (1993), a sexy, sun-drenched, and highly energetic film adaptation of Shakespeare's battle-of-the-sexes comedy, featuring Branagh and Emma Thompson as the bickering but lovelorn Benedick and Beatrice; *A Midwinter's Tale* (1995), a black-and-white semi-autobiographical comedy about a group of actors who stage a low-budget production of *Hamlet* in the English hinterlands; and, crowning his twenty-four-year-long obsession with the play, an epic, Super Panavision 70mm, full-text film version of *Hamlet* (1996).

In the midst of a hectic shooting schedule for Barry Sonnenfeld's *Wild Wild West* (1999), in which he plays a lead role, Branagh graciously made time available so *Cineaste* could question him about his Shakespearean filmmaking efforts.

Gary Crowdus: Our first question is easy because it's multiple choice.

Kenneth Branagh: [Laughs.] I usually find those the most difficult.

GC: You have commented that, after seeing a play, you are often haunted by cinematic images suggested by the play. Is this because of a) the overactive imagination of a longtime film buff; b) a desire to translate the play into a film version because it would be seen by many more people than would see a stage play; or c) the belief that, in terms of dramatizing a play's themes or exploring its subtext, the cinema actually offers more expressive artistic means than the theater.

KB: It's a combination of all of the above. I suppose I would disagree with the last point. I don't know that the cinema offers more expressive means, but it certainly offers different means. It's obviously a medium that many more people see, and many people would choose to experience Shakespeare, or perhaps even be able to afford to experience Shakespeare for the first time, only through that medium. Certainly an overactive film buff imagination is involved, as well as a terrific desire to share one's enthusiasm for something that seems to demand rediscovery.

For many people there continues to be the sense that this writer and his work, which has such Masterpiece status, is something to fear and dread, something that will somehow expose their lack of learning or intelligence. My experience has been that when people have had a good experience with Shakespeare, beyond perhaps just the snob factor and the feeling of cleverness, it's something that can open up a certain part of them that, from this point on, starts to be much less intimidated by great works of literature.

I'm simply attempting, as part of what a lot of other people are doing as well, to allow Shakespeare to be seen without prejudice, and without the implicit assumption that I believe it will be good for you or better than any other piece of cultural entertainment you may experience—and in the belief that this work deserves its place. For my money, what's important is the way in which Shakespeare unlocks that part of us which is currently rather bereft of poetry or mystery, something that is expressed with the ongoing obsession with New Age philosophies or philosophical books attempting to exercise that part of us seeking some kind of spiritual fulfillment.

I believe these plays, written by a great poet, affect us, in conscious and unconscious ways, spiritually. Once you start talking this way, it all starts to sound a little highfalutin, but the fact is—and one has seen proof of this in performance and in reaction to films—that people have been moved beyond what they necessarily, consciously can articulate. That mysterious power of a great poet, working through words in the way that music can affect us, is a marvelous thing to unleash because it's difficult to find that in cinema or in writing these days. That's very important to me.

GC: In each of your three Shakespearean films to date, you had previously played the lead role on the stage, but in an interpretation directed by someone else. When you directed your own film version, you were obviously free to develop your own interpretation of the play and the character, but to what extent did you find it necessary to more fully elaborate your interpretation simply because you were doing a cinematic version? In other words, does the cinema demand a more fully developed interpretation of the play on the part of the director?

KB: I don't know if it demands it, but it invites it, and I think this changes depending on the circumstances of the play. With *Hamlet* [1996], for instance, there is an invitation there to see whether the cinema can provide a stronger experience of what's clearly a large part of the central character's personality, which is the expression of his inner life, his interior life. In the theater, that's brought about chiefly by the personality of the actor playing Hamlet. That remains the case in film, but it seems to me that in the theater this experience of his inner life is a combination of the relationship between actor and audience and the audience's imagination, what they choose to receive and how they identify with the performance and their view of Hamlet, even if they're seeing it for the first time.

But in the cinema, I felt it was legitimate to be more strongly interpretive about that inner life. I felt we could usefully illustrate, for instance, some more explicit confusion, torment perhaps, and guilt on Hamlet's part about his relationship with Ophelia, and this would become a cornerstone of our inflection of the piece. In a way, we're trying to do two things at once. One is to give a reading that addresses what I mentioned earlier, allowing the play to sing, if you like, for each individual viewer, so you're not confining it too much. But at the same time you want to inflect it and somehow direct the audience into what you hope will not be some sort of reductive area where you're instructing them to understand one narrow idea of yours, which, next to the vastness of the play, is tiny. I felt that a balance needed to be struck.

I've certainly tried to experiment with the level to which I interpret strongly, without denying parts of the play that could otherwise reveal themselves to the audience. The other extreme is a kind of laid-out, uninflected play, which, in a way, can be more dangerous. It's important to find the fine balance between telling the story in a way that concedes that many people may be seeing it for the first time, and not necessarily know what's going to happen, so clarity about the plot is important, and yet at the same time trying to interpretively address those issues that your experience tells you have perhaps been unclear, sometimes because of the circumstances of theater. This was one obvious issue for me in making the film of *Hamlet*.

GC: One of the terrific things about the film is that you get a much better understanding of the characters' relationships and motivations. The fact that you can make it clear that Hamlet and Ophelia have been intimately involved, for example, is very beautifully done cinematically, and it makes the relationship between them, and her later descent into madness, much clearer.

KB: My view is that it did and, even if people familiar with the play felt this was a debatable point, it nevertheless sharpened up an overall view of the drama, trying to strike the balance we talked about earlier but also including other theatrical experience. For instance, when I have been in the theater, we were often involved in question-and-answer sessions in schools or after performances, and younger audiences are usually very concise about where they feel the difficulty in the play exists. With *Hamlet* there was often a great deal of questioning about the character of Gertrude, and why, despite her apparent importance in the scheme of things, she's given so little to say. In the theater it's actually difficult to keep her in focus, because she has so little to say even in important scenes, like the arrival of Rosencrantz and Guildenstern. Even in her great scene, the closet scene, she doesn't respond very often, but the film certainly gave us the opportunity to see how she was with Claudius.

The film seemed to me a terrific invitation to do something that doesn't make redundant the debate about why Shakespeare chose to have her say so little. Yet she's referred to so often, in her sin or crime or however Hamlet chooses to characterize it, which is so hugely important to the story of the play that it seemed to me legitimate to try to bring her into a little more focus and see whether cinema, in doing that, affects the play in a positive or negative way. My feeling was that it was bound to make the drama more interesting. There was actually an invitation to a lot of the actors to try, without crassly point-making, to allow work that they'd done around subtextual thoughts to emerge in subtle ways.

GC: You clearly prefer to have as much rehearsal time as possible prior to shooting. Russell Jackson's essay on the making of *Hamlet* discusses how you developed exercises so that each actor could develop his character's backstory. Is this intended simply to generate more of an emotional through-line for modern actors, to make them feel more comfortable in the role, or is this something that might actually visibly translate in the performance?

KB: Both, I think. The greater sense an actor has of the kind of person his character is, then the more the actor can provide in his performance a sense of freedom and fluidity. In my films so far there's been no attempt, beyond some tiny specifics to do with understanding and modern usage of language, to improvise, and yet at the same time one wants to feel it's all as natural as possible. I don't feel actors can do that unless underneath their understanding of how the actual language is constructed, what each word means, there is a strong sense of who they are. It gives them confidence in performance.

When trying to strike this balance between clarity and interpretive nuance, however, one of the key contributions comes from the actors in rehearsal, when we can perhaps discover a moment where, in another world, you might want to ask Shakespeare to write six lines to explain something for you. But in identifying such a need on the part of the actor, you can offer a close-up or some moment of business discovered in rehearsal, that in cinematic terms does perhaps offer some kind of interpretive insight; and so not to rehearse is to deny that possibility. Many discoveries are made in rehearsal and this combination of specifics, which you may choose to include in how you shoot the picture, plus a more general sense of a deeper understanding, a greater sense of reality, a greater comfort level in saying sometimes difficult things—all of this I think does translate. That feeling of confidence and knowledge is something you can't quite put your finger on, but you know it when it's there, because everything is just much easier to understand. I think practice goes a long way in Shakespeare, even if it's only the practice of rehearsal.

GC: It's quite clear from the casting of your Shakespearean films, especially *Much Ado about Nothing* [1993] and *Hamlet*, that you believe it's not only possible but in fact preferable to present Shakespeare by combining classically trained English stage actors with American or European film actors with little or no prior experience in Shakespeare. Would you explain why you prefer this approach and how you go about making it work effectively, especially when you have to deal with actors with such a wide variety of acting experience and techniques?

KB: It can be difficult. It goes back to what we were just talking about, in trying to achieve this comfort level, a sense that the people you're watching are not concerned about sounding Shakespearean or proper; they're simply being in front of you, and happening to talk in a heightened language. There are many ways to achieve this. Sometimes it's by casting people who, your instinct tells you, are very close to the kind of character you want them to play, or who you feel have an intuitive understanding of such a character, or who have an intuitive understanding of cinema and are comfortable in front of a camera in a way that is not necessarily the case with classically trained theater actors. Therefore trying to find confident actors is important, actors who will not be intimidated, whatever discipline they come from, and who, if they come exclusively from the world of film, will be prepared to engage in the rehearsal process. The catching up in terms of practice, of actually saying this stuff over and over again, is something they're prepared to do.

I also like the clash, if you like, of accents and sounds, so that we don't try to homogenize the sound of Shakespeare, which again, in its clichéd form, is equated with some kind of overblown theatrical delivery, usually English in accent. That actually can be very seductive, and I think as actors we can all be rather vain and enjoy hearing the sound of our own voices, in a kind of mythic connection with some old actor-laddy tradition. Somehow it feels proper and sometimes it's hard to shake oneself out of that. In casting different groups of people, however, you start to do that shaking, you start to create a more level playing field. I think it's true that sometimes for the British classical tradition there's a nervousness about filmmaking, about the ability to simply be in front of the camera. It's been my experience occasionally that it's harder for some of those theater actors to take advantage of a moment given to them where they may not speak, but where there's a chance to say something about the character. Often they're much more comfortable with lots of lines.

For me this approach helps to keep things exciting in the rehearsal process, it means that questions are asked from quite different cultural viewpoints, and the performances and the whole execution of the piece are debated from all sorts of angles, from interior characterological reasons to apparently superficial technical questions about whether a line or a phrase needs to be said in one breath. For some people that's enough somehow, in the process of experiencing it, to lead them towards the emotional connection with this or that thought. So we try to approach the matter from every possible angle, given, as the sociologists say, the current state of knowledge. Having many different views involved makes the rehearsal process exciting and it also means that each time you do something, there is not an attempt to find a style that one would create throughout more of these films in the future, but to find what works now, at the moment when you're doing it. International casting helps keep performance alive and exciting and different.

GC: Would it be unfair to ask whether you have more difficulty in getting stage actors to deliver the verse naturally, or in training non-Shakespearean actors to learn how to deal with the verse without getting totally intimidated by technique?

KB: It's really specific to individual actors and the nature of the roles themselves. Suffice it to say that everybody finds that there is something to learn. It's continually challenging, sometimes frustrating, to make a long, wordy piece sing with the excitement, passion, and poetry you have felt in reading it on the page, but which suddenly have dissipated when you start being self-conscious and strutting around. Even with the best of intentions, this is tricky for anybody. So the difficulties are pretty widespread, and they can vary.

Sometimes classically trained actors also happen to enjoy enormously the luxury of the less laborious style of delivery that they can employ. I'd use Derek Jacobi as a specific example of someone who has enormous theatrical experience, but who took real relish in the intimacy that he could use for the role of Claudius, particularly in those few moments available to him, in the full-text version, that give away his guilt. Somehow they were able to be couched in the film version with a degree of effectiveness that's not always possible in the theater, where asides remain big, and you have to go down front. But I wouldn't say, beyond those broad generalizations, that it's harder for one type of actor or the other, because people experience the difficulty to different degrees. To be quite honest, I experience both myself.

GC: You're part of a generation of Shakespearean actors who've rejected the old-fashioned declamatory style of Shakespearean acting in an attempt to make the verse sound more natural, more realistic, almost conversational, but without completely losing its musical qualities. Is this the Royal Shakespeare Company (RSC) approach, or your own personally developed approach? For example, did you ever study with John Barton?

KB: Very briefly, because our time at Stratford didn't really coincide. I did value every form of textual analysis that was made available to us there through the experience of other directors and other actors. I've always been resistant to allying myself to what might be called a school of verse-speaking, or coming up with any particular policy for speaking verse, beyond attempting to address every possible option in discovering what a particular line or speech means. To do that, I use whatever means are available, either technically or by looking through every Folio and Quarto version, by checking out punctuation offered by different editors, and by thinking—in a way this is more where I come from—about the kind of person the text seems to indicate this character is.

GC: One of the key elements of the RSC approach is a very in-depth, comprehensive understanding of almost every word in the text.

KB: One of the dangers, though, is that it's hard not to become self-conscious about that, and I have certainly been guilty on stage in the past, with the best of intentions, of attempting to pass on my homework. What this can lead to is a very arch delivery in which there are little upward inflections as you wish to draw attention to some internal rhyme scheme or some tiny brush stroke of understanding that analysis has led you to believe is very fully there. In performance, this can sometimes be dangerous because, quite frankly, it can end up in a mannered delivery where it feels as though the actor is delivering a lecture about what he's saying rather than living it.

The experience of actually performing Shakespeare is one that starts to teach you that, while all this understanding is helpful, probably necessary—although it's true that intuitive performers can sometimes be a fantastic vessel, and need not necessarily understand everything that they say or the full meaning of it yet somehow still allow themselves to transmit meaning to the audience—what's very important to grasp is the lightness of touch that is required, and that is something I have found a little more easily achievable in the cinema. It doesn't require less breath or less effort or less concentration or less applied intelligence, but because you don't have to shout so much, you're less liable to be trying terribly hard to show everybody what you've learned. Those are the dangers of overanalysis. You need to let all that go and somehow trust that your understanding, as a vessel, serving a piece of text with everything available to it, is something that the audience will somehow intuit, that they will receive the richness of your understanding—but you have to somehow trust that you don't need to bang it out. When you do, I think it produces a kind of arch Shakespearean acting that, because of its emphasis on the complexities of the text, alienates people.

I also think that in the theater generally, and with Shakespeare particularly, you have an obligation. Part of the bargain you strike, when the audience buys a ticket, is that you must communicate the play to them. Your job must be to give to the audience any understanding you possess of the character and the story. And the overt presence of an overanalytical approach is something that can set the actor back on himself. I'm not anti-analysis, I'm very much for it; it's just that what makes this work challenging, particularly in film, is somehow trying to produce the art that hides the art.

GC: I interviewed Ian McKellen last week and he said somewhat the same thing, that the challenge for the actor is to master this technical understanding, but then, once you're on stage or before the camera, to make sure the audience is not aware of that at all.

KB: Absolutely, and I find that a particularly interesting challenge. It's something that I try to pass on to actors I work with. I do wish to hear the consonants, I do wish to feel that it's all crisply delivered—yet unselfconsciously, as well, that it just *is*. As somebody like Benson or Irving said, you've got to speak loudly and stay natural.

GC: In light of the fact that you write the screenplays for your Shakespearean films, as well as direct and act in them, would you talk a bit about the roles played by Russell Jackson and Hugh Crutwell?

KB: Russell is someone with a very rich understanding of the textual history of Shakespeare's plays and an immense knowledge of Shakespearean performance, so he's a useful bridge between academia and his own knowledge of the ways in which, somehow, the play simply works, or how this difficult bit that the actor is having trouble understanding—and that no amount of textual analysis will clarify—works as well. So Russell is a reference point for actors in rehearsal who, for instance, may have an issue with having to perform a much shorter version of a speech or a piece of prose. Often they'll go to him and talk about the whole speech and sometimes, as a result of that, I will be led to understand that perhaps I cut too deeply or that I need to restore a line or two that continues an idea inside the language that I had underestimated in terms of its importance for the actor.

And for those interested, and they usually always are, there is a lot of talk about the meaning, or the change in meaning, of particular words, especially in anything where Shakespeare is punning or being satirical. That can lead into more general conversations about the Elizabethan world picture, the use of language and conceits, and the whole Elizabethan cosmos, which can sometimes be useful to bring into rehearsal. If you're doing something like *Henry V* [1989], for instance, it's useful to talk about the concept of honor as understood by people of the time, to talk about the concept of a Christian king, to bring this into rehearsal for the sake of the actors' imaginations, so that sometimes they can understand the real, direct import of things that otherwise may seem to emerge more casually from the play for us.

Hugh Crutwell is there not only for me but also for those who wish to partake of his extensive knowledge of the plays. He was a principal of the Royal Academy of Dramatic Art for about twenty years, so, apart from his own professional theatergoing, he had huge exposure to all the Shakespeare plays many times over during that period. He's also seen, at many stages of their careers, a whole generation of experienced Shakespearean actors that includes Jonathan Pryce, Ralph Fiennes, Mark Rylance, and Juliet Stevenson. They'd probably all agree with me that he's a ruthless and savage seeker of the truth in acting, particularly in Shakespeare, and he has many now tested and challenged and pretty passionately held views on some of the plays and the motivations of the characters. He's by no means an oracle, and he freely confesses that he doesn't sit in some guru-like position, but he is a lively debater, an erudite man who certainly, from my point of view as director, will challenge anything that he feels is gratuitous or that steps outside what might be legitimately involved in the overall interpretation.

I remember when we were doing a stage production of *King Lear* and, for reasons best known to myself, in the storm scene—for which we were presenting genuine precipitation; we had real rain and wind—I wanted to bring Richard Briers as King Lear onto the stage, carrying a makeshift cross of boughs he had constructed for himself. I remember we spent a month arguing about exactly why I should do this, and, in the end, I suppose my rather feeble answer was, "I think it's effective." But Hugh felt that it was drawing a Christian image across a pagan play, it did not pay off, and that it was gratuitous, ineffective, and distracting. Finally, to be perfectly honest, I agreed with him. He'd have been perfectly happy for me to do it, but over such points and other issues of interpretation, he holds a strongly argued, passionate point of view. He also has very good taste in acting from take to take as we shoot, and he's there to keep an eye on me, but also to offer up that kind of healthy critical assessment of both my performance and that of the other actors. It's been very valuable for me, in doing both jobs, acting and directing, to have him there so that the other actors, if they feel remotely undernourished by their director because of my other responsibilities, can have another voice to listen to.

Hugh's and Russell's knowledge is extensive and, while I have hopefully developed improved intuitions and knowledge about this whole period, the plays, the characters, and the structure of the language, I find that I remain chiefly a practitioner, and I feel like a beginner every time. The practical side of executing these things, in fact, keeps me from turning into the academic bookworm I sometimes wish I could be, so I'm very grateful that Russell and Hugh are there, filling in the many areas of knowledge that I don't have.

GC: You've commented that it was during the postproduction of *Henry V* that you discovered the enormous creative possibilities that film editing offered in terms of elaborating one's interpretation of the play. Could you talk about that a bit?

KB: The power of the close-up, well acted, in a Shakespearean film seemed to me very striking. If you were remotely interested in pursuing the internal life of any of the characters, there was a real invitation to the actors to take advantage of that. In *Henry V*, the fact of my relative youth then, as distinct from the more mature performance of Laurence Olivier in the other film—which I mention only because there is another film, not by way of comparison or any other way—made me surprised at how strongly it all played, from the earliest rushes, and we shot the film more or less in continuity. I found it exciting to see how little I had to do, and it seemed to me that involved responding to the doubt in the language of *Henry V* early on, and the caution, the nervousness, the youth, the guilt, and all sorts of other things that were different from what Olivier chose to emphasize about Henry's leadership qualities amidst the feel of a wonderful, celebratory pageant that his film had.

For us, the film offered a chance to more realistically get inside the lives of the people on the campaign, to go for a dirtier, more realistic sense of what it was like to go across country in the rain. Seeing people in that kind of scenario was also helpful because it immediately changed your whole perspective. It seemed to me very untheatrical and quite revelatory at the time. The actors themselves responded to it, and then performances changed in magnitude—would that be the word?—or in the level of intimacy. There was a sense of release. Many of them had been in the play before, there were about four or five Henry Vs there—Michael Williams had played the role, Ian Holm had played it, Jacobi had been in it before—and they all responded to the sense of having to do less by way of projection and simply allowed the intelligence and wit of the characters to emerge. They also felt they could respond more to the environment, for there was just a reality to it which was exciting.

GC: How much of your interpretation was influenced by historical readings you did on the real Henry V and his exploits in France? I know you've read John Keegan's *The Face of Battle* [1976], for example.

KB: Yes, and that is a strong tonic to resist the idea of banners and flags and celebration, when you read eyewitness accounts, as it were, of the battle and begin to understand that there were so many deaths by suffocation because people's bodies piled up on each other, and learn about the kinds of noises that were heard from the battlefield for hours and days afterwards from people dying very, very slowly—the awfulness of all that. I remember our having a rehearsal discussion and talking about how people would like to go. Would you like a nuclear bomb to fall on you, or would you like six inches of cold steel, during combat, in terrible, face-to-face conditions, on a tightly packed, wet, sodden battlefield, where arrows are raining down on you, and where it was necessary to hectically keep revolving and fighting in a way that was bound to produce chronic fatigue over a period of hours? Is that the way to go? I think those influences were important.

I also felt that a general feeling of unease, of conspiracy, of political uncertainty, that level of reality which we could see in our normal lives and that fascination with what goes on behind closed doors, how politicians can rationalize one brutal, violent act by reference to some other apparently important policy—all of it helped galvanize the film and get us away from any sense of some sort of chivalric pageant.

GC: I think that comes out very clearly. From the opening scene, you get a very clear impression that not only is Henry being manipulated by the clergy, but also by his own uncle, Exeter, and other wealthy nobles who obviously stood to benefit from a foreign war.

KB: Yes, it's a rather unfortunate position to be in, where the very people that you need to lean on, the people with whom you're stuck in terms of your confidants, are also people with their own personal agendas. This is something that Henry needs, at the same time as he is aware of it in its fullest complexity, so it all makes for a very interesting scenario, very potent drama. It was something we chose to exploit with the atmosphere of the smoky, dark room, something we just picked up from reading. The reality of rooms like that was that they were very smoky, because they weren't great with chimneys and ventilation, and it all added to the mystery and the sense of pressure.

GC: I loved some of the film's other textural details, such as, during the long tracking shot across the Agincourt battlefield, the enraged French women who at one point try to attack Henry.

KB: We were trying to make a film of some commercial or watchable length but also still trying, in a cinematic way, to complete the picture, to make it as complex as possible. There's no question that many did not regard Henry as the savior, and that such a battle also involved tragic consequences for all sorts of other people tangentially involved. That tracking shot was an attempt, after having put the audience inside the battle, to suddenly stand back for a moment and say, "Look what happened!"

GC: "This is a victory?"

KB: Yeah, exactly . . .

GC: In terms of your political fleshing out of the film, since you kept in the political betrayal of Cambridge, Scroop, and Grey, the threats of rape, murder, and pillage at the gates of Harfleur, and the hanging of Bardolph, why did you decide to cut Henry's order to kill the French prisoners?

KB: Well, it's the subject of much debate, as you know, both historical and textual, and to have stuck with everything that represented the real king historically would have been fighting against so much else in the play. I felt that we could achieve a sense of Henry's ruthlessness or brutality without it and make for clearer drama. On one level, it felt appropriate, because to have him do that at that point was to be utterly inconsistent with the rest of what we were presenting as a troubled and ambiguous character. It seemed to me that it would unduly draw attention from such ambiguity and suddenly make him one kind of character, and that this would be dramatically less interesting.

GC: But its absence, for those who know the play, is almost underlined by Henry's outrage at the killing of the baggage boys. It seemed to me, given the overall grittier tone you were aiming at, that retaining that scene would add to the complexity of the characterization. I know you wanted to emphasize the Christian nature of the king, but ruthlessness on the battlefield does not necessarily contradict, even during that era, a deep sense of religiosity.

KB: It's a debatable point, and it was something we argued about at the time. In the end, I felt that it was appropriate for the dramatic shape of what we were doing, in terms of pictures—showing the camp being attacked just beforehand—and that it added up dramatically. As I think about it, you may well be right about its actual impact had we included it.

GC: It's only a few lines, but the impact is stunning. It wouldn't be necessary to illustrate the way they were actually killed, which was pretty gruesome, as Keegan explained. The more historical readings you do, the more you realize that, despite all the ambiguities and complexities that Shakespeare brought into the play, it was still a fairly sanitized portrait.

KB: Yes, indeed. It may well be that one was swayed by what one would refer to as a kind of a cinematic logic in regard to the hero, so I confess that that may well have had an impact.

GC: Russell Jackson, in his diary on the making of *Hamlet*, wrote that you often encouraged actors to do a variety of takes, using slightly different emotional colorings or registers. Did you also do that for yourself, and what did that mean in terms of shaping the final version in the editing room?

KB: The idea behind asking people to do such a thing relates to what we were talking about earlier. One can't improvise, but one wants as much life and spontaneity as possible and that, for me, is a valuable commodity. It's really in the pursuit of that that one would encourage extra takes. My experience with playing the part so often was that there were some clear anchor points in my interpretation that had developed—if I played it again now maybe it would be different—but at that point there were certain things that I felt sure of about my Hamlet. Although central to the performance, however, they were not limiting in terms of how one actually said lines or approached scenes, as long as a central core understanding of what one was playing was there.

So the encouragement of different kinds of takes really aimed at trying to be as alive in each scene as possible, trusting that my understanding of the part would, could, and should ring out as newly minted as possible. This was also affected by how the lines were being given back to me, and the interpretation and sense of character that I was receiving from the other actors. There was a large part that was unknown about how this actual group would present this story. We knew the kind of world we were setting it in, and the kinds of feelings we had about the characters, but moment to moment we wanted the drama to live as strongly and passionately as possible. So I encouraged a great deal of freedom in that way, believing that the action one is playing in any particular scene is otherwise understood.

For example, in the closet scene, let's say that "Hamlet tries to convince Gertrude of her guilt." Well, he can do that in many ways—he can mock her, he can shout at her, he can harangue her, he can plead with her, he can tease her—with the overall objective that somehow he wants to make her suffer or feel guilty or make her understand or confess, or whatever it is that one had decided upon. I enjoyed that very much, so, when I arrived each day, it was a kind of blank sheet. Factors like where we set it, and how swiftly or slowly we played it, were the things that started to affect how everything came out that day, with our fingers crossed about believing that the understanding of the scene and the character was already deep in the system.

GC: Patrick Doyle's score for *Hamlet* seemed to come in for a lot of criticism, especially in the feeling that some of the soliloquies or other key passages were musically underlined for the audience. The only part that seemed to me to be questionable, and it's more a question of the mix, was on the "How all occasions do inform against me" soliloquy, where I felt the music competed with the verse in what was an otherwise spine-tingling scene.

KB: Well, he was definitely led that way by yours truly. I felt that it was an epic moment in a play where that particular beat, if it remains in the production, is somehow undervalued. It seemed to me that, in the wake of Hamlet's having killed for the first time, mistakenly, and with our being brought into this speech through a sort of summing up of his understanding of his predicament as he perceived it at that time, and given where he was and what he was seeing—it seemed that this was a huge moment, and so I wanted from Patrick a huge, stirring anthem.

GC: It comes up at the intermission break.

KB: Sure, there's a theatrical element to it as well. This whole question of the use of music in our films has been something of a thorny subject, really, since the first one, and the same debate has ensued. My respect for the spoken word is great, but I have followed my instinct about music, and it's part of what I have felt up to this point makes for a translation from the theater into the cinema. Maybe it is too obvious a way of somehow leading people by the nose, and some people might find it either intrusive or even faintly patronizing, but I've listened to my instinct about what I thought was correct.

I think it's a question of taste, and for my taste it has been appropriate, although I have to say it's something about which I debate with myself continually, right up to and through things like the very thing you mention, the actual mix of that cue, in the mixing stage. In the end, one follows one's instinct about, "Well, I think the effect of this is worth just straining for a little bit." I think it is questionable, and it's something I think carefully about each time I do it, and to date I haven't chosen to resist my desire for seizing on those moments that, when they do work, I think work well.

I'd say, for my money anyway, that the St. Crispin's Day theme underneath Shakespeare's speech in *Henry V*, for example, works spectacularly well, catching as it does the source of instantaneous connection with emotions that the script, the text itself, addresses. Some would argue that, "Well, that would happen anyway," but I would argue that we helpfully accentuate it in a way that the cinema invites us to do. But I do accept and continue to consider the view that we play sometimes a little fast and loose, so it continues to be a real subject of concern for us.

GC: You must have been glad that, for a change, you had only to act in Oliver Parker's film of *Othello* [1995], and not direct it as well...

KB: I was.

GC: ... because you've got to concentrate on performing one of Shakespeare's most compelling, but also one of his most ambiguously motivated, villains. How did you deal with that problem as an actor? Or did you not perceive it as a problem?

KB: I chose not to perceive it as a problem. One comes at these things in all sorts of different ways. I'd been in the play once before, as a very young amateur actor playing Cassio, and so I'd listened and watched, in ways that are sometimes very helpful when you're in another part in a play, because you hear it from a different perspective. You can choose to scratch the surface or dig deeper into the vast reams of literature that exist on all these plays and all these characters. With Iago, it's particularly dense and, although I began that process, I was very quickly frightened off. I found that, in a way, I wished not to explain him, that he was what he was, and I took his words at the end at face value: "What you know, you know." And I thought, well, what I know is what I know from the text.

GC: So rather than coming up with some sort of inner device for yourself—for example, to play him as clinically paranoid...

KB: No, I did not seize, for instance, in any character-defining way, on his suspicion that Othello had slept with his wife. I did take at face value his immense disappointment and bitterness at being passed over but decided that this was also, aside from its personal characteristic, the evaluation of a soldier who realized that Othello had made really a very stupid decision. I suspected Iago believed that had more to do with Othello's outsider feeling that he was suddenly being welcomed into the Establishment and ought to do those things that were appropriate, like getting the right face in the job of Lieutenant.

It seemed to me that this was a real enough starting point, and then to allow his occasional delight in the ease with which he could manipulate what he would regard as Othello's vanity to sort of self-propel itself. But in that character, almost more than anything I'd done, I was playing it absolutely moment to moment, and thinking on my feet, as I think he does, and then realizing that he enjoys it enormously. It's enormously daring to be as outrageous as he turns out to be. It was a very, very enjoyable role to play.

GC: You perform most of the role in big close-up, in asides to the camera.

KB: Although I'd been faced with the issue before, this was the first time that I'd actually been involved, through Oliver's decision, in actually talking directly to the camera, as opposed to having monologues essentially sort of overheard, which is mostly what I've chosen to do. I found that rather releasing. It's an unusual relationship to have with the audience and with the camera, and, again, it's an intimacy that film afforded that I suspect would not have been quite the same on stage. It felt very familiar and comfortable in some way to play that role. In a way it sort of played itself.

GC: You not only played a lot of his asides directly to the camera, but also developed that relationship through physical gestures, such as obscuring the camera lens with your hand at several points. Was this something of your own devising?

KB: No, this was strictly Oliver. He had a very strong idea of how he wanted to present that relationship between Iago and the audience.

GC: He had previously played the part himself on stage.

KB: He had, indeed, and knew the play very well. He'd also enjoyed playing that role enormously. There's something releasing about it, for Iago is without any sense of morality.

GC: As a character, he's very close to Richard III.

KB: Yes, less of an actor probably, less self-conscious, I think; there's less of a flourish to him, but he's a little more deadly, in a way. There's less overt, self-conscious wit, but the character is immensely powerful, immensely compelling. It seemed to me that it was all in the text, and then, given the way that Oliver wanted to present Iago's relationship with the audience, that it was my job probably to do as little as possible.

GC: So just play the text and let the contradictions and ambiguities take care of themselves?

KB: Absolutely. I felt that very strongly and played him extremely in terms of his mood swings and his believability in relationship to the other characters, his empathy with them. I felt that, because of its chilling effect, this was a great thing to play.

GC: I've heard it said that you go through a long period of "marination" in regard to ideas about possible Shakespearean film projects. We've read about your plans for a musical version of *Love's Labour's Lost* [2000], and maybe a film version of *Macbeth*. Are you thinking of another Shakespeare film?

KB: I am at the moment trying quite seriously to formalize a little more what I clearly understand now is something that I wish to continue to do, which is to make these kinds of films. Indeed, the very two you've mentioned are in the process of being planned, with *Love's Labour's Lost* being the first of them. I hope to make that very much sooner rather than later, but setting it up in such a way to perhaps even set up three at once, and do them year by year. That's the cunning plan.

GC: Will the current renaissance of Shakespearean film production make it easier for you to make another Shakespeare film? At the very least, you must be terribly relieved that you no longer have to carry the banner alone.

KB: Very much so. I think it just goes to show that a good film is a good film, and a good Shakespeare film is a good Shakespeare film and people will go to see them. It remains difficult to raise money for any kind of film and, with every Shakespeare film, including the four I've been involved with in one way or another, it's been difficult. Such templates as there are for box-office success, the most conspicuous of which is Baz Luhrmann's 1996 film of *Romeo* *and Juliet*, tend to make people want to somehow reproduce those elements, either by casting the same actors or by doing it in the same way...

GC: That's the Hollywood mentality.

KB: ... even though people know that it's necessary for there to be new ideas and new versions and interpretations, so there's always this strange contradiction. There's now much more evidence that Shakespearean films can be successful and profitable but, at the same time, as you can imagine, *Love's Labour's Lost* as a musical is a tough sell—but not impossible. The problem is always trying to find the circumstances under which you believe you can do the film well, not being compromised by those factors that wish it to become something that, from the outside, looks comfortingly commercial. That doesn't mean the two things are mutually exclusive at all.

But I feel more strongly than ever the need to have, for want of a better phrase, creative freedom, the freedom to cast whom I wish and to do the film in exactly the way I wish. In the case of *Love's Labour's Lost*, there are a number of factors involved in such a movie that make it scary for financiers. Nevertheless, my desire for this kind of freedom is paramount, so one is currently trying to find the way to make the film one wants to make and have enough popular success, obviously, to do the next one, which would be *Macbeth*, and, after that, *As You Like It* [2006].

Bibliography

Branagh, Kenneth. *Beginning*. London: Chatto and Windus, 1989.

Crowl, Samuel. *Shakespeare at the Cineplex: The Kenneth Branagh Era*. Athens: Ohio University Press, 2003.

Crowl, Samuel. *The Films of Kenneth Branagh*. Westport, Conn.: Praeger, 2006.

Hatchuel, Sarah. *A Companion to the Shakespearean Films of Kenneth Branagh*. Winnipeg, Canada: Blizzard, 1999.

Weiss, Tanya. *Shakespeare on the Screen: Kenneth Branagh's Adaptations of* Henry V, Much Ado about Nothing, *and* Hamlet. New York: Peter Lang, 1999.

White, Mark J. *Kenneth Branagh*. London: Faber and Faber, 2005.

Americans Abroad

"Screenwriters, Critics, and Ambiguity: An Interview with Joseph Losey," by Jason Weiss. From *Cineaste*, 13.1 (1983): 46-47.

After directing some shorts for MGM, Joseph Losey (1909-84) made his first important film, *The Boy with Green Hair* (1948), for RKO. While he was filming *The Prowler* (1951) in Italy, he was summoned to testify before the House Un-American Activities Committee, the congressional committee charged with rooting out Communist subversion in the motion-picture industry. Unwilling to subject himself to the committee's well-known intimidation tactics, Losey decided to seek exile in Great Britain. In the following years he used a pseudonym—"Joseph Walton"—for his films, which were of minor quality. He then regained his prestige with the thrillers *Chance Meeting* (1959) and *Concrete Jungle* (1960).

Since he had been blacklisted by Hollywood, Losey decided to remain in Europe, where he worked for the rest of his life—mostly in England. Three of his films were based on adapted screenplays by Harold Pinter (*The Servant*, 1963; *Accident*, 1967; *The Go-Between*, 1970). Other notable films include *Eva* (1962), with Jeanne Moreau; *Modesty Blaise* (1966), with Monica Vitti; *The Assassination of Trotsky* (1972), with Richard Burton; *The Romantic Englishwoman* (1975), with Glenda Jackson and Michael Caine; *Mr. Klein* (1976), with Alain Delon; the Mozart opera *Don Giovanni* (1979); and *The Trout* (1982), with Isabelle Huppert.

The following interview took place in Paris, in the fall of 1982.

Jason Weiss: You consider *The Trout* [1982] to be your most open-ended film. To what extent did the actors fill out the characters?

Joseph Losey: A great deal, more than usual, for a variety of reasons. We worked almost entirely on location, so we were together not only for the shooting, but also for the hotels, the meals, and travel, which helps. Another reason is that the script was never completely finished, so there's a degree of improvisation. I normally try to work this way anyway, but I think in this case it was more so.

JW: What are the most significant differences between your film adaptation and Roger Vailland's novel?

JL: The book was from 1964, the film from 1982. That's a difficult stretch, because there's a big difference between the sixties, the seventies, and the eighties as decades. It's not a big enough difference to make the film a period piece if you did the novel, but it is a big enough difference so that a lot of things that were acceptable in the novel are not acceptable in a 1980s film. So we had the period thing to cope with, in terms of motivation and explanation, and even how the picture looked. Vailland was talking about multinationals in a funny, naïve way. Now everybody knows a good deal more about them and they're more or less taken for granted. Also, he placed all of this in Hollywood, treating multinationals who had nothing to do with the movies—a subject that would now not be very important. I needed a completely different environment; I wanted to find a country where there was an extended, traditional background with a modern Western position on top of all that tradition.

JW: Would you talk about your work with screenwriters, about how some of the collaborations differed?

JL: I'm glad you brought this up, but it's a big subject. It seems obvious that you don't know that Franco Solinas died this week, suddenly, without any warning. It's an immense personal and professional loss for me. I've worked with Tom Stoppard, David Mercer, Harold Pinter, Jorge Semprún. I'm sure I'm forgetting some, but in my opinion Solinas was among the best. I think he was one of the top half-dozen in the world; he did many of the great films of our time, such as *The Battle of Algiers* [1966] and *Burn!* [1969]. He did *Mr. Klein* [1976] with me. He'd just finished a new film for Costa-Gavras. He wrote two other scripts, one for me and one for Costa-Gavras, neither of which could get mounted. So it's really a tragic, horrible death: he was only fifty-five. With Franco, of course, it was a different way of working, because he always wrote in Italian, although the films were always intended for an English audience. *Mr. Klein* was an exception, but that also was written in Italian and then translated into French.

Pinter is the man with whom I've had the longest collaboration, and the one to whom I am the very closest personally. Working with him is mostly talking things out for months or even a year, and then everything gets written quite quickly. We did have trouble initially, however, in entering into the team spirit of things. Harold and I had a long, long night of heavy drinking before the start of *The Servant* [1963], and we simply were not getting along. Finally, we agreed to part company at dawn and to come back together later in the day to see where we stood. Luckily, it worked out fine and, since then, we've always gotten along perfectly... except when there's a cricket scene to shoot. Harold is a big fan, and I can't stand the bloody game. Still, I think I can play it better than he can.

With Stoppard there's less talk and even quicker writing, but not always of the same level. With Mercer it was much as with Pinter. Mercer was more unpredictable—extraordinary moments and then sometimes he was quite bad. He was also in his middle fifties when he died. Jorge Semprún was not an important collaborator of mine. I don't think he was terribly interested in *Roads to the South* [1978]. I like him personally, but I didn't get a great deal from him. Monique Lange was very pleasant to work with on *The Trout*; we worked together all the time. She contributed a lot to the film, mostly poetic and philosophical things, but very good, and big departures from Vailland.

JW: Are there any more projects you have in mind with Pinter?

JL: He wrote the Proust screenplay, of course, which has been published very successfully [*The Proust Screenplay*, 1977], but we haven't been able to get the money to film it. We've talked about several other projects, but none of them have yet come about.

JW: What is the latest stage of the Proust project?

JL: The latest stage is that it was published and put on the shelf. That probably will be it, because the script that would have cost six or seven million dollars in 1970 now would cost twenty-five or twenty-six million, and people are afraid. As Lew Grade said, when it was presented to him, "Who the hell is Proust (pronouncing as in 'owst')?" The locations are disappearing and the cast is enormous, so it all becomes terribly expensive, no matter how modestly you do it. But I think this could be a very commercial film. It's one of the greatest screenplays ever written, perhaps the best.

JW: Is it true that you've been seeking Rockefeller money to finance the Proust project?

JL: Nelson Rockefeller and I are not total strangers. I was a classmate of his at Dartmouth. I recall him as a very handsome kid, one who belonged to the best fraternity, and I can still remember his family coming to visit him in a spectacularly huge green Pierce-Arrow. Not too long ago, I wrote to him, trying to interest him in my plan to film *Remembrance of Things Past*, and I got a letter back from him saying, "I am so pleased with your many successes, so very proud of you. But you must realize that a man in my position has his priorities." It was the most pompous thing I have ever read.

JW: Has Bertolt Brecht's work influenced your own?

JL: I learned a great deal from him, but the only thing of Brecht's I've done is *Life of Galileo*, which I've done twice on the stage—once in Los Angeles, once in New York—and once as a film [*Galileo*, 1975]. That took nearly thirty years to get made as a film, from the time I first did it in the theater in Hollywood.

I think Brecht may even have learned something from me. He came to see the *Living Newspaper* [produced by the Federal Theatre Project, under the WPA, in the mid-1930s], of which I was a co-founder and director of several plays. He was immensely impressed and felt very much that it was related to the political theater of the twenties in Germany.

JW: How did you feel about Brecht personally?

JL: I adored Brecht. He had a marvelous sense of humor, and he was a strict disciplinarian with everyone, including himself. He was vain and arrogant and absolutely sure of his own genius. He ate very little, drank very little, and fornicated a great deal. He was an eccentric-looking man, with very piercing eyes and a high-pitched giggle. He always wore denim clothing but tailored denim, very elegant. And his cigar was so foul that a kind of stench preceded him wherever he went.

We had rows. I once threw the script of *Galileo* at him and said I was quitting. I went home and did some gardening and then the phone rang. It was Charles Laughton saying, "Please come back." "I will," I said, "if Brecht apologizes to me." Laughton hung up and after a while he called back saying, "Brecht says please come back and he also says you should know Brecht never apologizes." I went back and nothing more was ever said about the row.

JW: One of the reasons you found time to mount *Galileo* in Hollywood, and a year later on Broadway, was that your movie career had hit a snag named Howard Hughes—isn't that true?

JL: Yes, Dore Schary, the head of RKO, wanted me to sign a seven-year contract, but I was afraid of getting trapped. "You have nothing to worry about," he said. "I'll be here to protect you." So I signed, Schary got the sack, and a studio-full of people stood atremble at the thought of having been left at the uncertain mercy of the mysterious Howard Hughes.

Hughes never came to the studio, but I used to get messages from him every morning, pieces of yellow paper with scribbled notes. I'm afraid I threw them all out, since I had no idea that they might one day be of historical significance. There were those who did get to see him, though. Nicholas Ray would sometimes be summoned in the middle of the night. But the only time I saw him was the day he splattered all over Beverly Hills in that plane he designed.

I got scribbled notes from Hughes, but movies I didn't get. There was already an anti-Communist crusade going on in Hollywood, and Hughes had this script called *I Married a Communist*, which he offered to directors as a test of their patriotism. Thirteen directors turned it down before it finally got made in 1949 [by Robert Stevenson], but I happened to be the first. The only movie I directed at RKO was *The Boy with Green Hair* [1948], and I did that before Schary left the lot.

JW: Your films employ a certain measure of ambiguity, whether in terms of the relationships between characters or their motives, thus enriching a film's texture—the way ambiguity works in poetry sometimes. Has this also made the reception of some of your films more difficult?

JL: Obviously. It's nice that you say that the ambiguity makes the work richer, because commercially minded people find it makes the work less rich in terms of their financial takings. That's because they are not out to explore, or to communicate, or to enrich anyone except themselves.

JW: Why did you maintain the ambiguity of Mr. Klein's being Jewish?

JL: That was the whole point. To show his own sense of, "It couldn't happen to me, it might happen to me, it could happen to me, it's happening to me." As almost a transfer and assumption of another personality, it couldn't be any other way. There's no reason to say he was or wasn't Jewish, but it's perfectly clear that he wasn't. Maybe Americans don't know that, because to them the name Klein is automatically Jewish. In Europe the name Klein is not necessarily, not even often, Jewish.

JW: Do you feel fantasy elements can be used in a film to make political points, as in the anti-war *Boy with Green Hair*? You haven't done many films like that since.

JL: No, but there wasn't much opportunity to. Even in *The Boy with Green Hair*, the fantasy element would've been more easily applicable to an anti-racist theme than to an anti-war theme, so, as is, it was pushed in a slightly distorted direction. *The Damned* [1963] is not really fantasy, if you like, but it is science fiction. And it's highly political. For me *The Damned* is a stronger anti-war statement by far, and based very much in an attitude and awareness of class than *The Boy with Green Hair*. It all depends on how much you're allowed to say. *The Boy with Green Hair* was just on the edge of what one could say then.

JW: Like your 1950 film, *The Lawless*—a tough indictment of racial prejudice and mob violence, which featured Gail Russell.

JL: Gail Russell had the most beautiful eyes I ever saw, except for Elizabeth Taylor's, and she was a lovely, painfully insecure girl. She used to say to me, "I never wanted to act. I'm absolutely terrified of acting." The fact was that she simply could not work without alcohol. The studio gave me strict orders not to let her near a drink, and so we had to keep doing the very first scene over and over because Gail couldn't get it right. She finally came to me, shaking uncontrollably, and said, "I'll never get this scene right if you don't get me a drink." So I got her a drink. Gail was a very sweet, sad girl, and she never did any harm to anyone. Everything was done to her. I deeply regret her death. She was a pathetically vulnerable woman whose life was wasted by her suicide.

JW: You just mentioned Elizabeth Taylor in connection with Gail Russell. How was it to work with her—and with her husband, Richard Burton?

JL: I succeeded in directing the first movie of the Burtons—*Boom!* [1968]—but not to make money. I've enjoyed working with them, though there is no doubt that their star behavior is sometimes tiresome and disgusting. Yet they have behaved very well with me. It's unfortunate that they have cultivated the kind of image they have. It's just not what they're really like. I'm especially fond of Elizabeth. Actually, they're better separate than together. I was quite pleased with Elizabeth in *Secret Ceremony* [1968], and I think I had success with Richard in *The Assassination of Trotsky* [1972], too. And I assume that if I ever work with them again, it will be separately.

JW: Do you feel that any of your films have been misread by critics and other opinion-makers?

JL: *Don Giovanni* [1979] was completely misappreciated by most Americans, but not in Europe or in England. *Secret Ceremony* was perhaps misread. Certainly it was totally misread by Hollywood. They just weren't interested in that kind of reading. The people that were distributing the film, not necessarily the audiences seeing it, wanted a more popular reading.

JW: How would you characterize your relations with critics?

JL: I've had very few problems with critics, because I think it's usually unworthy and useless to dispute with them. But when a critic goes out of his way three different times, with half page at a time, to attack something, and disregards letters that I know have been written to him, then that's another matter. Then he is using his power to impose his own lack of appreciation or difference of opinion, and it's an abuse of the press.

JW: Many critics consider *The Prowler* [1951] to be your finest film.

JL: The screenplay, you know, was written in secret by the blacklisted Dalton Trumbo, shortly before he began his prison sentence for refusing to cooperate with the House Un-American Activities Committee. As a sort of joke, we used Trumbo's voice for the disc jockey who's never seen in the movie, the husband of

Evelyn Keyes who gets murdered by Van Heflin. It was our little way of protesting.

Heflin played a corrupt cop in *The Prowler*, and some "patriots" voiced the opinion that this lacerating portrait of an authority figure—and the society that nurtured his greed—was unduly savage. But we consciously set out to make a film about the inculcation of false values. We had the cop say, "All you need is a hundred thousand bucks, a Cadillac, and a blonde"—a philosophy that I would say anticipated the present dilemma in the United States, the belief that it makes no difference how you make it so long as you make it.

JW: Why has the response to your films been greater here in France and in England?

JL: In the first place, my most mature work has been done here. It's also a much more cinema-conscious world, and a more educated one, by virtue of the fact that they've got better films. There's much more exchange of real information about filmmaking and film viewing and film criticism here than elsewhere, up to now. It's beginning to happen elsewhere. I've been invited, for example, to the San Francisco Film Festival and to Chicago, but never at times when I could go.

JW: How does Hollywood look to you now?

JL: I think it's in the hands of the money-brokers and the agents, both the actors' agents and the CIA.

JW: Do you have any particular desire to work in the States again?

JL: Oh, sure, naturally. I come from that background. I'm probably more deeply rooted, more strongly and more educatedly, than a lot of those people who make it impossible to work there. Of course I want to, but whether I will ever be able to is another matter.

JW: It was *The Servant* that first brought you back to your native land, right?—when it was selected to play the inaugural New York Film Festival in 1963.

JL: Yes, that's right. I returned to the U.S. with a certain amount of trepidation. After all, I had been gone for thirteen years and now had a family in England, so I certainly didn't want to be detained in America. When I got off the plane, I felt very strange. I was given the VIP treatment and the customs man thought I must be somebody very special. "Welcome to the home of the brave and the land of the free," he said. "You must be kidding," I answered.

JW: In the not-so-free 1950s, did you in fact refuse to testify before the House Un-American Activities Committee.

JL: No. I was named by the Committee when I was in Italy making *Stranger on the Prowl* [1951], with Paul Muni. It was announced that they had a subpoena for me, but I was in no hurry to rush back and pick it up.

JW: Who could have turned your name in to the Committee?

JL: Charles Laughton turned my name in to the FBI. He went to them and denounced Brecht and me.

JW: But why would Laughton do such a thing?

JL: Why did anybody talk to the FBI? To save their own necks. Laughton was a naturalized American, so maybe they threatened to have his citizenship revoked. He never pretended to be a brave man, so we can't condemn him for being a coward. But we can condemn him for being dishonest. In his authorized biography, he claimed that he had been duped by Brecht and me. That wasn't true. He always knew where we stood. I was furious and horrified when I read that book.

Laughton sometimes rather scathingly referred to me as his conscience, something he insisted he didn't need. He had a schizophrenic character, definitely a Jekyll and Hyde from one day to the next. I never saw him again, though somebody I know told me that he died with great courage. He had been a Catholic and, when we were doing *Galileo*, he temporarily went back to the Church and made a confession. He said it helped him in playing his role. But when he died, he did not take refuge in religion, and he died a horrible death by cancer of the spine. Obviously, there are contradictions in the man, which is what *Galileo* itself is all about.

JW: Will the time come again when Americans of seeming integrity are reduced by fear to playing the role of informer?

JL: Well, the House Un-American Activities Committee was disbanded in 1975, and supposedly they destroyed the records they kept on 750,000 citizens. But I doubt it. I suspect the reason they disbanded the committee was so that they can set up another one, one that has not been so thoroughly discredited. I think it can happen again.

JW: You must have breathed a deep sigh of relief when Richard Nixon, a man well remembered from the days of Red-Scare hysteria, walked out of the White House.

JL: I was absolutely delighted, but I must say that his resignation was a long time coming.

JW: At one point during your blacklisting, by the way, you were hired to work anonymously on a British psychological thriller called *The Sleeping Tiger* [1954], in which Alexis Smith, as a sexually tense married woman, surrenders herself to a cad played by Dirk Bogarde. I've heard that she had a rough time on the picture.

JL: Poor Alexis did have a rough time, and I have nothing but admiration for the courageous way in which she handled herself. It was the height of the blacklist and the producers did not have the decency to tell her what she was getting into. Alexis became scared silly, but she refused to back out of the picture. We were both staying in an English country inn, and one night—as we're having supper together in the grill—who should walk in but Ginger Rogers. Ginger Rogers! I left the inn the next day.

Bibliography

Caute, David. *Joseph Losey: A Revenge on Life*. New York: Oxford University Press, 1994.

de Rham, Edith. *Joseph Losey*. London: André Deutsch, 1991.

Gardner, Colin. *Joseph Losey*. Manchester, U.K.: Manchester University Press, 2004.

Hirsch, Foster. *Joseph Losey* Boston: Twayne, 1980.

Leahy, James. *The Cinema of Joseph Losey*. New York: A. S. Barnes, 1967.

Palmer, James, and Michael Riley. *The Films of Joseph Losey*. Cambridge, U.K.: Cambridge University Press, 1993.

"Only Connect: James Ivory on *Howards End*," by Matt Zoller Seitz (2016: previously unpublished in book or magazine form).

The first film by James Ivory (born 1928) was *Venice: Theme and Variations*, a documentary that the *New York Times* named as one of the best non-theatrical films of 1957. In 1961 he founded Merchant Ivory Productions with producer Ismail Merchant and Ruth Prawer Jhabvala, the screenwriter for many of their productions. Their first theatrical release was *The Householder* (1963), based on a novel by Jhabvala.

The film producer-director team of Merchant and Ivory celebrated their thirty-fifth anniversary as creative partners in 1996 and, along with screenwriter Jhabvala (who wrote the majority of their films), were identified by the *Guinness Book of World Records* as cinema's longest-running partnership. The two had produced an unequaled string of impressive low-budget adaptations of complex novels by such authors as Henry James, E. M. Forster, and Kazuo Ishiguro, and were known for their films' richly textured cinematography and Ivory's ability to evoke brilliant performances from some of the world's finest actors. These revolutionary filmmakers were heralded by literary and movie enthusiasts as the team that both revitalized film adaptations and introduced more sensitive and thoughtful character portrayals to the cinema.

Among Ivory's best known films are *The Europeans* (1979), *The Bostonians* (1984), *Heat and Dust* (1983), *Maurice* (1987), *Shakespeare Wallah* (1965), and three films that garnered Academy Award nominations, including a trio of best director nominations: *A Room with a View* (1985), *Howards End* (1992), and *The Remains of the Day* (1993). His subsequent pictures include *Jefferson in Paris* (1995), *Surviving Picasso* (1996), *The Golden Bowl* (2001), and *The City of Your Final Destination* (2009).

Matt Zoller Seitz spoke to James Ivory about *Howards End*—his version of Forster's classic novel that opened again nationally in

2016 in a 4K restoration—about hits and flops, and about his long collaboration with his two main filmmaking partners, screenwriter Ruth Prawer Jhabvala and producer Ismail Merchant.

Matt Zoller Seitz: Did you have an inkling when you were directing *Howards End* [1992] that it was going to work out as well as it did, much less that people would be interviewing you about it almost twenty-five years later?

James Ivory: Well . . . we hoped for that, you know! We had certainly been successful with the other two Forster films we'd done, *Maurice* [1987] and *A Room with a View* [1985]. We thought people would like this one and respond to it. It's a long film, two hours and twenty minutes. A length like that doesn't always bode well. But yes, we had hopes for it.

MZS: How many years had you been thinking about doing a film version of the novel?

JI: It wasn't something that I had wanted to do for a long, long time. It was a wonderful book and all, but it wasn't something I'd thought about for years and years before we made it.

But our writer, Ruth Prawer Jhabvala—it was very much in *her* mind. After we had done *A Room with a View* and *Maurice*, she urged us to think about *Howards End* as another candidate for adaptation.

MZS: Did the book pose any particular problems as a subject for film adaptation?

JI: [Laughs.] Well, fortunately, because I wasn't the screenwriter, I didn't have to face that kind of struggle, and that kind of winnowing out of the best storytelling material. I just didn't have to face that! Because I knew Ruth knew what to do, you see? I'd done so many films together already with Ruth and Ismail Merchant, some based on very complicated novels, like *The Bostonians* [1984], so I could just leave her at it and be confident.

Of course when I saw her script of *Howards End* for the first time, I probably did the usual yelling: "Where's this? Where's that?" You know. But that always happens with adaptations. We'd do that, and then we'd have a bit of a re-think. Ruth or Ismail would tell me,

"That's a good bit, but there's just not room," and I'd accept it. That's how we worked.

The great thing about Ruth was she was a very good fiction writer, a novelist herself. She had a very strong storytelling sense. Sometimes when you have a really good writer on a film, that person's storytelling sense can be better than the director's own. There were some things about the book that she felt she could improve in the screenplay, some aspects that were fine for the novel but that would have to be fleshed out for the movie.

MZS: Like what?

JI: For example, she felt that the characters of a certain social class in *Howards End*, particularly Leonard and Jackie Bast, were people Forster didn't know very well, so they didn't come across that strongly in the novel itself. She felt they had to be deepened a bit, because of the way the story pivots around Leonard and his rise and fall. Ruth knew we had to know them better, that we had to see them alone more, and sense the physical hold Jackie had on Leonard. So she built them up and made them into working-class people who were sort of living on the edge.

MZS: She didn't approve of Forster's handling of the Basts?

JI: Not so much *approve*; it was more a matter of recognizing that Forster just didn't have a sense of who they were, because he lacked a great deal of knowledge about people like that. I haven't re-read the novel since we did the film, so at the moment I couldn't tell you whether I think her sense of that was accurate or not, but at the time I thought she was probably right.

MZS: That was really a remarkable run that you and Ruth Prawer Jhabvala and Ismail Merchant had there, from 1985 when *A Room with a View* came out all the way through *The Remains of the Day* in 1993. The quality of most of those films is pretty high, in particular the period pieces. During that period you were making, well, not quite one movie a year, but—

JI: No, not by that point—but we were productive, you're right. You know, if you look at the output going back much further than 1985, you see that sometimes we made more than one in a year, right through the seventies and pretty much all through the eighties.

We slowed down a bit in the nineties, but there were still instances where we did more than one movie in the same year.

MZS: What are the factors that go into a run like that, for a filmmaker? Is it luck? Timing? Box office?

JI: All of that, but honestly, I'm not entirely sure exactly what goes into that kind of a run! It's quite something. I've seen it happen with other directors. Sometimes there's a period in which, if they're lucky, they get the financing where they can make two films in a year. Jean-Luc Godard was like that for a while. And Nicholas Ray.

Some of it probably has to do with satisfaction. You know, if the filmmakers were satisfied with the film they just made, they could jump right in and make another one, instead of lingering on the last one. We did that a few times. And you know, sometimes the theatrical films were interspersed with films we made for television.

MZS: *A Room with a View* seemed as if it kicked things up to a new level for you and your collaborators. I've never seen anything like that happen in my lifetime, where a little period piece strikes a nerve and just keeps making more and more money, staying in theaters forever. Not even *Howards End* had the sort of staying power that *A Room with a View* did.

JI: That's true! We had films before that the public liked very much, films that had a wonderful critical reception or that did very well at the box office. *Heat and Dust* [1983] was one of those, and *The Europeans* [1979] was another. And earlier, you could probably say that, in a way, *Shakespeare Wallah* [1965] was that kind of success. But you're right: *A Room with a View* really set us up with the people who give you money to make movies.

MZS: Why is that? Was it just a matter of the money-people looking at the box office returns and going, "Wow, these people know how to make hits"?

JI: There's that, but there's also the matter of how much you spend on a movie. See, nobody understood how we were able to make a film like *A Room with a View* so cheaply, for about $3.2 million, and have it look as good as it did.

MZS: What was your secret?

JI: For one thing, actors didn't ask for that much money, because they liked us. They wanted to play interesting roles in films derived from intelligent material. So they didn't charge the kinds of money they'd charge other kinds of producers.

Also, we shot a lot in Florence, which was not that expensive. And we took the money we saved on casting and locations and spent it on the production, instead of being cheap about the crew. We believed all along in getting the best crew available. The best cameramen, the best production designer. We never stinted on the crew. The actors complained a bit about being underpaid sometimes, but we really wanted to make sure we could afford the best technicians to make them all look as good as possible, and keep everybody happy.

That's why relatively inexpensive films like *A Room with a View* and *Howards End* look the way they do, because the people on the crew were experts and we were paying them appropriately.

MZS: I grew up in Dallas, and there's a movie theater there, the Inwood, where *A Room with a View* played for thirteen months, and *Howards End* for seven. Those were really long runs for the eighties and nineties, a period when films could still have long runs in theaters, and they would be unthinkable today, when even hit films rarely stick around for more than a couple of months. Clearly, something about these films struck a nerve. And it wasn't just in Dallas. I heard about that kind of thing happening in other theaters across North America—where your movies hit, and, for whatever reason, just kept on playing and playing.

JI: Yes, and it really was something! *A Room with a View* played in the Paris Theater in New York for more than a year. That was amazing, and we were amazed. The success of that film really encouraged the studios to finance our projects. Occasionally they would offer something to us, something that we didn't develop ourselves. *The Remains of the Day* was that kind of movie, one that was offered. *Surviving Picasso* [1996] was another.

MZS: Why did they start offering you their own projects?

JI: Because they thought we had the magic formula! They thought we had some kind of secret for making a good film for very little money that would become very profitable.

And so we moved on to do a string of studio features in the nineties. We had two unsuccessful studio films that slowed down our run a bit. One was *Jefferson in Paris* [1995], which didn't cost that much money. The next was *Surviving Picasso*, which did. They didn't do well at the box office, didn't do well with critics. That slowed us down. Somehow we managed to raise the money for a few more features. But we didn't get to do more *studio* features until we made *Le Divorce* [2003] for Fox.

MZS: *Mr. and Mrs. Bridge* [1990] was part of that great run, a very good film with two great lead performances, by Paul Newman and Joanne Woodward, but that just did O.K. and never became a hit.

JI: There was another flop in there, too: *Slaves of New York* [1989], based on the 1986 book by Tama Janowitz. And there was also a studio film in there: *Mr. and Mrs. Bridge*, which we did for Miramax.

MZS: I don't know if it means anything, but it's interesting to me that some of your best-known and most financially successful films were funded independently.

JI: Yes, although that can be a difficult process in its own way, as you know. And you might be surprised how things came together on some of our movies. *A Room with a View*, for instance—on that one we had Japanese investors, even though it was an English story!

MZS: What do you think of the film, honestly, now that a lot of time has elapsed? Are there things that make you cringe, that you would do differently? Things that you're particularly happy with, where you think, "Yes, that's about as good as it could have been"?

JI: I'd have to think about that.

Recently I've been thinking more about the process of adaptation. You know, since *Howards End* was restored, I saw it at Cannes, and then I saw it again the other night in New York, and it did make me want to go back and read the novel again, though, as I told you, unfortunately I haven't done that as yet. I'm curious to see exactly where we diverge from the novel and where we're faithful to it. I like the film a lot, but I can't remember all the things we changed!

Well, I mean—I remember *some* of them. For instance, there's a scene where Leonard and Helena Bonham Carter's character, Helen Schlegel, go out on the boat, and they talk a bit and then they make love. Well, obviously that's not in the novel. That's not the sort of scene Forster would do! So I'm curious to see if I can pinpoint exactly where during the process Ruth decided that we should go out on our own during that scene.

Also, the dialogue—it was tricky. That whole book is full of the most wonderful dialogue, but we couldn't use much of it. Ruth had a sort of a dictum about dialogue. She felt that if you had ten lines of very good dialogue in a novel you would be doing well if you could keep three or four of them, just to bring the book down to size.

I can say, also, that I look at *Howards End* differently today because now it calls up all these associations with time. When I saw the film last week again, while watching it I was pleased. But I was also thinking to myself, *I don't know if I could put something like that together in such a way now.*

Of course it goes without saying that so many people I know who were involved with that movie are gone, so of course a film version of *Howards End* would be different in that way if we tried to do it today. But I also wondered if I would have the strength to carry out such a complicated film. There are so many different characters and plot lines and stuff!

So I felt all that while watching it again. But mainly I felt pleasure, really, realizing that so much of it seemed to be . . . well, I won't say that *nobody* else could have done it. There are moments, just as in any film, where you say to yourself, "Oh, I shouldn't have done that," or where you can't even really evaluate what's on the screen because you're too busy thinking back to the time when you shot it, and remembering, "Oh—that was *not* a good day." But I will say that I look on *Howards End* with approval.

MZS: Did you have any inkling that Emma Thompson, who plays Margaret Schlegel, would go on to become a kind of cultural institution, much less that she'd win awards for her screenwriting as well as her acting? She was named Best Actress at the Academy Awards for this performance.

JI: I didn't really think like that. I never had such a thought when we were making our films. I don't think about Oscars or anything like that, really, when we're making movies.

But yes, there was a point during the shooting when I said to myself, "Wow, she's so good that there are people who are sure to notice this."

MZS: And they did notice her. They noticed the movie, too: the viewers, the critics.

JI: Yes, they did. We had eight Oscar nominations for *A Room with a View*, so I thought, "Maybe we'll get some for this one, too." And we did very well: nine nominations for *Howards End*.

MZS: I wonder if your thoughts about a film's characters change after the film is done and you have a few years to sit with them and think about them.

JI: How do you mean?

MZS: Well, the character of Helen, for instance: when I saw it back in 1992 I had such a huge crush on Helena Bonham Carter that I think it clouded my sense of that character. I didn't see her as particularly destructive. But watching it again, I did. Helen is practically a nice *femme fatale*. She brings so much misery into the lives of the Basts, and she does it in the name of helping people and doing the right thing.

JI: Sometimes I have that kind of reaction. Sometimes, also, I think about what would happen to the characters after the end of our story. I do have schemes worked out for various characters.

You know, the interesting thing about Helena is, early on she was cast as this wholesome, beautiful girl, and that's definitely how she was in *A Room with a View*. But it turned out that she had an incredible facility for playing dangerous or even violent characters, eccentrics, psychopathic killers and these sorts of fairy-tale villains.

MZS: In *The Lone Ranger* [2013] she plays a brothel madam with a Gatling gun for a leg, and you buy it. That's not a role I would have imagined her in when I was watching *A Room with a View* back in 1985 or 1986.

JI: Exactly, yeah! You know, we worked with her three times. She's so good! She's also in *Maurice*. She has one scene in there where she's watching a cricket match, talking about which of the boys should get a haircut.

MZS: Anthony Hopkins was so terrific early on as volatile, menacing characters or just really dynamic ones, but starting in the nineties he entered this phase where he was playing depressed or repressed or distant men, and he was so great at it that he started to get typecast a little. I wonder if his performance in *Howards End* contributed to that? And maybe also *The Remains of the Day* right after that.

And I wonder why you cast Hopkins as this character in the first place? It seems like an obvious choice now, but it didn't then. The last thing he'd done right before you cast him in *Howards End* was *The Silence of the Lambs* [1991], where his character eats human flesh and wears another man's face as a mask.

JI: That's a funny story: I had never paid very close attention to him in the earlier part of his career. I was talking to one of the actors from *Maurice*, James Wilby, who is English. I said, "We need to find somebody to play the character," and I described what sort of character he was. And James said, "Oh, get Anthony Hopkins, he'd be perfect." And I had never thought of him at all until James mentioned him!

So then we contrived to get a screenplay to him directly, through one of the sound editors on *The Silence of the Lambs*, and he read it, and he said "yes." He was keen on it from he beginning, no hesitation.

Then we did *The Remains of the Day* with him. That was a film that was originally going to be made by other people. Tony had heard about the book and the screenplay, and he approached Sony and said he was interested in doing that part.

MZS: And the film didn't get made.

JI: But then after *Howards End* we inherited *The Remains of the Day* from Sony, and they immediately said to us, "What would you think about Anthony Hopkins doing this part?"

MZS: That's funny! I guess they'd seen *Howards End* by that point? Or maybe it was just that he was the Oscar winner Anthony Hopkins and it was a whole different ball game.

JI: I don't know, but whatever the explanation, they were very deferential!

And then a few years later, we were doing *Surviving Picasso*, and Tony was the right age and physical type, and we thought in many ways that he was the best possible person for the role. And he said "yes" very quickly. The last feature we made together, *The City of Your Final Destination* [2009], was also one where he said "yes" immediately, as soon as we sent him the script.

MZS: It must be nice to have relationships like that with other artists, where you trust each other to such a degree that one of you can ask and the other will say "yes," and not even feel as if there has to be a discussion.

JI: Yeah, it's a great feeling! Sometimes you get lucky with people like that—where you not only know they're wonderful artists who will give you what you need, but also that you get along with them, that you like and respect them. Tony could be a little difficult at times, and there were moments on the set where he'd kind of flare up. But every actor does that in various ways; it's not unusual at all. And you knew that no matter what, there would be a special quality that an actor like him would bring to a part, just by virtue of who he is as a person.

MZS: What were your favorite scenes to do in *Howards End*, and what scenes do you think turned out the best?

JI: I tended to enjoy shooting the close, personal scenes that were done either in the Wilcoxes' house across the street from the Schlegels, or in the Schlegel house where they could look out the window and see the Wilcoxes. I liked those a lot, and they weren't hard to do, particularly.

And I like watching those scenes the most, too, of all the scenes in the film, because of the interaction between the two sisters and the brother, and the interaction between Leonard Bast and his wife, and the interaction between Margaret and the elder Mrs. Wilcox, played by Vanessa Redgrave. Anything going on in either of those houses, I'd name as my favorite scene to watch as well as to shoot.

MZS: Do you do postmortems on films that don't connect with critics or audiences, and if so, what questions do you ask, and what do you learn about the films, and about your own choices?

JI: I think about that in regards to the films we made later in the nineties. We had two films about heroes, *Jefferson in Paris* and *Surviving Picasso*, where we didn't show the heroes as being particular heroic. They both were heavily involved with women, and we showed them both as being mired in sex, you might say. That's not the vision of those men that a lot of people who are interested in them would prefer to have, and I think that hurt us.

And then on *Surviving Picasso*, we had a lot of trouble with Picasso's estate. We got involved, embroiled, in a legal dispute with them, which you might have read about in the papers.

MZS: Right. Picasso's estate objected to the film's depicting him as a womanizer, so they wouldn't give you permission to show actual Picassos in the movie, and you had to use work by Matisse and Braque to give a sense of the period.

JI: Yes. Things like that affect the health of a film.

And on *Jefferson in Paris*, we had all this stuff about his slave mistress and slave children. That was a story that had been widely known, going back quite a long ways, to when Jefferson ran for president the second time. It was not an unfamiliar story, really. But throughout the American South there were comments to the effect of, "Jefferson was much too fine a man to have had a relationship like that." Well, to me that was a racist remark. But it says a lot that people would need to feel he wasn't capable of something like that.

Both that film and *Surviving Picasso* were very expensive compared to some of our other films. They did not do well at the box office, especially *Jefferson in Paris*.

I still wonder if we could have done something different to get around our problems on *Surviving Picasso*. Maybe we could have put it together in a different way, I don't know. Maybe it wasn't interesting enough. Maybe we should have made it more explosive, as Picasso's art was. These are the things you think about!

MZS: Are you working on something new?

JI: Right now I'm involved in producing a film in Italy, based on a 2007 novel by André Aciman titled *Call Me by Your Name* [2017]. I also wrote the screenplay to that. And I am involved in a film version of Shakespeare's *Richard II*. That's what we're hoping to do next, a film of *Richard II* with Tom Hiddleston and Damian Lewis as Richard and Bolingbroke.

Bibliography

Long, Robert Emmet. *The Films of Merchant Ivory*. Rev. ed. New York: H. N. Abrams, 1997.

Pym, John. *The Wandering Company: Twenty-One Years of Merchant Ivory Films*. London and New York: British Film Institute/Museum of Modern Art, 1983.

Pym, John. *Merchant Ivory's English Landscapes: Rooms, Views, and Anglo-Saxon Attitudes*. New York: H. N. Abrams, 1994.

"'All Film Is Fantasy': An Interview with Richard Lester," by *Sight and Sound*, under the sponsorship of *The Guardian* and the British Film Institute, Nov. 8, 1999 (previously unpublished in book or magazine form).

Richard Lester (born 1932) is an American filmmaker who successfully transferred the fast-cut, stream-of-consciousness style of television commercials to the big screen. A childhood piano prodigy, Lester continued his musical activities while pursuing a psychology degree at the University of Pennsylvania. He traveled to Europe in 1954, ostensibly as a "roving correspondent" for a newspaper syndicate, and paid his way by playing guitar and piano. Within a year he was at London's Independent Television Studios, again as a composer and director. He hosted his own one-shot "Dick Lester Show" in 1956, which, though a disaster, led to a series of choice directorial assignments on the various television projects of "The Goon Show" co-creators Spike Milligan and Peter Sellers. Also during this period, Lester began directing commercials, an activity to which he would periodically return throughout his career.

While working on Milligan's TV series "A Show Named Fred," Lester provided frantic, non-sequitur filmed segments. These came to fruition in his theatrical-film directorial début, the short *The Running, Jumping, & Standing Still Film* (1960), which featured Milligan and Sellers in a series of surreal sketches and sight gags. Lester graduated to features with *It's Trad, Dad!* (1962), a low-budget capitalization on Britain's then current traditional jazz craze. When he directed his first studio-financed film, *The Mouse on the Moon* (1963), the following year, he continued to rely upon working methods he had honed for television, including the cost-saving use of multiple cameras. Because of this work, Lester was chosen to direct the Beatles' first film, *A Hard Day's Night* (1964). Though tightly scripted by Alun Owen, the film possessed a charmingly spontaneous, improvisational energy that not only encapsulated the dizzy euphoria of "Beatlemania," but also influenced moviemaking in general during the 1960s. Described by critic Andrew Sarris as "the *Citizen Kane* of jukebox musicals," *A Hard Day's Night* was followed by another enjoyable Beatles-Lester collaboration, *Help!* (1965).

With the exception of *Petulia* (1968), a comparatively straightforward account of an extramarital affair in contemporary San Francisco, Lester's other 1960s movies—the "swinging London" spoof *The Knack* (1965), an adaptation of the Broadway musical *A Funny Thing Happened on the Way to the Forum* (1966), the wickedly satiric anti-war pieces *How I Won the War* (1967) and *The Bed-Sitting Room* (1969)—were cut from the same stylistic cloth as the director's two Beatles pictures. His later films were more "mainstream" than his earlier efforts, though no less visually stunning. These included the all-star swashbucklers *The Three Musketeers* (1973), *The Four Musketeers* (1974), and *Royal Flash* (1975), the revisionist *Robin and Marian* (1976), the bittersweet historical romance *Cuba* (1979), and the lavish comic-book derivations *Superman II* (1980) and *Superman III* (1983).

After *The Return of the Musketeers* (1989), Lester virtually retired from filmmaking, reportedly disheartened by the on-set accidental death of a longtime colleague, the comic actor Roy Kinnear. He was briefly coaxed back to work by former Beatle Paul McCartney, who engaged the director's services for the concert feature *Get Back* (1990).

Sight and Sound: How did Walter Shenson end up owning 100% of *A Hard Day's Night* [1964]?

Richard Lester: United Artists thought the Beatles would be a spent force by the summer of '64.

SS: Only off by thirty-five years!

RL: Walter didn't know who they were and I only knew them through a freakish accident, but I did know their music. They had seen my 1960 short *The Running, Jumping, & Standing Still Film*; they had heard that *It's Trad, Dad!* [1962] was not an obscenity, it was actually passable; and they knew that I used to play piano rather badly and we felt we could get on together. They weren't really bothered too much about who was doing the film. United Artists felt that as long as it came out by June, they would put the money up.

It cost £180,000 to make *A Hard Day's Night* and we started filming in March; we shot for six-to-seven weeks. We had three weeks and four days to cut the picture, dub it, and get a final print, which was not a lot of time. And then there was the famous story that UA said they liked it a lot but they were going to have to dub it because no one would understand the voices, so we had to fight over that one. But in the end, for some ungodly reason, the Beatles kept on going.

SS: How long did it take to decide on the idea of "a day in the life" as opposed to an Elvis Presley, traditional-type of movie?

RL: Alun Owen, the person who was with me in that ill-fated venture into commercial television, was by that time a successful director. You never knew where Alun was from: he was either Irish, Welsh, or from Liverpool, depending on whom he was talking to and whom he was hoping to write for. At one point John Lennon got very fed up with him and said, "Why should I listen to you, you're nothing but an amateur Liverpudlian," to which Alun replied, "Don't you think that's better than being a professional Liverpudlian, John?" This was very dangerous because you should never mess with John.

But when we decided that Alun should write the script for us, Walter Shenson and I followed the Beatles to where they were doing their first performances in Paris, and we all stayed on one floor of the George V Hotel. Just being with them for a period of a long weekend, the script was writing itself in front of us. It would have taken an idiot not to use that energy and what was happening, and also it was the most logical thing to have four people who were not actors play themselves in situations and conditions that were normal to them. They were used to doing press conferences, they were used to running from their fans, they were used to getting in and out of cars, they were used to being shouted at and pushed around. All we were asking them to do was to do what they normally did.

SS: But apparently the first shot of the first day was a little hectic even by your standards.

RL: What happened is that we were mobbed. There was obviously a mole in our production department who was letting everybody know where we were shooting from day to day. So when we went to get on the train—we were going back and forth to the West

Country—we were absolutely mobbed, and because I was there first I grabbed the handheld camera and started filming anything I could, and the boys ran and got on the train and there are shots of it in the film. They're wearing the wrong clothes and the poor script supervisor, who was used to rather sedate and gentlemanly movies, saw what was going on and thought this would never cut it: they're in the wrong clothes, they came in the wrong way, and the baggage car is in the wrong place. She wrote this long note in which she stated, "If this carries on a second day, I'm not going to last a week."

But what happened was, by the end of the first day we had shot a massive amount of material, so we dumped the boys off somewhere near Reading to escape, and we came back to Marylebone station and the clapper loader got all the film we'd shot that day in a pile of tins. Unfortunately, he was very fond of the Beatles—he dressed like them, he was their age, and he had dark hair that was cut in a Beatles cut. He was thinking, "I'll just get this to the labs and they'll process it and we'll see how the first day's work has gone." He gets off the train and suddenly he sees the crowd and he really panicked for his life, and he threw the cans as they were about to attack him. So we lost about two-thirds of the first day's shooting because it was on unprocessed negative. It was under the train, it was on the floor, it was everywhere.

A Hard Day's Night was one of those great films that will never happen again to anyone in their lifetime. United Artists were in profit before we'd even finished shooting. Brian Epstein was a lovely fellow but not a great businessman and he'd given the rights to the album, *A Hard Day's Night*, to UA. The advance sales on the album—the film was out before the album was out—were more than it cost UA to make the film. So the film was in profit before we *began* shooting. I don't think that's happened again, although George Lucas can probably contradict me.

SS: The train sequences on the film were the first sequences you shot. How were they? The Beatles, were they nervous? Did they fall into it quickly?

RL: Nervousness was never something I would ever associate with the Beatles, ever. *A Hard Day's Night* was relatively unscathed by marijuana, but even then they were quite relaxed about the shooting. They knew themselves. They didn't often remember to bring their scripts with them: they got left in other people's cars or taxis or nightclubs. But apart from that technical problem they were very relaxed about what they were doing. Other people were nervous beside them. I remember in *Help!* [1965] dear old Frankie Howerd had a scene that we eventually had to cut out because the boys were just so foreign to the way he worked. Frankie, who gave the illusion of being a great ad-libber, really liked everything to be under his control and down pat. He just couldn't deal with it at all and he and the Beatles were not a marriage made in heaven.

SS: Why is George Harrison the best actor?

RL: I just think George came without any highs and without any lows and he always got it right; he nailed it and walked off and waited for the next time. He was very calm.

SS: Because in that scene where he goes into the producer's office, there isn't a line there that he doesn't absolutely drive home. He's perfect.

RL: I think Paul McCartney probably cared most about acting because he had a girlfriend who was an actress [Jane Asher], and she was very interested in the theater, and I think Paul suffered a great deal from that because he realized what could go wrong a little more than the others. I remember John in the first few weeks of *How I Won The War* [1967], when he was playing the part of someone else, not himself, and I went up to him and said, "John if you wanted to do this, you really could be very good at it"; and he said, "Yeah, but it's fucking stupid, isn't it? That's thirty-two years ago, and I haven't found an answer to it yet."

SS: You said George was the best actor, so why did you choose John Lennon for *How I Won the War*?

RL: I was looking to use John's energy and sarcasm, his intellectual curiosity. That's not to say George didn't have those qualities, but if you say those are the three characteristics of a Beatle that you want, I think your instinct would have to be to go to John. I think that on the basis of what John did and his disinterest in doing, it was a good choice—if indeed hiring a Beatle in a non-Beatle role was ever a good idea.

SS: In *A Hard Day's Night* during the press conference scene, when the reporter asks John Lennon what his hobbies are, what did he write on her pad?

RL: I have no idea. Was it zeroes and crosses? I do remember that when things didn't seem to be too funny, we'd sometimes switch the questions so that the answer went to the wrong question, and we got a few laughs that way.

SS: After *A Hard Day's Night*, people would often be accused of "doing a Richard Lester."

RL: The only time was in the late '70s or maybe early '80s. Related to this, I was sent a vellum scroll from MTV saying that I was the "spiritual father" of MTV—and I immediately demanded a blood test!

SS: Was the audience in *A Hard Day's Night* specially selected for the stage show?

RL: We knew how kids would respond. All I did was stick six cameras in the audience. I had one with me, and I ran from one set-up to the other. You couldn't hear anything. One of the camera operators lost two back teeth because the sound was so loud he lost the nerves of his teeth. I gave everyone exactly the same brief: "If you find anything interesting, get a piece that's long and pan off and try to make your pans useful. We'll just try to grab it like a documentary"—because that's all it was.

There weren't enough kids of that age with whom to fill the La Scala theater, so we went to an agency that had teenaged kids; it was run by Phil Collins' mother, and in fact somewhere in that audience is Phil Collins as an eleven-year-old boy. We said we're never going to fill up this audience with young people who are professionals, so just bring your friends. It's a totally spontaneous audience.

SS: Would it have been different if you had made a film about the Rolling Stones?

RL: I honestly don't know because I didn't meet the Stones until later. But one thing is sure, you shouldn't make *A Hard Day's Night*-like documentary of that kind with the Stones. There was something else much more interesting going on with them.

SS: Were you planning to follow *A Hard Day's Night* with *Help!*?

RL: No, I hadn't planned to do so. *The Knack* [1965], that came out of the blue. *A Hard Day's Night* came out in June and we went on holiday, and then a telegram came saying would I read something, and I did and thought it was something I could do.

SS: And the sequel had been discussed at that point?

RL: Yes, it was supposed to be three films, always.

SS: But you jumped on *The Knack* pretty quickly.

RL: It had been a successful stage play, by Ann Jellicoe, and Charles Wood and I deconstructed it and said, "Now we'll put it back together again and see what it is that we actually need." I think that is a good principle in general: instead of trying to open out a stage piece, you just explode the whole thing and slowly bring everything back down to earth; and you decide that when you need to be claustrophobic, you will be, and that worked fairly well for us. We started shooting *The Knack* in October and finished it in time for Cannes, by which time I was nearly finished shooting *Help!*

SS: You won at Cannes that year and you were on the jury the following year. That was the year Welles was there with *Chimes at Midnight* [1965] and you were approached at one point, weren't you?

RL: I had a phone call saying, "This is Harry Saltzman"—the Bond producer, also the producer of the Orson Welles film. "Would you come to the Carlton Hotel, suite 400." I thought, "Oh, terrific, this is the big league. I went up there, knocked on the door. Harry came out with no shoes on; behind him there were beautiful women, drink, there was champagne, there was Orson. He shut the door behind him and went out into the corridor with me and said, "Stop being rude to the other members of the jury." I said, "Harry, what do you mean? I haven't been mean to the other members of the jury and anything I've been saying to Peter Ustinov—who was also on the jury—has been translated for me and we're getting laughs." And he said, "You gotta relax. You understand? You know what I mean?" He turned and went back inside. I had no idea what he meant.

Only afterwards did I realize that he, I think, had been promised *Chimes at Midnight* was going to win the main prize—the Palme d'Or—and it became apparent that five of us thought it shouldn't win, and quite a lot of us were absolutely obsessed with a Danish film that we thought was terrific. With a view to that, we all decided to give a special award to Orson Welles for his contribution to the cinema, but not to that specific film, which the Cannes people did and that's the way it was announced.

While I was at Cannes my son was just four, and we were staying in a hotel just along the main street, and a young man came up to me and said, "I've got two films running tonight. I produced them and I'm in one and they cost only $30,000 each, but I'd really like you to come and see them." And I said, "Well I would, but I've tried before to get a babysitter at this time of night and we just can't get one." He said, "If you go and see my two films, I'll babysit for your son." I said, "Well all right, that seems fair enough. So he did and I did and I came back, said how much I had enjoyed the films, and he left and I didn't see him again for about fifteen years. I was in the Beverley Hills Hotel in Los Angeles, which has very dark and very cold, air-conditioned corridors that go endlessly away, and I'd just walked in from the light, couldn't see a bloody thing. I was walking to my room and a voice said, "Richard," and I said, "Who's that?"; and he said, "It's me, how's Dominic?"—my son. It was extraordinary to think that I hadn't seen someone for fifteen years and he'd remembered my son's name. The person I had entrusted to look after my son was somebody called Jack Nicholson!

SS: *Help!* was what many people expected the first Beatles film to be, in that it was a fictionalized knockabout piece. Was that a hard decision to come to?

RL: If you didn't want just to do a color version of *A Hard Day's Night* and you think, "Well, here are these people playing themselves and we don't want to see what they do in their work, we can't show you what they do in their life because that's X-rated, so what are we going to do with them?" We have, therefore, to make them passive responders to some external stimulus, and that was how *Help!* came about.

SS: How was that shoot different from the first?

RL: Just longer. I had more money and a bit more time. I had to learn to say to the crowd "Get out of the way" in three different languages. But it was no harder except that the boys had really discovered marijuana and there was a lot of smiling—more from them than from me. It was just as pleasant as *A Hard Day's Night*. It was very nice.

SS: So you jumped right into *A Funny Thing Happened on the Way to the Forum* [1966]. Was there a difficulty in translating farce onto film?

RL: Yes, I think there is a simple rule of thumb: if you can avoid it, do! I love theatrical farce but think it is the hardest thing to do on screen because good farce relies on the audience's understanding the geography of space. In film the minute you go to someone's close-up, that geography is lost.

SS: While you were finishing that film, you were preparing for one of your more creative, ambitious films, *How I Won the War*.

RL: Yes, I think it was one of the most ambitious and foolhardy things I've ever made. We said what we were doing was make an "anti-war film"—where a group of disparate people get together who don't like one another but through the preparation for battle become fond of each other and then die bravely. With the excitement of the guns and the bombs and the noise and the music the film sucks you in, and it is impossible to make a genuine anti-war film if you're showing the action of war, so we tried to use this Brechtian technique of alienation whereby, when you begin to like one of the characters, he suddenly turns to the audience and starts talking to you, or he comes out of character to break the hold that romanticized fiction has on an audience. The audiences then felt as if they were being manipulated and, as in the case of most Brechtian pieces, you say, "Get your hands off me, you've sucked me into liking this character and now he's lecturing me. What is this?"

Also, hiring John Lennon in a straight part, which I think he was perfectly capable of doing—well, nobody believed that he wouldn't pick up a guitar and play it and there was this disappointment that he didn't do that. There were decisions that were hard to make but I'm not sure I wouldn't do it in the same way again.

We went to Germany to borrow the tanks from the British army on the Rhine, and we were shooting a sequence over the bridge when the tank goes past and Michael Hordern is shouting, "On to Moscow." As each person died in the film, it was shot in black and white, but the film was tinted a different color for the Arnhem, Dieppe, Dunkirk, and El Alamain scenes; and when someone died, he was replaced, just as a platoon is always up to full strength, and the actors were dressed in uniform but dyed the appropriate color, with a stocking mask also of that color over their faces. So we were used to this, and we were shooting the tank sequence when the people from whom we'd borrowed the tanks came to watch, and they said, "What's that—are they supposed to be British soldiers?" Luckily my producer was quick-witted and said, "Oh, don't worry, that's a camera test for Technicolor!"

SS: So you were working on *Robin and Marian* [1976] and you got a call to work on *Juggernaut* [1974].

RL: A friend of mine said, "We've just fired our second director, we've got eighteen days before we shoot, and we've hired a Russian ship to come and find bad weather; can you come in and do it?" And I said, "Only if I can come in and rewrite the picture and recast it." And we rewrote it from scratch in two weeks and went to the captain and said, "Go to Land's End, turn right, and keep going until you find a force-8 gale," which he did, and we found the gale somewhere above the Shetlands. And we said, "Lovely, now take the stabilizers off," and he said, "Fine, nobody can go outside without a harness." We said, "But that's not in the script—they don't wear harnesses!"

And the other thing that happened was that we had to have an explosion to blow the funnel of the ship off, and the captain wouldn't allow us to do that. You're not allowed to bring dynamite aboard a commercial liner, but we did and we didn't say anything. On the last day of shooting, just as we were about to get back to Southampton, our producer got one of the world's first digital watches and had it inscribed with, "To Captain Alexandrov Dondua with grateful thanks from the cast and crew of *Juggernaut*," and we had a presentation ceremony with all the senior officers on the bridge, and just as the producer was handing the digital watch over to the captain at precisely 10 A.M., BOOM, we blew up the funnel with four cameras shooting it and a helicopter filming from up above; by that time it was too late to stop us and we docked at 11:30!

Hollywood decided this was going to be the year of the disaster movie. There were *Towering Inferno* [1974] and *Airport* [1974]. And we suffered because we were the first and there weren't any big scenes—it wasn't really a disaster movie. It was actually a rather small and controlled piece. I mean, we shot it in six weeks.

SS: It was scheduled for nine weeks.

RL: I like gardening. I like to go home early.

SS: Yes, this obsession with speed. You feel compelled to do the day's work no matter what.

RL: If someone gives me a call sheet with a list of numbers of what I've got to get through during the day, if I don't do it I'm almost physically ill and there's no reason for it. Even if I knew it wouldn't matter and there was enough money to do everything the next day. If someone says we didn't keep to schedule, I'm like this [physically shakes]. And I don't know why I'm like this; I think it's deep in my childhood. It's something you can't change, and when you hear about a director who's always been rather relaxed about the way he spends money and then says, "We're going to do a low-budget film," run like hell because he can't do it. Any more than I would be able to spend a lot of money foolishly.

SS: Robert Bresson once said, "Those who can work with the least can work with the most, but those who are accustomed to working with the most can never work with the least." And that's been true in my experience.

RL: Buñuel was absolutely like that. He used to give money back. He used to say, "Let me do what I want to do and that's all I'm going to spend."

SS: We'll backtrack slightly now to talk about your career prior to *A Hard Day's Night* and, most specifically, your work in television. You were in the States, in Philadelphia, weren't you?

RL: Yes, this was the very beginning of television, because what television there was in America was experimental until after the war, and I started in 1950, so they'd only had a few years of television work. Nobody knew quite what to do. In fact we were working out of a radio station, which meant they built the scenery on the second floor and we carried it up—because I was a stagehand at the time—to the fourth floor, where we would assemble it, and that's where the cameras were.

But the great thing about it is I was able to go from stagehand to floor manager to assistant director to director in a year, because there was just no one else to do it, and what people don't understand now about television is that we used to do about five shows a day. You'd do a news broadcast in the morning and next a sports program, then there'd be a give-away show, followed by a musical sequence of about half an hour and then a quiz show. And you would have a headset on and you had a row of buttons in front of you, and you just punched from one camera to another by yourself, and it all went by terribly quickly.

A year passed and at one point I was doing a live television Western five-and-a-half hours a week, with horses and stuntmen, and it was a nightmare. The reason that this is apposite is that it accustomed me (a) to work quickly; (b) to work with many cameras; and (c) to be hysterical. And I've carried all of that with me in my life and work.

So when I came to England at the very beginning of commercial television, it was easy for me because I was only doing one or two shows a week at most. It was really a holiday. It takes people of my age to remember what live television was like in those days, especially when you had Spike Milligan writing the script. You rehearsed all day and at eight at night the show went on live, and if anything went wrong there was nothing you could do to cure it. You would panic, you would shout, you had a continuous conversation with the backroom, in essence saying, "Something's gone terribly wrong here, the dog has just knocked over the set and the actors are sitting on the floor, and we've got no pay-off to the sketch, can you go to the news? Can you get us out?" And they'd just say, "Tell them to ad-lib. And the great thing about doing the Goon shows was that nobody noticed—nobody noticed anything!

That stood me in perfect stead for having to live a little bit by my wits and on my feet. Especially in something like *A Hard Day's Night* when we would go to shoot a sequence in Notting Hill and you'd get only one take to do it. Suddenly, out of nowhere, 2,000 kids would appear and completely block entrances and exits and the police would panic and say, "Just go away." So you would then have to find something to ad-lib with, or do, until somebody could find another street that was suitable where nobody knew we were coming. We'd put a car in, going one way, and have a car waiting to pick the boys up at the end of the take and go the other way; and we just hoped we would remember where we were supposed to be in the afternoon! There was a famous case in *Help!* where the boys had to run into Asprey's on Bond Street, and we cut the camera for two minutes, and then they ran out the other way. In that two-minute time sequence, John Lennon spent £8,000 in Asprey's!

SS: Now at the end of doing "The Goon Show" there was a one-time only show that was called "The Dick Lester Show"?

RL: At the very beginning of commercial television they had a half hour to fill between "Dragnet" and the first commercial pantomime, and they didn't know what to fill it with. Part of my deal to be able to stay in this country was that I was supposed to train new directors. I was twenty-two at the time, so I was passing on the wisdom of the ancients. Alun Owen was acting at this point and he joined me on the project. It was a test show for the director Philip Saville; it was his first job. But in any case when the time came to fill this slot, they said you do this test show, which was an ad-lib show. And without any pressure as a practice exercise it didn't go too badly, but when we did it on the air it was a nightmare; it was absolutely dreadful: nothing worked, no jokes came off. It was one of those moments you hope will never happen again. Yet we were the fourth-highest-rated program because nobody bothered to turn away from the "Dragnet" station before the pantomime, so we had this wonderful rating.

But the next day I came into the office feeling awful and there was a phone call and a voice said, "You don't know me but I saw your show last night and either that was the worst show there has ever been on British television, or you may be on to something." I said, "Do I have a choice?" and he said, "My name is Peter Sellers, would you like to come and have lunch with me?" and he decided that I would be the one entrusted with trying to take the radio Goon shows and put them on television.

SS: And Peter had recently purchased a camera.

RL: We did actually get the shows on and we did three series. At the end of the third, Peter bought a 16mm Pyer-Bolex—he was a mechanical freak, he liked toys of all sorts—and the fact that he wanted to try the camera out led to the making of *The Running,*

Jumping, & Standing Still Film, which is eleven minutes long, which we never planned to show to anyone but Peter was friendly with a man called Herbert Kretzmer, who used to be a newspaper television critic. He's now known as the man who wrote the English lyrics for *Les Misérables*. Peter showed Herbert the film, which had cost us £70 to make. We edited it on Peter's drum-kit, I wrote some music for it and I got some friends to play it, and it was all done very much as an amateur production, but they showed it to Herbert—who said, "I think you should try to get it on at the Edinburgh Festival."

And they showed it there and there was this man from San Francisco who said, "I'll show it at my festival." And then it got an Academy Award nomination, so the film that we had made for ourselves for no money—we had only the one copy—was an Academy Award-nominated film and I thought, "I've got a future now. I'm a contender." What happened is that everybody said, "We love the film, if we ever want a long version of that—well, it was a silent film, for God's sake—we'll let you know."

But nobody spoke to me for two years. Until a producer named Milton Sibotsky sent me a twenty-four-page script [for *It's Trad, Dad!*] and I said, "I think I can do something with it"—it was with pop-stars, with Gene Vincent and Helen Shapiro and a lot of trad bands ["trad jazz," short for traditional jazz, refers to the Dixieland and ragtime jazz styles of the early twentieth century], so I said, "I've been around this kind of music all my life, I think I know how to deal with it and as soon as you get a first draft screenplay, I'd be delighted to read it." He said, "That's the shooting script and you start in three weeks." I said, "But it's only twenty-four pages long," and he said, "You'll find a way to pad it out."

So we gathered these poor pop people with this feast of moveable sets behind them and shot three scenes a day. At the end of the last week of shooting, the Twist started—Chubby Checker and his first big Twist success. So I said to Milton, "I think it would be a great idea: we could be the first film in history to have the twist in it. He's in New York; I could go over and shoot him." And he said, "If you pay your own way over, you can go." So I did and we got him in the film, and that was one of the contributing factors to my getting *A Hard Day's Night*.

SS: You started to make commercials and you continued to do this between films.

RL: Yes, you can see from the kind of films I was making that I didn't get much of a chance to practice and do tests and to learn what new equipment was out. The great thing is that in the 1960s commercials were very much driven by technique, camera technique, the different use of lights, filters, and stock. Commercials enabled me to try things out. We were the first people to use a cameraman named David Watkin, who went on to do *The Knack*. We had an idea of using extreme whites in a very high-contrast stock, which we tried out. We went to Barbara Mullins' place to shoot a butter commercial for Ireland. In the end she looked like Lena Horne—you couldn't see her at all, she had just vanished: there was just black blob in a dress. The commercial was totally unusable.

But we learned enough from that disaster to paint one of the rooms white in *The Knack* and find out how we could manage to actually see the person's face. David obviously liked this because by the time we got to *Robin and Marian*, he managed to do some night shots of Audrey Hepburn in the most dramatic part of the film where we couldn't see her, either!

SS: Right after *It's Trad, Dad!*, which came out in 1962 and got pretty nice notices, you went on to do *The Mouse on the Moon* [1963], where you met Walter Shenson.

RL: Again, that was through Peter Sellers, who had done the first *Mouse That Roared* [1959], and he said, "I'm not going to do the second but I'll see you right." We didn't have enough money for sets, but Cornell Wilde had done a Lancelot/Guinevere thing at Pinewood and the sets hadn't been torn down, so we grabbed them and they became Ruhitania, where Margaret Rutherford lived.

SS: Did there come a time when you felt further away from your potential audience than when you started, and did you feel that your take on material and your take on society were becoming further removed just because of the societal changes taking place?

RL: Certainly changes in oneself. I always was aware that I would encounter a movie audience and think they were hamsters watching the screen because their metabolic rate had speeded up considerably more than mine. It's inevitable. And you end up wanting to do simple, pure films. Because you can't compete against the others. I could not set out now to do *A Hard Day's Night*. I would be the wrong person to do it. Learn not to try. If someone else can do it better, walk away.

SS: After *The Three Musketeers* [1973] you did *Robin and Marian*. You seem to like bleak takes on traditional ideas.

RL: Instead of filming the love scene, I'd like to see the maid taking the sheets off and taking them to the laundry the next morning. I'm more interested not in what the person seems to be but the other side of the myth.

SS: When you're doing a film that's set in the past, do you have a rule abut how to research and what to look for?

RL: Some of the best examples would be the Musketeers themselves. At the time when we were starting to do the duels, the first thing I did was to get books on the history of medicine at that time and the history of architecture, or whatever you can find out about how ordinary people lived, what they grew, etc. As far as dueling goes, almost all of the Hollywood duels were invented by mostly Hungarian fencers who were ex-Olympic fencers of the 1920s and 1930s, and they all used very small swords and they would parry on their back foot. If you look at any of Stewart Granger's, Errol Flynn's, and Fairbanks's films, that's the way it was.

But I found a book from 1615—*The Three Musketeers* was set in 1627—that tells you the sword was huge and you didn't parry with the blade, you parried with a main gauche that was a dagger or a cloak, your weight's on your front foot, and you hack with the sword—you didn't stab, you hacked. Now the minute you do that, the way the person fights is totally different from anybody else's fighting, but that was the way they fought. So give dear old Oliver Reed the instruction "hack at somebody," and he just went at it and terrified the stunt men he was fighting, who would be seen retching in the corner.

Another lovely Oliver Reed story is from when we did *Royal Flash* [1975]. He played Bismarck, and he was supposed to have a fight with a man who was a bare-knuckled prizefighter in England. So we got Henry Cooper to play the part and we staged the scene where the two of them were fighting in the very elegant Georgian dining room. But Oliver had gone to the stills photographer and said, "Keep your eyes open"—and he was obviously planning on going back to his pub and saying, "I decked the former heavyweight champion and here's the photograph to prove it." We'd practiced the moves, but once the cameras were rolling Oliver decided that he'd change a few of those moves. Henry, who was being the perfect film professional, was doing his best but slowly he was getting a little bit angry and a little bit concerned and finally at one point, where Oliver was flailing away at him, suddenly—and you can see it only if you slow the film down a great deal—Henry's fist traveled about that far [indicates short distance with his hands] so fast that nobody saw it, and Oliver was quiet and silent on the floor, gone. No photographs. Nothing.

SS: You've also talked about the cost of things in relation to other things during a particular time period.

RL: Yes, we used that in *Butch and Sundance: The Early Days* [1979], because normally you go to a Western and people load up their guns and go "boom, boom, boom"—next box of cartridges, please. But ammunition was really expensive, and when you look at a Western where men are just shooting randomly, well, they wouldn't have done that. It would have cost them six months' salary, and they didn't have that kind of money to burn.

SS: Now the *Superman* films [1980, 1983]. You were a producer on the first one, in 1978.

RL: I was a smiler because the other producers, they weren't talking to each other, so I had to make sure the film got made despite that, and then I got interested in it even though it was not the kind of material that I really ever thought I'd want to do. I realized how little I knew about the technologies that were available and were becoming available. All the opticals would soon be done electronically; by the time we had finished the third film, things were happening electronically. We were trying to do everything mechanically. We had Christopher Reeve on trampolines, we had wires, we had him dangling from a crane because we did it physically, and then we'd have to paint out and light the wire that he was hanging on so that no one could see it. Nowadays you just go in and [pretends table is computer keyboard] the wire just disappears. You kids have it so easy.

SS: Is there anything you miss about making films?

RL: No! It's awful to say but in the early days I used to have nightmares that I wasn't working, and in the last ten years I've been having nightmares that I *am* working and wake up white-faced thinking, "Oh, dear God."

SS: And does cinema hold any interest for you as an attender?

RL: Obviously less. You get out of the habit; it becomes harder. I do see quite a lot of things that I'm surprised are working as well as they do, and I see them with audiences and I know that they are working, but your metabolism changes, and I was always fairly narrow-minded about other people's films because I'm not good with genres. I keep being invited to horror film juries and it's agony, absolute agony. I can't judge the difference between one and the other; I can't see which is better. I was never good with erotic films, either, and I was never good with Westerns, so all the genre filmmaking is a complete loss to me.

SS: Your films are always very well cast and very well acted, yet you don't like to rehearse.

RL: I was never an actor, and therefore I don't presume to tell an actor how he should act. Film directing is largely very well-paid garbage collecting—you get rid of rubbish. You say to the composer, "I love that, I love that bit, but I don't like this." You say to the cameraman, "It's looking very good but wouldn't it be better if we didn't have that light from there?"

The same thing with an actor: you hire him because you think he understands the character and what you are trying to do. You say to him: "Do it, we'll film it. It works with someone like George C. Scott, whose first takes in *Petulia* [1968] were impeccable; his instincts were 100% right, and he's one of the best actors I've ever worked with. There are other actors who slowly come into their own, but basically you hire them because they should know what they are doing. All I can say to them is, "I don't think that line is working there, offer me something else." And just try by that process to mold the actor's work without presuming to be an actor-leading director.

SS: You weren't a big fan of auditions, either.

RL: I would never audition with a camera or with an actor and have him read anything. I would talk to him, go out for a meal with him, and if I felt he understood what the character was about, I would eventually hire him. Some people are terrific at auditions, and other people—like Michael Gambon—give the most terrible auditions yet are brilliant performers in the end, so you can't tell.

SS: What did you think of working with Spike Milligan?

RL: In terms of naked comedy, I've been very fortunate to have worked with Buster Keaton and Groucho Marx. But of all the people I've worked with, Spike was the most constantly inventive. An absolute nightmare to work with, especially during live television, but extraordinarily clever and creative: a brilliant mind. Quite unique.

SS: One final question: is *A Hard Day's Night* fantasy or reality?

RL: Film is a fantasy always masquerading as reality. We were choosing bits of a kind of reality; the Beatles' life was pretty unreal, so armed with the fact that it is Beatle-reality and that you're being screamed at from morning to night, we were trying to represent the mood and the feel of the way their life had become. They were prisoners of their own success. They were being pushed into cars, surrounded by people telling them what to do—and suddenly they break out of rooms with low ceilings and go play in a field. That was the structure, the spine, around which we wrote the film, and that was the Beatles' reality. But all film is fantasy.

Bibliography

Monaco, James. *The Films of Richard Lester*. New York: Zoetrope, 1974.

Rosenfeldt, Diane. *Richard Lester: A Guide to References and Resources*. Boston: G. K. Hall, 1978.

Sinyard, Neil. *The Films of Richard Lester*. Totowa, N.J.: Barnes and Noble, 1985.

Sinyard, Neil. *Richard Lester*. Manchester, U.K.: Manchester University Press, 2010.

Directors' Feature Filmographies

Michael Powell (1905-90)

Two Crowded Hours (1931)
My Friend the King (1931)
Rynox (1931)
The Rasp (1931)
The Star Reporter (1931)
Hotel Splendide (1932)
C.O.D. (1932)
His Lordship (1932)
Born Lucky (1932)
The Fire Raisers (1933)
Red Ensign, a.k.a. Strike! (1934)
The Night of the Party (1934)
Something Always Happens (1934)
The Girl in the Crowd (1934)
Lazybones (1935)
The Love Test (1935)
The Phantom Light (1935)
The Price of a Song (1935)
Someday (1935)
Her Last Affair (1935)
The Brown Wallet (1936)
Crown V. Stevens, a.k.a. Third Time Unlucky (1936)
The Man Behind the Mask (1936)
The Edge of the World (1937)
The Lion Has Wings (1939)
The Spy In Black, a.k.a. U-Boat 29 (1939)
Contraband, a.k.a. Blackout (1940)
The Thief of Bagdad (1940)
49th Parallel, a.k.a. The Invaders (1941)
One of Our Aircraft Is Missing (1942)
The Life and Death of Colonel Blimp (1943)
A Canterbury Tale (1944)
I Know Where I'm Going! (1945)
A Matter of Life and Death, a.k.a. Stairway to Heaven (1946)
Black Narcissus (1947)
The Red Shoes (1948)
The Small Back Room (1949)
Gone to Earth, a.k.a. The Wild Heart (1950)
The Elusive Pimpernel, a.k.a. The Fighting Pimpernel (1950)
The Tales of Hoffmann (1951)
Oh ... Rosalinda!! (1955)
The Battle of the River Plate, a.k.a. Pursuit of the Graf Spee (1956)
Ill Met by Moonlight, a.k.a. Night Ambush (1957)
Luna de miel (Honeymoon, 1959)
Peeping Tom (1960)
The Queen's Guards (1961)
Herzog Blaubarts Burg, a.k.a. Bluebeard's Castle (1964)
They're a Weird Mob (1966)
The Boy Who Turned Yellow (1972)
Age of Consent (1969)
Return to the Edge of the World (1978)

Carol Reed (1906-76)

It Happened in Paris (1935)
Midshipman Easy, a.k.a. Men of the Sea (1935)
Laburnum Grove (1936)
Talk of the Devil (1936)
Who's Your Lady Friend (1937)
Bank Holiday, a.k.a. Three on a Weekend (1938)
Penny Paradise (1938)
Climbing High (1938)
A Girl Must Live (1939)
The Stars Look Down (1940)
Night Train to Munich, a.k.a. Night Train (1940)
The Girl in the News (1941)
Kipps, a.k.a. The Remarkable Mr. Kipps (1941)
The Young Mr. Pitt (1942)
A Letter from Home (1941)

The Way Ahead (1944)
Odd Man Out (1947)
The Fallen Idol (1948)
The Third Man (1949)
Outcasts of the Islands (1952)
The Man Between (1953)
A Kid for Two Farthings (1955)
Trapeze (1956)
The Key (1958)
Our Man in Havana (1959)
The Running Man (1963)
The Agony and the Ecstasy (1965)
Oliver! (1968)
The Last Warrior, a.k.a. *Flap* (1970
Follow Me, a.k.a. *The Public Eye* (1971)

David Lean (1908-91)

In Which We Serve (1942, with Noël Coward)
This Happy Breed (1944)
Blithe Spirit (1945)
Brief Encounter (1945)
Great Expectations (1946)
Oliver Twist (1948)
The Passionate Friends (1949)
Madeleine (1950)
The Sound Barrier (1952)
Hobson's Choice (1954)
Summertime (1955)
The Bridge on the River Kwai (1957)
Lawrence of Arabia (1962)
Doctor Zhivago (1965)
Ryan's Daughter (1970)
A Passage to India (1984)

Charles Crichton (1910-99)

For Those in Peril (1944)
Dead of Night (1945)
Painted Boats (1945)
Hue and Cry (1947)
Against the Wind (1948)
Another Shore (1948)
Train of Events (1949)
Dance Hall (1950)

The Lavender Hill Mob (1951)
Hunted, a.k.a. *The Stranger in Between* (1952)
The Titfield Thunderbolt (1953)
The Love Lottery (1954)
The Divided Heart (1954)
Man in the Sky (1957)
Law and Disorder (1958)
Floods of Fear (1959)
The Battle of the Sexes (1959)
The Boy Who Stole a Million (1960)
The Third Secret (1964)
He Who Rides a Tiger (1965)
A Fish Called Wanda (1988)

Lindsay Anderson (1923-94)

This Sporting Life (1963)
The White Bus (1967)
If... (1968)
O Lucky Man! (1973)
In Celebration (1975)
Look Back in Anger (1980)
Britannia Hospital (1982)
The Whales of August (1987)

Karel Reisz (1926-2002)

Saturday Night and Sunday Morning (1960)
Night Must Fall (1964)
Morgan: A Suitable Case for Treatment (1966)
Isadora (1968)
The Gambler (1974)
Who'll Stop the Rain (1978)
The French Lieutenant's Woman (1981)
Sweet Dreams (1985)
Everybody Wins (1990)

John Schlesinger (1926-2003)

A Kind of Loving (1962)
Billy Liar (1963)
Darling (1965)
Far From the Madding Crowd (1967)
Midnight Cowboy (1969)

Sunday Bloody Sunday (1971)
Visions of Eight (1973)
The Day of the Locust (1975)
Marathon Man (1976)
Yanks (1979)
Honky Tonk Freeway (1981)
Privileged (1982)
Separate Tables (1983)
An Englishman Abroad (1983)
The Falcon and the Snowman (1985)
The Believers (1987)
Madame Sousatzka (1988)
Pacific Heights (1990)
A Question of Attribution (1991)
The Innocent (1993)
Cold Comfort Farm (1995)
Eye for an Eye (1996)
The Tale of Sweeney Todd (1998)
The Next Best Thing (2000)

Ken Russell (1927-2011)

French Dressing (1963)
Billion Dollar Brain (1967)
Women in Love (1969)
The Music Lovers (1970)
The Devils (1971)
The Boy Friend (1971)
Savage Messiah (1972)
Mahler (1974)
Tommy (1975)
Lisztomania (1975)
Valentino (1977)
Altered States (1980)
Crimes of Passion (1984)
Gothic (1986)
Salome's Last Dance (1988)
The Lair of the White Worm (1988)
The Rainbow (1989)
Whore (1991)
The Fall of the House of Usher: A Gothic Tale for the 21st Century (2002)

Tony Richardson (1928-91)

Look Back in Anger (1959)
The Entertainer (1960)
Sanctuary (1961)
A Taste of Honey (1961)
The Loneliness of the Long Distance Runner (1962)
Tom Jones (1963)
The Loved One (1965)
Mademoiselle (1966)
The Sailor from Gibraltar (1967)
The Charge of the Light Brigade (1968)
Laughter in the Dark (1969)
Hamlet (1969)
Ned Kelly (1970)
A Delicate Balance (1973)
Dead Cert (1974)
Joseph Andrews (1977)
A Death in Canaan (1978)
The Border (1982)
The Hotel New Hampshire (1984)
Blue Sky (1994)

Nicolas Roeg (born 1928)

Performance (1970)
Walkabout (1971)
Don't Look Now (1973)
The Man Who Fell to Earth (1976)
Bad Timing (1980)
Eureka (1983)
Insignificance (1985)
Castaway (1986)
Track 29 (1988)
The Witches (1990)
Cold Heaven (1991)
Two Deaths (1995)
Puffball (2007)

Ken Loach (born 1936)

Poor Cow (1967)
Kes (1969)
Family Life (1971)
Black Jack (1979)
The Gamekeeper (1980)

Looks and Smiles (1981)
Which Side Are You On? (1984)
Fatherland (1986)
Hidden Agenda (1990)
Riff-Raff (1990)
Raining Stones (1993)
Ladybird, Ladybird (1994)
Land and Freedom (1995)
Carla's Song (1996)
The Flickering Flame (1997)
My Name Is Joe (1998)
Bread and Roses (2000)
The Navigators (2001)
Sweet Sixteen (2002)
Ae Fond Kiss . . . (2004)
The Wind That Shakes the Barley (2006)
It's a Free World . . . (2007)
Looking for Eric (2009)
Route Irish (2010)
The Angels' Share (2012)
Jimmy's Hall (2014)
I, Daniel Blake (2016)

Stephen Frears (born 1941)

Gumshoe (1971)
Bloody Kids (1979)
A Change of Seasons (1980)
The Hit (1984)
My Beautiful Laundrette (1985)
Prick Up Your Ears (1987)
Mr. Jolly Lives Next Door (1987)
Sammy and Rosie Get Laid (1987)
Dangerous Liaisons (1988)
The Grifters (1990)
Hero (1992)
Mary Reilly (1996)
The Van (1996)
The Hi-Lo Country (1998)
High Fidelity (2000)
Liam (2000)
Dirty Pretty Things (2002)
Mrs. Henderson Presents (2005)
The Queen (2006)
Cheri (2009)
Tamara Drewe (2010)

Lay the Favorite (2012)
Muhammad Ali's Greatest Fight (2013)
Philomena (2013)
The Program (2015)
Florence Foster Jenkins (2016)
Victoria and Abdul (2017)

Peter Greenaway (born 1942)

The Falls (1980)
The Draughtsman's Contract (1982)
A Zed and Two Noughts (1985)
The Belly of an Architect (1987)
Drowning by Numbers (1988)
The Cook, the Thief, His Wife, and Her Lover (1989)
Prospero's Books (1991)
The Baby of Mâcon (1993)
The Pillow Book (1996)
8½ Women (1999)
The Tulse Luper Suitcases, Part 1: The Moab Story (2003)
The Tulse Luper Suitcases, Part 2: Vaux to the Sea (2004)
The Tulse Luper Suitcases, Part 3: From Sark to the Finish (2004)
Nightwatching (2007)
Goltzius and the Pelican Company (2012)
Eisenstein in Guanajuato (2015)
Walking to Paris (2017)

Mike Leigh (born 1943)

Bleak Moments (1971)
Hard Labour (1973)
The Permissive Society (1975)
Nuts in May (1976)
Abigail's Party (1977)
Kiss of Death (1977)
Who's Who (1978)
Grown-Ups (1980)
Meantime (1983)
Four Days in July (1985)
High Hopes (1988)
Life Is Sweet (1990)

Naked (1993)
Secrets and Lies (1996)
Career Girls (1997)
Topsy-Turvy (2000)
All or Nothing (2002)
Vera Drake (2004)
Happy-Go-Lucky (2008)
Another Year (2010)
Mr. Turner (2014)

Terence Davies (born 1945)

The Terence Davies Trilogy (1984; three short films: "Children", "Madonna and Child", and "Death and Transfiguration")
Distant Voices, Still Lives (1988)
The Long Day Closes (1992)
The Neon Bible (1995)
The House of Mirth (2000)
The Deep Blue Sea (2011)
Sunset Song (2015)
A Quiet Passion (2016)

Pawel Pawlikowski (born 1957)

The Stringer (1998)
Last Resort (2000)
My Summer of Love (2004)
The Woman in the Fifth (2011)
Ida (2013)
Cold War (2017)

Kenneth Branagh (born 1960)

Henry V (1989)
Dead Again (1991)
Peter's Friends (1992)
Much Ado about Nothing (1993)
Frankenstein (1994)
In the Bleak Midwinter (1995)
Hamlet (1996)
Love's Labour's Lost (2000)
Listening (2003)
The Magic Flute (2006)
As You Like It (2006)
Sleuth (2007)

Thor (2011)
Jack Ryan: Shadow Recruit (2014)
Murder on the Orient Express (2017)

Joseph Losey (1909-84)

The Boy with Green Hair (1948)
The Lawless (1950)
The Prowler (1951)
M (1951)
The Big Night (1951)
Stranger on the Prowl (1951)
The Sleeping Tiger (1954)
A Man on the Beach (1955)
The Intimate Stranger (1956)
Time Without Pity (1957)
The Gypsy and the Gentleman (1958)
Blind Date (1959)
The Criminal (1960)
Eva (1962)
The Damned (1963)
The Servant (1963)
King and Country (1964)
Modesty Blaise (1966)
Accident (1967)
Secret Ceremony (1968)
Boom! (1968)
Figures in a Landscape (1970)
The Go-Between (1971)
The Assassination of Trotsky (1972)
A Doll's House (1973)
The Romantic Englishwoman (1975)
Galileo (1975)
Mr. Klein (1976)
Roads to the South (1978)
Don Giovanni (1979)
The Trout (1982)
Steaming (1985)

James Ivory (born 1928)

The Householder (1963)
Shakespeare Wallah (1965)
The Guru (1969)
Bombay Talkie (1970)
Savages (1973)

Autobiography of a Princess (1975)
The Wild Party (1975)
Hullabaloo Over Georgie and Bonnie's Pictures (1976)
Roseland (1977)
The Europeans (1979)
The Five Forty-Eight (1979)
Jane Austen in Manhattan (1980)
Quartet (1981)
Heat and Dust (1983)
The Bostonians (1984)
A Room with a View (1985)
Maurice (1987)
Slaves of New York (1989)
Mr. and Mrs. Bridge (1990)
Howards End (1992)
The Remains of the Day (1993)
Jefferson in Paris (1995)
Surviving Picasso (1996)
A Soldier's Daughter Never Cries (1998)
The Golden Bowl (2001)
Le Divorce (2003)
The White Countess (2005)
The City of Your Final Destination (2009)

Butch and Sundance: The Early Days (1979)
Cuba (1979)
Superman 2 (1980)
Superman 3 (1983)
Finders Keepers (1984)
The Return of the Musketeers (1989)
Get Back (1990)

Richard Lester (born 1932)

It's Trad, Dad! (1962)
The Mouse on the Moon (1963)
A Hard Day's Night (1964)
The Knack ... and How to Get It (1965)
Help! (1965)
A Funny Thing Happened On the Way to the Forum (1966)
How I Won the War (1967)
Petulia (1968)
The Bed Sitting Room (1969)
The Three Musketeers (1973)
Juggernaut (1974)
The Four Musketeers (1974)
Royal Flash (1975)
Robin and Marian (1976)
The Ritz (1976)

General Bibliography of British Cinema

Adair, Gilbert, and Nick Roddick. *A Night at the Pictures: Ten Decades of British Film*. London: Columbus Books, 1985.

Aitken, Ian, ed. *The Documentary Film Movement: An Anthology*. Edinburgh, U.K.: Edinburgh University Press, 1998.

Aldgate, Anthony, and Jeffrey Richards. *Best of British: Cinema and Society from 1930 to the Present*. Rev. ed. London: I. B. Tauris, 1999.

Aldgate, Anthony. *Censorship and the Permissive Society: British Cinema and Theatre, 1955-1965*. New York: Oxford University Press, 1995.

Aldgate, Anthony, and Jeffrey Richards. *Britain Can Take It: The British Cinema in the Second World War*. 1994. London: I. B. Tauris, 2007.

All Our Yesterdays: 90 Years of British Cinema. Ed. Charles Barr. London: British Film Institute, 1986.

Allon, Yoram, et al., eds. *Contemporary British and Irish Directors: A Critical Guide*. London: Wallflower, 2001.

Armes, Roy. *A Critical History of the British Cinema*. London: Secker and Warburg, 1978.

Arnold, Kevin, and Wambu Onyekachi. *A Fuller Picture: The Commercial Impact of Six British Films with Black Themes in the 1990s*. London: British Film Institute, 1999.

Ashley, Walter. *The Cinema and the Public: A Critical Analysis of the Origin, Constitution, and Control of the British Film Institute*. London: Ivor Nicholson and Watson Limited, 1934.

Ashton, Bridgette. *British Cinema: A History*. Huntingdon, U.K.: Elm, 1993.

Atwell, David. *Cathedrals of the Movies: A History of British Cinemas and Their Audiences*. London: The Architectural Press, 1980.

Auty, Martin, and Nick Roddick. *British Cinema Now*. London: British Film Institute, 1985.

Babington, Bruce. *British Stars and Stardom: From Alma Taylor to Sean Connery.* Manchester, U.K.: Manchester University Press, 2001.

Baillieu, Bill, and John Goodchild. *The British Film Business.* West Sussex, U.K.: Wiley, 2002.

Balcon, Michael. *Twenty Years of British Film, 1925-1945.* New York: Arno Press, 1972.

Bamford, Kenton. *Distorted Images: British National Identity and Film in the 1920s.* 1980. London: I. B. Tauris, 1999.

Barber, Sian. *The British Film Industry in the 1970s: Capital, Culture, and Creativity.* Basingstoke, U.K.: Palgrave Macmillan, 2013.

Barnes, John, and Richard Maltby. *The Beginnings of the Cinema in England, 1894-1901.* 5 vols. Exeter, U.K.: University of Exeter Press, 1996-98.

Barnes, John. *Pioneers of British Film.* 1983. London: Bishopsgate Press, 1988.

Barnes, John. *The Rise of the Cinema in Great Britain.* London: Bishopsgate Press, 1983.

Barr, Charles. *British Cinema: A Very Short Introduction.* Oxford, U.K.: Oxford University Press, 2016.

Barrow, Sarah, and John White, eds. *Fifty Key British Films.* London: Routledge, 2008.

Bell, Emma, and Neil Mitchell. *Directory of World Cinema: Britain.* Bristol, U.K.: Intellect, 2012.

Bell, Melanie. *Femininity in the Frame: Women and 1950s British Popular Cinema.* London: I. B. Tauris, 2010.

Bell, Melanie, and Melanie Williams, eds. *British Women's Cinema.* London: Routledge, 2010.

Benyahia, Sarah Casey. *Teaching Contemporary British Cinema.* London: British Film Institute, 2005.

Berry, David. *Wales and Cinema: The First Hundred Years.* Cardiff, U.K.: University of Wales Press, 1996.

Betts, Ernest. *The Film Business: A History of British Cinema, 1896-1972*. London: Allen and Unwin, 1973.

Bird, John H. *Cinema Parade: Fifty Years of British Film Shows*. Birmingham, U.K.: Cornish Bros., 1947.

Blandford, Steven. *Film, Drama, and the Break-up of Britain*. Bristol, U.K.: Intellect, 2007.

Bloom, Abigail Burnham. *The Literary Monster on Film: Five Nineteenth-Century British Novels and Their Cinematic Adaptations*. Jefferson, N.C.: McFarland, 2010.

Boot, Andy. *Fragments of Fear: An Illustrated History of British Horror Films*. Rev. ed. London: Creation, 2000.

Border Crossing: Film in Ireland, Britain, and Europe. Ed. John Hill, Martin McLoone, and Paul Hainsworth. Belfast: Institute of Irish Studies, 1994.

Bourne, Stephen. *Black in the British Frame: The Black Experience in British Film and Television*. London: Continuum, 2001.

Bourne, Stephen. *Brief Encounters: Lesbians and Gays in British Cinema 1930-1971*. London: Cassell, 1996.

Boyce, Michael W. *The Lasting Influence of the War on Postwar British Film*. New York: Palgrave Macmillan, 2012.

Britain and the Cinema in the Second World War. Ed. Philip M. Taylor. New York: St. Martin's Press, 1988.

British Cinema. Ed. Kenneth A. Hurren. London: S. Evelyn Thomas, 1948.

British Cinema and Thatcherism: Fires Were Started. Ed. Lester Friedman. 1993. London: Wallflower, 2006.

The British Cinema Book. Ed. Robert Murphy. 2nd ed. London: British Film Institute, 2001.

British Cinema History. Ed. James Curran and Vincent Porter. London: Weidenfeld and Nicolson, 1983.

British Cinema in the 1960s: An Educational Resource. Ed. Wendy Hewing. London: British Film Institute, 2003.

British Cinema of the '90s. Ed. Robert Murphy. London: British Film Institute, 2000.

British Cinema, Past and Present. Ed. Justine Ashby and Andrew Higson. London: Routledge, 2000.

British Historical Cinema: The History, Heritage, and Costume Film. Ed. Claire Monk and Amy Sargeant. London: Routledge, 2002.

Brown, Julie, and Annette Davison, eds. *The Sounds of the Silents in Britain.* New York: Oxford University Press, 2013.

Brown, Simon, et al., eds. *British Colour Cinema: Practices and Theories.* Basingstoke, U.K.: Palgrave Macmillan, 2013.

Bruce, David. *Scotland the Movie.* Edinburgh, U.K.: Polygon, 1996.

Brunel, Adrian. *Nice Work: The Story of Thirty Years in British Film Production.* London: Forbes Robertson, 1949.

Brunsdon, Charlotte. *London in Cinema: The Cinematic City since 1945.* London: British Film Institute, 2007.

Buchanan, Judith, et al. *British Film.* Oxford, U.K.: Maison Française, 1999.

Burns, James McDonald. *Cinema and Society in the British Empire, 1895-1940.* Basingstoke, U.K.: Palgrave Macmillan, 2013.

Burrows, Elaine, et al., eds. *The British Cinema Source Book.* London: British Film Institute, 1995.

Burrows, Jon. *Legitimate Cinema: Theatre Stars in Silent British Films, 1908-1918.* Exeter, U.K.: Exeter University Press, 2003.

Burton, Alan, and Steve Chibnall. *Historical Dictionary of British Cinema.* Lanham, Md.: Scarecrow Press, 2013.

Burton, Alan, and Laraine Porter. *Scene Stealing: Sources of British Cinema before 1930.* Trowbridge, U.K.: Flicks Books, 2003.

Burton, Alan, and Laraine Porter, eds. *The Showman, the Spectacle, and the Two-Minute Silence: Performing British Cinema before 1930.* Trowbridge, U.K.: Flicks Books, 2001.

Burton, Alan. *Pimples, Pranks, and Pratfalls: British Film Comedy before 1930.* Trowbridge, U.K.: Flicks Books, 2000.

Burton, Alan, and Julian Petley. *Genre and British Cinema.* Trowbridge, U.K.: Flicks Books, 1998.

Butler, Ivan. *Cinema in Britain: An Illustrated Survey.* South Brunswick, N.J.: A. S. Barnes, 1973.

Butler, Ivan. *"To Encourage the Art of Film": The Story of the British Film Institute.* London: R. Hale, 1971.

Butler, Margaret. *Film and Community in Britain and France: From* La règle du jeu *to* Room at the Top. London: I. B. Tauris, 2004.

Carrick, Edward. *Art and Design in the British Film: A Pictorial Directory of British Art Directors and Their Work.* London: D. Dobson, 1948.

Casey, Sarah. *Teaching British Cinema since 1990.* London: British Film Institute, 2004.

Caughie, John, and Kevin Rockett, eds. *The Companion to British and Irish Cinema.* London: Cassell, 1996.

Chanan, Michael. *The Dream That Kicks: The Prehistory and Early Years of Cinema in Britain.* London: Routledge and Kegan Paul, 1980

Chapman, James. *The British at War: Cinema, State, and Propaganda, 1939-1945.* London: I. B. Tauris, 1998.

Chapman, James, and Christine Geraghty, eds. *British Film Culture and Criticism.* Trowbridge, U.K.: Flicks Books, 2001.

Chapman, James. *Past and Present: National Identity and the British Historical Film.* London: I. B. Tauris, 2005.

Chibnall, Steve, and Robert Murphy, eds. *British Crime Cinema.* London: Routledge, 1999.

Chibnall, Steve, and Julian Petley, eds. *British Horror Cinema.* London: Routledge, 2002.

Chibnall, Steve. *Quota Quickies: The Birth of the British "B" Film.* London: British Film Institute, 2007.

Chibnall, Steve, and Brian McFarlane. *The British "B" Film*. London: British Film Institute/Palgrave Macmillan, 2009.

The Cinema of Britain and Ireland. Ed. Brian McFarlane. London: Wallflower, 2005.

Cinema: The Beginnings and the Future: Essays Marking the Centenary of the First Film Show Projected to a Paying Audience in Britain. Ed. Christopher Williams. London: University of Westminster Press, 1996.

Claydon, E. Anna. *The Representation of Masculinity in British Cinema of the 1960s:* Lawrence of Arabia, The Loneliness of the Long Distance Runner, *and* The Hill. Lewiston, N.Y.: Edwin Mellen Press, 2005.

Conrich, Ian, and Julian Petley. *Forbidden British Cinema*. Trowbridge, U.K.: Flicks Books, 2000.

Cook, Pam. *Fashioning the Nation: Costume and Identity in British Cinema*. London: British Film Institute, 1996.

Cook, Pam. *Gainsborough Pictures, 1924-1950 (Rethinking British Cinema)*. London: Cassell, 1998.

Coultass, Clive. *Images for Battle: British Film and the Second World War, 1939-1945*. Newark: University of Delaware Press, 1989.

Craig, Edward, and Roger Manvell. *Art and Design in the British Film: A Pictorial Directory of British Art Directors and Their Work*. New York: Arno, 1972.

Cross, Robin. *The Big Book of British Films*. London: Sidgewick and Jackson, 1984.

Curran, James, ed. *British Cinema History*. Totowa, N.J.: Barnes and Noble, 1983.

Dave, Paul. *Visions of England: Class and Culture in Contemporary Cinema*. Oxford, U.K.: Berg, 2006.

Dick, Eddie. *From Limelight to Satellite: A Scottish Film Book*. London: British Film Institute/Scottish Film Council, 1990.

Dickinson, Margaret, and Sarah Street. *Cinema and State: The Film Industry and the Government, 1927-1984*. London: British Film Institute, 1985.

Dissolving Views: Key Writings on British Cinema. Ed. Andrew Higson. London: Cassell, 1996.

Donnelly, Kevin J. *Pop Music in British Cinema: A Chronicle*. London: British Film Institute, 2001.

Don't Look Now: British Cinema in the 1970s. Ed. Paul Newland. Bristol, U.K.: Intellect, 2010.

Drazin, Charles. *The Finest Years: British Cinema of the 1940s*. 1998. London: I. B. Tauris, 2007.

Dupin, Christophe, et al. *Free Cinema*. London: British Film Institute, 2007.

Durgnat, Raymond. *A Mirror for England: British Movies from Austerity to Affluence*. 1971. New York: Palgrave Macmillan, 2011.

Dyja, Eddie. *Studying British Cinema: The 1990s*. Leighton Buzzard, U.K.: Auteur, 2010.

Ede, Laurie N. *British Film Design: A History*. London: I. B. Tauris, 2010.

The Encyclopedia of British Film. Ed. Brian McFarlane and Anthony Slide. 4th ed. Manchester, U.K.: Manchester University Press, 2013.

Ellis, Jack C. *British Film after the War, 1945-1963*. 4th ed. Boston: Allyn and Bacon, 1995.

Eyles, Allen. *Gaumont British Cinemas*. West Sussex, U.K.: Cinema Theatre Association, 1996.

Farmer, Richard. *The Food Companions: Cinema and Consumption in Wartime Britain, 1939-45*. Manchester, U.K.: Manchester University Press, 2011.

Fenton, Harvey, and David Flint, eds. *Ten Years of Terror: British Horror Films of the '70s*. Guildford, U.K.: FAB, 2003.

Field, Audrey. *Picture Palace: A Social History of the Cinema*. London: Gentry Books, 1974.

Fifty Key British Films. Ed. Sarah Barrow and John White. London: Routledge, 2008.

Fitzgerald, John. *Studying British Cinema: 1999-2009*. Leighton Buzzard, U.K.: Auteur, 2010.

Fitzsimmons, Linda, and Sarah Street, eds. *Moving Performance: British Stage and Screen, 1890s-1920s*. Trowbridge, U.K.: Flicks Books, 2000.

Flynn, Arthur. *Irish Film: 100 Years*. Wicklow, Irl.: Kestrel, 1966.

Fogg, Claire. *Family Values: Popular British Cinema and the Family, 1940-1949*. Leicester, U.K.: University of Leicester Press, 1998.

Forshaw, Barry. *British Crime Film: Subverting the Social Order*. Basingstoke, U.K.: Palgrave Macmillan, 2012.

Forshaw, Barry. *English Gothic Cinema*. Basingstoke, U.K.: Palgrave Macmillan, 2013.

Gaffney, Freddie. *Studying British Cinema: The 1980s*. Leighton Buzzard, U.K.: Auteur, 2011.

Geraghty, Christine. *British Cinema in the Fifties: Gender, Genre, and the "New Look"*. London: Routledge, 2000.

Gifford, Denis. *Entertainers in British Films: A Century of Showbiz in the Cinema*. Westport, Conn.: Greenwood Press, 2008.

Gifford, Denis. *British Cinema: An Illustrated Guide*. London: A. Zwemmer, 1968.

Gifford, Denis. *The British Film Catalogue*. Vol. 2: *Non-Fiction Film, 1888-1994*. London: Fitzroy Dearborn, 2000.

Gifford, Denis. *The British Film Catalogue*. 3rd ed. Vol. 1: *Fiction Film, 1895-1994*. London: Fitzroy Dearborn, 2001.

Gifford, Denis. *The Illustrated Who's Who in British Films*. London: B. T. Batsford, 1978.

Gillett, Philip. *Forgotten British Film: Value and the Ephemeral in Postwar Cinema*. Newcastle-upon-Tyne, U.K.: Cambridge Scholars Publishing, 2017.

Gillett, Philip. *The British Working Class in Postwar Film*. Manchester, U.K.: Manchester University Press, 2003.

Glancy, H. Mark. *When Hollywood Loved Britain: The Hollywood "British" Film, 1939-45*. Manchester, U.K.: Manchester University Press, 1999.

Glancy, Mark. *British Cinema and the Second World War: Audiences, Cinema-Going, and Popular Films*. Abingdon, U.K.: Taylor and Francis, 2011.

Gledhill, Christine. *Melodrama and Realism in Twenties British Cinema*. London: British Film Institute, 1991.

Gledhill, Christine, and Gillian Swanson, eds. *Nationalising Femininity: Culture, Sexuality, and British Cinema in the Second World War*. Manchester, U.K.: Manchester University Press, 1996.

Gledhill, Christine. *Reframing British Cinema, 1918-1928: Between Restraint and Passion*. London: British Film Institute, 2003.

Goble, Alan. *The Complete Index to British Sound Film since 1928*. London: Bowker-Saur, 1999.

Gough-Yates, Kevin. *Somewhere in England: British Cinema and Exile*. London: I. B. Tauris, 2001.

Gray, Michael. *Stills, Reels, and Rushes: Ireland and the Irish in Twentieth-Century Cinema*. Dublin: Ashfield, 1999.

Gray, Richard. *Cinemas in Britain: A History of Cinema Architecture*. Farnham, U.K.: Lund Humphries, 2011.

Griffiths, Robin. *British Queer Cinema*. London: Routledge, 2006.

Hacker, Jonathan, and David Price. *Take Ten: Contemporary British Film Directors*. New York: Oxford University Press, 1991.

Hallenbeck, Bruce. *The Hammer Vampire: British Cult Cinema*. Bristol, U.K.: Hemlock Books, 2010.

Hammond, Michael. *The Big Show: British Cinema Culture in the Great War, 1914-1918*. Exeter, U.K.: University of Exeter Press, 2006.

Hammond, Michael, and Michael Williams. *British Silent Cinema and the Great War*. Basingstoke, U.K.: Palgrave Macmillan, 2011.

Harper, Sue, et al. *British Film Culture in the 1970s: The Boundaries of Pleasure*. Edinburgh, U.K.: Edinburgh University Press, 2013.

Harper, Sue. *British Cinema of the 1950s: A Celebration*. Manchester, U.K.: Manchester University Press, 2003.

Harper, Sue, and Vincent Porter. *British Cinema of the 1950s: The Decline of Deference*. New York: Oxford University Press, 2003.

Harper, Sue. *Picturing the Past: The Rise and Fall of the British Costume Film*. London: British Film Institute, 1994.

Harper, Sue. *Women in British Cinema: Mad, Bad, and Dangerous to Know*. New York: Continuum, 2000.

Harris, Ed. *Britain's Forgotten Film Factory: The Story of Isleworth Studios*. Stroud, U.K.: Amberley, 2012.

Herbert, Stephen. *Who's Who of Victorian Cinema: A Worldwide Survey*. London: British Film Institute, 1996.

Higson, Andrew. *Film England: Culturally English Filmmaking since the 1990s*. London: I. B. Tauris, 2011.

Higson, Andrew. *British Silent Cinema*. Exeter, U.K.: University of Exeter Press, 2011.

Higson, Andrew. *English Heritage, English Cinema: Costume Drama since 1980*. New York: Oxford University Press, 2003.

Higson, Andrew. *Young and Innocent: The Cinema in Britain, 1896-1930*. Exeter, U.K.: Exeter University Press, 2002.

Higson, Andrew. *Waving the Flag: Constructing a National Cinema in Britain*. New York: Oxford University Press, 1995.

Hill, John. *Sex, Class, and Realism: British Cinema, 1956-1963*. London: British Film Institute, 1986.

Hill, John. *British Cinema in the 1980s: Issues and Themes*. 1999. New York: Oxford University Press, 2005.

Hill, John, and Julian Petley. *British Cinema and Television in the Twenty-First Century*. Edinburgh, U.K.: Edinburgh University Press, 2012.

Hill, John, and Julian Petley. *Film in Britain in the New Millennium*. Edinburgh, U.K.: Edinburgh University Press, 2012.

Hindmarsh, Justin. *British Cinema, Style and Context: An Examination of British "New Wave" Films*. Leicester, U.K.: University of Leicester Centre for Mass Communication Research, 1997.

Hochscherf, Tobias, and James Leggott, eds. *British Science-Fiction Film and Television: Critical Essays*. Jefferson, N.C.: McFarland, 2011.

Hockenhull, Stella. *Aesthetics and Neo-Romanticism in Film: Landscapes in Contemporary British Cinema.* London: I. B. Tauris, 2011.

Hogenkamp, Bert. *Deadly Parallels: Film and the Left in Britain, 1929-1939.* London: Lawrence and Wishart, 1986.

Holmes, Susan. *British Film and Television Culture in the 1950s: "Coming to a TV Near You".* Bristol, U.K.: Intellect, 2005.

Hunter, I. Q., et al., eds. *The Routledge Companion to British Cinema History.* London: Routledge, 2016.

Hunter, I. Q. *British Science-Fiction Cinema.* London: Routledge, 1999.

Hunter, I. Q., and Laraine Porter. *British Comedy Cinema.* New York: Routledge, 2012.

Hunter, I. Q. *British Trash Cinema.* Basingstoke, U.K.: Palgrave Macmillan, 2013.

Hunter, Jefferson. *English Filming, English Writing.* Bloomington: Indiana University Press, 2010.

Huntley, John. *British Film Music.* New York: Arno Press, 1972.

Hurd, Geoff. *World War II in British Films and Television.* London: British Film Institute, 1984.

Hutchings, Peter. *Hammer and Beyond: The British Horror Film.* Manchester, U.K.: Manchester University Press, 1993.

Jaén, Susana Onega, and Christian Gutleben. *Refracting the Canon in Contemporary British Literature and Film.* Amsterdam: Rodopi, 2004.

Jaikumar, Priya. *Cinema at the End of Empire: A Politics of Transition in Britain and India.* Durham, N.C.: Duke University Press, 2006.

Jones, Graham, and Lucy Johnson. *Talking Pictures: Interviews with Contemporary British Film-Makers.* London: British Film Institute, 1997.

Jones, Stephen G. *The British Labour Movement and Film (1918-1939).* London: Routledge and Kegan Paul, 1987.

Kerry, Matthew. *The Holiday and British Film.* Basingstoke, U.K.: Palgrave Macmillan, 2011.

Kirkup, Mike. *Contemporary British Cinema: A Teacher's Guide*. Leighton Buzzard, U.K.: Auteur, 2004.

Kitson, Claire. *British Animation: The Channel 4 Factor*. Bloomington: Indiana University Press, 2008.

Klein, Michael, and Gillian Parker, eds. *The English Novel and the Movies*. New York: Ungar, 1981.

Korte, Barbara. *Bidding for the Mainstream?: Black and Asian British Film since the 1990s*. Amsterdam: Rodopi, 2004.

Landy, Marcia. *British Genres: Cinema and Society, 1930-1960*. Princeton, N.J.: Princeton University Press, 1991.

Lant, Antonia. *Blackout: Reinventing Women for Wartime British Cinema*. Princeton, N.J.: Princeton University Press, 1991.

Lay, Samantha. *British Social Realism: From Documentary to Brit-Grit*. London: Wallflower, 2002.

Le Corff, Isabelle, and Estelle Epinoux. *Cinemas of Ireland*. Newcastle-upon-Tyne, U.K.: Cambridge Scholars, 2009.

Leach, Jim. *British Film*. New York: Cambridge University Press, 2004.

Leggott, James. *Contemporary British Cinema: From Heritage to Horror*. London: Wallflower, 2008.

Lovell, Alan. *The British Cinema: The Unknown Cinema*. London: British Film Institute, 1969.

Low, Rachael, and Jeffrey Richards. *History of British Cinema*. London: Routledge, 1997.

Low, Rachael. *The History of the British Film, 1896-1906*. London: Allen and Unwin, 1948.

Low, Rachael. *The History of the British Film, 1906-1914*. 1948. London: Routledge, 1997.

Low, Rachael. *The History of the British Film, 1914-1918*. 1950. London: Routledge, 1997.

Low, Rachael. *The History of the British Film, 1918-1929.* 1971. London: Routledge, 1997.

Low, Rachael. *The History of the British Film, 1929-1939: Films of Comment and Persuasion of the 1930s.* 1979. London: Routledge, 1997.

Low, Rachael. *The History of the British Film, 1929-1939: Film Making in 1930s Britain.* 1985. London: Routledge, 1997.

Low, Rachael. *The History of the British Film, 1929-1939: Documentary and Educational Films of the 1930s.* 1979. London: Routledge, 1997.

Low, Rachael, and Roger Manvell. *The History of the British Film, 1948-1971.* London: Allen and Unwin, 1973.

MacKenzie, S. P. *British War Films, 1939-1945: The Cinema and the Services.* London: Hambledon and London, 2001.

MacKenzie, S. P. *The Battle of Britain on Screen.* Edinburgh, U.K.: Edinburgh University Press, 2007.

MacKernan, Luke. *Topical Budget: The Great British News Film.* London: British Film Institute/National Film Archive, 1992.

MacKillop, I. D., and Neil Sinyard. *British Cinema of the 1950s: A Celebration.* Manchester, U.K.: Manchester University Press, 2003.

MacKillop, James. *Contemporary Irish Cinema.* Syracuse, N.Y.: Syracuse University Press, 1999.

Macnab, Geoffrey. *Searching for Stars: Stardom and Screen Acting in British Cinema.* London: Cassell, 2000.

Macpherson, Don, and Paul Willemen. *Traditions of Independence: British Cinema in the Thirties.* London: British Film Institute, 1980.

Making History: Art and Documentary in Britain from 1929 to Now. London: Tate Publishing, 2006.

Manvell, Roger. *New Cinema in Britain.* London: Studio Vista, 1969.

Masterworks of the British Cinema. Intro. John Russell Taylor. New York: Harper and Row, 1974.

Mather, Nigel. *Tears of Laughter: Comedy-Drama in 1990s British Cinema*. Manchester, U.K.: Manchester University Press, 2006.

Masterworks of the British Cinema. Ed. Sidney Gilliat et al. London: Faber and Faber, 1990.

Mayer, Geoff. *Guide to British Cinema*. Westport, Conn.: Greenwood Press, 2003.

Mayer, J. P. *British Cinemas and Their Audiences: Sociological Studies*. 1948. New York: Arno Press, 1978.

McArthur, Colin. *Scotland Reels: Scotland in Cinema and Television*. London: British Film Institute, 1982.

McFarlane, Brian. *Twenty British Films: A Guided Tour*. Manchester, U.K.: Manchester University Press, 2015.

McFarlane, Brian. *The Cinema of Britain and Ireland*. London: Wallflower, 2005.

McFarlane, Brian, and Anthony Slide, eds. *The Encyclopedia of British Film*. London: Methuen, 2003.

McFarlane, Brian. *An Autobiography of British Cinema: As Told by the Filmmakers and Actors Who Made It*. London: Methuen, 1997.

McFarlane, Brian. *Sixty Voices: Celebrities Recall the Golden Age of British Cinema*. London: British Film Institute, 1992.

McGillivray, David. *Doing Rude Things: The History of the British Sex Film, 1957-1981*. London: Sun Tavern Fields, 1992.

McIlroy, Brian. *World Cinema 4: Ireland*. London: Flicks, 1988.

McLoone, Martin. *Irish Film: The Emergence of a Contemporary Cinema*. London: British Film Institute, 2000.

Miles, Peter, and Malcolm Smith. *Cinema, Literature and Society: Elite and Mass Culture in Interwar Britain*. London: Croom Helm, 1987.

Miller, Elizabeth Carolyn. *Framed: The New Woman Criminal in British Culture at the Fin de Siècle*. Ann Arbor: University of Michigan Press, 2008.

Missing Believed Lost: The Great British Film Search. Ed. Allen Eyles and David Meeker. London: British Film Institute, 1992.

Monks, Robert. *Cinema Ireland: A Database of Irish Films and Filmmakers, 1896-1996*. Dublin: National Library of Ireland, 1996.

Mulgan, Geoff, and Richard Paterson. *Hollywood or Europe?: The Future of British Film*. London: British Film Institute, 1993.

Mundy, John. *The British Musical Film*. Manchester, U.K.: Manchester University Press, 2006.

Murphy, Robert, ed. *British Cinema: Critical Concepts in Media and Cultural Studies*. New York: Routledge, 2013.

Murphy, Robert, ed. *The British Cinema Book*. 2001. London: Palgrave Macmillan, 2010.

Murphy, Robert, et al. *Directors in British and Irish Cinema.*1996. *A Reference Companion*. London: British Film Institute, 2006.

Murphy, Robert. *British Cinema and the Second World War*. New York: Continuum, 2000.

Murphy, Robert, ed. *British Cinema of the '90s*. London: British Film Institute, 2000.

Murphy, Robert. *Realism and Tinsel: Cinema and Society in Britain, 1939-1949*. 1989. New York: Routledge, 1992.

Murphy, Robert. *Sixties British Cinema*. London: British Film Institute, 1992.

Murray, Jonathan, et al. *Scottish Cinema Now*. Newcastle-upon-Tyne, U.K.: Cambridge Scholars, 2009.

Napper, Lawrence. *British Cinema and Middlebrow Culture in the Interwar Years*. Exeter, U.K.: Exeter University Press, 2009.

Nationalising Femininity: Culture, Sexuality, and British Cinema in the Second World War. Ed. Christine Gledhill and Gillian Swanson. Manchester, U.K.: Manchester University Press, 1996.

Nelmes, Jill. *The Screenwriter in British Cinema*. London: British Film Institute, 2013.

Neville, Carl. *Classless: Recent Essays on British Film*. New Alresford, U.K.: Iff Books, 2010.

New Questions of British Cinema. Ed. Duncan Petrie. London: British Film Institute, 1992.

Newland, Paul. *Don't Look Now: British Cinema in the 1970s.* Bristol, U.K.: Intellect, 2010.

Nowell-Smith, Geoffrey, and Christophe Dupin. *The British Film Institute, the Government, and Film Culture, 1933-2000.* Manchester, U.K.: Manchester University Press, 2012.

Oakley, Charles Allen. *Where We Came In: Seventy Years of the British Film Industry.* London: Allen and Unwin, 1964.

O'Pray, Michael, ed. *The British Avant-Garde Film, 1926-1995: An Anthology of Writings.* Luton, U.K.: University of Luton Press, 1996.

Orr, John. *Romantics and Modernists in British Cinema.* Edinburgh, U.K.: Edinburgh University Press, 2010.

Owen, Alistair. *Story and Character: Interviews with British Screenwriters.* London: Bloomsbury, 2003.

Palmer, Scott. *British Film Actors' Credits, 1895-1987.* Jefferson, N.C.: McFarland, 1988.

Park, James. *British Cinema: The Lights That Failed.* London: B.T. Batsford, 1990.

Park, James. *Learning to Dream: The New British Cinema.* London: Faber and Faber, 1984.

Perkins, Roy, and Martin Stollery. *British Film Editors: The Heart of the Movie.* London: British Film Institute, 2004.

Perry, George C. *The Great British Picture Show.* 1974. Boston: Little, Brown, 1985.

Petley, Julian, and Duncan J. Petrie. *New British Cinema.* Trowbridge, U.K.: Flicks Books, 2002.

Petrie, Duncan J. *Creativity and Constraint in the British Film Industry.* New York: St. Martin's Press, 1991.

Petrie, Duncan J. *New Questions of British Cinema.* London: British Film Institute, 1992.

Petrie, Duncan J. *The British Cinematographer*. London: British Film Institute Publishing, 1996.

Petrie, Duncan J., and Nick Pettigrew. *Inside Stories: Diaries of British Film-Makers at Work*. London: British Film Institute, 1996.

Petrie, Duncan J. *Screening Scotland*. London: British Film Institute, 2000.

Petrie, Duncan J. *Contemporary Scottish Fictions—Film, Television, and the Novel*. Edinburgh, U.K.: Edinburgh University Press, 2004

Pettitt, Lance. *Screening Ireland: Film and Television Representation*. Manchester, U.K.: Manchester University Press, 2000.

Phillips, Gene D. *Major Film Directors of the American and British Cinema*. London: Associated University Presses, 1990.

Pines, Jim. *Representation and Blacks in British Cinema*. London: British Film Institute, 1991.

Pirie, David. *A New Heritage of Horror: The English Gothic Cinema, 1946-1972*. 1973. London: I. B. Tauris, 2009.

Porter, Laraine, and Bryony Dixon. *Picture Perfect: Landscape, Place, and Travel in British Cinema before 1930*. Exeter, U.K.: Exeter University Press, 2007.

Powell, Danny. *Studying British Cinema: The 1960s*. Leighton Buzzard, U.K.: Auteur, 2009.

Powell, Danny. *Studying British Cinema: The 1970s*. Leighton Buzzard, U.K.: Auteur,

Propaganda, Politics, and Film, 1918-45. Ed. Nicholas Pronay and D. W. Spring. London: Macmillan Press, 1982.

Quinlan, David. *British Sound Films: The Studio Years, 1928-1959*. Totowa, N.J.: Barnes and Noble Books, 1985.

Quinn, Paul. *B Films as a Record of British Working-Class Preoccupations in the 1950s: The Historical Importance of a Genre That Has Disappeared*. Lewiston, N.Y.: Edwin Mellen, 2008.

Rattigan, Neil. *This Is England: British Film and the People's War, 1939-1945*. Madison, N.J.: Fairleigh Dickinson University Press, 2001.

Reekie, Duncan. *Not Art: An Action History of British Underground Cinema.* Plymouth, U.K.: University of Plymouth Press, 2003.

Rees, A. L. *A History of Experimental Film and Video: From Canonical Avant-Garde to Contemporary British Practice.* 1999. Basingstoke, U.K.: Palgrave Macmillan, 2011.

Re-viewing British Cinema, 1900-1992: Essays and Interviews. Ed. Wheeler Winston Dixon. Albany: State University of New York Press, 1994.

Richards, Jeffrey. *The Age of the Dream Palace: Cinema and Society in Britain, 1930-1939.* London: Routledge and Kegan Paul, 1984.

Richards, Jeffrey, and Anthony Aldgate. *Best of British: Cinema and Society, 1930-1970.* Oxford, U.K.: Basil Blackwell, 1983.

Richards, Jeffrey, and Anthony Aldgate. *Best of British: Cinema and Society, 1930 to the Present.* London: I. B. Tauris, 1999.

Richards, Jeffrey. *Films and British National Identity: From Dickens to Dad's Army.* Manchester, U.K.: Manchester University Press, 1997.

Richards, Jeffrey. *Cinema and Radio in Britain and America, 1920-60.* Manchester, U.K.: Manchester University Press, 2010.

Rigby, Jonathan. *English Gothic: Classic Horror Cinema, 1987-2015.* Cambridge, U.K.: Signum, 2015.

Robertson, James C. *The Hidden Cinema: British Film Censorship in Action, 1913-1975.* 1989. London: Routledge, 1993.

Robertson, James C. *The British Board of Film Censors: Film Censorship in Britain 1896–1950.* Kent, U.K.: Croom Helm, 1985.

Rockett, Kevin, ed. *The Irish Filmography: Fiction Films, 1896-1996.* Dublin: Red Mountain Press, 1996.

Rockett, Kevin, et al. *Cinema and Ireland.* Syracuse, N.Y.: Syracuse University Press, 1988.

Rogue Reels: Oppositional Film Making in Britain, 1945-90. Ed. Margaret Dickinson. London: British Film Institute, 1999.

Rose, James. *Beyond Hammer: British Horror Cinema since 1970.* Leighton Buzzard, U.K.: Auteur, 2009.

Russell, Ken. *Fire over England: The British Cinema Comes under Friendly Fire.* London: Hutchinson, 1993.

Russell, Patrick. *100 British Documentaries.* London: British Film Institute, 2007.

Ryall, Tom. *British Popular Cinema.* Sheffield, U.K.: Pavic, 1991.
Ryall, Tom. *Britain and the American Cinema.* London: Sage, 2001.

Sadoff, Dianne F. *Victorian Vogue: British Novels on Screen.* Minneapolis: University of Minnesota Press, 2010.

St. Pierre, Paul Matthew. *Music Hall Mimesis in British Film, 1895-1960.* Madison, N.J.: Fairleigh Dickinson University Press, 2009.

Sargeant, Amy. *British Cinema: A Critical History.* London: British Film Institute, 2005.

Scott, Ian. *From Pinewood to Hollywood: British Filmmakers in American Cinema, 1910-1969.* Basingstoke, U.K.: Palgrave Macmillan, 2010.

Sedgwick, John. *Popular Filmgoing in 1930s Britain: A Choice of Pleasures.* Exeter, U.K.: Exeter University Press, 2000.

Semenza, Greg M. Colón, and Bob Hasenfratz. *The History of British Literature on Film, 1895-2015.* New York: Bloomsbury, 2015.

Sexton, Jamie. *Alternative Film Culture in Inter-War Britain.* Exeter, U.K.: Exeter University Press, 2008.

Shafer, Stephen C. *British Popular Films, 1929-1939: The Cinema of Reassurance.* London: Routledge, 1997.

Shail, Robert. *British Film Directors: A Critical Guide.* Carbondale: Southern Illinois University Press, 2007.

Shail, Robert. *Seventies British Cinema.* Basingstoke, U.K.: Palgrave Macmillan, 2008.

Shaw, Tony. *British Cinema and the Cold War: The State, Propaganda, and Consensus.* London: I. B. Tauris, 2001.

Sheridan, Simon. *Keeping the British End Up: Four Decades of Saucy Cinema.* London: Reynolds and Hearn, 2005.

Shiach, Don. *Great British Movies: The Best British Films to Watch, 1929-2005.* New York: Oldcastle, 2015.

Simpson, M. J. *Urban Terrors: New British Horror Cinema, 1997-2008.* Bristol, U.K.: Hemlock Books, 2012.

Sixty Voices: Celebrities Recall the Golden Age of British Cinema. Ed. Brian McFarlane. London: British Film Institute, 1992.

Slide, Anthony. *Fifty Classic British Films 1932–1982: A Pictorial Record.* Mineola, N.Y.: Dover, 1985.

Slide, Anthony. *The Cinema and Ireland.* Jefferson, N.C.: McFarland, 1988.

Slide, Anthony. *"Banned in the USA": British Films in the United States and Their Censorship, 1933– 1966.* London: I. B. Tauris, 1998.

Smith, Gary A. *Uneasy Dreams: The Golden Age of British Horror Films, 1956-1976.* Jefferson, N.C.: McFarland, 2006.

Smith, Justin. *Withnail and Us: Cult Films and Film Cults in British Cinema.* London: I. B. Tauris, 2010.

Spicer, Andrew. *Typical Men: The Representation of Masculinity in Popular British Cinema.* London: I. B. Tauris Publishers, 2001.

Stead, Peter. *Film and the Working Class: The Feature Film in British and American Society.* 1990. London: Routledge, 2013.

Stokes, Jane C. *On Screen Rivals: Cinema and Television in the United States and Britain.* New York: St. Martin's Press, 2000.

Street, Sarah. *British Cinema in Documents.* London: Routledge, 2000.

Street, Sarah. *Transatlantic Crossings: British Feature Films in the United States.* New York: Continuum, 2002.

Street, Sarah. *British National Cinema.* 1997. London: Routledge, 2008.

Street, Sarah. *Colour Films in Britain: The Negotiation of Innovation, 1900-1955.* London: British Film Institute, 2012.

Street, Sarah, et al. *British Colour Cinema Companion.* London: British Film Institute, 2013.

Sutton, David. *A Chorus of Raspberries: British Film Comedy, 1929-1939.* Exeter, U.K.: Exeter University Press, 2000.

Swann, Paul. *The British Documentary Film Movement, 1926-1946.* Cambridge, U.K.: Cambridge University Press, 2008.

Sweet, Matthew. *Shepperton Babylon: The Lost Worlds of British Cinema.* London: Faber and Faber, 2005.

Swynnoe, Jan G. *The Best Years of British Film Music, 1936-1958.* Rochester, N.Y.: Boydell Press, 2002.

Taylor, B. F. *The British New Wave: A Certain Tendency?* Manchester, U.K.: Manchester University Press, 2006.

Taylor, John Russell, and John Kobal. *Portraits of the British Cinema: Sixty Glorious Years, 1925-1985.* London: Aurum, 1985.

Taylor, Philip M., and Andrew Kelly. *Britain and the Cinema in the First World War.* Abingdon, U.K.: Carfax, 1993.

Twenty Years of British Film, 1925-1945. Michael Balcon et al. London: Falcon Press, 1947.

The Ultimate Film: The UK's 100 Most Popular Films. London: British Film Institute, 2005.

The Unknown 1930s: An Alternative History of the British Cinema, 1929-39. Ed. Jeffrey Richards. London: I. B. Tauris, 1998.

Upton, Julian. *Offbeat: British Cinema's Curiosities, Obscurities, and Forgotten Gems.* London: Headpress, 2013.

Vermilye, Jerry. *The Great British Films.* Secaucus, N.J.: Citadel Press, 1978.

Walker, Alexander. *Hollywood, England.* London: Harrap, 1986.

Walker, Alexander. *National Heroes: British Cinema in the Seventies and Eighties.* London: Harrap, 1985.

Walker, John. *The Once and Future Film: British Cinema in the Seventies and Eighties.* London: Methuen, 1985.

Warren, Patricia. *British Film Studios: An Illustrated History.* London: B. T. Batsford, 1995.

Warren, Patricia. *British Cinema in Pictures: The British Film Collection*. London: B. T. Batsford, 1993.

Warren, Patricia. *The British Film Collection, 1896-1984: A History of the British Cinema in Pictures*. London: Elm Tree Books, 1984.

Wells, Paul. *British Animation: A Critical Survey*. London: British Film Institute, 2002.

Williams, Tony. *Structures of Desire: British Cinema, 1939-1955*. Albany: State University of New York Press, 2000.

Wollaeger, Mark A. *Modernism, Media, and Propaganda: British Narrative from 1900 to 1945*. Princeton, N.J.: Princeton University Press, 2006.

Wood, Jason, and Ian Haydn Smith. *New British Cinema: The Resurgence of British Film-making*. London: Faber and Faber, 2015.

Wood, Linda. *British Films, 1927-1939*. London: British Film Institute, 1986.

Young and Innocent?: The Cinema in Britain, 1896-1930. Ed. Andrew Higson. Exeter, U.K.: University of Exeter Press, 2002.

Index

A.B.C.: see Warner Brothers
Abigail's Party, 208
À bout de souffle: see *Breathless*
Absurdism, 28
Academy Awards, 20, 45, 69, 73, 75, 93, 138, 229, 231, 314, 320-322, 339
Accident, xiii, 304
Aciman, André, 324
Ackroyd, Barry, 129
Acting, 123-127, 134, 139, 209, 214-222, 228, 234, 240-241, 255, 286-294, 296-297
ACTT (Association of Cinematograph, Television, and Allied Technicians), 37
Adorée, Renée, 34
The Adventures of Robin Hood, 34
Afghanistan War, 123
Against the Wind, 41-42
The Age of Innocence, 261
The Agony and the Ecstasy, 20
Agutter, Jenny, 113
Airport, 335
Alfie, xii
All or Nothing, 224-225, 227, 232-233, 244
All That Heaven Allows, 263
Allen, Jim, 135
Allen, Woody, 156
Altered States, 82
Altman, Robert, 237
Amis, Kingsley, 92
Anarcho-syndicalism, 115
Anderson, Gillian, 261
Anderson, Lindsay, x-xiii, xv, 45-58, 61, 70, 77, 157, 166, 211, 346
Anderson, Paul Thomas, 273
Angela's Ashes, 143
Angels and Insects, xiv
Anglo-Irish War, 117
Another Country, xiv

Another Year, 209
Anouilh, Jean, 99
Antonioni, Michelangelo, xii, 83
Apollonianism, 204
Armageddon, 226
Ashcroft, Peggy, 28
Asher, Irving, 4
Asher, Jane, 330
Ashes to Ashes, 68
Asquith, Anthony, x, 263
The Assassination of Trotsky, 304, 310
As You Like It, 27, 302
Atherton, William, 74
Atkinson, George, 3
Attenborough, Richard, 34
Audley, Maxine, 10, 15
Austen, Jane, 63
Auteurism, 55-58, 80, 137
Avant-gardism, 106
"The Avengers," 36
Aykroyd, Dan, 261

Bachelard, Gaston, 112
The Back Crack Boy, 139
Bacon, Francis, 15, 28
Badlands, 154
Bad Timing, 101-102, 107, 257
Badt, Karen, 192-206
BAFTA (British Academy of Film and Television Arts) Awards, 70, 116-117, 266
Bagenal, Philip, 49
Bakker, Jim, 53
Bakker, Tammy Faye, 53
Balcon, Michael, ix-x, 40, 44
Ballon rouge, Le, 210
Barber, Samuel, 264
Baronova, Irina, 43
Barry, Philip, 49
"Barrytown Trilogy," 139
Bartok, Bela, 83

Barton, John, 289
Bates, Alan, xiii, 69, 86
The Battle of Algiers, 305
BBC: see British Broadcasting Corporation
Bearing, Robert, 21
The Beatles, 326-330, 333, 338, 344
Beckett, Samuel, 99
The Bed-Sitting Room, xiii, 327
Beecham, Thomas, 12
The Believers, 75
Bell, Alexander Graham, 221
Bellini, Gentile, 206
Bellini, Giovanni, 206
The Belly of an Architect, 194
Ben Hur, 3
Bennett, Alan, 55-56, 78, 140-141, 144
Benson, Frank, 291
Bergman, Ingmar, 257
Berlin Film Festival, 70
Bevan, Tim, 143
BFI: see British Film Institute
Bicycle Thieves, 128, 257
The Big Flame, 115, 135
The Big Parade, 34
Billion Dollar Brain, 82, 84
Billy Elliot, 143
Billy Liar, xii, 69, 71-72, 79, 274
Black, Jack, 153
Black, Karen, 74
The Black Mask, 2
Black Narcissus, 2, 10
Blair, Tony, 122
Bleak Moments, 181, 208, 212, 221, 229
Blethyn, Brenda, 209
Blewitt, Bill, 39
Blithe Spirit, x
Blow-Up, xii, 83
The Blue Lamp, 44
Blue Velvet, 205
Blunt, Emily, 275
Bogarde, Dirk, 36, 313
Bogart, Humphrey, 106
Bogdanovich, Peter, 57-58
Bond, Edward, 102

Bonet, Lisa, 152
Book of the Dead (Egyptian), 259
Boom!, 310
Boorman, John, 27
Borges, Jorge Luis, 205
The Bostonians, 314-315
Boulting, John, 92
Boulting, Roy, 92
Bowie, David, 101, 103, 111
The Boy Friend, 82
The Boy with Green Hair, 304, 308-309
Boyle, Danny, xiv
Bradley, David, 124, 126
Braine, John, xi, 92
Branagh, Kenneth, xv, 185, 282-302, 349
Braque, Georges, 197, 324
Brazzi, Rosanno, 28
Bread and Roses, 116, 132
Breathless, 96, 210-211
Brecht, Bertolt, 97, 307-308, 312, 334
Bremner, Ewen, 218
Bresson, Robert, 336
Breton, André, 209-210
The Bridge on the River Kwai, 27-28, 33
Bridget Jones's Diary, 230
Brief Encounter, x, 28, 254
Briers, Richard, 292
Britannia Hospital, 45-46, 50-52, 167
British Broadcasting Corporation (BBC), 7, 16, 69, 76, 80, 82-83, 88, 91, 115, 128, 130, 137, 142, 155, 158, 211, 240, 266
British Council, 274
British Film Institute (BFI), 7, 36, 80, 249-250, 326
British Lion Films, 93-94
British Museum, 112
Broadway, 308, 327
Brown, Pamela, 6-7, 10, 15
The Browning Version, x, 263
Bruckner, Anton, 252, 255, 258
Bryanston: see British Lion Films
Buñuel, Luis, 67, 81, 241, 336
Burden, Hugh, 7

Burn!, 305
A Burnt-Out Case, 90
Burrows, Anthony, 139
Burton, Richard, 93-94, 304, 310
Buscemi, Steve, 228, 230
Bush, George W., 122
Butch and Sundance: The Early Days, 342
Byron, Kathleen, 10

Cage, John, 200
Caine, Michael, xiii, 84, 304
Call Me by Your Name, 324
Calvino, Italo, 205
Cammel, Donald, 104, 111, 231
Cannes Film Festival, xi, 116-117, 319, 332-333
A Canterbury Tale, 5, 8
Capitalism, 120, 147-148
Capriccio, 87
Caravaggio, 55
Cardullo, R. J., 115-135, 208-247, 249-280
Carla's Song, 116-117, 122
Carlyle, Robert, 117
Carter, Helena Bonham, 319, 321
Cartlidge, Bill, xiv
Carve Her Name with Pride, 14
Castaway, 108-109, 112
The Catcher in the Rye, 273
Catholicism, 90, 139, 201, 231, 258-259, 265, 312
Cathy Come Home, 115-117, 126
Cavalcanti, Alberto, ix, 37, 39
Chamberlain, Neville, 5
Chamberlain, Richard, 89
Chance Meeting, 304
The Changing Room, 45
Channel 4, 46, 235
Chaplin, Charles, 212
The Charge of the Light Brigade, 93, 274
Chariots of Fire, xiii, 47
Checker, Chubby, 339
Chekhov, Anton, 51, 92, 253, 260

Chicago International Film Festival, 311
"Children": see *The Terence Davies Trilogy*
Chimes at Midnight, 332
Chinatown, 268
Chitty, Alison, 232
Christianity, 90, 102, 240, 276, 292, 296
Christie, Agatha, 8
Christie, Julie, xiii, 69, 71, 101, 113
Chungking Express, 150
Churchill, Winston, 4-5, 8
CIA (Central Intelligence Agency), 311
Cineaste, 137, 139, 282, 304
Cinema Journal, 208
Cinematograph Film Act, ix
Cinéma vérité, 267
Citizen Kane, 34, 83, 258, 327
The City of Your Final Destination, 314, 322
Clarke, T. E. B., 44
Clayton, Jack, xi, xv, 92, 211
Cleese, John, 36
Clements, John, 43
Close Encounters of the Third Kind, 34
Close, Glenn, 138
Coen, Ethan, 81
Coen, Joel, 81
Cold War, 201
Cole, Sidney, 36-44
Collins, Phil, 331
Colonialism, 206, 256
Columbia Pictures, 48, 81
Comedy, x, 3, 16, 36, 40, 42, 82-83, 133-134, 209, 218, 223, 227-228, 254, 257, 272, 276, 280, 282, 327, 344
Communism, 46, 130, 271-272, 304, 308
Concrete Jungle, 304
Conrad, Joseph, x
Conservative Party, 130
Considine, Paddy, 276
Contraband, 5

The Contractor, 45
The Cook, The Thief, His Wife, and Her Lover, 179, 192-194, 201, 203
Cooper, Henry, 341-342
Coppola, Francis Ford, 2-3, 5, 17
Corman, Roger, 101
Cornelius, Henry, x, 40
Costa-Gavras (Konstantinos Gavras), 305
Cotten, Joseph, 11, 21-24
Courtenay, Tom, xiii, 69
Coventry Drama School, 249
Coward, Noël, x, 22, 27, 254
Crawford, Joan, 263
Crichton, Charles, x, xv, 36-44, 164, 346
Crimes of Passion, 82
Cronenberg, David, 193, 205
Crowdus, Gary, 282-302
Crutwell, Hugh, 291-293
Cuba, 327
Cubism, 197-198
Cukor, George, 74
Culver Studios, 3
Curtis, Jamie Lee, 36
Cusack, John, 139, 153
Czech Renaissance, 131, 266, 273

Dafoe, Willem, 228
Dahl, Roald, 101
Dalrymple, Ian, 4
The Damned, 309
Dance Hall, 44
Dance of the Seven Veils, 83, 87-88
Dangerous Liaisons, 55, 138, 156, 158
Daniels, Stan, 53
Dardenne, Jean-Pierre, 128
Dardenne, Luc, 128
Darling, 69, 71, 79
Dartmouth College, 307
Darwin, Charles, 204
Darwinism, 196, 202, 204
Davies, Terence, xiv-xv, 182, 249-265, 349
Davis, Bette, 51, 263

Davis, Judy, 28-30
The Dawn Patrol, 34
Day-Lewis, Daniel, 143-144, 157
The Day of the Locust, 69, 72-74
Days of Heaven, 154
Days of Hope, 115-116
Dead Give Away, 70
Dead of Night, 39-40, 43
"Death and Transfiguration": see *The Terence Davies Trilogy*
Debussy, Claude, 83
Decline and Fall, 90
The Deep Blue Sea, 60, 249, 262-264
Delaney, Shelagh, xi, 96
A Delicate Balance, 93
Delius, Frederick, 83-84
Delon, Alain, 304
Deneuve, Catherine, 144
Denham Studios, 17, 37
De Niro, Robert, 6, 125
de Paul, Judith, 34
Descartes, René, 199
De Sica, Vittorio, 128, 257
The Devils, 82, 89-90
The Devils of Loudon, 82, 89
Devine, George, 92
A Diary for Timothy, 54
Dickens, Charles, x, 20, 27, 129, 212
Dickinson, Emily, 250, 265
Dickinson, Thorold, x
"The Dick Lester Show," 326, 338
Dietrich, Marlene, 144
DiMaggio, Joe, 106
Dines, Gordon, 38
Directing, 21, 104, 123-128, 135, 145, 209, 214-215, 221-222, 241, 268-271, 310, 343
Dirty Pretty Things, 139-140, 146-151, 177, 280
Disney, Walt, 16
Distant Voices, Still Lives, xiv, 182, 249, 254, 259
Divorce, Le, 319
Doctor Zhivago, 27, 104

Documentary, ix-x, 39, 45, 54, 60-61, 69-70, 76, 82-83, 115, 123, 226, 240, 249, 254, 260-262, 267-268, 273-274, 279, 314, 331
Donat, Robert, 11
Dondua, Alexandrov, 335
Don Giovanni, 304, 310
Donohue, Amanda, 110
Don Quixote, 195
Don't Look Now, 101, 103, 106, 109-110
Door, Bonnie, 52-53
Doyle, Patrick, 298
Doyle, Roddy, 139
"Dragnet," 338
The Draughtsman's Contract, 192, 203
Drowning by Numbers, 204
Duchamp, Marcel, 200, 206
Duel in the Sun, 11
du Maurier, Daphne, 101
Duncan, Isadora, 60-61, 83
Durran, Jacqueline, 232

Ealing Studios, x, 36-44, 257
The Earthsea Trilogy, 6, 17
Eco, Umberto, 198
The Edge of the World, 3, 15-16
Edinburgh Festival, 280, 339
Einstein, Albert, 106
Eisenstein in Guanajuato, 194
Eisenstein, Sergei, 194
Ejiofor, Chiwetel, 149
Elephant Boy, 36
Elgar, Edward, 83
Eliot, George (a.k.a. Mary Ann Evans), 63
Eliot, T. S., 110, 250
Elizabethanism, 99, 292
Elstree Studios, 94
Emma, xiv
Encountering Directors, 19
Enfield, Shirley, 99
Enigma, 141
The Entertainer, xii, 92-94, 96-99, 172
Epstein, Brian, 329

Eugene Onegin, 89
Eureka, 107, 109
European Film Awards, 116
The Europeans, 314, 317
Eva, 304
Evans, Max, 153-154
Expressionism, 17

Faber & Faber, 101
The Face of Battle, 294
Fahrenheit 451, xii, 101
Fairbanks, Douglas, 34, 341
Falklands War, 48, 282
The Fallen Idol, x, 19, 21, 50
The Fall of the Louse of Usher, 82
The Falls, 200-201, 203
Family Life, xiv, 115-116, 133
Far From the Madding Crowd, 69, 71-72, 75, 170
The Far Pavilions, 34
Farce, 13, 27, 53, 334
Farrar, David, 10, 17
Fascism, 139, 201, 226
Father Brown, x
Faulkner, William, 93
FBI (Federal Bureau of Investigation), 312
Federal Theatre Project, 307
Feher, Friedrich, 13
Fellini, Federico, 81
Feminism, 151
Ferrer, Mel, 13
Fielding, Henry, 93
Fiennes, Ralph, 292
Film Comment, 27, 82
Film Criticism, 45, 192
FILMEX (Los Angeles International Film Exposition), 33
Film4: see Channel 4
Film noir, 19, 106, 137
Film Quarterly, 92
Films and Filming, 2
Finch, Peter, 103
Finney, Albert, xiii, 55, 60, 99, 138

FIPRESCI (International Federation of Film Critics), 116
Fires Were Started, ix, 54
A Fish Called Wanda, 36, 50
Florence Foster Jenkins, 139
Flynn, Errol, 34, 341
Ford, Dan, 57
Ford, John, 52, 54, 56-58, 154
Forman, Milos, 273
Forrest, Frederic, 3
Forster, E. M., 27-29, 31-32, 314, 316, 319
Forsyth, Bill, xiv
For Those in Peril, 36, 38-39
49th Parallel, 2, 8
Four Days in July, 208, 240
The Four Horsemen of the Apocalypse, 33
The 400 Blows, 211, 257
The Four Musketeers, 327
Four Quartets, 110, 250, 263
Fowles, John, 63-65
Fox, James, xiii, 102
Frampton, Hollis, 193, 204-205
Francis the Talking Mule, 257
Frears, Stephen, xiv-xv, 47, 54-56, 81, 137-159, 176, 213, 230, 280, 348
Free Cinema Movement, x-xii, 45, 55, 60, 62, 70
French Dressing, 82-83
The French Lieutenant's Woman, 60, 62-67, 168
French Revolution, 201
Freud, Sigmund, 65, 203-204
Freudianism, 154, 203
Friedman, Lester, 45-58
Fukuyama, Francis, 122
Fuller, Buckminster, 200
A Funny Thing Happened on the Way to the Forum, 327, 334
Furie, Sidney J., xii

Gainsborough Pictures, 21
Galileo, 307
Gallagher, Tag, 57
The Gambler, 60, 67

Gambon, Michael, 203, 344
Gandhi, xiv, 34
Garfunkel, Art, 101-102
Garnett, Tony, 211
Garr, Teri, 3
Gatling, Richard, 321
Gaumont Pictures, 27
Genevieve, x
Get Back, 327
Gibbon, Lewis Grassic, 250
Gilbert, John, 34
Gilbert, W. S., 208
Gilliat, Sidney, 19
Girard, René, 193
Gish, Lillian, 51
Glory! Glory!, 51-53
The Go-Between, xiii, 187, 304
Godard, Jean-Luc, 96, 204-205, 210-211, 317
Godden, Rumer, 10
The Golden Bowl, 314
Gone to Earth, 11
"The Goon Show," 326, 337-338
G. P. Putnam's Sons, 19
Grade, Lew, 307
Granger, Stewart, 341
Grant, Hugh, 141
Grease, 158
Great Depression, 139
Great Expectations, x, 28, 33
Greek Tragedy, 240
Green, Walon, 153
Greenaway, Peter, xv, 178, 192-206, 249, 348
Greene, Graham, x, 19, 21-22, 90
Grierson, John, ix, 267
The Grifters, 139, 153, 155-156
Grigg, James, 8
The Guardian, 121, 326
Guernica, 108
Guin, Ursula Le, 6
Guinness, Alec, x, 28, 33, 250
Guinness Book of World Records, 314
Gumshoe, 55, 138
Guthrie, Woody, 121

Hall, Peter, 74
Halliwell, Kenneth, 138
Hamer, Robert, x, 27
Hamlet, x, xiv, 32, 186, 282, 284-287, 289, 296-298
Hammett, 2-3
Hammett, Dashiell, 2-3
A Handful of Dust, xiv, 90
Hanks, Tom, 78
Happy-Go-Lucky, 208, 223-224
Happy Together, 150
A Hard Day's Night, xiii, 191, 326-334, 336-337, 339, 341, 344
Hardy, Thomas, 22, 62-63, 72, 80
Harrison, George, 330
Harry Potter, 195
Hauer, Rutger, 109
Hayworth, Rita, 264
HBO: see Home Box Office
Heat and Dust, xiv, 314, 317
Heflin, Van, 311
The Heiress, 261
Help!, 327, 330, 332-333, 338
Helpmann, Robert, 12
Hemming, Lindy, 232
Henry V, x, 185, 282, 292-296, 299
Hepburn, Audrey, 340
Hepburn, Katharine, 28
Hero, 138, 156
Hidden Agenda, 115-116
Hiddleston, Tom, 324
High Fidelity, 139, 151-156
High Hopes, xiv, 212, 227, 229, 237, 243
High Noon, 80
Hiller, Wendy, 6
The Hi-Lo Country, 138, 153-156
Hines, Barry, 133, 135
The Hit, 55, 137-138
Hitchcock, Alfred, 10, 15, 71, 75, 137, 157, 226, 230
Hitchens, Christopher, 141
Hitler, Adolf, 88
Hobson, Valerie, 4-5, 43
Hoffman, Dustin, 75, 79, 138, 156-157
Holiday, 49

Hollywood, ix, 2-3, 5, 20, 28, 49, 72, 93-94, 131-133, 138-139, 155-156, 193, 209-210, 213, 221, 228-231, 235-236, 244, 257, 260-261, 302, 304-305, 307-308, 310-311, 335, 341
Holm, Ian, 294
Holocaust: see World War II
Holt, Tim, 106
Home, 45
Home Box Office (HBO), 51-53
Hopkins, Anthony, 321-323
Hordern, Michael, 334
Hornbeck, William, 37
Hornby, Lesley (a.k.a. Twiggy), 91
Horne, Lena, 340
Horrocks, Jane, 216
The Householder, 314
The House of Mirth, 249, 260-261
House Un-American Activities Committee (HUAC), 304, 310, 312
Howard, Leslie, 8
Howard, Trevor, 23
Howards End, xiv, 189, 314-324
Howerd, Frankie, 330
How I Won the War, xiii, 327, 330, 334
Hue and Cry, x, 40-42, 165
Hughes, Howard, 308
Humanism, 51, 131, 235
Hunted, 41
Huppert, Isabelle, 304
Huston, John, xii, 106
Hutton, Betty, 84
Huxley, Aldous, 82, 89

I Am a Camera, 14
Ice Age, 112
Ida, 266, 277
I, Daniel Blake, 117
An Ideal Husband, xiv
If..., 45, 48-49, 166, 211
I Know Where I'm Going, 6
I Married a Communist, 308
The Importance of Being Earnest, x
Impressionism, 128, 197, 255

In Celebration, 45
Independent Television Studios, 326
Indiana Jones, 34
Ingram, Rex, 3, 13
Insignificance, 106
Intervals, 192, 194
In the Mood for Love, 150
In This World, 280
In Which We Serve, x, 27
IRA: see Irish Republican Army
Iraq War, 123
Irish Republican Army (IRA), 19
Irving, Henry, 291
Isadora, 60-61, 83-84
Isadora, the Biggest Dancer in the World, 83-84
Ishiguro, Kazuo, 314
Istanbul Film Festival, 139
It Happened One Night, 3
It's a Free World, 122
It's Trad, Dad!, 326-327, 339-340
Ivory, James, xv, 188, 314-324, 349-350

Jackson, Glenda, xiii, 69, 72, 85, 89-90, 304
Jackson, Pat, ix
Jackson, Russell, 286, 291, 293, 296
Jacobi, Derek, 289, 294
Jagger, Mick, 101
James, Henry, 314
Jane Eyre, xiv, 7
Janowitz, Tama, 319
Jarman, Derek, 54-55, 107
Jarmusch, Jim, 273
Jason-Leigh, Jennifer, 228
Jefferson in Paris, 314, 319, 323-324
Jefferson, Thomas, 324
Jellicoe, Ann, 332
Jennings, Humphrey, ix, 54, 262
Jesse, Bill, 133, 135
The Jewel in the Crown, 34
Jhabvala, Ruth Prawer, 314-316, 320
Joanna, xii
Johnson, Celia, 28
Jones, Jennifer, 11

Jordan, Neil, xiv
Joseph Andrews, 93
Joyce, James, 195, 199
Judaism, 79, 105, 139-142, 201, 203, 209, 240, 272, 309
Juggernaut, 335
Jules et Jim, 211
Julia, 80
Jungianism, 204

Karas, Anton, 24-25
Kar-wai, Wong, 150, 270
Kawalerowicz, Jerzy, 89-90
Keaton, Buster, 212, 344
Keegan, John, 294, 296
Kennedy, Harlan, 27-34
Kennedy, Madge, 74
Kerr, Deborah, 10
Kes, xiv, 115, 124, 126, 133, 135, 175
Keyes, Evelyn, 311
Kind Hearts and Coronets, x, 259-260
A Kind of Loving, xii, 69-72, 79, 169
King Kong, 60
King Lear, 292
Kinnear, Roy, 327
Klee, Paul, 197
Kline, Kevin, 36
The Knack, xiii, 191, 327, 332, 340
Kneale, Nigel, 96
Knight, Esmond, 6, 11
Knight, Steven, 146
Korda, Alexander, ix, 3-4, 11-12, 19, 22, 36
Korda, Zoltan, 4
Krasker, Robert, 19
Kretzmer, Herbert, 339
Krish, John, 90
Kubrick, Stanley, xii, 34, 81, 88
Kureishi, Hanif, 55, 138, 141, 144-145, 151
Kurosawa, Akira, 81, 257

Labour Party, 130-131, 210
Ladybird, Ladybird, 115-116, 124, 135
The Ladykillers, x

Lahr, John, 138
Lancaster, Burt, 264
Land and Freedom, 116-117, 122
Lange, Monique, 306
Lassally, Walter, 95
The Last of England, 55
The Last Picture Show, 260
Last Resort, 184, 266, 273, 275, 277-280
Last Year at Marienbad, 105
Laughton, Charles, 308, 312
Launder, Frank, 19
Laurel and Hardy, 212
The Lavender Hill Mob, x, 36, 41, 44, 165
The Lawless, 309
Lawrence, D. H., 31, 80, 82, 84-86
Lawrence of Arabia, 27, 33, 101, 104
Lawrence, T. E., 28
"Lazy Sunday Afternoon," 272
Lean, David, x, xv, 17, 19-20, 27-34, 54, 101, 104, 163, 254-255, 346
The Leather Boys, xii
Leftism, 115-116, 132, 237
Leigh, Mike, xiv-xv, 128, 137, 142, 144, 180, 208-247, 267, 348-349
Leigh, Vivian, 263
Lenczewski, Ryszard, 277
Leninism, 115
Lennon, John, 328, 330-331, 334, 338
Lester, Dominic, 333
Lester, Richard, xiii, xv, 77, 190, 326-344, 350
Letter From an Unknown Woman, 261, 263
Lewis, Damian, 324
Lewis, Mark, 13, 17
Liam, 139-143, 145
Life, 102
The Life and Death of Colonel Blimp, 2, 5, 7, 161
A Life in Movies, 2
Life Is Sweet, 208, 216, 223, 227, 232, 243
Life of Galileo, 307, 312

Linden, Jennie, 86
Linney, Laura, 261
The Lion Has Wings, 4
Listen to Britain, ix, 54, 262
Lisztomania, 82
Literature/Film Quarterly, 60, 208
Little Dorrit, xiv
Littlewood, Joan, 129
Litvak, Anatole, 263
Livesey, Roger, 7
Living Newspaper, 307
Lloyd, Phyllida, 230
Loach, Ken, xiv-xv, 115-135, 137, 142-143, 155, 175, 210-212, 237, 267, 275, 347- 348
Lockhart, Ted, 38
London Can Take It, ix
London Films, 36
The Loneliness of the Long Distance Runner, xii, 93
The Lone Ranger, 321
The Long Day Closes, xiv, 183, 249, 259
Look Back in Anger, xi, 45, 70, 92-94, 96-98
Looking for Eric, 117, 127, 133
Lopez, Sergi, 148-149
Lord of the Rings, 195
Losey, Joseph, xii, xv, 186, 304-313, 349
The Loved One, 93
Love's Labour's Lost, 301-302
Loves of a Blonde, 273
Lucas, George, 329
Lucia, Cynthia, 137-159
Lucky Jim, 92
Luhrmann, Baz, 301
Lyme Regis Society, 63
Lynch, David, 205

Macbeth, 301-302
Macdonald, Richard, 71-72
Mackendrick, Alexander, x
MacLaine, Shirley, 69
Madame Sousatzka, 76
The Madness of King George, xiv

Madonna (Louise Ciccone), 69
"Madonna and Child": see *The Terence Davies Trilogy*
Magnificent Obsession, 263
Mahler, Gustav, 254-255, 258
MAI (Multilateral Agreement on Investment), 120
Major, John, 116
Malick, Terrence, 154, 270
Malkovich, John, 138, 158
Mamoulian, Rouben, 11
Manichaeism, 267
The Man in the White Suit, x
Mann, Christopher, 3
Mansfield Park, xiv
The Man Who Fell to Earth, 101, 103, 105-107, 111
The Man Who Knew Too Much, 157
Marathon Man, 69, 74-75, 79
The March on Russia, 45, 51
Mare Nostrum, 13
Marks, Leo, 14
Martin, Valerie, 157
Marx Brothers, 212
Marx, Groucho, 344
Marxism, 115, 118, 237
Mary Reilly, 138, 156-157
"The Mary Tyler Moore Show," 53
The Masque of the Red Death, 101
Massey, Anna, 15
Massine, Léonide, 12
Matewan, 127
Matisse, Henri, 256, 324
The Matrix, 226
A Matter of Life and Death, 2, 5, 9
Maurice, 314-315, 321, 322
Mayer, Louis B., 230
McCartney, Paul, 327, 330
McCarthyism, 73
McDowell, Malcolm, 48-49
McGovern, Jimmy, 139, 142-143, 145
McKechnie, James, 7
McKellen, Ian, 291
McKeown, Joseph, 139
Meantime, 238

Melodrama, 11, 119
Mendes, Sam, 230
Menges, Chris, 150
Mercer, David, 60, 305-306
Merchant, Ismail, 314-316
Merchant Ivory Productions, 314
Meredith, Burgess, 74
Metamorphosen, 87
The Method: see "Acting"
Metropolitan Opera (New York), 13
MGM (Metro-Goldwyn-Mayer Studios), 3, 304
Mickiewicz, Adam, 271
Midnight Cowboy, 69, 71-73, 75, 77-79
A Midsummer Night's Dream, xiv
A Midwinter's Tale, 282
Miller, Arthur, 99
Milligan, Spike, 326, 337, 344
Milyukova, Antonina, 89
Minghella, Anthony, 67
Ministry of Information, 9
The Minnesota Review, 115
Miramax, 319
Misérables, Les, 339
Modernism, 27
Modesty Blaise, 304
Modigliani, Amedeo, 255
Mohyeddin, Zia, 33
Momma Don't Allow, xi, 92
Monger, Chris, xiv
Monitor, 82-83
Monroe, Marilyn, 91, 106
Moore, Henry, 65
Moore, Michael, 193
More, Kenneth, 263
Moreau, Jeanne, 304
Morgan: A Suitable Case for Treatment, xii, 60-61
Mother Joan of the Angels, 89-90
Mountbatten: The Last Viceroy, 34
The Mouse on the Moon, 326, 340
The Mouse That Roared, 340
Mozart, Wolfgang Amadeus, 304
Mr. and Mrs. Bridge, 319

Mr. Klein, 304-306, 309
Mr. Turner, 209
Mrs. Dalloway, xiv
MTV (Music Television), 331
Much Ado about Nothing, xiv, 282, 287
Mullan, Peter, 117
Mullins, Barbara, 340
Muni, Paul, 312
Murdoch, Rupert, 142
The Music Lovers, 82, 85, 88-89, 171
My Beautiful Laundrette, xiv, 47, 55, 138, 140-144, 151, 155, 157, 177
My Darling Clementine, 57
My Name Is Joe, 116-118, 134
My Summer of Love, 184, 266-267, 269-270, 273-280

Naked, xiv, 208, 216-218, 222, 227, 232, 241, 243
National Film Finance Corporation, 94
National School of Film and Television, 249
National Theatre, 209
Naturalism, 69, 107, 209
The Navigators, xiv
Nazism, 5, 87-88
Neame, Ronald, 17
Ned Kelly, 93
The Neon Bible, 249, 261
Neorealism (Italian), x, xii, 128, 131, 274
New Cinema (British), xii, xiv
Newman & Sinclair (film cameras), 38
Newman, Paul, 319
New Wave (British), 60, 92, 211-212
New Wave (Czech): see Czech Renaissance
New Wave (French), xi-xiii, 95, 99, 210
New York Film Festival, 256, 311
New York Times, 314
The Next Best Thing, 69
Next of Kin, x
Nicaraguan Revolution, 117
Nichols, Dudley, 58

Nicholson, Jack, 333
Nietzsche, Friedrich, 88
Nightwatching, 194
Nijinsky, Vaslav, 84
Nine Men, 42-43
Nixon, Richard, 313
Norris, Patricia, 154
Nugent, Frank, 58
Nureyev, Rudolf, 84
Nuts in May, 208

O'Connor, Donald, 257
Odd Man Out, 19, 25, 50
O Dreamland, xi
Oedipus the King, 111, 202
Of Time and the City, 249, 260-261
Oh... Rosalinda!!, 12-13
Oklahoma!, 80
"The Old Crowd," 56
Oldman, Gary, 111-112
Oliver!, 20, 50
Oliver Twist, x, 20, 33, 293
Olivier, Laurence, x, 8, 28, 32, 94, 99, 282
O Lucky Man!, 45
Olvidados, Los, 241
One from the Heart, 3
One of Our Aircraft Is Missing, 7, 15, 27
On Golden Pond, 51
Open City, 128
Ophüls, Max, 263
Orton, Joe, 138
Osborne, John, xi, 45, 70, 92-94, 96-97
Oscars: see Academy Awards
Othello, 97, 299-300
O'Toole, Peter, 28, 33
Outcast of the Islands, x, 19
Owen, Alun, 326, 328, 338
Oxford University, 45, 129
Ozu, Yasujiro, 241, 257

Pacific Heights, 75
Painted Boats, 39
Palmer, Ernest, 38
Pappy: The Life of John Ford, 57

Paramount Pictures, 73
Paris Theater (New York), 318
Parker, Alan, 47-48
Parker, Oliver, 299-301
A Passage to India, xiv, 27-34, 163-164
Passport to Pimlico, x
Pather Panchali, 235
Pathos, xiv, 83, 223, 310
Patton, George, 9
Pawlikowski, Pawel, xv, 183, 266-280, 349
PBS (Public Broadcasting Service, U.S.), 142
Peeping Tom, 2, 9, 13-15, 17, 160
Penguin Books, vii
Penn, Arthur, 77
Performance, 101-102, 104, 111, 174
The Perils of Pauline, 83
Petulia, 327, 343
Pfeiffer, Michelle, 138
Philadelphia, 78
Phillips, Gene D., 82-91
Philomena, 139
Picasso, Pablo, 108, 197, 255, 324
Pickles, Vivian, 83
The Pillow Book, 192, 197
Pinewood Studios, 17, 340
Pinter, Harold, 60, 64, 66, 68, 304-306
"Play for Today," 226
Poitier, Sidney, 149
Polanski, Roman, xii, 268
Pollock, Griselda, 113
Poor Cow, 116
Pop Goes the Easel, 83
Pope, Dick, 223, 232
Populism, 222
Portman, Eric, 8-9
The Portrait of a Lady, xiv
Postmodernism, 193-194, 196
Poststructuralism, 193
Potter, Sally, 67, 249
Powell, Columba, 14
Powell, Michael, xv, 2-17, 19, 27-28, 160, 257, 345
Prague Spring (Czechoslovakia), 131

Precious Bane, 11
Pre-Raphaelites, 63
Presley, Elvis, 328
Pressburger, Emeric, 2, 4, 7-8, 10, 13-14, 19, 257
Pre-Victorians, 63
Previn, André, 89
Price, Dennis, 8-9
Prick Up Your Ears, xiv, 55, 138
Prix d'Italia, 267
Prokofiev, Sergei, 83
Proust, Marcel, 306-307
The Proust Screenplay, 306-307
The Prowler, 304, 310-311
Pryce, Jonathan, 292
Psycho, 15, 71
Puffball, 101, 110, 112
Puffin Books, 6
Puttnam, David, 47-48, 81
Pygmalion, x, 27

Les Quatre cents coups: see *The 400 Blows*
The Queen, 139
A Quiet Passion, 250, 265

RADA: see Royal Academy of Dramatic Art
Radford, Basil, 40
Raining Stones, 116, 133-134
Rambo, 258
Rank, J. Arthur, 17, 102
Rationalism, 204
Rattigan, Terence, x, 60, 249, 262-264
Rau, Santha Rama, 32
Ray, Nicholas, 308, 317
Ray, Satyajit, xiii, 235
Reade, Walter, 93-94
Reagan, Ronald, 46, 107
Realism, xi, xiv, 68, 96-97, 128, 193, 210, 243, 251, 273, 280, 289, 294
Reality TV, 273
Redgrave, Michael, 264
Redgrave, Vanessa, xiii, 61, 69, 93, 323
Red River, 153

Red Scare, 313
The Red Shoes, 2, 9, 12-13
Reed, Carol, x, xv, 17, 19-26, 50, 161, 345-346
Reed, Oliver, 86-87, 109-110, 112, 341-342
Reeve, Christopher, 342
Reisz, Karel, x-xiii, xv, 60-68, 70, 77, 83-84, 93-94, 99, 157, 167, 211, 346
The Remains of the Day, xiv, 314, 316, 318, 322
Rembrandt (Harmenszoon van Rijn), 194, 205
Remembrance of Things Past, 307
Renaissance, 197
Renarde, Le (*The Vixen*): see *Gone to Earth*
Renoir, Jean, 10, 137, 228
Repulsion, xii
Requiem for a Nun, 93
Resnais, Alain, 105, 204, 206
The Return of the Musketeers, 327
Reynolds, Debbie, 260
Richard II, 251, 324
Richard III, x, 300
Richardson, Tony, xi-xiii, xv, 61, 70-71, 84, 92-100, 172, 211, 347
Richelieu, Cardinal (Armand Jean du Plessis), 90
Riff-Raff, xiv, 116, 124, 133, 135, 176
Ríu Carmen Pérez, 60-68
The River, 10
RKO Pictures, 304, 308
Roads to the South, 306
The Robber Symphony, 13
Roberts, Julia, 138, 156-157
Roberts, Oral, 53
Robin and Marian, 327, 335, 340-341
Rocco and His Brothers, 257
Rock, Crissy, 116, 124, 135
Rockefeller, Nelson, 307
Roeg, Luc, 102
Roeg, Nicolas, 27, 53, 72, 101-114, 173, 257, 347
Rogers, Ginger, 313

The Rolling Stones, 331
The Romantic Englishwoman, 304
Romanticism, 27
Romeo and Juliet, 301-302
Room at the Top, 92-93, 211
A Room with a View, xiv, 314-319, 321
Rossellini, Roberto, 128
Rossetti, Dante Gabriel, 83
Roundabout Theatre, 68
Royal Academy of Dramatic Art (RADA), 124, 217, 282, 292
Royal Air Force (RAF), 4, 82
Royal College of Art, 81
Royal Court Theatre, xi, 45, 92
Royal Flash, 327, 341
Royal Shakespeare Company (RSC), 217, 282, 289-290
The Running, Jumping, & Standing Still Film, 326-327, 338-339
Rushbrook, Claire, 219
Russell, Gail, 309-310
Russell, Ken, xv, 82-91, 107, 170, 347
Russell, Theresa, 112-113
Russian Revolution, 99
Rutherford, Margaret, 250, 340
Ryan's Daughter, 27-28
Rylance, Mark, 292

Sabu (Dastagir), 4
Salinger, J. D., 273
Salt, Waldo, 72-73
Saltzman, Harry, 84, 94, 332
Salzburg Festival (Austria), 81
Sammy and Rosie Get Laid, xiv, 138, 140, 144, 151
Samuels, Charles Thomas, 19-26
Sanctuary, 93
Sanders of the River, 36
San Francisco International Film Festival, 229, 311
Sarris, Andrew, 327
Sartre, Jean-Paul, 99
Satire, xi, 50-53, 80, 227, 291
Saturday Night and Sunday Morning, xi, 60, 93-94, 98-100, 168, 211

Savage Messiah, 82
Saville, Philip, 338
Sayles, John, 127
La Scala theater (Milan), 331
Schary, Dore, 308
Schlesinger, John, xii-xiii, xv, 69-81, 83, 169, 346-347
Scorsese, Martin, 2, 81
Scott, George C., 343
Scott, Ridley, 47
Second World War: see World War II
"Secret Agent," 36
Secret Ceremony, 310
Secrets and Lies, xiv, 181, 208-209, 219, 228, 231, 242-244
Seitz, Matt Zoller, 314-324
Sellers, Peter, 326, 338-339
Selznick, David, 11, 21-22
Semprún, Jorge, 305-306
Sense and Sensibility, xiv
Sentimentalism, 3, 79, 143, 150, 210, 255-256
Separate Tables, 264
Sequence, 45, 60
Serbian Epics, 267
"The Serenata to Shelley," 13
The Servant, xii, 187, 304, 306, 311
Seurat, Georges, 255
Seventh Symphony, 252
"The Sewing Machine," 84
Shakespeare in Love, xiv
Shakespeare Wallah, 314, 317
Shakespeare, William, x, 63, 74, 97, 212, 217, 282-302, 324
Shapiro, Helen, 339
Shaw, Bernard, x
Shearer, Moira, 10, 12
Shenson, Walter, 327-328, 340
Shepard, Sam, 74
Sheridan, Jim, xiv
Sherwin, David, 49
She Wore a Yellow Ribbon, 57
Shilovsky, Vladimir, 89
Shostakovich, Dmitri, 255, 258
"A Show Named Fred," 326

Sibotsky, Milton, 339
Sight and Sound, 45, 80, 326-344
Signoret, Simone, 42
Signs and Meaning in the Cinema, 58
The Silence of the Lambs, 322
Sillitoe, Alan, xi, 93-94, 98
Sim, Alastair, 250
Simmons, Jean, 28
Singer, Paris, 84
Singin' in the Rain, 257, 260
Sirk, Douglas, 263
Sixth Symphony, 89, 258
Slaves of New York, 319
The Sleeping Tiger, 313
Slocombe, Douglas, 38-39
The Small Back Room, 16
Small Faces, 272
Smith, Alexis, 313
The Snapper, 139, 142
Socialism, 46, 210, 212, 237, 239
Social realism, xi-xiii, 45, 115, 137, 211-212
Social Services, 116
Solinas, Franco, 305
Solondz, Todd, 193
A Song of Summer, 83, 88
Sonnenfeld, Barry, 282
Sony Pictures, 322
The Sound of Music, 87
"Space: 1999," 36
Spanish Civil War, 117
Spanish Revolution: see Spanish Civil War
Spielberg, Steven, 34
The Spy in Black, 4
Stalinism, 116
Stapleton, Oliver, 154
Stephenson, Robert Louis, 157
Stevenson, Juliet, 292
Stevenson, Robert, 308
Stewart, Eve, 232
Stewart, Scott, 45-58
Stezaker, John, 101-114
Stoppard, Tom, 305-306
Storey, David, xi, 45

The Stranger in Between, 36
Stranger on the Prowl, 312
Strauss, Richard, 83, 87-88, 90
Strohm, Walter, 3
Sturridge, Charles, 90
Sullivan, Arthur, 208
Summertime, 27
Sundance Film Festival, 81
Sunday, Bloody Sunday, 69, 72, 77-79
"Sunday in the Park," 76
"Sunday Night Film," 82
Sunset, 49
Sunset Boulevard, 223
Sunset Song, 250
Superman III, 327, 342
Superman II, 327, 342
Surrealism, 16-17, 132, 210, 326
Surviving Picasso, 314, 318-319, 322-324
Sutherland, Donald, 74
Swaggart, Jimmy, 53
Swanson, Gloria, 192, 223
Sweet, John, 5, 9

The Tales of Hoffman, 2, 12-13
Tarzan's Greatest Adventure, 104
A Taste of Honey, xii, 93, 95-96, 98-99, 173, 211, 274
Tate, Reginald, 7
Tautou, Audrey, 147
Taviani, Paolo, 81
Taviani, Vittorio, 81
"Taxi," 53
Taylor, Elizabeth, 309-310
Tchaikovsky, Pyotr Ilyich, 82, 88-89
Tearle, Godfrey, 7
Television vs. film, 36, 46-47, 53-56, 70-71, 76, 78, 83, 85, 87-89, 91, 115, 127, 130, 133, 138-139, 142-143, 145, 199, 208, 211-213, 226, 234-235, 257, 260
The Tempest, 6
Ten Little Indians, 8
The Terence Davies Trilogy, 249, 251, 254-256, 259

Tess of the D'Urbervilles, 22
Thalberg, Irving, 230
Thatcher, Margaret, 46, 48, 107, 116, 131, 147, 155, 158, 201
Thatcherism, 55, 140, 210
Theater vs. film, 52, 74, 97-98, 125, 130, 195, 233-234, 257, 282-302
Thewlis, David, 217-218
The Thief of Bagdad, 4, 36
Things to Come, 36
The Third Man, x, 19-26, 162
This Happy Breed, 255
This Sporting Life, xii, 45, 211
Thompson, Emma, 320
The Three Musketeers, 327, 341
Thursday's Children, 45
The Times Literary Supplement (London), 6
The Titfield Thunderbolt, x, 36
Tom Jones, 93
Tommy, 82
Toole, John Kennedy, 249, 261
Topsy-Turvy, 208, 227-229, 231-232
Toronto International Film Festival, 267, 280
Totem and Taboo, 203
Towering Inferno, 335
Towne, Robert, 268
Track 29, 107, 110-112
Tragedy, 28, 48, 83, 108, 143, 295, 305
Train of Events, 43
Trainspotting, 273
Trapeze, 20
The Treasure of the Sierra Madre, 106
Trees Lounge, 230
Trevelyan, John, 88
Trotsky, Leon, 115, 130
The Trout, 304, 306
Truffaut, François, xii-xiii, 101, 144, 211, 257
Truman, Michael, 44
Trumbo, Dalton, 310
The Tulse Luper Suitcases, 180, 192-197, 199-201
Turner, J. M. W., 209, 255

Turner, Paul, xiv
Twelfth Night, xiv
Twentieth Century-Fox, 93, 319
Two Thousand Years, 209
2001: A Space Odyssey, 9, 34, 88

Ulysses, 195, 199
United Artists (UA), 89, 327-329
United Nations (UN), 121
University of Pennsylvania, 326
Ustinov, Peter, 332

Vailland, Roger, 305-306
Valentino, Rudolph, 34
Valli, Alida, 21-23
The Van, 139
Vaudeville, 209, 212
Veidt, Conrad, 4-6
Venice Film Festival, 192, 194
Venice: Theme and Variations, 314
Vera Drake, 208, 218, 244-247
Verswijver, Leo, 69-81
Vertical Lists, 200
Victorianism, 62-63, 65-66, 228
Vidor, King, 34
Vietnam War, 201
Vincent, Gene, 339
Vincentis, D. V., 153
Viola, Bill, 205
Violin Concerto, Op. 14, 264
Visconti, Luchino, 257
Vitti, Monica, 304
Vivre sa vie, 211

WACs (Women's Army Corps), 9
Walbrook, Anton, 6, 8, 13
Walkabout, 101-102, 110, 174
A Walk Through H, 203
Walton, Joseph: see Joseph Losey
Warner Brothers, 72, 93, 102
Warner, Jack, 41-42
War Office, 8
War Requiem, 55
Warsaw University, 274
Waterhouse, Keith, 69

Watkin, David, 340
Watt, Harry, ix, 39, 42-43
Waugh, Evelyn, 90
The Way Ahead, x
Wayne, Naunton, 40
The Way to the Stars, x
We Are the Lambeth Boys, 60
Webb, Mary, 11
"The Wednesday Play," 130
Weiss, Jason, 304-313
Welch, Raquel, 74
Welcome to Sarajevo, 279
Weldon, Huw, 83, 88, 90
Welles, Orson, 21-23, 34, 137, 156, 332-333
West End (theatre), 92
Western (film), 342-343
Western Approaches, ix
West, Nathanael, 72
The Whales of August, 45, 50-51
Wharton, Edith, 249, 261
Where Angels Fear to Tread, xiv
Whisky Galore, x
White Mischief, xiv
Whiting, John, 89
Whore, 82
Wilby, James, 322
Wilde, Cornell, 340
Wilde, Oscar, x
Wilder, Billy, 81
Wild Wild West, 282
Williams, Michael, 294
Williams, Tennessee, 99
Williams, Tony, 2-17
Wilson, Harold, 130
The Wind That Shakes the Barley, 117, 122
The Wings of a Dove, xiv
The Winslow Boy, x
Winterbottom, Michael, 279-280
The Witches, 101
Wittgenstein, Ludwig, 279
A Wizard of Earthsea, 6
Wollen, Peter, 58
The Woman in the Fifth, 266, 277

Women in Love, 82, 85-87, 90-91, 171
Wong, Benedict, 150
Wood, Charles, 332
Woodfall Film Productions, 92, 94
Woodward, Joanne, 319
Wooland, Norman, 32
Wordsworth, William, 204
World Expo 1958 (Brussels World's Fair), 76
The World Is Ever Changing, 101
World War I, 7
World War II, ix-x, xv, 19, 87, 206, 282
WPA (Works Progress Administration), 307
Wright, Basil, ix
Wuthering Heights, xiv
Wyler, William, 5, 26, 80

York, Michael, xiii
York, Susannah, xiii
Young, Colin, 92-100
Young Veteran, 37

Zanuck, Richard, 93
Zarathustra, 87-88
Zellweger, Renée, 230
Zinnemann, Fred, 80
Zionism, 212
Zoetrope Studios, 2, 4
Zola, Emile, 129

www.ingramcontent.com/pod-product-compliance
Lightning Source LLC
Chambersburg PA
CBHW070715160426
43192CB00009B/1196